Acknowledgments

If you have nothing to tell us but that on the banks of the Oxus and the Jaxartes, one barbarian has been succeeded by another barbarian, in what respect do you benefit the public?

Voltaire, 1764

If we have come anywhere close to benefiting the public, credit must be shared with many friends in Uzbekistan for all their kind help and hospitality.

Calum MacLeod
My thanks to Tanya and Stas Nikiphorov, Greg Grosenick and Melanie Reimer, Victor Tsoy, Asia Travel, Uzbektourism, Uzbekistan Airways, Dr Lola Babakhanova (Tashkent) and Ludmilla Kosogorskaya (Samarkand). My parents Janice and Iain MacLeod were a bedrock of love and enthusiasm. *Katta rakhmat* to Keith and Margarita Silver of the ABC in Tashkent for help during the 1998 research trip. Last and yet foremost, eternal thanks to my wife, Zhang Lijia, who made possible our first trip in 1992 and who provided support, research and advice every step of the *plovfest* that followed.

Bradley Mayhew
My thanks to Noila Kasijanova (Bukhara), Svetlana (Khiva), Salvatore Amodeo, Peace Corps (Bukhara / Osh), Price Waterhouse (Karshi), Designed Storage for technical assistance, Radi Bakayev of Asia Travel, the English Faculty at Termez University, Uzbekistan Airways, Ludmilla Kosminsk (Hotel Bukhara), and finally thanks to Kelli Hahn for patience and endurance beyond the call during our 1996 trip.

Calum MacLeod and Bradley Mayhew graduated in Oriental Studies (Chinese) from Wadham College, Oxford University (1988–1992). Calum has travelled extensively through Russian and Chinese Central Asia, China and Indo-China. He contributes to a range of publications and is the Beijing Chief Representative of Batey Burn & Co. Ltd. Bradley has travelled and trekked across Chinese and Russian Central Asia, Tibet, Iran and Ladakh. He has led adventure tours along the Silk Road and is the author/co-author of Lonely Planet guides to Tibet, Pakistan, the Karakoram Highway, the Indian Himalaya and Southwest China. Calum and Bradley have lectured on Central Asia to the Royal Geographical Society.

(Preceding page) *Tamerlane's Tomb, Gur Emir, Samarkand*

UZBEKISTAN
The Golden Road to Samarkand

Text and photography by
Calum MacLeod and Bradley Mayhew

Odyssey Publications Ltd, 1004 Kowloon Centre, 29–43 Ashley Road,
Tsim Sha Tsui, Kowloon, Hong Kong
Tel. (852) 2856 3896; Fax. (852) 2565 8004; E-mail: odyssey@asiaonline.net

Distribution in the United Kingdom, Ireland and Europe by
Hi Marketing Ltd, 38 Carver Road, London SE24 9LT, UK

Distribution in the United States of America by
W.W. Norton & Company, Inc., New York

Library of Congress Catalog Card Number has been requested.

ISBN: 962-217-582-1

Grateful acknowledgment is made to the following authors and publishers:

William Heinemann Ltd and Aitken, Stone & Wylie for
The Lost Heart of Asia by Colin Thubron, © 1994

Secker & Warburg Ltd for
Red Odyssey by Murat Akchurin, © 1992

Oriental Literature Publishing House, Moscow,
for *Uzbek Poetry* by Khamza Niyazi

Penguin Books Ltd for
Eastern Approaches, by Fitzroy Maclean, © 1991

Century Travellers for
Turkestan Solo, by Ella Maillart, © 1934

Editor: Adam Nebbs
Series Co-ordinator: Jane Finden-Crofts
Design and maps: Tom Le Bas
Cover Concept: Margaret Lee

Practical information, such as telephone
numbers and opening hours, is notoriously
subject to change. We welcome corrections
and suggestions from guidebook users, together with additions and critiques; please
write to:

Odyssey Publications Ltd
Room 1004, Kowloon Centre
29–43 Ashley Road, Tsim Sha Tsui
Kowloon, Hong Kong
E-mail: odyssey@asiaonline.net

Photography by Calum MacLeod (pages 1, 5, 16, 19, 26, 27, 34, 35, 42, 49, 53, 59, 66, 75, 84,
97, 104, 108, 109, 112, 118, 122, 127, 134, 139, 147, 150, 158, 159, 163, 166, 175, 182, 190,
191, 210, 225, 228, 254, 262, 267, 273, 291, 294, 295, 299) and Bradley Mayhew (pages 13, 30,
71, 89, 143, 203, 214, 229, 237, 243, 250, 251, 258, 276, 284, 285, 305, 309, 313)

Production by Twin Age Ltd, Hong Kong
Printed in China

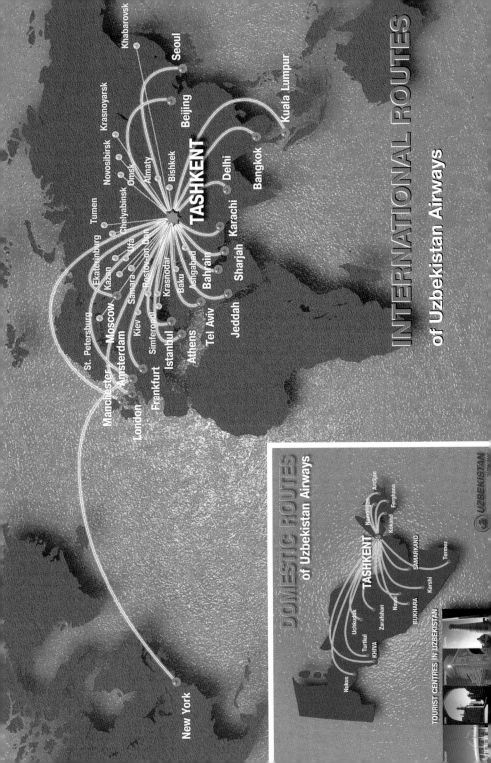

INTERNATIONAL ROUTES
of Uzbekistan Airways

Khabarovsk
Seoul
Krasnoyarsk
Kuala Lumpur
Beijing
Novosibirsk
Omsk
Bangkok
Almaty
Bishkek
Delhi
Tumen
Chelyabinsk
Ekaterinburg
Karachi
TASHKENT
Kazan
Ufa
Samara
Rostov-on-Don
Sharjah
St. Petersburg
Krasnodar
Baku
Ashgabad
Bahrain
Moscow
Kiev
Amsterdam
Simferopol
Jeddah
Manchester
Istanbul
Tel Aviv
London
Frankfurt
Athens

New York

DOMESTIC ROUTES
of Uzbekistan Airways

Namangan
Andijan
Fergana
TASHKENT
Kokand
Nukus
Uchkuduk
Turtkul
Zarafshan
Navoi
SAMARKAND
Termez
KHIVA
BUKHARA
Karshi

TOURIST CENTRES IN UZBEKISTAN

UZBEKISTAN

Contents

MAPS

MAP KEY

——— Main road		—··— Provincial boundary	
——— Secondary road		▟▙▟ City wall	
═▬═▬ Railway		⋊ Bridge / pass	
—·— National boundary		∴ Ruins	

A NOTE ON SPELLING

Since independence restored the status of local languages, Central Asian names and spellings have undergone de-Russification and de-Sovietization. Kirghizia became Kyrgyzstan, its capital dropped the Bolshevik Frunze for the earlier Bishkek, and the Kazakh capital Alma Ata reverted to the earlier Almaty. As their statues fell, Lenin and Marx were removed from countless street signs. This guide adopts the latest versions wherever they have entered common use. Transliteration remains a considerable problem, such as the Uzbek 'o' (a) and 'kh' (h) sounds, for literature on Central Asia features multiple spellings. In general, with apologies for inconsistencies, this guide follows the most well-known transliterations for place and people names, e.g. 'Ashkhabad' for the Turkmen capital, not the newer 'Ashgabat', and 'Tamer-lane', not the Uzbek 'Amir Timur'.

Introduction

Once you have become the companion of the road, it calls you and calls you again...the road lies outside the door of your house full of charm and mystery. You want to know where the roads lead to, and what may be on them, beyond the faint horizon's line.'

Graham, Stephen; *Through Russian Central Asia*, (1916)

The Golden Road to Samarkand, the Royal Road from Noble Bukhara, the Silk Roads through Transoxiana from the Ferghana Valley across the Kyzyl Kum desert to Khiva and the Khorezm oasis. Their call embraces over two millennia of travels of conquest, commerce and plain curiosity.

From the West came Alexander the Great, Genghis Khan erupted from the East, while Tamerlane made his home the heartland of Central Asia, the remarkable historical and architectural legacy inherited by modern-day Uzbekistan. She is a young nation who has outlived her Soviet sire, but her roots are ancient, steeped in the legends of the steppe. These lands saw the wax and wane of countless empires, mounted nomad versus settled farmer. Islam came this way to flower and outshine anywhere in the Muslim world. The Uzbeks themselves emerged from Turco-Mongol tribes in the 14th century. Polarized into the warring khanates of Bukhara, Khiva and Kokand, they provided the most exotic, perilous and coveted playing fields of the Great Game, the 19th-century war of stealth between the tsarist and British empires.

A glance at a map seems to belie Uzbekistan's role as ethnic and cultural melting pot. Surely Central Asia's vast expanse kept apart the civilizations at its edge? Those barriers were broken by the greatest trade routes in history, the fragile threads of the Silk Road. Wending their way over mountain and wasteland, myriad teams of merchants braved this key stretch of the long haul from China to Rome. Camel caravans laden with silk, spices and news searched for the guiding minarets of oasis paradises, lighthouses for their ships of the desert. Convening in bazaar and caravanserai, nomad met settler, Persian met Turk and Chinese met Sogdian in a fertile exchange of goods and ideas—religious, intellectual and artistic.

Nature has bestowed this harshly arid land with two channels of hope; the Amu Darya and Syr Darya, sweeping down from the Roof of the World, the high Pamirs and Tian Shan to the east, bringing the desert to life up to Khorezm and the Aral Sea. The Greeks knew them as the Oxus and Jaxartes; between their middle reaches lay Transoxiana, the Arab Mawarannahr, the 'land beyond the river'. Its illustrious centres, Samarkand and Bukhara, arose beside the Zerafshan, the aptly-named 'gold-strewer', for water is the most precious commodity in the region.

In the seventh century, golden peaches sent to Tang Dynasty China from the kingdom of Samarkand epitomized enigmatic mystery. Today her romance still works its magic, alluring the traveller with a dreamlike quality. Follow your heart to be rewarded with a passage back to the 14th century, to the brilliant blues of Tamerlane's capital, mirror to his empire's wealth and breadth, monument to his own immortality. Six days away by camel, the riches of Bukhara span a thousand years. Boasting a different mosque for every day of the year, drawing the finest minds of the East with its cultural and commercial vitality, the city well deserved the title Bukhara the Holy. Everywhere else, it was said, light shone down from heaven; in Bukhara the light shone up. Khiva, the third of Uzbekistan's foremost architectural ensembles, stems from a later period when the region first attracted the Russian tsars. Preserved as a living museum of mud walls and minarets, it is frozen in a time when a visit required months of travel through desert and the prospect of days without water paled into insignificance at the sight of the man-stealing Turkomans, hungrily roaming for slaves.

Wherever one treads in Uzbekistan, one follows the footprints of some of the greatest travellers in history—from Chinese pioneers seeking blood-sweating horses or enlightenment from India, to Arab scholars like ibn-Battuta, the Marco Polo of the Muslim world. To Tamerlane's court in 1404 journeyed the Spanish ambassador Clavijo; the English merchant Jenkinson also survived the trials of Transoxiana in the 16th century. But this remained remotest Tartary. It took the Great Game players to carve out western Turkestan and fill in the huge blanks on the map. Growing awareness of the exotic dangers on the road to Samarkand spurred the adventurous and the eccentric; in 1898, Robert Jefferson rode his bicycle 6,000 miles from London to Khiva, "because so many people said it was impossible".

The Tournament of Shadows, as the Russians termed the Game, brought Turkestan under tsarist suzerainty. The Bolshevik revolution brought more thorough attempts to civilize, educate and remould the land and its people. National delimitation created the five republics we know today: Kazakhstan, Kyrgyzstan, Tajikistan, Turkmenistan and Uzbekistan. Brand new states, without historical precedent, they have been subject to successive waves of Russification, Sovietization and modernization. The effects are ever-present; Russian is the most useful language for the traveller and concrete jostles with sun-dried brick in the centre of Samarkand.

Yet many traditions of Uzbek life have weathered the storm. Women walk resplendent in the bold stripes of their tie-dyed *ikat* gowns, topped with brightly patterned scarves. Older men retain the quilted *khalat* coats, embroidered skullcaps and leather boots. Drinking tea for hours, they swap stories at the local *chaikhana* teahouses, enjoying shashlik kebabs and melons from the bazaar. Islamic beliefs have survived 70 years of Soviet atheistic bullying. Loyalties lie with family, clan, village and oasis and respect for one's elders, the *aksakal* or whitebeards, is still a cornerstone of society. Perhaps the most welcome tradition for the traveller is the Uzbeks' renowned hospitality, as warm as ever, for 'the guest is the first person in the home'.

The declaration of independence on 24 August 1991, took few more by surprise than Uzbekistan itself, as the nation stumbled away from the political vacuum of the Soviet implosion. The reawakening is now fully underway. Mosques springing up at every turn mark the resurgence of Islam. The Silk Road is reviving as travel and trade cross borders long forbidden. The Great Game has recommenced, sparking a rush by neighbouring countries to promote their brand of Islam in a climate thirsty for both aid and the Koran. Businessmen too are drawn by 20th century silk—gold, oil, gas and minerals. As nationalism replaces communism, the old heroes and poets of the golden age of Transoxiana return as symbols of national pride. The land beyond the river is recovering its past.

History

Its blend of desert, steppe, oasis and river valley places Uzbekistan at the heart of the complex interaction of nomadic culture and oasis settlement that patterns the history of Central Asia. Over 100,000 years ago, primitive man was engraving caves in the region with scenes from his hunting lifestyle, but the haze of pre-history only begins to clear in the second millennium BC, when Bronze Age metallurgy developed the bronze bit, enabling horse riding. Mounted tribes sponsored contacts between the farming south and the livestock-breeding north. An Aryan Indo-European race from the north led the first known migration into the territory of present-day Uzbekistan. From 800 BC their successors, the Scythians (to the Greeks) or Saka (to the Persians), swept all before them into a loose nomadic dynasty from the Ferghana Valley to the Khorezm oasis. These tent-dwellers matured during the Iron Age into skilled craftsmen, but their chief legacy was horseback archery. On top of such military advantage, they set standards of terror for barbaric waves through the centuries. Victories were toasted with the blood of slain enemies, their skulls used as drinking vessels.

The first Achaemenid Emperor of Persia, Cyrus the Great, sought to end their raids and, despite his death in 530 BC fighting the Messagetae clan near the Aral Sea, his conquests proved lasting. Persian kings divided Turan (outer Iran) south of the Syr Darya into three satrapies: Khorezm, Sogdiana (the Zerafshan and Ferghana Valleys) and Bactria (southern Uzbekistan, Tajikistan and Afghanistan). Achaemenid influence speeded the process of urbanization already underway and installed the state religion, Zoroastrianism, the worship of an all-powerful god through fire offerings. Its origin may have been local for both Khorezm and Bactria claim the site of the revelation of mysterious prophet Zoroaster, 'one who possesses golden camels'. In the sacred book *Avesta*, the supreme deity declares, "The second among the best localities

Sogdian mural, Samarkand, 7th century

and countries, I, Ahura Mazda, created Gava, the abode of the Sogdians".

In 329 BC, the Sogdian capital, Samarkand, an oasis on the Zerafshan river, fell to Alexander the Great. Having vanquished the Persian empire, the Macedonian hero had floated his forces across the Oxus on twig-filled hides and dragged them over the perilous Hindu Kush to the south. Yet once he had departed to found his easternmost Alexandria at the mouth of the Ferghana Valley, Sogdian ruler Spitamenes led his people in a guerilla war that delayed the Greeks for two years. To ease local dissent, Alexander married the daughter of a Sogdian leader, the captive, beautiful Roxana, who bore him his only son.

His generals were encouraged to do likewise and, after Alexander's death in 323 BC, one of them established his eastern empire as the Seleucid Dynasty. Although many states broke away in the mid-third century BC, as the Parthians rose to the west, Hellenistic culture was promoted through the Graeco-Bactrian kingdom for another hundred years until the invasion of Yuezhi nomads from the east. They had been forced from China by the Huns of the Mongolian steppe, the scourge of the Han Dynasty. In 138 BC Emperor Wudi dispatched Zhang Qian to Ferghana to seek alliance against the Huns, as well as supplies of the valley's renowned heavenly horses, so swift they sweated blood. The envoy brought back neither, although there was news of high demand for Chinese silk. Subsequent campaigns secured the horses, subdued the Huns and opened the fledgling Silk Road. From the first century AD trade prospered from Chang'an (Xi'an) to Rome as Central Asia enjoyed stability under the Yuezhi Kushan clan, masters of a vast empire centred on what is now northwest Pakistan. Their famous King Kanishka promoted Buddhism and the Sogdians relayed it to China, in what was just one aspect of a fruitful cultural and commercial exchange. The hegemony of Sassanian Persia from the third century boosted Sogdian fortunes, for the new power demanded a shift in world trade from Kushan southern routes to a more northerly itinerary through Sogdiana.

Fresh nomadic incursions by the Khidarites and Khionites culminated in the Hephthalites, or White Huns, from the Altai mountains. In the fifth century they devoured the Sassanian eastern empire while the Black Huns and their infamous King Attila ravaged Europe. In turn they fell to the Turks by the mid-sixth century. This latest nemesis from Mongolia and eastern Siberia formed the largest nomadic empire yet seen and introduced enduring ethno-linguistic traits. Yet the Sogdian city-states of Ferghana and Zerafshan proved resilient. Their merchants dominated the trade routes and their artists absorbed the traditions of far-off lands. All religions were present: Zoroastrianism, Buddhism, Nestorian Christianity, Judaism and Manichaeism.

THE VICTORY OF ISLAM

The next invasion, the first from the west for a millenium, was designed to end such diversity. To the Arabs, conquerors of the Sassanids, this territory was Mawarannahr, the Land Beyond the River (Oxus/Amu Darya), and they determined to cross it with the Prophet Mohammed's bold new creed. Eastern expeditions began in 649, but full annexation awaited the energetic campaigns of Qutaiba ibn-Muslim, governor of Khorasan, the eastern province of Persia. Between 706 and 713, he took Bukhara, Samarkand, Khorezm and Tashkent. On campaign in Ferghana in 715, Qutaiba's rebellion against the new Ummayad caliph in Baghdad, a personal enemy, brought assassination by his own troops. His death and the weakened state of the caliphate ensured a stormy century of Sogdian and Turkic revolt against the new religion and its overlords.

The Chinese threatened to absorb the region into the Tang realm, until another Arab general routed them at Talas (Dzhambul, Kazakhstan) in 751, securing a Muslim future for the peoples of Central Asia. The new Abbasid caliphate ruled from Khorasan, but authority lay in the hands of increasingly independent governors. In the ninth century, the Iranian Saman aristocracy rose to prominence. Ismail ibn-Ahmad, ruler of Bukhara from 875, purged Tahirid and Saffirid influence to unite Central Asia under the Samanid dynasty. There followed a century of remarkable political, cultural and economic growth. Sunni Islam was firmly established as Bukhara attracted the greatest scholars and poets of the age. Ibn-Sina (Avicenna) wrote his famed medical encyclopedia, the *Qanun,* and Rudaki made the city the birthplace of Persian literature.

Such prosperity could hardly escape the attentions of Turkic nomads. In 999, the Karakhanids overran Transoxiana, while the Ghaznavids took Khorasan and Khorezm. However, these were Muslim Turkic dynasties, recently converted, and they sought to maintain urban civilization. By the mid-11th century, another Turkic tribe, the Seljuks, had reduced them to vassals. They continued west to conquer Byzantine Anatolia, forcing Baghdad to acknowledge the power of their Grand Sultan of Islam, based in their capital Merv (Turkmenistan). But in 1141 the illustrious Seljuk Sultan Sanjar met defeat near Samarkand by the next challenge from the steppe.

As the Mongol Karakhitai won control of a huge swathe of territory from western China to the Aral Sea, news of their victories over the Muslims reached Europe as the legend of Prester John, a king of the Orient rushing to save Christendom. Growing Volga trade gave Khorezm the strength to overthrow these pagans in the name of Islam in the early 13th century. The arrogant Khorezmshah Mohammed saw himself as a second Alexander when he marched from Urgench to liberate Samarkand in 1212, thereby removing the Karakhitai barrier between the Muslim world and the most notorious nomads of all time.

THE MONGOL STORM

The boy Temujin was born of a Mongol chief around 1167 north of the Gobi desert. Through bitter struggle he removed all rivals, notably the tribe of Tartars, whose name East and West would adopt for the united hordes Temujin gathered in 1206. They proclaimed him Genghis Khan, master of 'all the people with felt tents', and China was but the first to suffer his fury. After the Khorezmshah's governor at Otrar slaughtered a Mongol merchant caravan in 1218, Genghis dispatched three envoys to Mohammed's court. When Mohammed killed one and burnt the others' beards, he sealed his fate. Contemporary historian Juvaini hardly exaggerates the result: "For every drop of their blood there flowed a whole Oxus; in retribution for every hair on their heads, it seemed that a hundred thousand heads rolled in the dust at every crossroads."

The Mongol horsemen were deadly archers, able to ride for days and nights on end, sleeping in the saddle, nourished by the blood of their steeds. Strategies like the feigned retreat overcame numerical inferiority, while massed ranks of prisoners formed protective walls from enemy arrows. By 1221 Genghis Khan's domains spread from China to the Caspian and the grand cities of Central Asia lay in ruin. His successors pushed even further, simultaneously challenging the Japanese and the Germans from the greatest land empire the world has ever seen.

Their campaigns left some five million dead, yet in their wake the Mongols established the Pax Mongolica, over a century of stability and recovery of which Marco Polo was a witness and beneficiary. As the *yam* horse relay system speeded communications to a level surpassed only by 19th-century engineers, the Silk Road traveller could march with impunity "from the land of sunrise to the land of sunset with a golden platter upon his head". Before his death in 1227, the Great Khan divided his realm between his four sons. Most of Uzbekistan fell within the *ulus* of Chagatai, his second son. Initial hostility to Islam faded as subsequent rulers adapted to local Turkic culture and by the 14th century their language was known as Chagatai Turkic. Fragmentation of power sparked wars among various fiefs, brilliantly exploited by the Turkicized Mongol Tamerlane.

TIMURID TRANSOXIANA

Born near Samarkand, in the heart of Transoxiana, in 1336, he survived youthful trials, like Genghis Khan, to dominate his homeland by 1370. 'As there is only one God in Heaven, so there should be only one king on earth' was a chronicler's explanation of the fearless ambition that raged from India to Russia, smashing Urgench,

Mullah outside the Gur Emir, Samarkand

TAMERLANE, CONQUEROR OF THE WORLD

The last nomadic emperor to shake the world was born in 1336 to a minor chief of the Barlas clan near Kesh, south of Samarkand. The first of countless legends reports the infant Timur—'iron', a common name in Central Asia—was born with blood-filled palms, an omen predicting his hands would slay many. His family was of Mongol stock, part of the ruling aristocracy of the fragmented Chagatai Ulus, but settled into local Turkic and Islamic culture. From his childhood he honed the skills of the steppe—horsemanship, sword-craft and archery. His prowess and nobility attracted a band of warriors with whom he rustled sheep and raided caravans.

In 1360, court chronicles introduce Timur to history as the astute young man who welcomed a Mongol invasion and succeeded as Barlas' chief. Mixed fortune filled the next decade with adventures by wit and sword. From arrow wounds to his right leg and arm grew the appellation Timur-i-Leng, Timur the Lame, and the English corruptions Tamburlaine and Tamerlane. When he caught his assailant 20 years later, he had him strung up for target practice. By 1370, after clever political and military manoeuvering, he became lord of Transoxiana and master of Samarkand. Lack of direct descent to Genghis Khan limited Tamerlane to Amir (commander), for Turco-Mongolian tradition necessitated rule through a puppet khan. Marriage to his rival's Mongol widow promoted him to *guregen* (royal son-in-law) and after his death a mythical geneology carved on his tombstone traced common ancestry with the illustrious khan back to the maiden Alangoa, ravished by a moonbeam.

An early title, Conqueror of the World, showed Tamerlane shared his forebear's boundless ambition. Over the next 35 years he personally led his mounted archers as far afield as Moscow and Delhi, less than the Mongolian realm, but still the greatest extent ever conquered by a single ruler. "The whole world is not large enough for two kings" he explained as he plundered Khorezm, Khorasan, Persia, Syria, Asia Minor and Russia. Sacked cities like Baghdad and Damascus lent their names to villages near Samarkand, where he fashioned an imperial capital beyond compare with the loot and craftsmen gathered on campaign.

His brilliance as a strategist and the loyalty of highly mobile troops overcame all opposition. Estimates suggest 17 million people died in a trail of blood and suffering, marked by pyramids of skulls, that surpassed even Mongol barbarity. In 1383, 2,000 troublesome citizens of Isfizar (Iran) were piled alive one upon another and cemented into clay towers. In 1398, on the outskirts of Delhi, he killed 100,000 Hindu prisoners, lest they hamper his attack, before massacring an equal number within the city. In 1402, after the sack of Smyrna (Turkey), he bombarded the escaping Christian fleet using knights' heads as cannon balls.

Despite their success, Tamerlane's conquests appear haphazard and repetitive, compared to the clean sweep of Genghis Khan, for he rarely consolidated them with permanent administration. Only in the last years of his life did he carve out fiefs for his descendents, yet his jealousy of power and the cohesive role of his charisma built an empire that could not long survive him. His career had pervasive influence. Defeat of one-time protégé Toktamish in 1395 so weakened the Golden Horde that Russia came to discard the Mongol yoke, eventually annexing Tamerlane's heartland itself. Capture of Ottoman Sultan Bayezid the Thunderbolt in 1402 delayed the fall of Constantinople for half a century, allowing Greek scholarship the time to reach Italy and birth the Renaissance. Although he encouraged agriculture and irrigation, concentration of trade on Samarkand and decimation of other centres reduced the economic base for later empires, exacerbated by the fall of the Silk Road.

As for the man himself, contemporaries speak highly of his sharp intellect and thirst for knowledge. Illiterate but fluent in Turkic and Persian, he pursued aggressive debate with scholars of history, medicine and astronomy. He played chess with a passion, named his son Shahrukh (king-knight) during a game and doubled the pieces on the board. His relationship with Islam reveals his opportunism, for at home he cultivated both official clergy and popular sheikhs and elsewhere his religious zeal hid political goals.

The good citizens of Samarkand were granted tax exemptions after plunder-rich victories and enjoyed the ruler's pleasure grounds during his frequent absences. Spanish ambassador Clavijo observed in 1404: "Good order is maintained in Samarkand with utmost strictness and none dare fight with another or oppress his neighbour by force: indeed as to fighting that Timur makes them do enough but abroad." Tamerlane's death in 1405 denied history a spectacular showdown with Ming China, whose emperor he derided as 'King Pig'. Genghis Khan's fame may be wider, but Tamerlane's legacy shines brighter, for he took a Samarkand of sun-dried brick and left it the architectural pearl of Central Asia.

Tiling detail, Shah-i-Zinda, Samarkand

Baghdad, Damascus, Herat and Delhi. Meticulous planning enhanced classic nomadic warfare, concluded by brutality on an unprecedented scale. With the plunder and slave-artisans of conquered lands, Tamerlane raised his capital Samarkand to its greatest heights.

On his death in 1405, en route to savage China, his fragile empire collapsed to its core: his son Shahrukh ruled eastern Persia, while his grandson, Ulug Beg, made Samarkand an intellectual centre. In 1449 Ulug Beg's preference for science over politics and religion met Islamic reaction and a son bent on patricide. His nephew avenged him but soon fell to Tamerlane's great-grandson, Abu Said, helped by Uzbek khan Abul Khair. A descendent of Shayban, Genghis Khan's grandson, Abul Khair had united the nomadic Turco-Mongol tribes on the steppes of today's Kazakhstan. His grandson, Mohammed Shaybani, a brilliant warrior and poet who campaigned with a travelling library, eclipsed Timurid authority by seizing Khorezm, Samarkand, Bukhara and Tashkent by 1505. Tamerlane's great-great-great-grandson Babur fought back bravely until defeat, by Shaybani's relatives in 1512, sent him south to found the Mogul Empire in India.

Under Abdullah Khan, ruler of Bukhara from 1557 to 1598, the Shaybanid Uzbek dynasty, the last great empire of Transoxiana, reached its peak. A relative by marriage from Astrakhan succeeded him to form the Astrakhanid dynasty, while a Shaybanid branch ruled Khorezm from Khiva, following the demise of Urgench. During the 17th century, the Uzbek clans continued to settle into oasis life, merging with the earlier inhabitants, Turkic and Iranian (Tajik), until the name Uzbek was used for the whole population. The Turkomans and Karakalpaks to the east and the Kazakhs to the north retained the nomadic ways of stockbreeders.

The strength of Shi'ite Saffavids in Persia cut off Central Asia from the cultural and intellectual stimulus of the Sunni Islamic world. Declining caravan trade further isolated the region, for the Silk Road had succumbed to sea routes and robbers plagued merchants by land. In 1740 the Uzbeks had little answer to the artillery of Nadir Shah of Persia, who conquered all the major cities before leaving his protégé to found the Mangit dynasty in Bukhara. The next occupation would not be so brief.

THE GREAT GAME

As Peter the Great strove to modernize Russia, rumours of gold on the Oxus persuaded him to send an expedition to Khiva. It was slaughtered on arrival in 1717, yet two years earlier the first of a line of forts, built at the edge of the northern steppe, began a slower but more effective colonizing drive. Russian generals exploited the incursions of the Mongol Oirots by offering protection to the Kazakh Khans. By the mid-19th century their lands were under Russian control. The rest of Central Asia was fractured into three warring khanates: Bukhara, Khiva and Kokand in the Ferghana Valley, where a resurgent branch of the Shaybanid dynasty overcame Kazakhs, Kyrgyz and religious orders in the 18th century. The fierce rivalry of the khanates greatly weakened resistance against the common enemy.

This was the era of Great Game diplomacy and adventure, for the British Empire saw Russia's southward expansion aimed straight for India, the jewel in its crown. To map out the geographical and political mysteries of the no-man's-land between them, both sides sent spies on 'hunting trips' or 'scientific surveys'. Harbouring a closet of disguises, armed with little more than languages, unshakeable self-confidence and hidden agendas, British officers played hide-and-seek across desert and mountain with tsarist soldiers and nomadic bandits. Some never returned, but survivors excited Europe and worried London with tales of evil despots and fabled cities. While an advance on India appealed to many Russian Great Game players, more immediate aims included a secure southern frontier, trade development and the liberation of Russian slaves. Just as America tamed its Wild West, Russia spread like a flood across the eastern steppe to become the world's fastest growing imperial state, averaging an increase of 140km^2 every day. In 1864 Foreign Minister Gorkachev justified the conquests on humanitarian grounds: "The position of Russia in Central Asia is that of all civilized states which are brought into contact with half-savage nomad populations possessing no fixed social organisation."

Despite assurances the Russian Bear was sated, Tashkent fell the following year. In 1867 General Konstantin Kaufmann arrived as first governor general of Russian Turkestan, the 'land of the Turks', a term first used after Turkic invasions in the sixth century. This veteran of Caucasian campaigns orchestrated the annexation of the khanates, with modern firepower and tactics more than compensating for modest numbers. In 1868 Samarkand fell and Bukhara became a Russian protectorate, followed by Khiva in 1873. Once Kokand was taken in 1876, the conquest of the area was completed by the occupation of Turkoman fortresses to the southwest, Geoktepe in 1881 and Merv in 1884. The Game crescendoed as the two continental empires were taken to the brink of war and then spilled over into the high passes of the Pamirs, but by the end of the century defendable and defined borders had been largely established and rivalries put to rest by the 1907 Anglo-Russian Convention.

In the early years of Russian Turkestan the Russians were more intruder than invader, content to ignore rather than transform, but the infidel victory had shaken religious confidence and given cause for reflection. In the region's turbulent transition to modernity a medley of ideas ranging from *jadid* religious reform to Muslim nationalism, from pan-Islam to pan-Turkism fomented in the desert oases as tensions spread: in 1898 a local Sufic master led an armed insurrection in Andijan; in 1910 Sunni-Shi'ite tensions exploded into sectarian violence; in 1916 rumours of forced conscription into World War I was met with violent, mass resistance; and in 1918 an autonomous Muslim government was set up in Kokand, to be suppressed at the estimated cost of 14,000 lives.

The Disappearing Horse

My faithful follower now whispered in my ear, "We are to have a great feast tonight. The guide's brother-in-law has a horse that is not very well. The animal is to be killed directly, and we are to eat him." Later on, an enormous cauldron was suspended from a tripod across the fire. A heap of fagots was piled upon the embers, and a dense smoke filled the tent. Large pieces of the unfortunate quadruped were now thrown into the pot by the guide's wife, who officiated as cook. The host and the rest of the party superintended the operations with the greatest interest.

"Will there be anything else to eat?" I enquired.

"No," was the answer of my surprised Tartar. "What more would you have? We might eat two sheep at a time; but a horse—no. There will, perhaps, be enough left for breakfast, praise be to God for his bounty!" and the little man, opening his mouth from ear to ear, licked his lips in anticipation of the banquet.

A portion of the steed and some rice were given to me in a slop basin. The rest of the party, calling upon Allah to bless the entertainment, squatted around the cauldron, and thrust their hands into its seething contents, which speedily vanished down their throats. A cunjurer, or fire-king at a village fair, might have swallowed swords or flames, pokers or daggers, but he would have had no chance whatever if pitted to eat horse against my guide's brother-in-law. I thought, when for the second time the cauldron had been emptied, that this would have suffised. But no, for each man strove to outdo his neighbour. Belts and broad sashes were loosed from around the loins, and Nazar, who had made up his mind that he ought to eat for his master as well as himself, was actually swelling before my eyes, and becoming wheezy in his utterances.

I hoped that this would wind up the entertainment, but the feasters were far from having any such intention. The sounds of gorging going on steadily throughout the night announced to me that my follower would very likely be wrong in his conjecture, and that ere breakfast-time all the horse would have disappeared.

Captain Frederick Burnaby, A Ride to Khiva.
Travels and Adventures in Central Asia. 1876

The violence continued with the chaos, anarchy and famine of the October Revolution as Bolsheviks, cut off from Moscow, struggled in a tug of war with White Russians, British agents, Muslim freedom fighters and 40,000 European prisoners of war. The civil war was largely a European affair, fought largely on Muslim soil, but as it became clear that the Bolsheviks harboured no more intention of Muslim independence than the tsarists before them, a *basmachi* resistance movement rose up from the sides of the Ferghana Valley. The movement was given focus by the tenuous but enigmatic leadership of Enver Pasha, son-in-law of the Turkish Caliph and self-styled Prince of Islam, funded by the deposed emir of Bukhara from his exile in Afghanistan and united under the banner of Islamic *jihad,* but it rapidly fragmented and dissolved into clan rivalries as the Bolsheviks tightened their stranglehold on the region. It may have been joked that Bukhara and Khiva were so remote that the 1917 Revolution took three years to arrive, but by 1920 General Frunze's troops had stormed Central Asia's Islamic citadels and transformed them into people's republics inside the Soviet Republic of Turkestan.

MOHAMMEDOV: THE SOVIETIZATION OF CENTRAL ASIA

As if to purge the memory of life under the Tartar yoke, the New Russians dominated the area like few previous overlords. In 1924 the Turkestan ASSR was carved up by the then Commissar of Nationalities, Joseph Stalin, into four ethnic republics and Uzbekistan was born. National Delimitation created nationalities out of what had traditionally been only settler Sart and nomad. It was a policy of divide and rule, couched in terms of national liberation, that was trusted to diffuse the rallying calls of pan-Turkism and pan-Islam.

Having created these new identities, the Soviets promptly set about destroying them. As socialism developed into communism, it was argued, so transient ethnic national identities would 'draw together' and merge to form *Homo Sovieticus*—new Soviet Man. Policy swung from the virulent repression of Stalin and Krushchev to the relative leniency of Brezhnev and Gorbachev and was dependent upon wider political events. But Uzbekistan was essentially a land of merchant begs and mullahs and both of these groups needed to be addressed if Turkestan was to be economically and culturally integrated with the rest of the state. Marx turned his eye to Mohammed.

After early concessions to Islam to win the support of local Muslims, a series of anti-religious drives, a Movement of the Godless, swept through Uzbekistan from the late 1920s to culminate in the terrible purges of Stalin in 1937. Groups of women and statues of Lenin were unveiled in mass meetings; bride price (*kalym*) and polygamy were made illegal. The *hadj* to Mecca, ownership of the Koran and the holy medium of Arabic were all banned in an attempt to prise open the grip of Islam. A wave of anti-religious propaganda turned madrassah into anti-religious museums and minarets into beacons of socialism. By 1942 the number of mosques had fallen from

THE SCIENTISTS

Abu Ali ibn-Sina (980–1037), 'The Prince of all Learning', or Avicenna as he is better known in the West, was the finest medic in the world of his day. As an eighteen-year-old self-taught medic and metaphysicist he cured Sultan Nur of Bukhara and was granted the keys to the finest library in the Islamic world. In the course of the next 30 years he systemized the knowledge of his time in his philosophical encyclopedia and translated Aristotle into Arabic. His *Qanun*, or 'Medical Canon', laid out the position of the main internal organs and blood system, touched upon the existence of bacteria and, when translated into Latin in 1543, became a text book for western medicine until the 19th century, even quoted by Chaucer in his *Canterbury Tales*.

Like al-Beruni, he was a religious man who believed earth was the gift of God and that the light of the stars influenced events on earth and he did not shun political life. Upon the fall of the Samanids, Sina fled to Gurganj where he worked for the next 17 years, much of the time with al-Beruni who often assisted him in the Frankenstein-like stealing of dead bodies for medical experimentation. Even his death in the Persian town of Hamadan was a medical experiment for, as he felt life ebbing away, he ordered his body anointed with an elixir of 40 selected oils. After 39 oils his dying body was again flush with life. The 40th was tragically spilt. Even the great medic could not cure his own mortality.

Al-Beruni (973–1048) was ahead of his time. He knew the earth was round 500 years before Columbus, he knew that the earth went round the sun half a milennium before Copernicus. He plotted the formation of 1,029 stars, estimated the distance to the moon and the radius of the earth, correct to within 12 miles, and announced to a superstitious world the true reason behind an eclipse of the sun. He was astronomer, historian, poet, geographer, pharmacolgist, minerologist and walking encyclopedia.

Born in Kath he served in the Academy of Learning in Gurganj where he was friends with ibn-Sina before he was taken captive to the Ghaznavid court in Afghanistan where he died.

25,000 in 1917 to 1,700, *waqf* religious lands had been confiscated and mullahs deprived of their income.

World War II brought to the region not only a wave of deported peoples and evacuated heavy industry, but also a shared Soviet experience and a conciliatory package of religious concessions. In 1943 the Muslim Spiritual Board of Central Asia was set up and a series of registered clerics were allowed to go through the motions of official Islam under the watchful eye of the party central. Yet the rise of official Islam merely spurred the growth of a parallel Islam. Clandestine Sufic brotherhoods such as the Nakhshbandi, Yassawiya and Kubrawiya, with their itinerant mullahs and personal *zikr* form of prayer, had since Mongol times worn the mantle of defenders of the faith. In the face of this modern onslaught, they formed a silent conspiracy of faith around clandestine teahouses, mosques and holy cemeteries. Infamous anti-state brotherhoods such as the Hairy Ishan were frequently purged (32 leaders were executed in 1936), but popular traditions merely spread in the theological vacuum. Islam went underground and its roots grew deep.

It was not only mullahs but also merchants and nomads that the Soviet state had to tame. In 1928 land was forcibly collectivized into *kolkhoz* or state farms. By 1937 the proportion of collectivized land had leapt from 1.2 per cent to 95 per cent. Over a million people died in Central Asia, as nomads resisted sedentary life, slaughtering their herds and fleeing to China. Epic irrigation schemes such as the Grand Ferghana and Karakum Canals were dug to feed the centre's demand for cotton self-sufficiency. Central Asia became a producer of primary products that were manufactured, sold and profited from in European Russia. Spiralling cotton quotas crescendoed in the 1970s and were met at any price. Or so it seemed. In reality, statistics were falsified, the silence of over 2,500 Central Party officials (including Brezhnev's son-in-law) was bought and the president of the republic, Sharif Rashidov, managed to siphon off over $2 billion from ten million tonnes of cotton that were never picked. He built 30 mansions for Brezhnev's six state visits and then sold them on the black market, while a colleague spent over $100,000 of state funds on her son's wedding celebrations. Corruption was endemic and Tashkent gained infamy as a centre of the union's underworld.

The cotton scandal was only one of many that rocked Uzbekistan in the 1980s as Gorbachev's *perestroika* unlocked a Pandora's box of snowballing state secrets and nationalistic grievances. In the wake of the Chernobyl disaster, the scale of the Aral Sea disaster began to emerge as the true cost of the cotton monoculture. Reports of the systematic murder of Uzbek recruits in the Soviet army incensed a republic already uneasy about a war with Muslim Afghanistan. In 1989 the state-sponsored mufti of Tashkent was sacked for womanizing, drinking alcohol and 'insufficient knowledge of Islam' only to see his replacement fired two years later for 'financial misdeeds'. In the mood of growing nationalism, the centre became the outside and

Dressed for a pilgrimage, Daniel's Tomb, Afrosiab, Samarkand (top)
Tajik chaikhana rhythms, Mavlono Lutfullo Park, Chust, Ferghana Valley (bottom)

The Shir Dor Madrassah from inside the Tillya Kari facade, Samarkand (top)
New Khokkimiyat (Mayor's Office), Tashkent (bottom)

angry whispers amplified into political slogans. 'What the Russians gave us was little and we would have obtained it sooner or later anyway, what they took from us was great and we shall never get it back', went one. Policies that had changed local scripts from Arabic to Latin and then Cyrillic and that promoted Russian language as the medium of inter-ethnic communication were now seen merely as examples of Great Russian chauvinism. Soviet Uzbekistan stood head and shoulders above neighbouring Muslim countries vis-à-vis literacy rates, levels of health and infrastructure, but lagged behind Russia and that hurt inflamed pride. Rioting and ethnic strife broke out in the Ferghana Valley as economic hardships began to bubble to the surface. But as the Union trembled under the weight of economic and ethnic tensions, momentous events were to come not from within the republic but from without.

INDEPENDENT UZBEKISTAN

Russia may well fall to pieces, as many expect. Conolly, Capt. Arthur (1839)

In a March 1991 union-wide referendum, 90 per cent of Central Asia voted to retain the union. In August, however, Moscow shook to a hardline coup. And on September 30, as the revolution came crashing down from above, Uzbekistan reluctantly declared its independence and 1924's jigsaw borders suddenly became real international boundaries.

The Communist Party of Uzbekistan committed suicide and was reborn as the People's Democratic Party, the KGB became the National Security Service and the former chief of the Communist Party, Islam Karimov, was sworn in as president with one hand on his heart and the other on the Koran. An official opposition party called Birlik (Unity) was formed and promptly split into two. As Western journalists heralded the victory of ill-defined concepts such as democracy and freedom, the reaction of local people faced with chronic shortages of the most basic foodstuffs was understandably somewhat more cynical. As history's pendulum swung back to the Uzbeks, Russians began to leave at the rate of 700 per day. In the ideological vacuum, people are returning to an idealized past and Islam for consolation.

Today Karimov plays the strong clan leader warding off the twin bogeymen of fundamentalism and nationalism. Stability is the key word, following Tajikistan's collapse into civil war in 1992, and the renewal of conflict among the long-suffering Afghans in 1996. Kazakhstan and Kyrgyzstan present autocracy with greater style— the former boasts Central Asia's leading statesman, President Nazarbayev, and high-profile energy contracts, while the latter is the darling of international financiers, keen to build the Switzerland of Turkestan. Turkmenistan remains '99.9 per cent yes' country, where President Niyazov, or rather Turkmenbashi, 'Father of the Turkomans', enjoys a vigorous personality cult.

A flurry of international players, eager to stake a claim in what has been billed the return of the Great Game, have entered the political and economic linchpin of Central Asia. Tashkent's hotels have filled with Turkish businessmen keen to capitalize on ethnic and linguistic common ground and Western magnates drawn to the world's fifth-largest producer of cotton and eighth-largest miner of gold, whilst the Ferghana Valley has seen a fervent scurrying of Saudi Arabian, Iranian and Pakistani missionaries jostling for religious influence. China points to the successes of economic reform under tight political control, Turkey suggests a secular Western-backed model and Iran preaches a revolutionary fundamentalism, but all offer new models for a discredited system. Plans to reintegrate the region into its natural environment includes rail links to the Persian Gulf, a superhighway to Karachi and the Iron Silk Road to Beijing. Ancient religious, trade and cultural links are being redrawn as lifelines thrown to a disconnected past.

Faced with an uncertain future, Uzbekistan is trying to rediscover and recreate its identity, to rekindle what the Soviets tried to snuff out. Textbooks are being rewritten, streets renamed and a new set of myths employed. Lenin becomes Tamerlane and Tamerlane becomes an Uzbek. As locals will wryly tell you, in Uzbekistan only the past is as unpredictable as the future.

Land and People

GEOGRAPHY

The Republic of Uzbekistan, the 'land of the Uzbeks', forms the very centre of ex-Soviet Central Asia, for it alone borders each of the new republics—Kazakhstan to the north, Kyrgyzstan and Tajikistan to the east and southeast, Turkmenistan to the southwest, as well as Afghanistan to the south. Unlike some of their neighbours, the Uzbeks remain a clear majority in their republic, accounting for almost 75 per cent of the total population of 22.5 million. Most of its territory of 447,400 square kilometres (roughly the size of Sweden) lies between the two major rivers of Central Asia, the Syr Darya (Jaxartes) and the Amu Darya (Oxus).

The **Syr Darya** rises in remotest Kyrgyzstan before plummeting from the Tian Shan (the 'Mountains of Heaven') into the wide hollow of the Ferghana Valley in the northeast of Uzbekistan. Skirting the capital Tashkent, it completes a journey of 2,137 kilometres (1,335 miles) through southern Kazakhstan and the Kyzyl Kum (Red Sands) desert to the distant Aral Sea. For centuries it marked the northern limits of Transoxiana and the edge of the boundless nomadic steppe.

From its origins in the Hindu Kush, the **Amu Darya** cuts through the High Pamirs of Tajikistan to follow the Afghan border and trace a northwesterly path of 1,437 kilometres parallel to the Syr Darya, separating the Kyzyl Kum from the Kara Kum (Black Sands) of Turkmenistan, and in ancient times dividing the Persian and Turkic

Desert citadel Toprak Kala, Karakalpakstan

worlds. Along its lower reaches the river enters the Turan lowland and the Khorezm oasis. Its final course has changed many times, sometimes stretching west to the Caspian Sea across the Ust'urt plateau. Today it founders heavy with silt at the shrinking Aral Sea, victim of insatiable irrigation.

Steppe and desert plains account for two thirds of Uzbekistan, with the remainder of the country rising into the foothills and mountains of the western Tian Shan and Gissaro-Alay ranges in the east and southeast, where peaks along the borders of Kyrgyzstan and Tajikistan reach to 4,500 metres (14,750 feet). Its location between two major rivers has always ensured commercial and cultural prominence. Thousands of smaller streams expire in wasteland, but one, the **Zerafshan**, former tributary of the Amu Darya, first waters the most attractive oases in the region, Samarkand and Bukhara. The fertility of these river valleys has long supported greater populations than elsewhere in Central Asia, although the Uzbeks themselves are relative latecomers to oasis community and culture.

While less than ten per cent of Uzbekistan's territory is arable land, Soviet planners drew on tsarist experimentation to turn the republic into the Union's cotton production base. As the American civil war cut world cotton supplies, Turkestan was discovered to be ideal for cotton cultivation. Under Moscow's orders, irrigation networks stretching 150,000 kilometres (94,000 miles) were built in Uzbekistan to support a plantation economy supplying 70 per cent of the Soviet Union's cotton. In

1924, output totalled 200,000 tonnes; by 1980 this figure had risen to nine million tonnes. The sheer size of the irrigation system required to sustain this level of production has resulted in much of the water from the major rivers being diverted; deprived of its sustenance, the Aral Sea has been shrinking steadily, halving in size since 1960. [see page 312].

Despite the staggering environmental costs of the cotton monopoly, independent Uzbekistan desperately needs the revenue from its major crop. Some land is now being switched from cotton to less thirsty grain production, although the 1996 harvest of under four million tonnes still ranked Uzbekistan as the world's fourth-largest cotton nation. Other mainstays of the Uzbek economy include fruit and vegetables, animal husbandry and textiles, but it is the republic's mineral wealth that most excites foreign investors. In addition to being the world's seventh-largest gold producer, Uzbekistan harbours significant reserves of oil and natural gas, as well as uranium, silver, copper, zinc, coal and lead.

ETHNIC GROUPS
Nomadic migrations through the centuries make precise ethnic definition almost impossible. The ancient tribes of the Scythians, Sogdians, Khorezmians and myriad Turkic peoples formed the foundation for the later Uzbeks, Kazakhs, Kyrgyz, Turkomans and even Tajiks. History is also complicated by Soviet 'divide and rule' tactics, whereby common heritage was distorted into artificial 'nationalist' identities.

■ UZBEK
The Uzbeks are a predominantly Turkic people, Sunni Muslims of the Hanafi school, yet their ethnogenesis shows significant Persian and Turco-Mongol elements. The origin of the ethonym itself is in dispute. One view holds that the group name derives from Uzbek Khan (1282–1342), the last powerful ruler of the Golden Horde and responsible for its conversion to Islam, though the nomadic Uzbeks were never subject to him. Etymological argument states that the name means 'independent' or 'the man himself', from *uz*, self, and *Bek* or 'Beg', a noble title of leadership.

The process of the formation of the Uzbeks began in the 11th century and solidified in the 14th as a conglomeration of Turkic tribes. Their language, Chagatai or Old Uzbek, evolved at the same time. These nomads clashed with the Timurids, Ulug Beg and Babur, as they moved south from the Kazakh steppes to dominate Transoxiana in the 16th century. This Shaybanid Uzbek dynasty promoted the transition to sedentary life by merging with the earlier inhabitants in the 16th and 17th centuries, until the name Uzbek came to be used for the whole population.

By the early 20th century, the Uzbeks were yet to be consolidated into a nation. First and foremost an Uzbek was (and remains) a Muslim, while his next point of reference was his home town. The tsarist administration generalized the settled inhabitants of Turkestan as *Sarts*, or 'traders', a word of Sanskrit origin, to distinguish them from nomads. The Uzbeks comprised three major ethnic layers. The first was the urban population, oasis-dwelling Uzbeks intermingled with the original Persian (Tajik) inhabitants of Central Asia. The second and third layers were the semi-nomadic descendants of the pre-Shaybanid Turco-Mongol tribes and the Shaybanid Uzbek tribes. The latter two groups still preserve some tribal identity, such as the Kipchaks, Karluks, Mangit and Kungrat, ethnic groupings shared by other Turkic nations.

Soviet delimitation, "negative ethnic gerrymandering" in the words of American expert Edward Allworth, gave the Uzbeks the heart of Central Asia, less than the original Uzbek domains, but encompassing the historic power centres. Soviet historiography encouraged an anachronistic Uzbek nationalism, once firmly within the Russian fraternal embrace, but which has since taken on a life of its own. The belief that the glories of Transoxiana are an exclusive part of the Uzbek heritage, plus the Uzbeks' numerical superiority, leaves neighbouring republics wary of 'great Uzbek chauvinism'. At around 18 million strong, the Uzbeks are the third-largest nationality in the former Soviet Union. Uzbeks in Uzbekistan number almost 17 million, with substantial minorities in Tajikistan (23 per cent), Kyrgyzstan (12.9 per cent) and Turkmenistan (13 per cent). Up to two million Uzbeks inhabit northern Afghanistan, with another 25,000 in northwest China's Xinjiang Autonomous Region.

■ KAZAKH

Like the Uzbeks, the Kazakhs have a complex ethnic history stretching back to various nomadic tribes breeding livestock on the steppes of Turkestan long before the Mongols of Genghis Khan. A popular explanation derives the ethonym, first used in the 16th century, from *kaz* (goose) and *ak* (white), after the legend of a white steppe goose that turned into a princess who birthed the first Kazakh. Another version reads Kazakh as 'wanderer', descriptive of their mobile lifestyle, or rather 'outlaw', a term coined after the first united Kazakh confederation, the Kazakh Orda, split from the Shaybani Uzbeks in the 15th century.

Resisting Uzbek advances, the Kazakhs built a steppe empire that defined 'Kazakh' as the tribes to the north of the Syr Darya and Uzbeks as the tribes to the south. In the 17th century the Kazakh groups were unified into three federations—the Great, Middle and Little Hordes. The wide, indefensible expanse of the Kazakh steppes, lacking in natural boundaries, meant that they were the first of the Central Asian peoples to be colonized by the Russians. The Soviets exploited the vast territory for nuclear testing until popular pressure stopped tests at the Semipalatinsk site in 1990.

Today, Kazakhstan reveals a clear divide between the industrialised, Russified north and the more traditional south. While the Kazakhs are mostly settled, their nomadic cultural past remains deeply embedded in the national consciousness. Mongol physical features are more pronounced than in the Uzbeks and the patrilateral lineages of the Kazakh hordes form an integral part of contemporary society. As with fellow nomads, the Kyrgyz and Turkomans, the Kazakhs are Sunni Muslim, although Islam contends with shamanist beliefs and never dominated the grasslands and mountains of Central Asia as it did the oases and valleys.

The Kazakhs represent only 42 per cent of the republic's population of 17 million, with the Russians close behind at 36 per cent and another 100 ethnic groups forming the remainder. Some 800,000 Kazakhs inhabit northern areas of Uzbekistan, with a further 1.2 million in northwest China.

■ KYRGYZ

White felt *ak-kalpak*, the yurt-like headgear of the Kyrgyz, symbolize a proud nation of mountain nomads. One translation of their name is 'indestructible', for about 93 per cent of Kyrgyzstan's territory comprises the lofty mountains of the Tian Shan and Altai ranges. The Kyrgyz know them as the 'Wings of the Earth', a remote refuge from countless invasions.

Their origins lie along the Yenisei river in southern Siberia, source of another translation of Kyrgyz, 'forty clans', though this better describes the assimilation of indigenous tribes during the slow migration southwest. After falling under Turkic and Mongol suzerainty, the Kyrgyz became a distinct people by the 16th century. Yet even by the 20th century little was known of them. Their Kazakh cousins were called Kirghiz, or Kirghiz-Kazakh, while the true Kyrgyz were called Kara (black) Kirghiz.

Fierce resistance to the World War I draft, and later collectivization, brought violent repression, but industrialization and Russification has spared most of the Kyrgyz' beautiful homeland. The oral epic *Manas*, traditional sports such as falconry, eagle-hunting and *baiga* (polo with a goat carcass) remain important cultural denominators. The Kyrgyz account for 52.4 per cent of the republic's 4.4 million population, with Russians at 21.5 per cent and Uzbeks at 12.9 per cent. About 200,000 Kyrgyz are spread around the ethnic jigsaw of the Ferghana Valley and another 150,000 live over the border in Xinjiang, China.

■ TURKOMAN (TURKMEN)

For centuries, the 'man-stealing Turcomen' were the scourge of travellers in western Central Asia. Unscrupulous slave-traders, the Turkomans ravaged merchant caravans and sleeping oases in the hunt for loot and human flesh. Harsh desert wasteland characterizes most of present-day Turkmenistan, yet archaeologists have recorded agricultural settlements over 5,000 years old. The modern Turkomans are descended from the Oghuz Turkic tribes of the Mongol Altai region who migrated to this part of Khorasan in the tenth and eleventh centuries.

Although its etymology is unclear, the ethnym 'Turkoman' had replaced Oghuz

People of Uzbekistan

by the 13th century. By the 14th and 15th centuries, these warrior nomads had attained a recognizable ethnic identity, but tribal divisions were still uppermost. Four centuries later, the major groupings included the Tekke, Sariks, Salors, Yomuts, Ersary and Goklen. Harassment from the Persians and the warring Uzbek khanates frequently pressed the Turkomans into mercenary service, leaving little opportunity for a stable indigenous empire to establish itself.

Russian colonization met its stiffest test in pacifying these formidable masters of desert warfare. Today, the Tekke, resplendent in shaggy, Persian-lamb *papakha* hats, remain the most powerful Turkoman tribe. Despite the republic's undeniable mineral wealth, Turkmenistan attracts equal attention for its Stalinist personality cult, centred on President Niyazov, chiefly renowned for bestowing fine Turkoman steeds on foreign dignitaries. Turkomans comprise 72 per cent of the total population of 4.2 million, followed by an equal number of both Russian and Uzbeks (13 per cent each). Over 300,000 Turkomans live across the border in Iran, with another 400,000 in Afghanistan.

■ TAJIK

Tajikistan, like Kyrgyzstan, is predominantly a mountain state: some 76 per cent of its territory rests high in the Pamir mountains, a world of yaks and glaciers rarely dipping below an altitude of 3,000 metres (10,000 feet). Most similarities end there, however, for the Tajiks are the odd men out of Central Asia—Indo-European, Iranian-speaking, with almond eyes, pronounced noses and heavy beards. This ethno-linguistic oasis predates the arrival of the Turks by at least a millenium.

During the sixth and seventh centuries BC, Transoxiana was already peopled by east Iranian stock: the Bactrians, Sogdians and Scythians. Despite centuries of diverse cultural invasion, this Persian influence has dominated sedentary life. Derived from the Arabic tribal name *Taiy*, the Sogdian word *Tazik* was used for the Arab invaders and by the 11th century came to mean the Islamicized, Persian-speaking population, as opposed to the Turkic peoples of the region.

The Tajiks were increasingly marginalized to the southeast of the Uzbek domains, though Persian maintained its status as the premier literary language. Squeezed by the legacies of the Uzbek khanates, the Tajiks received the leanest slice of national delimitation, losing their historic centres of Samarkand and Bukhara to Uzbekistan. The complex divide between Tajikistan's pro-communist, industrialized north and the poorer, more Islamic south exploded just nine months after independence in a sorry confusion of ethnic, regional and political loyalties. For the rest of Central Asia, Tajikistan is held up as an example of the evils of political and religious liberalization. Tajiks comprise almost 59 per cent of the republic's population of 5.4 million, followed by Uzbeks at 23 per cent and Russians at 11 per cent. Another four million Tajiks inhabit northern Afghanistan (outnumbering Afghans) and a further one million live in Uzbekistan.

■ OTHERS

The Turkic **Karakalpak**, numbering over 400,000, occupy an autonomous republic within northwestern Uzbekistan [see Nukus p309-314]. The **Russian** population percentage in Central Asia declines steadily with every new assertion of the republics' independence. In 1989, the Russians accounted for 8.3 per cent of the population of Uzbekistan; this had dropped to 6.9 per cent by 1994—a combination of low birth rates and large-scale emigration. Many of the other non-native peoples, such as **Ukrainians**, **Belorussians**, **Volga Germans** and **Koreans**, often deported to Central Asia in the 1930s and during World War II, have also found cause to leave. Other inhabitants of Uzbekistan include **Uighurs**, the Turkic people based in Xinjiang, **Dungans**, Muslim Chinese immigrants, and relatively small numbers who still identify themselves as **Tartars**, **Persians**, **Arabs**, **Jews**, **Gypsies** or **Turks**.

Art and Architecture

The rich architectural inheritance of Uzbekistan is endowed with some of the most audacious buildings in the Islamic world. They are the legacy of a series of Central Asian rulers from the Turkic hordes to Tamerlane to the Khivan khans, who created breathtaking monuments to their own immortality in an attempt to leave an enduring mark on restless nomadic lands. The heavy swell of a melon dome, the graceful arch of a madrassah portal and the bold silhouette of a towering minaret form some of the most evocative images a traveller will carry away with him and sound the clearest echoes of past splendour.

Rich archaeological remains in the area preserve an intriguing mix of Hellenistic, Buddhist and Scythian influences in the laconic desert castles of Khorezm and Bactria and trace a development to the rich Sogdian palaces and wall paintings of Varakhsha and Afrosiab. But it was the arrival of Islam in the eighth century and its alien synthesis of styles that transformed the face of Central Asia as much as its soul.

Islamic architecture is historically the result of a fusion of ideology and wide-ranging local traditions by a desert people with little architectural tradition of their own. However, its eclecticism has been joined by a deep conservatism and a unifying ideology that has long favoured established forms and continuity of development. A madrassah from the 19th century differs little from one of the 15th century and a mosque from Samarkand shares many similarities with one in Marrakesh. For more than a millennium, Islam has dominated the function of buildings, their layout and their decoration.

Central Asia's desert environment has also profoundly affected its architecture. Whole towns are turned in on themselves in protection against desert storms and nomad raids. A lack of stone gave rise to a richly imaginative use of baked brick and

A TALE OF TWO LEADERS

Faizullah Khodjaev (1896–1938)

In 1907, the young Khodjaev left Bukhara with his father, a wealthy Uzbek trader, for a Moscow education that opened his eyes to the 'living anachronism' of Bukharan society. He offered his services and his father's fortune to the reformist Jadids who in 1916 re-formed into the Young Bukharan Party. After the Bolshevik failure to seize Bukhara, on Khodjaev's invitation, in late 1917, he escaped to Tashkent and only returned following the emir's flight in September 1920. As the head of the Bukharan People's Republic, Soviet

power in autonomous guise, he barely escaped assassination by *basmachi* leader Enver Pasha. He survived Moscow's 1923–4 purges of 'national communists' to become President of the Council of People's Commissars of Soviet Uzbekistan. In pursuing a lifelong goal of greater independence for Turkestan, Khodjaev fought against the cotton monoculture imposed on his republic. Slogans such as 'you cannot eat cotton' attracted Stalin's wrath—he was arrested in 1937 on trumped-up charges, appeared at a Moscow show trial of the 'Trotskyite and Rightist bloc' and was executed on March 13, 1938. Rehabilitation came in 1966, but Khodjaev remains a controversial figure in independent Uzbekistan, blessed by few memorials save for one of his father's beautifully decorated Bukharan homes, now open to the public.

Sharaf Rashidovich Rashidov (1917–1983)

Born in the year of the Russian Revolution to 'poor peasant' stock in Dzhizak, Rashidov worked as teacher, journalist and editor of a Samarkand daily. He fought in the Great Patriotic War until heavy wounds forced him home in 1942. Having published his war-time poetry, *My Wrath*, he rose to editor of a republican daily and head of Uzbekistan's Writers' Union in 1949. More significant was his election in 1950 to Chairman of the Praesidium of Uzbekistan's Supreme Soviet, and his promotion in 1959 to the top job, First Secretary of the Uzbek Communist Party. His 24-year tenure is synonymous with corruption, nepotism and Tashkent's monumentalist architecture. With Brezhnev in the Kremlin condoning the antics of his Central Asian power-base, Rashidov and his mafia network falsified figures to earn $2 billion profit for cotton never grown. Fiefdoms were granted to loyal cronies like Akhmadzhan Adylov, feudal lord of a private estate, harem and underground torture-chamber deep in the Ferghana Valley. Rashidov's death in office spared him public humiliation following satellite discovery of empty cotton fields and widespread arrests, executions and suicides. Yet such was Uzbek resentment at the Russian media's treatment of the 'Uzbek affair' that many see Rashidov as a strong leader who defied Moscow and won. After independence he has re-emerged as a national hero with statues in Tashkent and Dzhizak testifying to father-figure status.

made the development of the brick cupola a natural choice in a land chronically lacking in timber. Desert heat inspired cool summer *iwans*, suburban gardens and a love of freshwater canals.

Several innovations have also steered the course of local architectural development. The introduction of fired brick in the ninth and tenth centuries gave buildings not only a far greater solidity than before, but also a rich medium of decoration that was ideally suited to the harsh desert light. The series of corner arches that appeared for the first time at Tim, near Samarkand, eased the move from a square base, through an eight- and sixteen-sided layer of transition, to a round dome and paved the way for the great turquoise domes of Samarkand and Bukhara. The technology of mono-chrome tilework, first brought to the Kalon Minaret in Bukhara in the 12th century to emphasize exterior monumental inscriptions, soon expanded into the revelry of Timurid polychromatic tilework. The full resources of Tamerlane's empire brought a cosmopolitanism and monumentality to Timurid architecture. It also introduced the ribbed dome, the high drum and the double dome (employed so successfully in the Gur Emir), the tendency to ensemble architecture and the new madrassah design of monumental portals flanked by towering minarets.

Today the blues of Samarkand, the khakis of Bukhara and the greens of Khiva reflect Central Asia's staggered architectural evolution. Samarkand offers the most spectacular, Bukhara the widest variety, Khiva the most homogenous.

Mosques form the cornerstone of religious and social life in Central Asia. Their relatively bare interiors, devoid of the Christian distractions of furniture, sculpture or music, require only a *mihrab* niche set in a *qiblah* wall to point the direction of Mecca, a *minbar* pulpit from where an imam can address his congregation, and a clean, carpeted space used for daily prayer. Prayer also requires ablution and, in a desert faith like Islam, mosques stood to benefit by combining religious ritual with a clean water supply. In Central Asia's rather relaxed version of social Islam, mosques thus soon grew into social centres providing school, notice board and meeting place. Mosques are divided by function and structure into district *guzar* mosques, built on a personal scale to service approximately 60 households; *jummi* or Friday mosques, such as the Kalon in Bukhara, required to accommodate the entire male population of a city for its most important lunchtime service; and *namazgokh* or holiday mosques, open air arenas catering to both town and country during important Islamic festivals. Minarets summon the faithful to the mosque and provide an eloquent example of the synthesis of engineering, art and imagination working in tight constraints. Their height ranges from 60 metres to 10, from the fragile taper of Vabkent to the cylindrical tower of Khiva to the vertical ribs of Jarkurgan.

Mausoleums have largely followed the pattern first set in 997 by the portal and dome of the Arab Ata mausoleum of Tim, but have nevertheless expanded into a range of styles from Khorezmian conical tent designs to monumental streets of tombs, as seen in the Shah-i-Zindah. Most contain a tomb chamber (*gurkhana*) and prayer hall (*ziaratkhana*) and have provided clandestine shelter for popular Islam during troubled times.

Madrassah are religious colleges run under state sponsorship and most conform to a set pattern. Twin flanking mosque and lecture rooms lead into a four *iwaned* square courtyard lined by *hujra* cells.

Decoration in Central Asian art has been straightjacketed by Islam's prohibition in the Hadiths of figural art. In its place geometric and later arabesque designs thus developed in a mind-spinning fusion of science, mathematics and art. *Girikh* pentagons inscribed in stars and continually dividing floral motifs were inscribed on grids and transposed onto tile to cover entire façades. Calligraphy also gained a primary position in tile and brick decoration as a sacred vehicle of divine communication. Of the various decorative scripts used, the angular Kufic was most favoured by the Timurids, although the rounded, cursive *Thulth* script is also widely used, often with its stems elongated and interwoven with floral designs to produce a foliated script.

Tilework however remains the most spectacular medium of Central Asian decoration and the Timurids its most accomplished masters. Faïence mosaic, which was carved in soft clay, individually coloured and fired, then assembled on a mortar base like a jigsaw, gradually gave way to polychrome tiles, which had their floral designs painted directly onto the tile before it was glazed. Both still conformed to the non-figural traditions of Islam and were characterized by their deep turquoise hue (turquoise—the colour of the Turks). Yet bold breaks with tradition can be seen in the lions and faces of the Shir Dor and Divanbegi madrassah and in the yellow and brown hues imported from Iran and Azerbaijan. Other forms of decoration to look out for include carved alabaster *ganch* and *kundal* and *chaspak* painting techniques, which respectively use heavy mineral paint and three dimensional carved wood set on sub-coloured ganch to decorate the interiors of mosques and royal buildings.

Facts for the Traveller

Getting There

In modern times, Uzbekistan's capital Tashkent has pursued its traditional crossroads role to become the communications hub of Central Asia and a mid-point transit stop for trans-Asian long hauls. Road, rail and air routes converge to make the city the major starting point and base for regional travel. With independence has come ever wider international access, enabling foreign tourists to forego the time-honoured delay in Moscow and fly to Tashkent direct, or trace the Silk Road by train, bus or boat from Russia, China, Iran and Azerbaijan, through the neighbouring republics of Kazakhstan, Kyrgyzstan and Turkmenistan. Recent upgrading of the Samarkand, Bukhara and Urgench airports enables international charters to fly directly to these cities.

AIR

Thanks to its extensive network, modern aircraft and improving in-flight service, **Uzbekistan Airways** (Havo Yullari) enjoys a growing reputation among the plethora of carriers to emerge from the former Soviet airline Aeroflot. Direct Tashkent flights include: London (4 times a week); Delhi (6); Frankfurt (3); New York (1) via Amsterdam; Bangkok (2); Sharjah (3); Istanbul (2); Karachi (2); Tel Aviv (2); Kuala Lumpur (1); Jeddah (1); Beijing (1); Seoul (2); Moscow (daily) and destinations throughout the CIS; e.g Almaty (3 weekly); Bishkek (1); Ashkhabad (1). Flights to and from Moscow (other than on Transaero) are still considered domestic and so operate from Moscow's Domodedovo Airport, not the international Sheremetyevo. Those transiting through Moscow therefore have to transfer between airports.

For information and bookings contact Uzbekistan Air in: (area codes in parantheses)

China: 304, CITIC Rear Bldg, 19 Jianguomenwai Dajie, Beijing, tel. (10) 65006442

Germany: 125 Buroraum, 216 Merkurhaus, Hauptbahnhof 10, 6000 Frankfurt-Am-
    Main, tel. (69) 27100265

India: Rm 20, Hotel Janpath, New Delhi, tel. (11) 3327042 or 3320070 ext. 2020

Israel: 1 Ben Yehuda St, Tel Aviv, tel. (3) 5104685

Malaysia: 130-131, 1st Floor, Plaza Berjaya (Negaria Complex), 12 Jalan Imbi, Kuala
    Lumpur, tel. (3) 2447506

Pakistan: F-13/1 Block-9 KOA Scheme-5, Clifton, Karachi, tel. (1) 573901

Russia: 1U, 11/2 Kazachi Berulok, Moscow, tel. (095) 2382124

Thailand: 191/68, 15th Floor, CTI Tower, 191 Rajadapasike Road, Klongtoey,
    Bangkok, tel. (2) 2615084/5

Turkey: 39/4 Jumkhuriat St, Istanbul, tel. (1) 2371993

Islam Khoja minaret, Khiva

UK: 72 Wigmore St, London W1, tel. (0171) 9351899. There is also a branch of Uzbektourism here; ask for Mr Alisher Akhmedov. For bookings contact Regent Holidays [see page 54] or HY Travel, 69 Wigmore St, tel. (0171) 9354775/8
USA: Suite 1401, 630 Fifth Avenue, New York, tel. (212) 4893954/6

From many countries tickets may be cheaper through travel agents than directly from the airline. Tickets to destinations such as Delhi and Bangkok via Tashkent can actually cost less than a flight to Tashkent alone, but stopovers are often forbidden.

Other airlines serving Uzbekistan include daily Aeroflot Moscow–Tashkent connections, Lufthansa (3 flights a week Frankfurt–Tashkent); PIA (2 flights a week Islamabad–Tashkent and Karachi–Tashkent); Air India (2 flights a week New Delhi–Tashkent); Turkish Airlines (3 flights a week Istanbul–Tashkent); Transaero (4 flights a week Moscow–Tashkent); Iran Air (1 flight a week Tehran–Tashkent); and Ariana Airlines (an intermittent 1 flight a week Kabul–Tashkent). British Airways is planning a London–Tashkent connection. For details of airline offices in Tashkent, see page 92.

Travellers should also consider Almaty a useful point of entry for its more lenient visa regime and growing international connections: British Airways (twice a week from London); Lufthansa (5 times, Frankfurt); Austrian Airlines (2, Vienna); KLM (2, Amsterdam); Xinjiang Airlines (2, Urumqi); Kazakhstan Airways (2, Beijing; 1, Delhi/ Frankfurt/Istanbul/Sharjah/Tehran/Tel Aviv).

THE IRON SILK ROAD—RAIL

The Trans-Siberian Railway is the most celebrated train epic, yet the 1990 completion of a line from Urumqi in northwest China to the Kazakh border opened another Sino-Russian connection, through the khanates of Central Asia. A minimum of three trains is necessary: Moscow–Almaty, Almaty–Urumqi, Urumqi–Beijing, though the wealth of sites along the route begs frequent diversions.

Trains depart from Moscow's Kazan Station (for Tashkent and Almaty) or Pavelets Station (Ashkhabad, Dushanbe) and trace a twin branched route through forest, steppe and desert via either Kazakhstan and the Syr Darya or Urgench and the Amu Darya, respectively. Direct trains to Tashkent take the Syr Darya route and take two and a half days, while the southern route gives the option of entering Uzbekistan at Urgench/Khiva or continuing to Ashkhabad. If you do wish to stop off at Urgench but do not already have a visa, you will be given three days transit grace by the local OVIR (the office of visas and foreign registration) until they come looking for fines.

Side routes into Uzbekistan also include the Transcaspian link from Turkmenbashi in Turkmenistan to Tashkent, and the Turk-Sib branch north, via Almaty, to connect with the Trans-Siberian at Novosibirsk. Trains also continue east from Almaty to Urumqi. For carriages and ticket types see Getting Around [page 47-48]. In 1996 another Silk Road connection was re-tied with the opening of the Mashad–Ashkhabad rail link. Now all that remains between travellers and yet another epic trans-continental rail link is the currently suspended Erzurum (Turkey)–Tehran line.

Overland Silk Road Routes

■ TO/FROM CHINA

The Sino/Central Asian border can be crossed at five places. Visas are not issued at the borders but China does have embassies in both Tashkent and Almaty, while Urumqi has a functioning Kazakh and a planned Uzbek consulate. [see pages 48-51]. When crossing into China it is imperative to explain that you will be leaving China by a different point of exit, as officials often restrict CIS citizens by stamping their visa with the condition that they exit by the same port of entry. Such a stamp guarantees considerable grief when you try to exit China from, for example, Beijing or cross into Hong Kong, as bureaucrats demand you return whence you came.

The main international crossing point at Dzharkent (former Panvilov)/Khorgos in Kazakhstan follows the Mongols' traditional gateway to Central Asia through the Dzungarian Gap and leads by road to the Chinese town of Yining and by rail via Dostyk to Urumqi and Beijing. Direct buses sometimes run between Urumqi and the Kazakh capital, Almaty. Otherwise take a bus to the nearest town to the frontier and then hitch or take a taxi the rest of the way. Taxis are not allowed into the four-kilometre stretch of no-man's-land. Two further Sino/Kazakh border crossings have also opened: Bachty/Tacheng and Maykopchagay/Jeminay (Altai). Further south, the Torugat Pass (3752m / 12,300ft) connects Kashgar (China) with Naryn (Kyrgyzstan) and Bishkek beyond. An occasional public bus makes the 36-hour run between Kashgar and Bishkek. If you hitch, remember that border guards are reluctant to let you cross the five kilometres (3 miles) of no-man's-land unless you have onward transport arranged, either with a Kyrgyz agency or Kashgar CITS. All visas must be in order and none are issued on the border. The imminent opening of a further crossing from Kashgar at Irkeshtam, near Sary Tash, also in Kyrgyzstan, will soon provide a much more convenient way of entering the Ferghana Valley via Osh, but similar transport problems will apply. From Kashgar, routes continue south along the Karakoram Highway into Pakistan.

■ TO/FROM CIS

Apart from the transcontinental railroads there are a number of off-beat ways of entering Central Asia and thus Uzbekistan. Ferryboats shuttle between Baku in Azerbaijan and Turkmenbashi (Krasnovodsk) in Turkmenistan and occasionally leave for Astrakhan in Russia, from whence cruise boats glide up the Volga into the Russian heartland. There is also an intriguingly remote route out of Central Asia via north-eastern Kazakhstan and a brief transit through the Russian Altai Mountains to the international border crossing with Mongolia and the remote town of Olgi beyond. The route requires ruthlessly efficient preparation and watertight paperwork, but promises spectacular scenery.

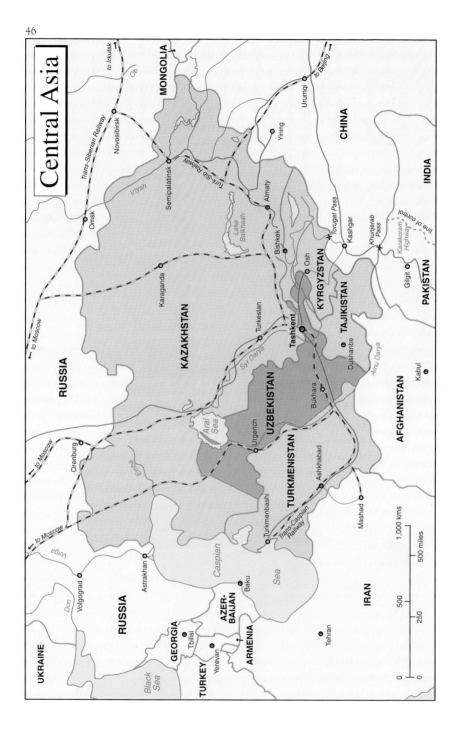

Central Asia

■ **TO/FROM IRAN**

There is an international border crossing at Bajgiran, 45 kilometres from Ashkhabad in Turkmenistan on the road to Mashad, that is presently open to local Khorasan traffic and that will inevitably (soon) open to international Silk Road travel. If the political situation in Afghanistan is ever stabilized and demilitarized, pipe-dream road and rail routes will hopefully again lead from Herat to Merv in Turkmenistan and Mazar-e-Sharif to Termez in Uzbekistan, and complete an overland route to Peshawar in Pakistan.

It is much to be hoped that something comes of 1994's grandly titled Samarkand Declaration, purporting to ease travel restrictions along the silken threads from China to Europe across Central Asia. To jump the gun, pack plenty of time, flexibility and a Great Game spirit, for you will be exploring a bold, new frontier of independent travel just as the fog of inner Asian isolation begins to lift. In times of frustration, remember that your encounters with bureaucracy will not bear comparison with those of the long-suffering populace.

GETTING AROUND

■ AIR

Uzbekistan Airways offers regular departures from Tashkent to all the republic's major cities and tourist destinations: Andijan, Bukhara, Ferghana, Karshi, Kokand, Namangan, Navoi, Nukus, Samarkand, Shakhrisabz, Termez, Urgench, plus regional capitals Almaty, Ashkhabad and Bishkek. Weekly Ferghana/Namangan–Urgench flights help avoid wasteful backtracking. Tickets can be bought at certain hotels or the city branch of Uzbekistan Airways. Foreigners must pay in U.S. dollars but rates remain reasonable, e.g. one-way Tashkent–Samarkand $50; Bukhara $62; Urgench $77; Ferghana $48; Termez $65. Return tickets are rarely sold, so book your return flight immediately on arrival. Domestic standards of service are somewhat below the airline's international efforts, so bring sufficient snacks and drinks. When checking in, it is quicker, safer and common practice to carry one's own luggage on board.

■ RAIL

While trains offer interesting routes into Uzbekistan, they compare poorly with the convenience and comfort of buses for domestic travel. Independence has cut services, yet the rising cost of air and bus tickets has increased the numbers of passengers. The *provodniks* (attendants) can be more concerned with crowding the corridors than keeping the samovar alive or the toilet sanitary. Heed local warnings never to lose sight of your belongings. Nevertheless, journeys can be fun as vodka and melon slices accompany international friendship to a slowly moving backdrop of desertscape and oases. The most reliable and well maintained connections are the Tashkent–Bukhara express trains which leave each city at 7pm nightly.

Ticket buying often requires outstanding patience. Check the information on the ticket window to ensure it sells tickets to your destination and that the next office break is a few hours away. In Tashkent, a foreigners' ticket office demands a dollar surcharge to the cheap sum price but dispenses with queues. Train numbers 001–149 are *skorry poezd* (fast trains), quickest of which are infrequent expresses; nos 151–169 refer to slower *skorostnoi poezd* (quick trains); nos 171–699 signify *passazhirskiy poezd* (passenger trains), stopping wherever they can. First class tickets are for the 'soft' car (*myagkiy vagon*) *liux* means a two-berth compartment. Four-berth *kupeyniy* can be soft or second class hard (*zhostkiy*). Third class is *platskartniy*, an open carriage with hard seats that change into bunks; fourth class *obshchiy* offers benches and little else.

■ ROAD
The most popular and convenient way to follow the Silk Road. A hardy fleet of red Hungarian Ikarus buses has been supplemented by blue joint-venture UzDaewoo vehicles. Seating is by ticket, though buses can pick up unfeasible numbers of people en route. For shorter journeys, booking tickets a day in advance is rarely necessary and often impossible. Check the signs above the ticket booths for your required destination. In larger bus stations be prepared to have your papers checked by OVIR. Minibuses soliciting custom outside offer faster, more expensive inter-city travel on major routes. Certain travel bottlenecks such as Kokand and Andijan can prove awkward to leave. Increasingly assertive independence has resulted in the suspension of many of the cross-republic bus services.

Taxis can often be persuaded to do long runs such as Khiva–Bukhara and offer the twin advantages of stop-offs and decreased time on the road. Bargain the opening price down to a sensible figure and agree on petrol costs. Indeed, obtaining enough petrol will be your driver's greatest challenge. Taxis are almost always cheaper than hiring a car from Uzbektourism. **Hitch-hiking** is a distinct possibility, but is almost always paid—all cars moonlight as taxis to cut fuel costs. It is again safer to establish a fare at the beginning of a ride. Potential pit stops at a relative's house for liquid refreshment are implicit.

City Transport is easiest by taxi or metro but, armed with a city map and a smattering of Russian or Uzbek, city buses, trolley buses, trams and *marshrutnoe* taxis (numbered minibuses which follow set routes and guarantee a seat) open up local life and offer a cheap and cheerful way to get around.

Visas

Apparently there was nothing to be learnt officially from Russian sources, but unofficially, and one by one, many little bits of information crept out.

Burnaby, Capt. Frederick; A Ride To Khiva. Travels And Adventures In Central Asia, (1876)

Over a century on and you may echo Burnaby's sentiments. Yet, as more Uzbek embassies open worldwide and the republic sheds more of its Soviet mind-set, visa procurement should stabilize into relative simplicity. Group tourists will have visas processed by their agency, but for individuals the visa challenge remains meeting or circumventing the Soviet-era requirements that one either book and pay in advance for transport and accommodation, or acquire an invitation from a 'host organization'. Independent travel is perfectly possible in Uzbekistan, as elsewhere in Central Asia, once the entry hurdle has been cleared. You will soon understand what the long-suffering locals have learnt over the past 80 bureaucratic years: 'without papers, you're a shit!'.

Camel at sunrise

Firstly enquire about the latest set of rules at the Uzbek embassy in (or nearest to) your country (see list below). Before the embassy issues a **tourist visa**, you may be directed to a travel agent authorized by the national company Uzbektourism. These agencies sell organized tours and also semi-packages, whereby you pre-book only part of your stay and complete it by yourself. The cheapest and most flexible options are offered by private travel agencies in Uzbekistan itself [see Tashkent, Samarkand and Bukhara chapters, pages 98, 180, 274], who can be reached by e-mail.

An alternative is to apply for a **business visa**, for which you do not need to be a business person. If not, however, you will require an official invitation from an Uzbek sponsor. In either case, your travel agency/sponsor must obtain approval for your visit from the Ministry of Foreign Affairs and notify you when approval has been communicated to the relevant Uzbek embassy to issue the visa. If there is no embassy in your country, it may be necessary to stop off elsewhere en route to Tashkent to process the visa. Most travellers now arrive in Uzbekistan with visas already stamped in their passports; it should be stressed that this is the recommended approach (and indeed the legally required approach if there is an Uzbek embassy in your country). Some continue to adopt the traditional, more risky method of matching up one's invitation letter with the copy (plus approval) in the files of Tashkent airport officials. Visa **costs** are: Three-day transit visa, US$20–40; up to seven days, $40; up to

30 days, $60; up to three months, $80.

Some travellers have risked arrival at Tashkent airport without visa or invitation. Most are sent straight back; the lucky few may negotiate a tourist visa or at least a transit visa—in which case you have three days to extend it or escape to another republic. When immigration officials fail to find your name on their lists, contend that your visa is still being processed. A friendly tone aids all negotiations, as does apologetic ignorance of the rules, though be warned that airlines may ask to see your visa or letters of invitation and approval at check-in.

Another approach is to make Uzbekistan part of a wider trip, such as an overland Silk Road journey, for in 1993 the Commonwealth of Independent States (CIS)—excluding the Baltic states, Moldova, Azerbaijan and Turkmenistan—agreed that holders of valid visas for one of the states are entitled to a **visa-free three-day stay** in any of the others. In theory you would then have three days in which to acquire a proper Uzbek visa. Thus the key is to enter the CIS at some point and head for Central Asia.

A way can usually be found to extend your stay, or if needs be you can disappear into a neighbouring republic. Bring ample passport photos and a flexible attitude, as enforcement is arbitrary. Almaty airport immigration now issues (expensive) visas on arrival. While it remains far from a failsafe route, in time this may prove a crucial breakthrough in the paper war.

Russia is an obvious starting point for a Turkestani foray. If you have no luck at the Uzbek embassy, Uzbektourism or the Travellers' Guest House (fax. 095 2807686) in Moscow, just get on a train to Tashkent. Arriving in Uzbekistan overland from another republic, you may escape detection. Not every train is checked, nor every public bus, as they cross borders of increasing national significance. When you need to face officialdom, probably at the insistence of hotel reception, go to the nearest branch of **OVIR**, the Office of Visas and Registration. In Tashkent, the city branch is located at 5 Navoi Street (tel. 569713 or 567365). Go in the morning with all the paperwork you can muster, i.e. contact a travel agency to act as your sponsor. This is also the place to go for a visa extension.

Likewise, an Uzbek visa should facilitate visits to the other countries party to the 72-hour agreement, though again enforcement is arbitrary. Of the other republics featured in this book, Kazakhstan and Kyrgyzstan can be visited without additional visas. Tajik police are generally unaware of the agreement, so a Tajikistan visa should be sought in Tashkent. Turkmenistan requires visas from all foreign visitors (available in Tashkent and also at Ashkhabad airport, but not at the borders).

Obtaining visas en route can often be easier than from your home country. With their strong links to Central Asia, Turkey and Pakistan are recommended for Central Asian visa hunters (so too is Brussels). All five republics have representation in Beijing and the Kazakhs have a visa-issuing consulate (currently for locals only) in Urumqi (tel. (0991) 3821203), in western China's Xinjiang Autonomous Region and the Uzbeks intend to open an office there. In future, Silk Road travellers heading east–west may be able to bypass Beijing altogether.

UZBEK EMBASSIES AND CONSULATES ABROAD INCLUDE:

China: 11 Beixiaojie, Sanlitun, Beijing, tel. (10) 65323621, fax. 65326304
Germany: Embassy, Deutschherrenstrasse 7, 53177 Bonn, tel. (0228) 9535715
        Consulate, Frankfurt, tel. (069) 740569, fax. 750541
India: Delhi, tel. (011) 6119034, fax. 6873246
Pakistan: Embassy, Islamabad, tel. (051) 820779, fax. 262144
        Consulate, Karachi, tel. (021) 572566, fax. 533884
Russia: 49 Bolshaya Polyanka, Moscow, tel. (095) 2300076, fax. 2388918
Turkey: 14 Ashmet Rashim, Chankiya, Ankara, tel. (4) 4392740
        Medusan Yokusu 61–63, Medusan Caddesi, Karakoy, Istanbul,
        tel. (212) 2527544/55, fax. 2934742
USA: 1746 Massachusetts Ave, Washington DC, tel. (202) 8875300, fax. 2936804
UK: 41 Holland Park, London W11 9DL, tel. (0171) 2297679, fax. 2297029

FOREIGN EMBASSIES IN TASHKENT INCLUDE:

Afghanistan: 6 Murtazaeva St, tel. 339171/342634
China: 89 Gogol St, tel. 338088/335375
France: 25 Akhunbaev St, tel. 335382/337406, fax. 336210
Germany: 15 Sharaf Rashidov St, tel. 344361/344530
India: 5 Alexei Tolstoy St, tel. 338267/333782
Iran: 20 Parkent St, tel. 688224/683725/686968
Kazakhstan: 20 Samatova St, tel. 335806/333705
Kyrgyzstan: 30 Samatova St, tel. 339841
Pakistan: 25 Chilanzar St, tel. 776977
Russia: 83 Nukus St, tel. 557954/553641
Tajikistan: 2 Mustakillik Square, tel. 548413
Turkey: 87 Gogolya, tel. 323525/322104
Turkmenistan: 16 Krasnodonsky Lane, tel. 547461
USA: 82 Chilanzarskaya St, tel. 771407/771132, fax. 406335
UK: 6 Murtsaeva St, Yunusabad, tel. 406288/406549/339847, fax. 406430

Customs, Registration and Police

On arrival at Tashkent airport, you will be asked to complete two copies of a form detailing your currency (cash and traveller's cheques). Keep the stamped copy returned to you for the duration of your stay. On departure, complete another copy and hand both copies in for officials to check you leave Uzbekistan with less money than when you entered. Early 1998 rules impose a one per cent fine if importing over US$10,000 cash equivalent. If there is a US$2,000-plus difference between your declared currency amount at entry and exit, you may be asked to show official exchange receipts. Customs staff are most concerned with preventing the export of antiques. Anything regarded as vaguely old will be questioned, so without a special licence it is not recommended to buy old souvenirs. Modern items like handicrafts, carpets and embroidery also draw suspicion, so keep receipts and battle hard over their recent manufacture. Travellers entering and exiting Uzbekistan overland are unlikely to be bothered by Uzbek customs. They will, however, face similar requirements to the above at their points of entry/exit into/from the CIS.

It is worthwhile keeping hotel receipts, as policemen/immigration officials can sometimes request them. In theory, all foreigners travelling, studying or working in Uzbekistan should register their presence and residence with the local OVIR. In practice, hotel staff register tourists automatically—when visas were separate pieces of paper, they would be stamped with the hotel's name and date. However, this regulation should not make you refuse the offer of staying with local families—one of the most enjoyable freedoms to follow independence. If officials notice a discrepancy in dates of receipts, fabricate a simple loss.

The most common complaints among independent travellers, after foul foodstuffs, concern Uzbek policemen, whose cold-war vigilance has lapsed into blatant profiteering. Police attention can result in somewhat arbitrary 'fines' (one of many uses for small denomination dollars). Request an English-speaker, discover the exact nature of your 'offence', bargain down their initial bid, demand a receipt and take a photo of the arresting officer. You may be let off with a warning or they'll throw you in the Bug Pit and your camera in the Lyab-i-Hauz. Police in Kazakhstan and Kyrgyzstan are slightly more approachable, while their colleagues in Tajikistan and Turkmenistan are best avoided.

Travel Agencies

Independent travel in Uzbekistan is perfectly possible, to varying degrees, but the time needed and the bureaucracy involved make pre-organized tours at present the most popular method of travel in Central Asia. The following tour companies either offer tours or can arrange personal itineraries.

Exodus Expeditions, 9 Weir Road, London SW12 OLT, UK, tel. (0181) 6755550, fax. (0181) 6730779. Exodus offers small, escorted group tours of Uzbekistan, overland expeditions and trekking trips in the Fan Mountains.

Explore Worldwide, 1 Frederick St, Aldershot, Hants GU11 1LQ, UK, tel. (01252) 319448, fax. (01252) 343170. Small group cultural, trekking and overland-style tours.

InnerAsia Expeditions, 2627 Lombard St, San Francisco, CA 94123, USA, tel. toll-free

Shir Dor madrassah, Registan, Samarkand

(800) 7778183. Adventure travel through Central Asia with extensions into the Ferghana Valley.

Intourist Ltd, Intourist House, 219 Marsh Wall, London E14 9FJ, UK, tel. (0171) 5388600, fax. (0171) 5385967. Totally revamped and privatized following the fall of the Soviet Union, Intourist now offers a series of tours to Uzbekistan and Central Asia and can pre-book individual, one-off accommodation and transport; also provides much-needed visa support.

Journeys, 4011 Jackson Road, Ann Arbor MI 48103, USA, tel. (313) 6654467

Mountain Sobek, 6420 Fairmount Ave, El Cerrito, CA 94530, USA, tel. (800) 2272384

Mir, Suite 210, 85 Washington St, Seattle, WA 98104, USA, tel. (206) 6247289 Can arrange visas, homestays and tours through representatives in Tashkent.

Regent Holidays, 15 John St, Bristol BS1 2HR, UK, tel. (0117) 9211711, fax. (0117) 9254866 Offers a range of Central Asia tours, plus personalized itineraries.

Steppes East, Castle Eaton, Swindon, Wiltshire SN6 6JU, UK, tel. (01285) 810267, fax. (01285) 810693, e-mail sales@steppeseast.co.uk. Personalized itineraries, group travel or trekking throughout Central Asia.

Voyages Jules Verne, 21 Dorset Sq, London NW1 6QG, UK, tel. (0171) 7235066. High-quality tours through Central Asia to China, including epic, continent-traversing luxury railway charters and occasional charter flights.

Various trekking companies offer Bukhara/Samarkand extensions to their treks in the Tian Shan or Pamirs of Kyrgyzstan and Tajikistan:

Himalayan Kingdoms, 20 The Mall, Clifton, Bristol BS8 4DR, UK, tel. (0117) 9237163

Karakoram Experience, 32 Lake Rd, Keswick, Cumbria CA12 5DQ, tel. (017687) 73966; PO Box 10538, Aspen CO 81612, USA, tel. toll-free (800) 4979675

Out There Trekking, 62 Nettleham Rd, Sheffield S8 8SX, UK, tel. (01742) 588508

REI, PO Box 1938, Sumner WA98390, USA, tel. (206) 8912631 or (800) 6222236

Sherpa Expeditions, 131A Heston Rd, Hounslow, Middlesex TW5 ORD, UK, tel. (0181) 5772717

Uzbektourism. A national company formed in 1992 on the basis of the local staff and facilities of Soviet travel agencies such as Intourist and Sputnik (which themselves were mere reincarnations of the wonderfully named Society for Proletarian Tourists). Although still focused on group tourists, with an instinctive distrust of individuals, attitudes are changing as post-independence flexibility influences the planning of new itineraries and activities. Adventure travel is gaining more emphasis: skiing, trekking, climbing, rafting and hunting. For the headquarters address, see Tashkent chapter [page 98]; branch offices are listed under individual cities. Moscow office: Rm 33, 5th Floor, 41 Bolshaya Polyanka St, tel. 2385632. UK office: 35 Wigmore Street, London W1, tel. (0171) 935-1899. US office: Suite 2308, 60 East 42nd Street, New York NY 10165, tel. (212) 9830382, fax. 9830390.

While Uzbektourism strives to dominate the indigenous travel industry, it finds itself in ever closer cooperation with private travel agencies. These represent the greatest hope for the future of Central Asian travel. They are usually staffed by enthusiasts, often ex-Intourist experts, who can provide up-to-date information, visa invitations, tailor-made itineraries, reasonable prices, knowledgeable guides and minimal bureaucracy. Dealing with these agencies direct often cuts out expensive Western middlemen, and while international communication can be frustrating, the advent of e-mail facilitates unprecedented efficiency. First choice operators inside Uzbekistan include Tashkent's **Asia Travel** (adventure@asia-travel.uz; www.asia-travel.uz) Moscow branch: 6, bldg.1, Vorontsovskaya St (tel/fax: (095) 9117732; azia_travel@usa.net), **Sairam Tourism** (silkroad@ sairamtour.com.uz), the new **Sam-Buh** (ravshan@sambuh.silk.org, and Bukhara's **Salom Travel** (raisa@salom.bukhara.silk.org). Consider too the **American Business Centre** in Tashkent (office@csabc.silk.glas.apc.org), for services from visa support to office space. See chapters on individual cities for further details.

Itineraries

Most 10–14 day tour itineraries cover the three main cities of Samarkand, Bukhara and Khiva and enter/exit via a tour of Tashkent. Excursions to Kunya Urgench, Shakhrisabsz or Pendzhikent are sometimes covered as good day trips. For those with more time, the Ferghana Valley loop offers many insights into modern Uzbekistan and the rewarding historical sites of the Royal Road between Bukhara and Samarkand are easily visited en route with personal transport. To get right off the beaten track, head down the Road south, to the rarely seen sights of Termez or deep into the heart of the Khorezm oasis.

Combination tours are becoming increasingly popular. A tour of CIS Turkestan is a natural extension of a visit to Uzbekistan (and largely covered in this guide) and the recently opened borders with China connect east and west Turkestan. International flight connections offer the opportunity of further cultural combinations, including a tour of pan-Turkic Istanbul/Uzbekistan, the ethnic threads joining Uzbekistan to Russian Dagestan, the architectural continuity of Iran/Uzbekistan and the historical links of Uzbekistan/Mogul India.

Health

Medical insurance, including emergency evacuation, should be a priority in trip preparation, for agreement is uniform on the horrific state of Central Asian healthcare. Although no vaccinations are officially required by the new republics, it is wise to check if and when you were immunized against: tetanus, diptheria and polio (ten years protection); typhoid (three years); cholera and hepatitis A (up to six months—

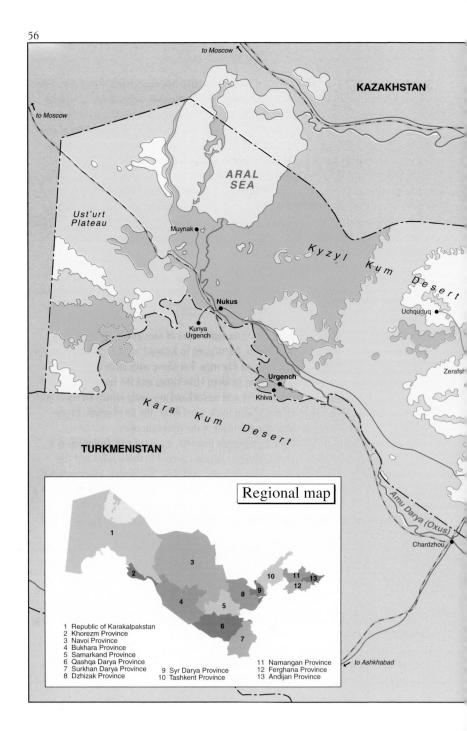

to Moscow

to Moscow

KAZAKHSTAN

*ARAL
SEA*

*Ust'urt
Plateau*

Muynak

K y z y l   K u m   D e s e r t

Uchquduq

Nukus

Kunya
Urgench

Zerafsh

Urgench

Khiva

K a r a   K u m   D e s e r t

TURKMENISTAN

Amu Darya (Oxus)

Chardzhou

Regional map

1

2

3

10   11   13
12

8   9

4

5

6

7

1 Republic of Karakalpakstan
2 Khorezm Province
3 Navoi Province
4 Bukhara Province
5 Samarkand Province
6 Qashqa Darya Province
7 Surkhan Darya Province
8 Dzhizak Province

9 Syr Darya Province
10 Tashkent Province

11 Namangan Province
12 Ferghana Province
13 Andijan Province

to Ashkhabad

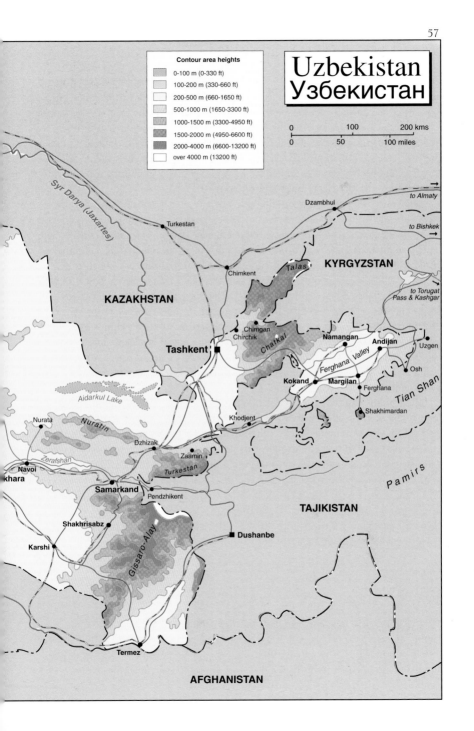

Uzbekistan
Узбекистан

Contour area heights

- 0-100 m (0-330 ft)
- 100-200 m (330-660 ft)
- 200-500 m (660-1650 ft)
- 500-1000 m (1650-3300 ft)
- 1000-1500 m (3300-4950 ft)
- 1500-2000 m (4950-6600 ft)
- 2000-4000 m (6600-13200 ft)
- over 4000 m (13200 ft)

0   100   200 kms
0   50   100 miles

Syr Darya (Jaxartes)

to Almaty

Dzambhul

to Bishkek

Turkestan

KYRGYZSTAN

Chimkent

Talas

KAZAKHSTAN

to Torugat
Pass & Kashgar

Chimgan
Chirchik

Chatkal

Namangan

Andijan

Uzgen

Tashkent

Ferghana Valley

Osh

Kokand

Margilan

Ferghana

Tian Shan

Aidarkul Lake

Khodjent

Shakhimardan

Nurata

Nuratin

Dzhizak

Zerafshan

Zaamin

Turkestan

Pamirs

Navoi

khara

Samarkand

Pendzhikent

TAJIKISTAN

Shakhrisabz

Gissaro-Alay

Karshi

■ **Dushanbe**

Termez

AFGHANISTAN

ask your doctor's advice). A vaccination for Meningococal Meningitis is also worth considering. Steer clear of animals to avert the risk of rabies, body fluid contact for hepatitis B and partially cooked food for salmonella. Water is the chief disease carrier, so minimize the danger by avoiding tap water, ice and local dairy products. When tea, boiled or bottled water are unavailable, purify tap water with iodine tablets. For food the basic rule is 'cook it, peel it or leave it'. Eat only hot, thoroughly cooked foods that have not been allowed to sit and cool. Locals avoid fish in months with no 'r'. Refuse raw foods like salads and peel fruit yourself.

In practice few people can sustain such a regime, so prepare for diarrhoea, the most common Central Asian complaint—even Alexander the Great got the runs on his approach to Samarkand. The best treatment is thorough rehydration, with boiled, bottled or purified water, soft drinks allowed to go flat and rehydrating solutions. Avoid fruit and greasy foods (admittedly a challenge in Uzbekistan) and stick to bread, biscuits, rice and boiled eggs with salt. Diarrhoea tablets merely block up your system, to be taken when you have to travel. The brave may try the local remedy— vodka and hot peppers. Sunburn and sunstroke are genuine dangers; reduce your time in the sun and wear hat, sunglasses and sunscreen. Altitude sickness can afflict anyone above 3,000 metres (10,000 feet). The symptoms of headaches and nausea should disappear after a couple of days; ascend slowly, eat and rest well, drink plenty of fluids (but no alcohol) and don't smoke. If they persist, descend immediately, for fatal conditions can quickly develop.

Medical kit: Aspirin/paracetamol/Tylenol; diarrhoea pills; rehydration powders; iodine tablets; antiseptic cream/wipes; antihistamine; dressing pads; bandage; plasters; cotton wool; tweezers; scissors; thermometer. To guarantee sterility, consider a pack of disposable syringes. Mosquito nets, insect repellent and sting relief are welcome in summer, though only southwestern Tajikistan necessitates malaria tablets. In an emergency inform hotel staff and call the Tashkent International Medical Clinic on (3712) 307312 or (371) 1852088, at 14 Mahmud Tarabi Street. Hard currency drugstores in Tashkent include Uzbekimpex at 33 Abdullah Tukaya Street and 6 Navoi St. First choice hospital in Tashkent is the No.1 Government Hospital at 40 Pochtovaya St, off Buyuk Ipak Yuli to the northeast.

Climate

Most visitors arrive in summer to bake in a dry country aptly termed 'the sunny republic', as every year brings over 300 days of sunshine and under 300 millimetres (12 inches) of rainfall. Uzbeks explain their sharply continental climate, born of desert and mountain isolation from the sea, in terms of two 40-day *chilla*; the summer ver-

Relieving the summer heat in one of Tashkent's many fountains

sion from 25 June to 5 August and winter from 25 December to 5 February. During the former, expect afternoon temperatures above 35°C (95°F); during the latter, they may fall to -30°C (-22°F), but most cities stay above -10°C (14°F). Travel is most pleasant from the brief spring that dusts the desert with floral colour until early June and from September to early November, when tree-lined streets shine in autumnal glory. Yet the burning heat of summer is offset by low humidity, relatively cool evenings and bazaar stalls crowded with fresh fruit, and winter too is dry and sunny; Samarkand's fabled domes sparkle white only briefly. Khorezm is painfully cold and often windy after the beginning of November and Termez bakes on the Oxus from June to September. Mountain areas are refreshingly cool in summer, freezing cold and snowy in winter.

Clothing

Light-coloured cotton garments are best for summer travel; trousers, long skirts and long-sleeved shirts prevent sunburn and respect Muslim sensibilities. Flesh must be covered when visiting any holy site and streetwear should also be conservative. A hat

Shashlik Surprise

Soon the shashlik was being thrust triumphantly from hand to hand. Dribbling blood and fat, it was tough as rope. But the three men swallowed each morsel wholesale, or clamped it between their teeth like mastiffs and worried it to and fro, until it separated with a noise like tearing sheets. They celebrated every mouthful with a carnivorous burp, and dipped gluttonously into mountains of radishes and olives. The brief respites between skewers resounded with an anticipatory grinding of gold and ivory molars and the smack of oily lips. They looked artless and timeless. At any moment, I thought, they might break into shamanistic chant or propose a raid . . .

Assiduously they plied me with the tenderest chunks of shashlik, but my teeth recoiled even from these. I smuggled them out of my mouth and secreted them wherever I could: in the bush behind me, under the sand between my knees, in my shirt pockets. Murad kept thrusting more at me, the point of his skewer threatening my chest. But he was grinning with hospitality. They all were. The big man detached the most succulent nuggets to press on me, with the crispest onions. But soon my pockets sagged with the telltale meat, and a betraying stain of fat was spreading across my shirt-front.

As I masticated despairingly on another hunk, I bit on something hard, and assumed it was mutton-bone. Then I realised that it was one of my own bones I was chewing. I had lost a tooth. Neurotically I ran my tongue back and forth over the gap. Nobody else noticed. I longed to inspect it in a mirror, but I could picture it well enough: the double rank of ivory now breached by a slovenly void, as obvious as a fainted guardsman. Viewed from the right, I might pass muster. But seen from the left, I thought, I must show a Dracula-like unreliablity. Would I be refused permits, visas, even hotel bedrooms, I wondered, on account of this lost incisor? Would conversations dry up the moment I grinned?

These broodings were halted by the arrival of soup. Murad elevated the cauldron above his head as if at a pagan Eucharist, while the calf's head bobbed obscenely to the surface. The big man skimmed off the fat and threw it on the sand. Then we drank and it was delicious. Fumbling in my rucksack, I found a packet of English cheese biscuits and passed them round complacently. They nibbled them without comment. Later I noticed Murad dropping his into the sand.

Colin Thubron, The Lost Heart of Asia, 1994

is a necessary accessory. Heat and dust make thick-soled walking shoes a better choice than flip-flops. In colder weather, bring warm boots and woollen layers, plus a down or Goretex jacket. When desert trekking, be ready for nightly temperature drops. If you leave lowland Uzbekistan for the mountains of Kyrgyzstan or Tajikistan, prepare well for intense cold, strong winds and heavy snows.

What to Bring

In 1899, Lord Curzon's recommendations for travellers to Central Asia included taking one's own pillow, air cushion, saddle, pith helmet, tinned spam and India rubber bath. The spam is still a good idea, but the rest may prove cumbersome. Bus luggage racks cannot accommodate large backpacks; keep valuables with you in a smaller bag and store the pack in the hold. Wear a concealed money-belt and don't leave valuables in your hotel room. Consider the following items: medical kit; mug; water bottle; Swiss army knife; bicycle lock (for luggage); torch/rape alarm; ear plugs for restaurant bands; sachets of coffee, ketchup etc for restaurant food; universal plug; all toiletries; batteries; film; toilet paper; washing powder; string clothes line; photocopy of passport; reading material; Russian phrasebook; postcards of home/ photos of family.

Money

The Uzbek *sum* is worth 100 *tiyin*, and is available in notes of 1, 3, 5, 10, 25, 50 and 100, proudly bedecked with Uzbek heroes and architecture, and trading at around 90 to the US dollar at official rates, and 170 at black market rates, in mid-1998. Elsewhere you find the Kazakh *tenge*, Kyrgyz *som* and Turkoman *manat* and Tajik *rouble*.

While the US dollar is Uzbekistan's alternative currency, be circumspect in public as it is *not* legal tender. Bring it in traveller's cheques *and* cash; the former can be swapped for sum at hotel exchange counters and some banks; the latter, preferably in crisp and new bills (1990 at the earliest), proves invaluable on many occasions. Visa cards enjoy growing acceptance and are ideal for emergencies. The National Bank for Foreign Economic Activity supplies dollars for Visa cards and traveller's cheques at most of its branches around the country. You will encounter numerous offers to change money privately at the current street rate—the black market has long been a key to survival for many people. If you accept, it is safer to change with someone you know, e.g. a friend or hotel employee. Prepare your dollars to conceal the temptation of a bulging money belt and hand them over only *after* carefully counting the sum.

When travelling off the beaten track, beyond the motherly (big-brotherly?) reach of Uzbektourism, remember to take sufficient cash. Apart from tourist-price hotels, local costs are very low by Western standards.

Photography

As ever, be prepared for minimal supplies—you may find imported colour print film at some hotels or sites, but try to bring sufficient film and batteries. If developing cannot await your return home, try Tashkent's TSUM and GUM department stores. Cameras and film should spend as little time as possible in direct sunlight; store film in a cooler bag lined with heat-reflective material like a survival blanket. Such a bag is useful in winter too, when film can become brittle—remember batteries die quickly in the cold. To avoid the risk of customs X-ray machines fogging your film, ask for them to be hand-searched. Dust from the desert or the many restoration projects will soon find its way into your lens, so protect it with a lens hood, also good for reducing flare, and a UV/skylight filter, also essential for snowscapes. Pack a blower brush and wet/dry lens-cleaning tissues.

Central Asia's intense sunlight allows for slower film (25–64 ASA) and great depth of field, yet over-exposure is a constant danger. Reduce it by bracketing below your camera's recommended exposure and shooting in the softer light of early morning or late afternoon. For snowscapes, over-exposure by up to two stops is necessary to keep them fresh and white. For colour film, especially transparencies, a polarizing filter is a welcome accessory, for it reduces reflections, thereby intensifying colour saturation and contrast, notably darkening skies. For black-and-white film, a red filter darkens skies and improves skin tones.

When taking pictures of people it is polite to ask permission first, though the results can be overly formal. For more natural portraits, try a telephoto lens or a 90° candid angle attachment. Be sensitive to Muslim attitudes—older people, particularly women, may be unwilling subjects. Ask before taking photos inside mosques and never take any during prayer time. In Islamic strongholds like Namangan, use your camera with considerable care. At many architectural sites, visitors may have to pay a fee to use still or video cameras and flash is often prohibited. Taking photos at borders, military installations or bridges is asking for trouble.

Communications

For **international calls** to Uzbekistan dial Uzbekistan's country code (7), the city code (see below) and the local number. To phone home, major hotels offer the most convenient service for a dollar surcharge and main city post offices offer a slower but cheaper service at local rates. Both switchlines have to book calls and the further one is from Tashkent the longer one has to wait. To dial home direct use 8-10 followed by your country code.

For **domestic calls** it is best to use your hotel (normally no charge) or post office. Hardly any public phones in Uzbekistan remain in working order and those that do accept only tokens or tiyin coins. Local codes include Tashkent (3712 for six-digit numbers, 371 for seven-digit numbers), Samarkand (3622), Bukhara (36522), Urgench (36222), Khiva (36237), Ferghana (37322), Kokand (43400), Andijan (37422), Shakhrisabz (37522), Termez (37622).

For calls to the CIS, simply dial 8 followed by the city code; Moscow (095), Almaty (3272), Bishkek (3312), Ashkhabad (3632), Dushanbe (3772) etc.

Few local phone lines can support international **fax** messages and these are normally relayed via Tashkent or Samarkand. Faxes can normally be sent from the main hotels and post offices. Telexes are cheaper and more reliable for international messages and are sent from main telecommunications offices. The desired message is normally displayed on a computer screen and should be checked before sending.

Uzbekistan's **post service** is not good, and postcards and letters can take a month or two to arrive home. Post restante can be received at the main hotels and is most reliable at the Hotels Uzbekistan and Samarkand. Western couriers operate out of Tashkent only [see Tashkent page 98].

Electricity

As with the rest of the ex-Soviet Union, Uzbekistan runs on 220 volt, 50c AC with a twin round plug. Bring a suitable adaptor.

Media and Information

Access to information remains limited in Uzbekistan, although the top hotels are introducing CNN and BBC World Service television. Russian speakers will find more evening entertainment and real news on Moscow's Channel 1 than on Uzbek television, though local Channel 3 offers an English news roundup of CNN and BBC broadcasts on weekend afternoons. Uzbek programmers are keen on song and dance; keep tuning in to catch the good news—cotton harvests and presidential decrees. If you pack a short-wave radio, find the BBC on 15.305/15.310/15.315 MHz and Voice of America on 7.205/7.290 MHz. Search the dial for the English services of Radio Moscow and Radio Tashkent. Foreign newsprint is hard to find. For English news of Uzbekistan and the region, hunt for the excellent *Central Asian Post*, weekly from Bishkek, sgi@imfiko.bishkek.su (www.bishkek_su/CAP/). For Uzbek-related websites see Recommended Reading [page 324].

Tashkent publishers have produced some highly detailed city and country maps since independence, though paper shortages challenge availability. Look for them in hotel lobbies and major bookshops [see Tashkent shopping page 91] and purchase all possible destinations whenever sighted. New books suffer the same problem. Future publications will include an English language series on Uzbek culture and history—a welcome addition to the current crop of political propaganda. Check the Recommended Reading guide [page 323] for suitable books to bring on your trip.

Longer-term visitors to Tashkent should quickly acquire a copy of the TWIG (Tashkent Women's International Group) *Guide to Tashkent*, packed with information and insights (nanci@nanci.silk.org). Shorter-term visitors too will enjoy the monthly recommendations of the *Odds & Ads* cultural periodical (same e-mail, available from some hotels, or direct from the UN building, at 4 Taras Shevchenko).

Time

Uzbekistan straddles two of the former USSR's 11 time zones: all nine provinces west of Tashkent are two hours ahead of Moscow time (and five hours ahead of GMT), as are Turkmenistan and western Kazakhstan. Tashkent and the three Ferghana Valley provinces join eastern Kazakhstan, Kyrgyzstan and Tajikistan three hours ahead of Moscow (and six hours ahead of GMT). The 24-hour clock is used for transport schedules, which no longer run on Moscow time.

Accommodation

While many hotels ebb into gentle decay long after their Stalinist prizes for architecture have been forgotten, their rooms remain generally clean and spacious with attached bathroom and a good chance of hot water (and often telephone, television and fridge, any one of which may still function). Post-independence foreign investment in Uzbekistan's travel industry means Tashkent, Samarkand and Bukhara now boast comfortable hotels offering a range of air-con rooms, bathrooms en suite, satellite TV (CNN and BBC), business and conference centres, health clubs, a selection of bars and restaurants, souvenir shops and travel agencies. Many mid-range places are also undergoing renovation. Most welcome of all are the numerous bed and breakfasts that have blossomed all over Uzbekistan in renovated private homes, offering tourists a cheap and fascinating entry into Uzbek and Tajik life.

At old-style hotels, after you have filled in a registration form hotel staff may request your passport in exchange for your room key during your stay. If this unsettles you, try offering other ID as key deposit, or reclaim it later by saying you need to change money/buy an airline ticket. Instead of a key, you may receive a pass to be swapped for the key with the *dezhurnaya* (floor lady). She may request the key each time you leave the building. Befriending the *dezhurnaya* can ensure a supply of tea or boiled water (a small fee may be appropriate). Remember to lock your door even when inside the room and never leave valuables lying around—ask if the hotel has a safe.

Group tourists are processed fairly efficiently from reception to room to restaurant. Individuals turning up unannounced often provoke a frustrating combination of surly service and dollar lust. High room rates conjured from thin air are no guarantee of high quality. Ask to see the room and, if bargaining fails, look elsewhere, for there are exceptions to the hostile-greedy brigade, though only certain hotels are permitted to receive foreigners.

This book makes every effort to highlight hotels offering visitors cheap, standard accommodation. The arrival of B&Bs and homestays with families marks a welcome breakthrough, though closures are common—enquire at travel agencies; hotel reception staff will sometimes offer a relative's place. Other possible alternatives to Soviet blocks include *turbaza* (tourist camps with chalets and campsites) and Young Pioneer Camps (*Pioneerski Lahgir*—where *Homo Sovieticus* was trained), staffed by teachers often happy to offer weary travellers a meal and a bed.

All room prices are given in US dollars, due to unstable rates of Uzbek inflation, but be aware that tourist hotels are legally required to accept sum only, on presentation of official exchange receipts or through exchanging at the hotel (Uzbektourism hotels are particularly strict). While the premium business hotels accept dollar credit card payment only, other hotels may allow payment in sum without official receipts, thereby opening up the more competitive market rate. You may wish to clarify this point prior to arrival. Except in the upmarket hotels, most rates are negotiable, depending on season, mood and suite size. The prices in this book serve only as a comparative guide; expect considerable changes, as with many aspects of Central Asian travel.

Melon Sea   *Shashlik vendor*

Food and Drink

"Have you tried our national dish?" is a common expression of genuine Uzbek hospitality that rapidly translates into a lengthy and revered process. *Plov* (or pilau) is the national pride and joy, for which an excuse is barely needed, from visiting guests and circumcision feasts to election day parties to make voting in the Party more appealing. Legend credits Alexander the Great with its invention, for he bade his cooks devise a substantial yet light campaign meal. Only the first requirement was met. Locals claim over 100 versions of *plov*, differing in rice and extras such as raisins or quince, and tuck in to the steaming mutton mound with their right hands, massaging the oily mix into bite-sized balls. It is believed that outdoor cooking, by men only, yields the best results. Staple number two is shashlik, mutton kebabs from smouldering charcoal grills. These are the skewers of life, the traveller's foremost companion across Central Asia. Connoisseurs enjoy the chunks of fat neighbouring each piece of meat and regulars relish the occasional variety of grilled liver. Your order is served on the skewer, usually in rounds of four or five, beneath raw onion and beside fresh bread.

Popular too are *manty*, small dumplings of chopped mutton and onion, topped with the Russian favourite *smetana* (sour cream) and *pelmeni*, filled ravioli rather similar to Chinese *jiaozi*. Energetic dough-tossing means *laghman* creation, a thick noodle soup with fried meat and vegetables such as potatoes, carrots and cabbage. Among various *shurpa*—more meat and vegetable soups—are *dymbul shurpa*, with sweetcorn, potatoes and stuffed peppers; *nakhot shurpa*, with chickpeas; and *chuchvara shurpa*, with large mutton dumplings. Other soups include *mastava*, rice and vegetables; *mampar*, meat, fried egg and chopped noodles; and *chalop*, a cool bowl of yoghurt with chives and cucumber. *Nakhot shurak* is a chickpea dish stewed with onion and meat; *dimnama* a chicken stew with potatoes, carrots and tomatoes; and *naryn*, a horsemeat and noodle soup. *Samsa* are meat and onion pastries (samosas) baked in clay ovens. Common appetizers are tomato and cucumber salads, enlivened with the sour cream dip *charka*, and cold meat platters featuring *kasy* horse sausage.

For many travellers *non* (nan) bread and fruit are the twin fat-free saviours of Uzbek cuisine. A bazaar has no claim to the name without baskets and prams of warm, fragrant, crispily-crusted yet soft-centred *non*. These unleavened roundels form the perfect shashlik partner and plate. They enjoy exalted status in Uzbek society [see Behaviour page 71-2], for legend claims rulers once paid the minters of coins in *non*, while the 11th-century scientist Avicenna recommended *non* and *plov* as cures for any debilitating disease. Wheatflour dough, sprinkled with sesame or poppy seeds, is thrust against the clay walls of a *tandyr* oven, falling only when baked to perfection. Besides the common variety of flatbreads, *obi-* or *uy-non*, (*lepyoshka* in Russian), fancier types are called *patyr*, baked from puff pastry flavoured with mutton fat to preserve freshness. Samarkand boasts over 20 different varieties of *non*, colourfully patterned as gifts for special occasions.

Fresh fruit is the bazaar's other main attraction. Over 1,000 years ago, the region's famous melons and grapes were packed in ice for export as delicacies. Even the briefest encounter will leave you in sympathy with Babur, great-great-great-grandson of Tamerlane, who recalled the exquisite taste of the fruit of his homeland long after becoming emperor of India. In summer and autumn look forward to a tempting array of peaches (*shaftoli*), apricots (*yorik*), plums (*alkhori*), apples (*alma*), cherries (*alcha*), raspberries (*malina*), strawberries (*kulupnay*), mulberries, persimmon, pears (*nok*), grapes (*uzum*), pomegranates (*anor*) and figs. A sea of melons (*kovun*) and watermelons (*tarvuz*) spills from truck and cart; expert buyers check for fragrance, the correct resonance on tapping and weight over size—the heavier the better. Other than fruit, an alternative pudding and widespread street snack is locally made ice-cream (*marozhni*), often delicious and always a flagrant violation of medical advice. *Semechka* sunflower seeds are a national obsession.

Drinks: To drink *chai* in a *chaikhana* is to follow a long and venerable Central Asian tradition. Hot green tea (*kok chai* in Uzbek; *zilyoni chai* in Russian) not only quenches thirst and cools the body, it also aids the digestion of greasy foods. In an Uzbek home tea may come with *halva* wheatflour sweets. Restaurants commonly serve bottles of mineral water or lemonade; ask to try *sok*, sweetened fruit juice, or *kompot*, a fruit concoction made from local berries. Streetside vending machines offer glasses of strangely flavoured water, but look instead for crowded *kvas*—tankers selling a refreshing brew made from bread and yeast. For breakfast, the drinking yoghurt *kefir* or *kalmak* is excellent. Coca-colonization has reached the underbelly of the evil empire, as Western brands of soft and alcoholic drinks make their mark.

Despite resurgent Islam, alcohol is readily available, in state and private shops, and publicly consumed. Vodka may prove the most enduring Russian legacy, normally drunk in units of 100 grammes with a grimace and a hastily snatched piece of sausage or tomato. Prepare your excuses well to avoid nightly excess, for when a bottle is opened your hosts expect it to be finished, one shot after another, as in the court of Tamerlane. Women may decline, but men face tremendous peer pressure. Export Stolinchnaya or Rasputin are the preferred brands. Chilled *champanski* (sparkling wine) is a welcome table guest and the only partner to caviar (*ikra*). Viniculture has a long history in this land—legend boasts that Samarkand grapes produced the world's first wine. Uzbektourism can arrange wine-tasting sessions, though the emphasis is on the very sweet. Shakhrisabz is reputed as the best local blend. Beer (*piva*) is sold on the street from bottles or tankers, where drinkers nibble *kurut*, hard balls of salted milk. Not to be missed is the nomadic speciality *koumis*, mare's milk fermented into a mildly alcoholic and thoroughly invigorating brew, said to cure all manner of ailments. Marco Polo, enjoying the Mongol original, thought it "like white wine, and very good to drink". William of Rubrick, however, was less impressed: "at the taste of it I broke out in a sweat with horror and surprise". Find it in all good Kyrgyz/Kazakh yurts or bazaar churns, ignore the smell and believe it improves with practice.

Restaurants: Only on festival days or at large family celebrations can the visitor hope to sample all of the above dishes. Home cooking always beats restaurant fare, so accept invitations with alacrity. For authentic Uzbek food search the older parts of town, within or close to a bazaar. First stop is the teahouse or *chaikhana*, a time-honoured place for men to gather on carpeted dais and swap the latest news over *chai* and Uzbek favourites like shashlik, *plov* and *laghman*. A fuller menu may be available at home restaurants, where people open their own doors for business. Hotel restaurants commonly serve starkly Sovietized Russian-Uzbek hybrids that do neither cuisine any favours, yet they are the easiest choice after a day on the road. Russian choices include: borscht (meat and vegetable soup), cutlets (anonymous breadcrumbed meat), *lul* kebab (round kebabs with onion), *tabak* (fried chicken), *galubtsi* (cabbage leaves) or *piertsi* (peppers), both stuffed with meat and rice, beefsteak or beef stroganoff, all accompanied by vegetables boiled without mercy and the infamous tomato and cucumber *salat turist*.

Hotel breakfasts, between 8 and 10am, are at most tea, *kefir*, fried eggs, bread and jam. Enquire about *bliny* pancakes and *kasha* porridge. Lunch is the heartiest meal of the day, from about 11am to 3pm. To locate your evening meal, from about 6 to 10pm, find the source of the wall of sound. That will be the restaurant band, rendering conversation and ordering all but impossible. Once you have a menu, look for items with marked prices as half of these may be available. Time is saved, and your diet restricted to three or four standards, by accepting the waiter's recommendations. Beware of billing for unwanted extras you thought were free.

You will not starve in Uzbekistan, but you run a high risk of terminal repetition and a liberal use of fats and oils often provokes disagreement with foreign stomachs. The eating advice in this book endeavours to discover variety in a world of monotony, e.g. Korean restaurants with welcome spice, flavour and minimal fat. Independence is rousing proprietorial dreams from Soviet slumber and turning them into restaurants to be savoured. As their custom is well-heeled, they offer the traveller an introduction to the *biznez* government elite, who prosper amid the difficult passage into the reality of nationhood.

Festivals and Holidays

When you wander in a residential area and hear the cry of *surnai* and *karnai* pipes, the twang of the *dutara* guitar and the rhythmic drumming of the *doira* tambourine, make haste to the celebration, for a *toi* is underway and stray foreigners are invariably welcome to join the fun. These are Uzbek family parties, among the traditions long attacked by Moscow, quietly condoned by local officials and joyfully reclaimed after independence. The wedding feasts of a grand *toi marosimi* can last a week, with the separate receptions of *fortillar toi* and *padar oshi* held for the relatives of bride and groom. A *beshik toi* is held on the ninth day after a baby's birth, when the infant is strapped to a colourful wooden cradle and the mother rises from her bed. *Sunnat toi* mark the circumcision of boys aged between seven and ten years old. This important ritual purifies the boy and declares his entry into Islam and the community. The richer the father, the more members of his *mahalla* he can invite for singing, dancing and mountains of *plov*. At large gatherings, guests sit at great trestles, segregated for men and women (though foreign women may be considered honorary men). The Islamic backdrop rarely curbs the flow of alcohol and eating continues until the host signals by cleaning his hands. Smaller holiday meals, for a birthday, new house or just the reception of guests, are called *dastarkhan* (literally 'tablecloth'), when a family sits round a piece of cloth laden with Uzbek dishes, sweets, fruit and *non*. Funerals normally take place the same day as death and, after the body has been washed and shrouded, a slow procession snakes its way through the streets to the cemetery, as every man (women do not attend) endeavours to carry the bier forward seven steps. At traditional funerals the young wear red and the old white. Professional mourners are employed, no meal is cooked in the house of the deceased for three days and mourning continues for a minimum of 40 days.

The most cherished public holiday, only rehabilitated in 1989, is **Navruz** ('new day'), the Central Asian new year that falls on March 21 in Uzbekistan. During this two-day festival of spring renewal, look for singing, dancing, the parading of seven special dishes beginning with an 's', including *sumalakh* (a wheat bran pudding cooked during an overnight party), *kurash* wrestling by burly *palvans* and epic poetry recital by wandering *bakshi* minstrels. Streets and bazaars fill with crowds seeking national dishes and handicrafts, and the festival culminates with a ritual ploughing of the first furrow of the year by the most respected *aksakal* in the village. While **Ramadan**, the Muslim month of daytime fasting, and the ensuing feast of **Rosaheid** are not strictly observed, many Uzbeks perform the feast of sacrifice, **Kurban Khait** or **Bayram**, and visit the graves of relatives, about a month after the end of Ramadan. Once the cotton harvest is in, collective farms may celebrate **Pakhta Bairam**. The dates of Ramadan depend on the cycle of the moon and are as follows:

1999	—	8/9 December	to	6/7 January
2000	—	28/29 November	to	27/28 December
2001	—	18/19 November	to	17/18 December
2002	—	8/9 November	to	7/8 December
2003	—	29/30 October	to	27/28 November

Other traditional entertainments for which no excuse is needed include skull-splitting ram fighting, frenzied *baiga* (a game of polo played with the decapitated corpse of a goat), Uzbek circuses featuring the high wire and the rather more decorous professions of bird fancying and backgammon. Mexican soap operas badly dubbed into Russian command a huge following throughout Central Asia.

Other days when government and business close are:

January 1: New Year's Day

March 8: International Women's Day; men greet women with the first spring flowers

May 9: Victory Day; to honour veterans and martyrs of the Great Patriotic War (World War II)

September 1: Independence Day; ex-Lenin Squares explode in celebration

December 8: Constitution Day; commemorating independent Uzbekistan's first constitution (1992)

Behaviour, Customs and Culture

As a guest in Uzbekistan you will be accorded much respect and shown great hospitality, for local families gladly seize the chance to welcome new friends from abroad after so many years of isolation. In return you should abide by the local codes of conduct: remove shoes before entering a mosque or home or sitting on a *chaikhana* bed; bare the minimum of flesh, particularly when visiting a holy site; respect the right of mosque/madrassah personnel to deny entry to women or non-Muslims; attempt no photography during prayer time. While Russian remains more useful, learning some important Uzbek phrases (see page 317) is an easy and greatly appreciated way to make friends; at the very least offer the traditional greeting *Assalam aleikum* (may peace be unto you).

An invitation to eat provides a welcome opportunity for a more genuine Uzbek repast, but be aware that in these hard times your host may be forced to make sacrifices for their hospitality. Gifts from abroad, postcards, coins and especially photos from home may mean little to you but will be well appreciated as tokens of friendship. Always accept when you are invited to wash your hands from water poured from a ewer.

Elderly people enjoy revered status in Uzbekistan. The old men who dominate the neighbourhood councils, *malhalla*, are respectfully known as *aksakal*, 'white beards'.

Chaikhana devotees, Lyab-i-Hauz, Bukhara

Make room for them and remember this is a firm handshake culture; perform it with your left hand over your heart. Likewise, when passing anything, use only your right hand. Foreign women can be honorary men in Uzbek households, but also have a unique opportunity to talk to women away from the pressures of a male-dominated society.

Chaikhana Etiquette Aboard the wooden dais (*kan*), be conscious of the great respect shown towards the round *non* bread. Before a family departure, like a son leaving for military service, he bites a fresh *non* which is hung up to safeguard his return, when he can finish it with his friends. At a meal, break the bread into pieces and share them round the table but never place non face-down, i.e. keep the patterned, seeded side uppermost. Never leave *non* on the ground or throw it away in public. Anyone who finds a piece on the ground should pick it up, kiss it and touch it to their forehead three times.

> *To study that part of their lives which is before the public eye, we must first pay a visit to the tea-booths, which are the resorts of all classes. The Bokhariot, and the remark applies indeed universally to all Central Asiatics, can never pass by a second or third tea-booth without entering, unless his affairs are very urgent indeed.*

> Vambery, Armenius; *Sketches of Central Asia*, (1868)

Tea should be brewed by pouring it three times into the *piala* cup and three times back into the pot. When pouring for the fourth time, do not fill another's cup to the brim (this signifies that it is time for him to leave) but instead pour less, more often. The first *piala*-full is normally used to wash and sterilize the cup and should be passed and received with the right hand. To cool the tea, swirling is preferred to blowing. A green, powdered tobacco known as *noz* is also taken at teahouses, skilfully shovelled under the tongue, rendering all attempts at even basic communication utterly futile.

At the end of a meal (or when passing a holy cemetery), the *fatiha*—the Muslim gesture of holding out cupped palms to receive God's blessings and then running hands over one's face—is generally performed as a sign of thanks and blessing.

Handicrafts and Costume

Traditional costume in Central Asia is an important component of cultural, ethnic and religious identity. Perhaps unsurprisingly, over the years many younger people have discarded traditional garb for Soviet shirts and Russian tracksuits.

The most striking piece of male attire is the long, striped, wrap-around cloak called a *chapan*, or *khalat* in Russian, tied around the waist by a *turma* sash. *Massi* slippers are worn over *kavish* soft boots so that only the overshoes need be taken off when entering a mosque or private house. The characteristic black-and-white Uzbek *doppe/doppillar* skullcaps (*tubyeiteka* in Russian), embroidered with stylized floral motifs, are worn almost universally to provide a religious as well as ethnic marker, while multi-coloured 'carpet' Tajik scullcaps are worn widely in Samarkand and Shakhrisabz. Both styles originally served as support for the traditional 40 folds of a white or blue *chalma* turban, but are worn today in their own right. In winter, skull-caps are generally swapped for warmer *karakul* fleeced *tilpaks*. In Khorezm, wild and woolly Turkoman dreadlock *chormas* bristle with past infamy, while white, felt Kyrgyz *kalpaks* speckle the fringes of the Ferghana Valley. Muslim headgear is universally rimless to avoid impeding daily prayer.

Women's dress centres around the mass-produced, but vibrant, tie-dyed *ikat* silks of the Ferghana Valley. *Kuljak* knee-length dresses are worn either alone or with *ishton* trousers, while violently embroidered skullcaps are reserved for unmarried girls. Married women generally wear coloured headscarves. Only in rural areas will you see older women wearing the traditional *chetvan* robe with arms tied behind the back. In parts of the Ferghana Valley Iranian-style *chador* dresses and veils (*paranja*) are returning with the rising Islamic tide.

In traditionally nomadic areas, wealth was worn in the saddle and on the hoof and Kazakh, Karakalpak and Turkoman carpets, saddlery, *koshma* felts, coral amulets and women's silver jewellery are particularly fine. Embroidery is also a long established art in Central Asia; witness the male-dominated profession of Bukharan gold embroidery or local variations of *suzaine* embroidered designs.

The Turkic peoples of Central Asia have long enjoyed fame as a blacksmith race (the most popular male name, Timur, means iron) and the tradition is preserved in most local bazaars in the form of *pichok* knives, *kumgan* ewers, *chillim* hubble-bubble pipes and chased metal plates. Brightly painted *beshik* cradles are also found and local styles of pottery persist in isolated pockets such as Gijduvan and Rishtan. Traditional musical instruments range from the guitar-like *dutara* (2 strings), *tanbur* (4 strings) and *rubab* (5 strings)—traditional accompaniment to the epic poetry of wandering bards—to the percussive *nagora* drum and *doira* ringed tambourine. The famed Bukharan carpet, however, rarely came from Bukhara itself but rather from the semi-nomadic lands of present day Turkmenistan and it is there that serious buyers should seek them out.

Tashkent

The capital of Uzbekistan, Central Asia's premier metropolis betrays little of its 2,000-year history as a crossroads of ancient trade routes. Romantic notions of a Silk Road oasis lie buried beneath the avenues of socialism. Yet this modern city of 2.1 million people, the fourth largest in the CIS after Moscow, St Petersburg and Kiev, holds much to arrest the curious traveller, from imposing squares, monumentalist architecture and fine museums, to the mud-brick maze of the old Uzbek town, autumn colours on dappled poplar lanes and the sweet spray of fountains on burning summer days.

The Tashkent oasis lies on the Chirchik river, within sight of the foothills of the western Tian Shan. Mountain meltwater feeds the river, in turn feeding the Syr Darya on whose middle reaches once lay the principality of Chach. Archaeologists battling myth and legend call its first capital Kanka, a square citadel founded between the fifth and third centuries BC, eight kilometres from the Syr Darya. By the seventh century AD, after the Sakas, Sassanians and Hephthalites, prominence shifted to the fertile Chirchik valley, focus of trade between Sogdian settlers and Turkic nomads. Over 50 irrigation canals nurtured more than 30 towns as Chach blossomed into an exporter of cattle, horses, gold, silver and precious stones. The seventh century remains of the ruler's fortress were found at Mingur-yuk, 'thousand apricot orchard', now deep in the Russian quarter of Tashkent. In 751, invading Chinese troops executed the prince of Chach, provoking the Arab invaders to crush them at Talas. Thereby the supremacy of Islam was established and Chinese hopes of Central Asian hegemony were terminated.

Under Samanid rule in the ninth century the capital became known as Binkath, Arab pronunciation turned Chach to Shash and city walls fortified its mosques. Merchants rested their caravans here after the hazardous journey from China over steppe and mountain, before continuing to Samarkand and Bukhara. Arab visitors described a verdant place of vineyards, bazaars and craftsmen. Karakhanid rule from the late tenth century maintained such prosperity and bequeathed a new, Turkish name: Tashkent, 'stone village'.

The Mongol tour of devastation arrived in 1219, although Genghis Khan discovered the Khorezmshah had sacked the city only five years earlier. Recovery quickened under Tamerlane and his successors in the 14th and 15th centuries, when the city's oldest extant buildings arose. During the next three centuries the Uzbeks, Kazakhs, Persians, Mongol Oirots and Kalmyks all clashed for possession, yet by the 18th century growing trade with Russia had expanded Tashkent into four quarters with a common bazaar. In 1780, Yunus Khodja, the chief of the Sheikhantaur quarter, ended internal strife by conquering the other three, Kukcha, Sibzar and Besh-Agach (the names survive today). He repelled Kazakh attacks, but his son lost Tashkent to the Khan of Kokand in 1809.

Tsarist Russia's steady progress southward brought Tashkent into view in October 1864. Behind crenellated walls, 16 miles round, lived a wealthy population of over 100,000 people served by some 300 mosques. Major General Mikhail

Fountain fun outside Tashkent circus

Chernaiev's first assault was beaten off, but the threat of the Bukharan emir stealing this prize and the prospect of Great Game glory back in St Petersburg persuaded him to try again in May 1865. Ignoring orders not to attack, he advanced his force of 1,900 men against the city's 30,000 defenders. On the night of 14 June, the Russians crept up to one of 12 city gates. Felt wrapping deadened the noise of gun wheels. Just before dawn, a diversionary attack lent the main party time enough to scale ladders and use a secret passage to open the gate from inside. Chaplain Malov led the charge, holding his Orthodox cross out high (and winning a military cross for valour). After two days of fighting, city elders chose surrender to save Tashkent from destruction by superior firepower. Chernaiev had lost only 25 men. For his daring, locals christened him Shir-Naib, Lion Viceroy. More importantly, Tsar Alexander's reaction was favourable. Chernaiev's disobedience had secured with little cost a key foothold in the imperial underbelly and British protests could be ignored.

To avoid further rushes of blood, Chernaiev was soon recalled. In autumn 1867 General Konstantin Kaufmann took up appointment as first governor general of Russian Turkestan. His grand palace stood at the heart of the canal- and poplar-lined Russian town with the radial layout of St Petersburg, founded to the east of the old, mud-bricked districts. The American diplomat Schuyler, visiting Tashkent in 1873, observed a clique-ridden, military society: "the officers have little resource but gambling and drinking, and in many instances young men have utterly ruined themselves, some even having to be sent out of the country—and a man *must* be bad to be exiled from Tashkent."

Electric trams connecting old and new Tashkent greeted English writer Stephen Graham in 1914. He delighted in this "fresh, fragrant city", where "cherries ripen by the 1st of May, and strawberries are seven copecks a pound", yet colonialism had its downside:

> With the coming of the Russians, the angel of death has breathed on all that was once the grandeur of the Orient at Tashkent . . . as the fine Russian streets were laid down, and the large shops opened, and the cathedrals were built, and the gardens laid out, the old uphill-and-down dale labyrinth of the Eastern city changed to a curiosity and an anachronism. It faded before the eyes . . . Poor old Tashkent, slipping into the sere and yellow leaf, passing away even as one looked, always decreasing whilst the new town is always increasing—there is much pathos in its destiny . . . Now Turkestan and Russian Central Asia are extremely loyal, peaceful and happy colonies.

Like most travellers, Graham was shielded both from Muslim anger at the neglect of Islam and the encroachment of Russian infidels, as well as from the seeds of revolution growing among the latter. The railway workers whose sweat had done so much to establish the Tsarist regime were among the first to respond to the Bolshevik clarion in November 1917. The provisional government was overthrown and Muslim opposition crushed. In April 1918, Tashkent became the capital of the Turkestan Autonomous Soviet Socialist Republic, yet Soviet suzerainty remained under threat from White Russians and Muslim *basmachi*. In January 1919, Bolshevik commissar Ossipov shot his fellow commissars and declared for the counter-revolution, but drunkenness and poor organization gave him but a single day in power. Four thousand executions followed and pools of blood lay frozen on the winter streets. At this time, Britain's last Great Game player was hiding in the Chimgan mountains outside Tashkent. Colonel F.M. Bailey had been closely watched ever since his arrival from Kashgar in August 1918. The feared Cheka (secret police) even set spies on his dog Zep and Bailey only escaped death and fled to Persia by his mastery of disguise and remarkable nerve. At one point the Bolsheviks assumed him dead for he had left his toothbrush behind, as no Englishman would (in fact he had two). During Bailey's stay, the city reverted from farce—"an Englishman passed through with a troupe of performing elephants he was taking to Kashgar"—to terror—"one man who had his piano nationalized lost his temper and broke up the piano with an axe. He was taken to gaol and shot." The face of the city suffered too: "You were given a coupon for fuel on your ration card. When you asked for your share of fuel you were shown a tree standing in the street and told to take it. Fortunes in paper money were made by the lucky owners of saws and axes."

In time the trees were replanted, but architecture was less lucky: city walls and gates were demolished along with countless mosques, madrassah and mausoleums. In 1930, the city won from Samarkand the capitalship of the Uzbek Soviet Socialist

Republic. Russian settlers, institutions and industries flooded in, particularly during the war years (1941–45), when evacuees from European Russia doubled the population to a million. "Like living on the back of a beserk camel" was how one journalist described the earthquake (7.5 on the Richter scale) and over 1,000 subsequent tremors that devastated Tashkent on 26 April 1966. Casualties were relatively low, but 300,000 were left homeless. The whole Union rushed to the task of reconstruction and the result is today's Tashkent, both the concrete grandeur of Moscow's 'beacon of socialism in the East', now brushed with a veneer of independence, and the old quarter to the west, alive with Uzbek tradition.

Sights

A WALK THROUGH MODERN HISTORY

"The historical-revolutionary monuments and sculptures are an organic part of the city's landscape and give Tashkent a cheerful air." The Soviet guidebook requires extensive revision, for independence has felled giants across the communist pantheon.

Head out from the Hotel Uzbekistan to leafy **Amir Timur Square**, where a statue of Tamerlane on horseback is but the latest political statement to mark Uzbekistan's rites of passage. On the death of governor general Konstantin Kaufmann in 1882, this military parade ground received his cannonball tomb, later moved to his cathedral as the square became a racetrack and promenading area for the well-to-do. In 1913 his statue returned, supported by two soldiers sounding the bugle and planting the flag of tsarist victory. The Bolsheviks renamed Kaufmann's square Revolution Garden and replaced him with a hammer and sickle, temporary obelisks and Lenin busts, until 1947 when Stalin arose, imposing and avuncular. In 1968, long after Joseph's disgrace and removal, came a gargantuan bronze head of Karl Marx, hair and beard cascading in the rush to communism. In 1993, at the close of the experiment his philosophy spawned, Marx was toppled by Tamerlane, rehabilitated from feudal despot to Uzbek hero.

Follow the direction of Tamerlane's horse, between 19th-century gymnasia, along Saiyelgokh Street, where portrait artists and *plov* hawkers compete for your custom, to the most eccentric reminder of tsarist Tashkent, the **former residence of Grand Duke N.K. Romanov** (1850–1917), a first cousin of Tsar Nicholas II, exiled here in 1881 for exploits involving the crown jewels. The firebrick building of dog and deer statues, domes and spires, is based on the outline of the double-headed eagle. In 1919 Romanov's widow showed British agent Bailey their house of many treasures, nationalized into a museum 'to show the people how the *bourjoui* lived in the bad old days'. In 1935 it became a Lenin Young Pioneers Palace and reopened only in the 1980s to

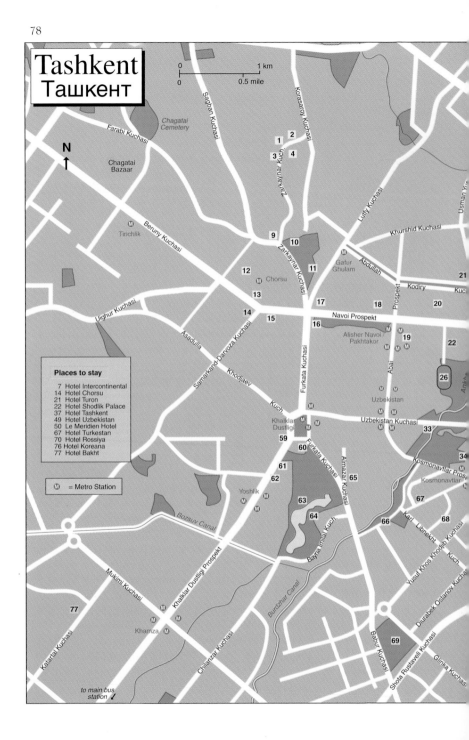

Tashkent
Ташкент

Places to stay

- 7 Hotel Intercontinental
- 14 Hotel Chorsu
- 21 Hotel Turon
- 22 Hotel Shodlik Palace
- 37 Hotel Tashkent
- 49 Hotel Uzbekistan
- 50 Le Meridien Hotel
- 67 Hotel Turkestan
- 70 Hotel Rossiya
- 76 Hotel Koreana
- 77 Hotel Bakht

Ⓜ = Metro Station

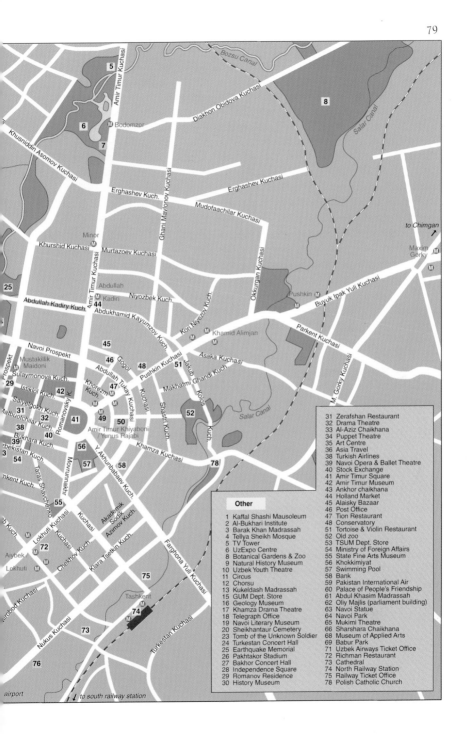

Other

1 Kaffal Shashi Mausoleum
2 Al-Bukhari Institute
3 Barak Khan Madrassah
4 Tellya Sheikh Mosque
5 TV Tower
6 UzExpo Centre
8 Botanical Gardens & Zoo
9 Natural History Museum
10 Uzbek Youth Theatre
11 Circus
12 Chorsu
13 Kukeldash Madrassah
15 GUM Dept. Store
16 Geology Museum
17 Khamza Drama Theatre
18 Telegraph Office
19 Navoi Literary Museum
20 Sheikhantaur Cemetery
23 Tomb of the Unknown Soldier
24 Turkestan Concert Hall
25 Earthquake Memorial
26 Pakhtakor Stadium
27 Bakhor Concert Hall
28 Independence Square
29 Romanov Residence
30 History Museum

31 Zerafshan Restaurant
32 Drama Theatre
33 Al-Aziz Chaikhana
34 Puppet Theatre
35 Art Centre
36 Asia Travel
38 Turkish Airlines
39 Navoi Opera & Ballet Theatre
40 Stock Exchange
41 Amir Timur Square
42 Amir Timur Museum
43 Ankhor chaikhana
44 Holland Market
45 Alaisky Bazaar
46 Post Office
47 Tion Restaurant
48 Conservatory
51 Tortoise & Violin Restaurant
52 Old zoo
53 TSUM Dept. Store
54 Ministry of Foreign Affairs
55 State Fine Arts Museum
56 Khokkimiyat
57 Swimming Pool
58 Bank
59 Pakistan International Air
60 Palace of People's Friendship
61 Abdul Khasim Madrassah
62 Oliy Majlis (parliament building)
63 Navoi Statue
64 Navoi Park
65 Mukimi Theatre
66 Sharshara Chaikhana
68 Museum of Applied Arts
69 Babur Park
71 Uzbek Airways Ticket Office
72 Richman Restaurant
73 Cathedral
74 North Railway Station
75 Railway Ticket Office
78 Polish Catholic Church

display a fabulous jewellery collection. After independence the lavish interiors attracted the Ministry of Foreign Affairs, closing the museum once more.

Ahead sprawls **Independence Square**, the largest city square in the former Soviet Union, flanked by public buildings and walls of fountains. It was first known as Cathedral Square, for near the first bank of fountains Kaufmann founded a splendid Orthodox church and bell tower. Disguised as a Romanian-Austrian POW, Bailey slipped in to celebrate Easter Eve in 1919, the last public service for over 70 years. The cathedral was destroyed in the early 1930s as the square turned Red. In 1936, Lenin mark I arrived to claim it in young, taxi-hailing mode. By 1974 and mark III, the elder statesman with greatcoat and manifesto, Tashkent's Lenin was the world's tallest, topping 30 metres from granite base to balding pate. He shuffled off in 1992, making way for a building block of nationalism: the giant globe showing only the independent Republic of Uzbekistan. May Day parades of Soviet power have been replaced by the singers, dancers and fireworks of 1 September, Independence Day.

Beside the globe stands the former Government House, first built in 1931 and now housing the **Bakhor Concert Hall** and the **Alisher Navoi Library**. Founded in 1870, the library is renowned for the Turkestan Collection, a vast encyclopedia of events 1867–1917. Here was the cannon-fronted **White House**, the governor general's residence from Kaufmann's time onward. Part of it survives at the library's rear, where the **Ankhor Canal**, one-time border of old and new Tashkent, meanders through a verdant swimming and leisure area. Just to the south is the ex-Yuri Gagarin Park, former home to a statue of the idolized cosmonaut. When Tory MP George Curzon visited in 1888, this was the governor's private garden, 'in which a military band plays, and to which the public are admitted three times a week. It contains shaded walks and sylvan retreats, a respectable cascade formed by an artificial dam, and a pit for bears, which was kept by Tchernaieff, who had a craze for animals, until one of his pets nearly bit off the leg of a Kirghiz'. Beyond Uzbekistan Street looms the **Presidential Palace**, occupying the site of the tsarist military fortress. A noonday gun once sounded from its battlements, but today only the gates remain, tucked away in an adjacent park.

Northeast of the globe burns the flame at the **Tomb of the Unknown Soldier**, killed during the 1941 defence of Moscow. Another essential stop on any wedding day video tour is the **Earthquake Memorial**, one block north past the Turkestan Concert Hall. A granite cube displays the time (5.22am) of the first tremor while an Uzbek man shields a woman and child from the earth opening up before them. Granite reliefs picture the reconstruction.

ALISHER NAVOI OPERA & BALLET THEATRE

Lenin's neon dictum 'Art belongs to the People' has gone, but the building remains a tribute to harnessing art for political gain. By 1940, Soviet planners had decided a

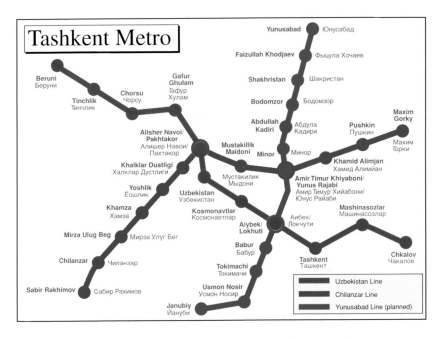

theatre would greatly enhance an area known as the Drunken Bazaar for its wine-soaked market. Japanese prisoners of war completed construction in 1947, while head architect Shchusev, designer of Lenin's mausoleum, reaped Stalinist prizes for his yellow-brick hybrid of classical and Central Asian styles. Beyond the marble lobby are six foyers dedicated to Tashkent, Samarkand, Bukhara, Termez, Khiva and Ferghana, all thickly dressed in stucco carving, themed motifs and murals from Navoi's poetry. Under a chandelier resembling a jewel-studded skullcap, the auditorium seats 1,400 for grand productions of Russian opera or Uzbek folk tales. Tickets are sold inside the columns of the main façade. The theatre occupies its own square opposite the Hotel Tashkent at 28 Mustafa Kamul Ataturk St (tel. 339081). To the south at 17 Uzbekistan St, is **TSUM**, the Central Department Store and barometer of economic progress as both Western and Eastern imports disturb the drab monopoly of Soviet fashion. Opposite is the **International Centre of the Union of Artists of Uzbekistan**, a showcase for modern art exhibitions, at 40 Prospekt Sharaf Rashidov (tel. 565346).

METRO

Tashkent's citizens are justifiably proud of their metro, Central Asia's first and bursting with decorative intent. Construction began in 1972 and five years later the first train rolled. Extensive rubber padding makes the system, 30 kilometres and growing,

as earthquake-proof as possible. Besides being the most convenient way to traverse
the city, and a cool escape from melting avenues, its stations cry out to be appreciated, though stirring Lenin and fraternal republic reliefs have now disappeared from
Mustakillik Maidoni (Independence Sq, ex Leneni) and Khalkar Dustligi (Friendship
of Peoples). Cotton is a common motif, from the mosaics of Pakhtakor (cotton worker) to the boll lamps of Uzbekistan; cupolas drip with gold leaf at Alisher Navoi,
while Kosmonavtlar offers ceramic discs of cosmonauts floating in a spectral sea.

Museums

STATE FINE ARTS MUSEUM OF UZBEKISTAN
16 Movorunnakhr St (tel. 1367345) (10am–5pm, closed Tuesday)
In 1974 this Soviet block was ready to receive the collection established in 1918 from
works confiscated from Grand Duke Romanov, an exiled cousin of the tsar, who in
turn had probably stolen them from St Petersburg's Hermitage. These are displayed
on the second floor and include European paintings and sculpture from the 15th–
20th centuries, notably Russian icons from Novgorod. Soviet artists like Benkov and
Volkov feature throughout, though independence has packed away more propagandist canvases in favour of colourful bazaar scenes. Uzbek art dominates the ground
and first floors: ceramics from the ninth to 17th centuries; tile fragments from Samarkand, Shakhrisabz, Bukhara and Khiva; finely carved wooden doors and shutters;
Bukharan court robes heavy with gold embroidery; ornate metalware and much more.
Behind the museum is the **Communards' Garden**, laid out in the 1880s and subsequently given over to the graves of heroes, notably Bolsheviks who died in revolutionary streetfighting in 1917, the 14 Turkestan Commissars who fell victim to
Ossipov's treachery in 1919, first Uzbek president Yuldush Akhunbabayev and first
Uzbek general Sabir Rakhimov.

MUSEUM OF APPLIED ARTS
15 Rakatboshi St (tel. 564042) (10am–5pm, closed Tuesday)
This museum is as popular for its setting as for its many beautiful exhibits. Tsarist
diplomat Alexandrovich Polovtsev expressed his appreciation of Uzbek architecture
by having his residence built by masters from Bukhara, Samarkand, Khiva, Ferghana
and Tashkent. He was transferred before completion in 1907, so never saw the finished courtyard of verandas and reception halls, vibrant with colour, ganch and
wooden carving. The *mihrab* niche in the main hall points in the opposite direction to
Mecca as Polovtsev desired decorative not functional Islam. Omar Khayyám quotes
frame two doorways: 'The world is a great caravanserai with two doors: one entrance

and one exit. Every day new guests come to the caravanserai.' Among the store of 19th–20th century embroidery are many items essential to a bride's dowry (traditional wedding rites empowered them to protect the young couple from evil): *suzaine* wall-hangings and variants such as *oi-palyak*, lunar sky, and *gulkurpa*, flower blanket. *Tubyeiteka* (skullcaps) display similar diversity in stitching, motifs and symbolism. Carved wooden furniture includes tables and *laukhi*, folding book stands, by Kokandian master Khaidarov. Other halls feature regional ceramics, metalware, musical instruments for festive occasions, such as *karnai* pipes and *doira* drums, and jewellery sets weighing up to 20 kilograms.

MUSEUM OF THE HISTORY OF THE PEOPLE OF UZBEKISTAN

3 Sharaf Rashidov Prospekt (off Independence Sq) (tel. 1335713). (Open 10am–6pm, closed Sunday).

In 1970, the centenary of Lenin's birth, Tashkent lauded the opening of this white marble shrine to the life of Vladimir Ilyich Ulyanov. For two decades Young Pioneers gazed at over 3,000 exhibits: carpets, statues, even a copy of blood-stained clothes from a 1920 assassination attempt. Independence has killed the cult in favour of a post-Soviet version. Besides contemporary propaganda, the core collection is from the now defunct Aiybek Museum, founded in 1876 as Central Asia's first and strong on archaeological explanation of the Uzbek heritage. Highlights include Uzbekistan's only complete Buddha figure (first/second century), a replica of the Osman Koran, an outsize seventh-century work, and reconstructions of Samarkand's Bibi Khanum mausoleum, Ulug Beg Observatory and Khorezm's Koi Krylgan Kala.

ALISHER NAVOI LITERARY MUSEUM

69 Navoi St (tel. 410275) (10am–5pm, closed Saturday)

A tall statue of the poet announces his museum. Born in Herat, Afghanistan in 1441, he was educated there, and at Meshed and Samarkand, and enjoyed illustrious careers in literature and politics. His skills extended to painting, music and sculpture, while his benevolence endowed countless mosques, schools and hospitals. An early work, the *Judgement of Two Languages*, proved that Chagatai, the eastern Turkish vernacular, could be as richly descriptive as Persian or Arabic. He remained a bilingual craftsman, writing poetry of romance, nature and philosophy in both Chagatai and Persian, but it was his development of the former that lends him the mantles Chaucer of the Turks and Father of Uzbek Literature. He died in Herat in 1501. The museum displays manuscripts and miniatures, as well as halls painted in the palace and garden scenes of his major work, the Khamsa quintet. Also featured are copies of the busts of Tamerlane and his son Shah Rukh, created by the archaeologist who examined their bones, and a model of the famous observatory of Shah Rukh's son, Ulug Beg.

Hand-woven Tamerlane carpets, Khudjum Embroidery Factory, Shakhrisabz

MUSEUM OF DEFENCE MINISTRY OF UZBEKISTAN

98 Akademik K. Abdullaev St (tel. 624646), (10am–5pm, closed Monday, Tuesday)
Set behind a giant, defiant Soviet soldier, thrusting his machine-gun skyward, this museum lies in a garden of military cast-offs. Inside are fascinating, as yet unreconstructed displays of Soviet might. Highlights include World War II posters and a telephone barking the orders of General Frunze.

TAMARA KHANUM MUSEUM

House 1, Flat 14, Pushkin-Bishkek St (tel. 678690), (10am–5pm, closed Sunday)
The last home of Uzbekistan's greatest dancer, Tamara Khanum (1906–1991), a Margilan-born Armenian who devoted her life to Central Asian folk dance and female liberation. Previously women could sing and dance only at home, while young boys played female roles in public performances. Tamara was among the first to perform unveiled. Among photos, paintings and posters are many of her beautiful costumes.

AMIR TIMUR MUSEUM

Northwest corner of Amir Timur Sq (tel. 1320212) (10am–5pm, closed Monday)
Erected in record time for Tamerlane's 660th birthday, the outsize ribbed dome conceals a bold interior where Timurid meets independent Uzbekistan. Of chief interest are reconstructions of his works.

GEOLOGY MUSEUM

1 Furkata St (tel. 450866), (10am–4pm, closed weekends)
A new museum of dinosaurs and minerals.

NATURAL HISTORY MUSEUM

16 Sagban St, Chorsu Sq (9am–5pm, closed Monday)
From cavemen and their paintings to cotton and dying seas.

Old Tashkent

SHEIKHANTAUR CEMETERY

Buried deep in institutes and factories north of Navoi's museum and street are three mausoleums dating back to the 15th century. They are the only survivors of a Muslim complex of mosques and madrassah founded in the 14th century with the burial of local saint Sheikh Khawendi Tahur (popularly Sheikhantaur). The largest is that of Yunus Khan, descendent of Genghis Khan, grandfather of Babur and sometime khan of western Mogulistan. In 1485 he resolved a Timurid squabble by taking Tashkent for himself. After his death in 1487, his son built this two-storey dome and portal

Wake Up!

Wake up, beloved Turkestan, and greet your happy days !
Be hale and hearty, Turkestan, we sing your triple praise !
Long years and glory, Soviet might, our land's defence and pride !
We have the age-old fetters shed and free is now our stride.
The sons of workers now may live as free and happy men,
To knowledge true our people turn, the door is open wide.

Oh, may they perish, mullah, bey, ishan with poisoned tongue,
Who wraps his turban up in gauze immeasurably long.
At last the time has come for us, the breaking of our dawn.
The men who work and till the soil are tied in friendship strong.

May all our children learn at school to sharpen mind and eye,
Let superstitions disappear and evil customs die.
May youth grow up in knowledge true as teachers wise and just,
May they spread learning far and wide, may learning reach the sky.

Can we forget the fiery days when happy freedom came ?
Who but the loyal Soviet friends could help us reach this aim ?
Should now this cause we disregard, oblivion this would mean,
No scholar would in future books seek for my country's name.

Today is not a day to laugh, and not amusement day.
"Our duty be our guiding staff", the slogan says today.
Arise, my brothers, work and fight, the time has come to wake.
The cornerstone of knowledge true let us in gladness lay.
Wake up, beloved Turkestan, and greet your happy days !
Be hale and hearty, Turkestan, we sing your triple praise !

Khamza Niyazi (1889–1929)
Uzbek Poetry

memorial. The blue tiles were restored in the 1970s. If the halls are locked, you may request the key from the **Uzbek Restoration Institute** at the rear. This is well worth a look itself, for here experts mould, fire, glaze and fire again tiles used in conservation projects across Uzbekistan, from the sky blue of Samarkand and Shakhrisabz to the more muted tones of Bukhara and Khiva. Visitors interested in restoration work may contact Director Rashod, 11 Kadiri St (tel. 411245).

The institute's *chaikhana*, nestling beneath Yunus Khan, displays beautiful Khivan wooden columns and a 19th-century ceiling from Tashkent's old town. In a small garden just to the east is the **Sheikhantaur mausoleum**, rebuilt in the 19th century according to the original design. Metal sheeting protects the brick dome from Tashkent's harsh climate and pollution. Behind is the **Kaldirgach Bey mausoleum**, built for a ruler of Mogulistan early in the 15th century and noted for its 12-sided pyramidal dome, spherical on the inside. Nearby is the **Shark Embroidery Factory**, at 78 Prospekt Abdullah Kadiri, a collective enterprise formed in the 1930s when Soviet planners brought Uzbek folk art out of the home and into mass production. Almost 3,000 women workers use machines and more traditional methods to decorate wall hangings (*suzani*), head dresses and skullcaps (*tubeiteka*) of velvet, satin, silk and cotton. A display room and gift shop reveal the changing motifs of recent times, from Lenin portraits to scenes of Mecca.

CHORSU

Emerge from Chorsu Metro into reassuringly Central Asian bazaar bustle. Here, at the Chorsu (four ways) crossroads, merchants through the ages have traded the wares of diverse lands. The bazaar was the local bastion of capitalism throughout socialism's tenure in these parts. Today it has rejected its Soviet moniker, October Market, for **Iski Juva** (old tower), after a nearby minaret that once marked the ruler's fortress. The great two-storeyed dome is Soviet-built, an extension of the local tradition of a labyrinth of covered stalls offering protection from summer's fierce rays. Dried fruit and nuts sell upstairs, fresh fruit, vegetables, sacks of herbs and spices downstairs, spilling outside into carpets, slippers, shawls, all manner of entrails and smoking shashlik.

Opposite the Hotel Chorsu is the **Kukeldash Madrassah**, built in the mid-16th century by the ruler's vizier, Kukeldash. After secular use as a Soviet warehouse and museum, the madrassah is reasserting a religious role as money from neighbouring *malhalla* restores the collapsed second storey, corner minarets and brightly tiled façade. Ask permission to view the inner courtyard of 38 student cells (*hujra*) that accommodate over 2,000 young men and women on five-year courses of Islamic study. Friday prayers take place on the entrance platform, near the ruined 15th-century **Jummi Mosque**, constructed by influential Islamic leader Khodja Akrar (1404–1492). This area formerly marked the city centre or *Registan* ('sandy place'), where public executions were held. Until the revolution, unfaithful wives were sewn into sacks and dashed to their deaths from the madrassah's 20-metre-high minarets. When you tire of dust and strife, head to Tashkent's premier soak, four acres of steaming tearooms at the blue-domed **Hammon baths**, west of the Hotel Chorsu on Uighur Street. Five bus stops further down at No. 372 is the **Sheikh Zein-ad-Din** mosque and mausoleum ensemble, the 16th-century remains of an extensive cemetery.

KHAST-IMAM SQUARE

Pick a lane like Zarkaynar, winding north from Chorsu bazaar to the holy heart of Tashkent. This is the least Russified or Sovietized part of the city, a maze of baked-mud walls bereft of fenestral intrusion into Muslim privacy. In many cases tradition-ally built houses survived the 1966 earthquake—only walls with windows or doors collapsed. Ladas rust under mud and timber entrance halls once reserved for horse and cart. Open doorways afford a glimpse of vine-shaded courtyards and quiet pros-perity. Councils of *aksakal* (white beards) in each neighbourhood, or *malhalla*, fos-tered community relations long before socialism arrived.

At length one reaches the Khast Imam Square and the **Barak Khan Madrassah**, founded in the 16th century by a descendent of Tamerlane who ruled Tashkent for the Shaybanid dynasty. The ornate façade of blue-tiled mosaic and Koranic inscrip-tion conceals a rose garden courtyard and 35 *hujra*. Tourists must request permission to view the interior, for this is the administrative centre of the Mufti of Uzbekistan, the head of official Islam in the Republic. Directly opposite Barak Khan is the **Tellya Sheikh Mosque**, first built in the same era and now employed as the city's chief Friday Mosque. Male visitors may petition the imam for the chance to see its beautiful Islamic library. The highlight is the immense Osman Koran, claimed to be the world's oldest; in 655 it was stained with the blood of the murdered Caliph Osman. In the late 14th century, Tamerlane brought it to Bibi Khanum's mighty lectern in Samarkand. General Kaufmann, tsarist conqueror of Turkestan, dispatched it to St Petersburg. After the revolution, the Bolsheviks returned it to Tashkent and in 1989 the Mufti finally secured control.

Just to the north is the **Abu Bakr Mohammed Kaffal Shashi mausoleum**, the grave of a local doctor, philosopher and poet of Islam who lived from 904 to 979. The portal, inner dome and arcade date from the 16th century, when his holy reputation attracted a cemetery. Barren women smear their faces with dust from his tomb in the hope he will end their curse. Opposite is the former Namazgokh Mosque, built in the 19th century for Islamic festivals and animal sacrifices. In recent times it became the **Imam Ismail Al-Bukhari Islamic Institute**, the highest Muslim seminary in the Soviet Union (senior to the only other authorized college, the Mir-i-Arab Madrassah in Bukhara). Where formerly only 25 trainee imams were accepted for four years of study, now up to 1,000 men and women, in separate shifts, attend two-year courses.

A half-hour wander west of Khast Imam, or a ten-minute walk north of Tinchlik metro, is **Chagatai Cemetery**, beside Chagatai bazaar at 319 Farabi Street. Left of the entrance lie buried the common people of the neighbourhood, a crowded mix of Muslim and Soviet-style remembrance. To the right are the servants of the people, the grand tombs of the dignitaries and celebrities of the Uzbek Soviet Socialist Republic, commemorated with deeply un-Islamic busts and engraved faces. Take a guide for a personalized history lesson: Hero of Labour **Turson Akhunova** (1937–1983), the first woman to drive a cotton-picking machine. She travelled widely, encouraging women to enter agriculture, until the chemical fertilizers sprayed on cotton fields gave her cancer; People's Writer **Mirza Aiybek** (1905–1968), among the first to assert Tamerlane's role in world civilization. Official persecution led to a stroke that robbed him of speech; **Shukur Burkhon** (1910–1987), the first Uzbek to play Othello. So impassioned was his performance, he almost strangled Desdemona for real; Uzbek president **Sharaf Rashidov** (1917–1983), lies beneath a marble tombstone of marked simplicity compared to the ostentatious structure which Gorbachev's anti-corruption drive removed from near the Lenin Museum.

MISCELLANEA

Khalkar Dustligi metro delivers you to yet another monstrous square, centred on the monumental marble of the **Palace of People's Friendship**, a 4,000 seater for political and musical displays. In front is a statue of the blacksmith Shamakhmudov and the 15 orphans from European Russia who he and his wife adopted during World War II. Behind the palace, beside yet more fountains, is the **Abdul Khasim Madrassah**, the heavily restored 19th-century college of a Tashkent man famous for his ability to recite the Koran by heart, a skill shared by all his children. Today the madrassah has a limited educational role but enjoys greater renown for its metalwork craftsmen, using *hujra* as workshops to produce 'antique' jewellery. Opposite is the vast **Navruz wedding house**, best visited during Saturday lunchtime when countless newlyweds and video-camera crews battle for champagne and floor space. Outside they weave through

Russian Cathedral, Tashkent

Lada, Moskvich and Zhiguli, festooned with bridal dolls, to make pilgrimage to the statue of 15th-century poet **Alisher Navoi**. His cupola offers a couplet of advice: 'Know, all human kind: the greatest curse is enmity; the greatest blessing—amity'. From here, one can view the boating and swimming lake of **Navoi Park** (ex-Komsomol), dug out by Leninist youth in 1939 in only 45 days, and the bright blue dome of the new **Oliy Majlis** (Uzbek parliament).

For a thorough fill of republican statistics and repackaged propaganda, visit the **UzExpoCentre**, formerly the VDNKh or Uzbek Exhibition of Economic Achievements beside the aquapark, in former Victory Park on the Bozsu Canal, north of the centre on Amir Timur St (metro Bodomzor). The main pavilion introduces educational, scientific, cultural and industrial progress, under President Karimov's promise that 'Uzbekistan is a great state in the future'. Towering to the north is the 375-metre (1,230 foot) **TV Tower** (open 10am–9pm, closed Mondays). Above the viewing platform at 100 metres are two revolving restaurants offering a leisurely panorama of leafy cityscape: new district Yunusabad to the north, Independence Square far to the south, the old town to the west and the **Botanical Gardens and Zoo** (open daily, 9am–5pm), new home to the zoo, on the Salar Canal to the east.

Just as the Muslims relish newly gained freedom to worship openly, Orthodox Christians turn to their church for salvation in these troubled and changing times. On Sunday mornings Russian babushkas revere icons with candles and prostration at the onion-domed **Cathedral**, first built as a small church in 1872. Address: 20 Avliyoota Kuchasi, west of Tashkent railway station.

Theatres

Alisher Navoi Opera & Ballet Theatre 28 Ataturk St (tel. 1333528)[see page 80-1]
Turkestan Concert Hall, 2 Prospekt Navoi (tel. 349945)
Tashkent's newest, boasting indoor spectaculars, music, dance and outdoor theatre.
Theatre Ilkhom, ('Inspiration'), 5 Pakhtakor St, below the Hotel Yoshlik
(tel. 412252 / 412241)
The brightest and best of experimental theatre, mime and farce.
Republican Puppet Theatre, 1 Afrosiab Avenue (tel. 567395)
Delightful theatre of Uzbek and international fables also featuring a puppet museum.
Bakhor Concert Hall, 5 Mustakillik Square
Home to the celebrated Bakhor Uzbek dance troupe and various music recitals.
Philharmonic Hall, 10 Provda Vostoka St
Renovation is supplying a third lease of life: built in 1913 as the Coliseum Theatre for circus shows, it became the Sverdlov Concert (and meeting) Hall after the Revolution.

Khamza Uzbek Drama Theatre, 30 Navoi St (tel. 1443542 / 1441751)
Mukimi Uzbek Musical Theatre, 187 Almazar St (tel. 453655 / 451633)
Young Spectators Uzbek Theatre, 8 Zarkaynar St (tel. 1443343 / 1443152)
Gorky Russian Drama Theatre, 28 Saiyelgokh St (tel. 1333205 / 1338165)
Circus, Khadra Sq (tel. 1442904). Weekend afternoon performances.

Sports

The hippodrome lies to the southwest, a short bus ride from Sabir Rakhimov Metro, though Sunday horse racing is a minor diversion to the riotous free market consuming the car park. For regional football clashes visit the 80,000 capacity Pahktakor (Cotton worker) Stadium, beside its eponymous metro. Swimming facilities include in/outdoor pools open 7am–8pm at 78 Abdullah Tukaya, behind Mekhrdzhon Park. A Turkish-built 'aquapark' with water slides and roller coasters makes for a fun afternoon, beside the UzExpoCentre on Amir Timur St (metro Bodomzor). To the north in the shadow of the TV tower is Savdo Stadium/Yunusabad Tennis Club: ten courts (two indoor), sauna and gym. Open 6am–11pm (tel. 346981). Ten-pin bowling can be found at Bowling Yuldus (tel. 351830) beside Holland Market, just north of Alaisky Bazaar entrance on Amir Timur Kuchasi. Try too the Jar tennis club beside the Hotel Chorsu. Pool tables can be found downstairs at Mir Burger, Saiyelgokh St. With the imminent opening of the Tashkent Lakeside Golf Club (tel. 302182) Uzbekistan gains its first course, wrapped around Lake Rohat at 1, Bektemir District, a short drive southeast from the city centre.

Shopping

Hotel souvenir shops introduce the basic range—carpets, paintings, ceramics and jewellery, but greater variety is available within the Applied Arts, State Fine Arts and History museums [see pages 82–3] or the Kuranti Art Salon at 2 Akhunbabayev St, beneath the clock built in 1947 to commemorate victory over Nazi Germany. For Soviet goods and the latest in imported dreams, visit the Main and Central Department Stores, GUM and TSUM, opposite the Kukeldash Madrassah and south of Navoi Theatre respectively. Opposite TSUM, look for paintings and handicrafts at the International Centre of the Union of Artists of Uzbekistan at 40 Prospekt Sharaf Rashidov. Two doors down is a gift and bookshop where you might try for the elusive map of Tashkent (and other cities). Another such store is at 13a Khamid Alimjan Sq (and metro); two more bookshops can be found at 14 & 16, Navoi Street. Saiyelgokh Street painters, between Tamerlane and the Zerafshan restaurant, offer portraits and bazaar scenes as well as Soviet souvenirs, while the Shark Embroidery Factory has a gift shop with gowns, skullcaps and wall-hangings. The Zumrad Cultural Centre for Uzbek crafts at 2 Kosmonovtov St (just west of the ongoing metro construction site which once was Lakhuti Street) is an important outlet for crafts, particularly ceramics and jewellery. Open Monday to Saturday, 10am to 7pm.

Tashkent Practical Information

TRANSPORT

■ AIR

Tashkent airport is located seven kilometres south of the city centre and is split into two terminals 250 metres apart: international (including all CIS flights) and domestic (Uzbekistan only). Both underwent welcome renovation in 1997–8. Arrivals are on the ground floor and departures on the first floor. A $10 departure tax is levied on some international flights (if not included in ticket price). A more comfortable (*liux*) arrival/departure lounge is available for $30–50 per person. Second floor offices include various airlines (potential tickets—see list below) and a branch of Uzbek immigration (potential visa extensions). A taxi to the Hotel Uzbekistan should not exceed $5, or take a bus from in front of the old terminal: bus 25 stops at Khokkimiyat (Mayor's office) near the Hotel Uzbekistan; bus 67 services the Hotel Rossia and bus 11 the Hotel Chorsu. All three connect with the metro.

The easiest place to buy CIS tickets is the airline ticket desk at the Hotel Uzbekistan, open daily 8am–6pm, tel. 333217 (minimum $5 surcharge). Uzbek Airways' ticket office for domestic and international flights is opposite the Hotel Rossiya at 9 Shota Rustaveli Kuchasi, tel. 563837 (open daily 9am–5pm; counter 22). For same-day CIS departures, try the international terminal. For airport information service call 548637.

Foreign Airline Offices:
Aeroflot, 5A Abdulla Qodyri St, Tashkent, Uzbekistan (tel. 415717)
Air Ukraine, Tashkent International Airport, 3rd floor, (tel. 509116, fax. 555689
Ariana (Afghan), Tashkent International Airport, 3rd floor, (tel. 555001, fax. 555001)
El-Al Israel Airlines, Tashkent International Airport, 3rd floor, (tel. 503409)
Imair Airlines (Azerbaijan), 25 Khalkar Dustligi Avenue, Embassy of Azerbaijan, Tashkent, Uzbekistan (tel. 313316, fax. 551753)
Kvant Global Sales Agency (Russian), 9 Kunaev St, Tashkent, Uzbekistan (tel. 563769 / 568343, fax. 561519)

* Tashkent has two telephone area codes: 3712 for six-digit numbers, 371 for seven-digit.

Lufthansa, Tashkent International Airport, 3rd floor, Lufthansa office (tel. 553420 / 1376065, fax. 553420)

Pakistan International Airlines, 4 Druzhba Narodov Avenue, Tashkent, Uzbekistan (tel. 453568 / 459192, fax. 453942). Tashkent International Airport, 3rd floor, PIA office (tel. 549215)

Transaero (Russian), Tashkent International Airport, 3rd floor, Transaero office (tel. 551505 / 504931). Reservations: 17 Pushkin St, Tashkent, Uzbekistan (tel. 1337638 / 1339935)

Turkia Havo Yullari (Turkish), 14 Otatyurk St, Tashkent, Uzbekistan (tel. 1525252 / 1525253, fax. 1320727). Tashkent International Airport, 3rd floor, Turkish Airlines office (tel. 548281 / 591537)

Uzbekistan Havo Yullari (Uzbekistan Airlines), National Air Company, 41 Movarounnakhr St, Tashkent, Uzbekistan (tel. 1335000 / 1339868, fax. 1331885 / 1367500)

Central Booking & Sales Office, 9 Kunaev St, Tashkent, Uzbekistan (tel. 563837 / 548794/066)

Tashkent International Airport (tel. 554858 / 546267)

Local/CIS Dispatcher (tel. 551954)

International Dispatcher (tel. 591556)

■ TRAIN

Tashkent Vokzal, officially the Severnay (North) Vokzal, is the station for northbound trains to Russia, Kazakhstan and Kyrgyzstan, plus various departures to Turkmenistan and the Ferghana Valley. It is south of the city centre on Turkestan Street (tel. 1997216) (metro stop Tashkent). Further southwest on Usman Nosir Street is the Yuzhni (South) Vokzal (tel. 1399113) for local trains throughout Uzbekistan, from Andijan to Termez to Nukus. Until the opening of the Janubiy stop on the new Yunusabad line, take the metro to Chilanzar and any bus south. Tickets for all destinations are sold on the ground floor of the Hotel Lokomotif at Tashkent station (entrance on platform side), but non-CIS passport holders may well be directed to the International Ticket Office at the right-hand corner of the main advance booking office, ten minutes' walk away at 51 Movarunnakhr St. Open everyday from 8am to 5pm, this office asks a $20 surcharge for its queue-free service and provides a money exchange desk.

■ BUS

The main long-distance bus station is the Tashkent *avtovokzal,* five minutes' walk through a bazaar from Sabir Rakhimov Metro (western terminus of the Chilanzar line). The further the destination the less frequent the buses, so consider buying tickets a day in advance. Particularly for inter-republic travel (e.g. Turkmenistan), the ticket-seller may request you first register with the station police upstairs. If you miss the last scheduled bus (usually late afternoon) to popular destinations like Samarkand or Andijan, try a night bus from in front of Yuzhni Vokzal. Despite its name, the Samarkand bus station opposite only runs buses within Tashkent Province.

CITY TRANSPORT

The Tashkent Metro [see map p81] runs from 5am to 12 midnight and should be your first choice whenever possible. Construction continues on a third line to bring most of the city within its reach. A flat fare applies, so buy a handful of tokens each time. Bus, trolleybus and tram networks connect the centre with the remotest suburbs—check routes with a city map and ask fellow passengers for advice. Officially marked taxis charge around 10 sum per kilometre, though the meter is often neglected and a full journey rate established through firm bargaining. A ride across town costs from $1–3. Bargaining is especially necessary when stopping a taxi at night or near a tourist hotel. It pays to take a map and the name of your destination written in Russian and/or Uzbek. Many locals use their cars as private taxis and few problems are reported. Again, agree the price first.

ACCOMMODATION

Hotel Inter-Continental Tashkent, 107A Amir Timur Kuchasi (tel. (371) 1325252, (3712) 407000, fax. 406459) (e-mail: tashkent@interconti.com) (*Metro Bodomzor*) Uzbekistan's first five-star hotel is the centrepiece of a business complex in the north of the city. Managed by Intercontinental, the hotel boasts an impressive range of business and leisure facilities: 246 rooms, Club IC floor, conference and banquet halls, business centre, health club and pool. Restaurants include the oriental Dome on the top floor, the Italian Allegro, the Los Amigos Mexican restaurant, and the first Irish pub in Central Asia. Single/double from US$255 to US$1,550 for the Presidential Suite. Room payment by credit card only; other services payable in sum.

Hotel Shodlik Palace, 5 Pakhtakor St (tel. 414222, fax 414404) (*Metro Pakhtakor*) A flagship for the benefits of foreign involvement, Shodlik's German management have turned the crumbling Hotel Yoshlik (the former House of Youth) into a smart and comfortable four-star establishment, with 107 rooms, conference, business and fitness centres, the French/Italian La Strada, The Gallery and Hemingway bar/bistro. Single/double from US$160/220, payable in sum by credit card.

Le Meridien Hotel, 2 Uzbekistan Ovozi St (tel. 406600, fax. 406319) (*Metro Amir Timur Khiyaboni*) Well located just behind the Hotel Uzbekistan, Le Meridien is the Forte-led transformation of the Indian-built Tata. The three-star hotel offers over 300 rooms, plus business centre (including Uzbekistan Airways desk), function rooms, health club, outdoor pool, Sheherazade and La Baguette restaurants, and the Salty Dog pub.

Single/double US$190/210, suites US$320; room payment by credit card only; other services payable in sum.

Hotel Uzbekistan, 45 Khamza St (tel. 1360077, fax. 406115) (*Metro Amir Timur*)
Intourist's 17 storey beacon of Soviet comfort has been rejuvenated by Malaysian renovation. The two-star hotel remains a group/delegation favourite, offering tour and ticket desks, business centre, pool, *chaikhana* (a local wedding favourite) and average restaurants. Singles/doubles in the well refurbished left wing cost US$120/160 (including breakfast); unrefurbished singles cost US$90.

Hotel Turkestan, 64 Navruz St (tel. 564535/1335954) (*Metro Kosmonavtlar*)
A quiet, luxury option beside a presidential dacha. Official introduction now appears unnecessary for rooms and suites from US$80–180. No English spoken.

Hotel Tashkent, 56 Buÿuk Turon St (tel. 1524375/1332735, fax. 406131) (*Metro Mustakillik Maidoni*)
Well-placed opposite Navoi Theatre, the one-star Tashkent offers large singles/doubles from US$45–60/75–90, including breakfast and dinner, bathroom and satellite TV.

Hotel Tsorbi, 1 Gorky Street (tel. 674382, fax 683843) (*Metro Maxim Gorky*)
A private, one-star hotel in the east of the city, with doubles for US$75.

Hotel Sayokhat, 115 Buyuk Ipak Yuli Street (tel/fax 686772) (*Metro Maxim Gorky*).
Also in the east with a wide range of services, including travel agency. Singles/doubles from US$42/124 including breakfast.

Hotel Chorsu, 1 Chorsu Square (tel. 427600, fax. 428700) (*Chorsu metro*)
Near Chorsu metro, bazaar and the heart of the old town is this three-sided concrete goliath. Malaysian investment has collapsed, abandoning the US$40/60 singles/doubles to further decay.

Hotel Rossiya, 2 Sapyerlar Sq (tel. 562963)
Awaiting renovation, the Rossiya is overpriced at $21/27–52 for single/double. Of the small hotels touted at the Rossiya's entrance, the best lies five minutes' walk behind the Rossiya at 32 Mirakilova St (tel. 554192). Clean rooms for $4–10 per night.

Hotel Turon, 5 Usman Yusupov St (tel. 415769)
On the corner with Abdullah Kadiri St. Basic singles/doubles for $30/48.

Hotel Bakht, 21 Katartal St, Chilanzar Kvartal 8 (tel. 789525) (*Metro Khamza*)
An excellent budget choice ten minutes' walk from Khamza metro. Fifty clean and spacious rooms ranging from $6–10 per night, with private or shared bathroom. Phone ahead, as it is often full.

Hotel Koreana, 6th floor, 73 Nukus St (tel. 542555, fax 543587)
Good budget choice; pristine rooms for US$40 (shared bathroom); sauna, billiards, *kimchi* and Daewoo cars all available in same building.

Sam Buh B&B, 21 Tsehovaya St (tel./fax 549174; ravshan@sambuh.silk.org)
Welcome addition to the Tashkent accommodation scene. Six clean, en suite doubles (US$70, plus breakfast) in a former Jewish *mahalla* south of the Hotel Rossiya. Host

A rising tide of skullcaps, Shah-i-Zinda

Ravshan offers an impressive range of services, from visas and airport pick-up to nationwide tours.

FOOD AND NIGHTLIFE

In most countries people eat out for the pleasure of sampling better-than-everyday cuisine. In Uzbekistan, however, you will often be reminded that staying in is a safer culinary bet. You can now combine the two by visiting the home restaurants of **Chagatai bazaar** along Akademik Sadikov St (metro Tinchlik). Long renowned for exceptional shashlik, the bazaar's air is pungent with grilled meat by 4am. A number of fresh dairy products are available to complete your breakfast. After 10am the grillers return home and open their doors until 10pm. Enquire after the celebrated *plov* of Babur Zakirov; **Ibodat** at No. 19 offers full restaurant set-up. For their splendid settings, two of Tashkent's *chaikhana* stand out from the crowd: the **Yunus Khan**, in the shadow of that blue-domed mausoleum on Sheikhantaur St, north of the Navoi Museum, and the **Sharshara**, beside the Burdzhar Canal at the end of Rakatboshi St, ten minutes' walk from the Museum of Applied Arts. Popular too is the **Ankhor Canal-bank chaikhana** on Navoi beside the Turkestan Concert Hall. Another area for home cooking, plus live bands, is Ivlieva St, southwest of the Hotel Rossiya, with Armenian/ European and Uzbek fare at **Klubik Rubika**, **Number One Café**, **Café Sevan** and others.

Rather than the Sovietized Uzbek-Russian cuisine of the Hotel Uzbekistan, walk past Tamerlane towards Independence Square along Saiyelgokh St, Tashkent's premier night food market and epicentre of nocturnal entertainment. Here is the cavernous **Zerafshan**, at 17 Matlubochi St (tel. 334376), popular for wedding banquets and dramatic cabaret, with the **Oasis Bar** and **Aphrodita Nightclub** upstairs, the **Beijing Restaurant** behind, and fast-food/pool tables at adjacent **Mir Burger** and nearby **Ardus FM Burger** (plus Turkish supermarket).

From the Hotel Uzbekistan head up Pushkin to dine with Tashkent's *champanski* and caviar set at **Tion**, No. 13 (tel. 1339117, reservations recommended). Le Meridien nearby offers its **Sheherazade** or **La Baguette** restaurants and a **Pizza Hona** for eat-in or take-away (tel. 455862). Behind it on Abdullah Tukay is **Kassandra** (tel. 1337561), with European fare, or continue north up Pushkin just over the Khamid Alimjan metro bridge for classical music and Uzbek cuisine at **Tortoise & Violin**, 11, Jakub Kolos (tel. 1364522). South of Le Meridien at 49 Khamza is the delightful **Opera** (tel. 1334185) with pricy Euro fare in a colonial-style building with garden. A cheaper bet, for excellent Turkish food is **Hilamin** ('Turkish Snack') five minutes walk down Lokhuti.

Three blocks north of the Hotel Uzbekistan is **Alaisky Bazaar**, a cornucopia of fruit, vegetables, sheep innards and Lada parts. Spring and summer coat stalls with cherries, raspberries, figs and melons. Hunt for *kukcy*, Korean cold noodles, courtesy of Stalin's deportation of Koreans from the Soviet Far East to Central Asia during World War II. Proper Korean restaurants include **Sam Yang**, beside Al-Khorezmi Sq., Massiv Chilanzar 11 (tel. 744571, 15 minutes' walk from Metro Chilanzar), and **Seoul**, 65 Shota Rustaveli, (tel. 531414, metro Tokimachi). Recommended is the Korean seafood buffet and opera at the **New World**, on the second floor of the Navoi Theatre. Nearby is the **New World Bakery & Pizza**, with the best baguettes and *pain au chocolat* in town. For pizza, try also **Zam Zam Pizzeria** at 27 Kunaev, across from the Hotel Rossiya.

Elsewhere, sample the first-rate, reasonably priced Middle Eastern **Al Delphin**, No. 3 Malyasovar St (tel. 340400, turn right north of Holland Market), inexpensive Turkish fare at **Effendim**, 30 Navoi Prospekt (tel. 1445549), the Pakistani **Hadra** inside the Hotel Hadra further along Navoi and up beside the circus at 56a Gafur Ghulam (tel. 442844, Gafur Ghulam metro), or the oriental flavours of **Restaurant Khitai**, at Almazar 8/2 (tel. 458670, Khalklar Dustligi Metro). The Intercontinental tempts with some of the best food in town—**The Brasserie**, Italian **Allegro**, Lebanese **Dome** and Mexican **Los Amigos**, while the Shodlik Palace boasts the French/Italian **La Strada** and relaxed **Hemingway Bistro**. Other good (expensive) places for western food include **Richman**, 16a Lokhuti (tel. 565038, metro Aiybek) and **Sogdiana**, 4 Buyuk Ipak Yuli (tel. 668666, metro Maxim Gorky).

Tashkent's nocturnal options have expanded with a number of nightclubs (expect $5–10 cover charge); big in 1998 was **Kizil Shom** (Red Sunset), not far from the popular **Lucky Strike bar**, tucked behind the shopping complex at 13A Khamid Alimjan (via the northeastern metro exit). Try also **Aphrodiat** (see above) or **Aladdin** in Independence Square (5, Rashidov, 1391516). For other pubs, try the **Salty Dog pub** in Le Meridien or the **Irish pub** in the Intercontinental. For all the latest recommendations, and theatre listings, obtain the monthly *Odds & Ads* periodical [see page 64].

MONEY

Most hotels have money-changing counters, likewise the airport and the International Railway Ticket Office near Tashkent Station. To get hard currency from traveller's cheques or Visa, head to rooms 42 and 8, National Bank for Foreign Economic Activity, 23 Akhunbabaev St (tel. 1336070, fax. 1333200, weekday mornings only). If you need to have money wired to you, or wish to open an account, try the Uzbek-Turkish joint venture UT-Bank, at 74 Chilanzar-3, tel. 771111, fax 406362.

COMMUNICATIONS

■ POST/PHONE/FAX

All the bigger hotels offer these facilities. The main post office is near Alaisky Bazaar at 7 Abdullah Tukay (open 8am–8pm), from where international phone calls can be made, but the Central Telegraph Office offers a cheaper, more extensive service, prepaid calls relayed to your room, plus fax/telegram/telex facilities, at 28 Prospekt Navoi (8–10pm daily, tel. 1443043).

■ BUSINESS SERVICES

American Business Centre (ABC), 41 Buyuk Turon St (tel. 406705, fax 406676, e-mail: office@csabc.silk.glas.apc.org). Part of the US Commercial Service, the ABC provides extensive help and expertise to visiting US business people.

Asian Business Agency (ABA Co.), 3/26 Babur St (tel. 541392, e-mail: aba@aba.bcc.com.uz)

Business Communications Centre, 16 Lakhuti St (tel. 565362, e-mail: bcctash@bcc.com.uz)

DHL, 42/125 Khalklar Dustligi (tel. 406169)

Xerox, K. Ataturk St, between Navoi Theatre and Zerafshan Restaurant (tel. 335425)

TRAVEL AGENCIES

Uzbektourism, 47 Khorezm St (tel. 1330733, fax. 1327948). This is the headquarters of the national tourist agency, situated behind the Hotel Uzbekistan, though their service bureau (tel. 332773) inside the hotel can provide most itineraries, including city tours with driver and interpreter. Russian/Uzbek speakers should try the branch office beside Metro Pakhtakor (tel. 441292)

Asia Travel, 40 Sharif Rashidov (tel. 1526728/26, fax. 562927, e-mail: adventure@asia-travel.uz). The pick of the new, private travel agencies, offering moderately priced tours of the city, republic and region, but specializing in adventure travel across the Tian Shan and Pamirs—trekking, climbing, skiing, caving and rafting, plus camel-trekking in the Kyzyl Kum desert. Phone ahead as the office is notoriously difficult to find.

Sairam Tourism, 16-a Movarounnahr St (tel. 1333559 / 1337411, fax 406937, e-mail: silkroad@sairamtour.com.uz)

Around Tashkent

ZENGI ATA MAUSOLEUM

This mausoleum complex 15 kilometres (9 miles) south of Tashkent ranks among the holiest sites in the province. **Zengi Ata**, or 'dark father', was the dark-skinned Sheikh

Ay Khodja, a 13th-century Sufic preacher and patron saint of shepherds. When American diplomat, Schuyler, attended the annual festival in 1873, crowds of pilgrims prayed and feasted while a native orchestra competed with a Russian military band:

Later on, to amuse the officers, the Russian prefect of the district had some women dance, much to the horror of the Mussulmans that a religious festival should be so profaned. It was one of those little things shocking to native feeling which not all Russian officials are careful enough to avoid. Such a dance was once before arranged on a public festivity when the governor-general was present, but he was deceived by the story that the women who danced were the wives of the chief natives, who did this in his honour, and he even presented them with some silver cups and souvenirs, which were found the next day in various brothels.

The post-Soviet religious climate permits veneration once more. Resident holy men are besieged for blessings by engaged couples and barren women. The latter come to the mausoleum of Zengi Ata's wife, **Ambar Bibi**, widow of his teacher—a disciple of Turkestan's Akhmed Yasawi [see page 103–5]—and patroness of women and mothers. Legend records how Tamerlane was rebuilding Yasawi's mausoleum in the late 14th century but a wall repeatedly collapsed. Yasawi appeared to him in a dream, entreating that Zengi Ata be honoured first, so Tamerlane had workers pass bricks along a great line from Turkestan to Tashkent. The two mausoleums date from that time, when Tashkent was a Timurid fortress. A madrassah courtyard was added in the 18th century, a mosque in 1870 and a polygonal minaret in 1914. Recent renovation has smartened the ensemble and, most impressively, Zengi Ata's portal, bright in multicoloured mosaic. Inside is the burial vault and marble tombstone, elegantly carved in Koranic inscription. Ambar Bibi lies in the cemetery beyond, where ostentatious Soviet tombs mingle with Muslim graves of traditional simplicity. To reach this green haven of quiet devotion, take bus 153 from Sabir Rakhimov metro for a 30-minute ride in the country.

CHIMGAN-CHARVAK

For heli-skiing or trekking, windsurfing or simply a lakeside barbecue, head to the capital's resort, the foothills of the western Tian Shan around Chimgan, 80 kilometres northwest of Tashkent. Once the tsarist governor-general had a house here, the social elite also built summer cottages, only for the Bolsheviks to requisition them for sick workers after the revolution. The Russian love of winter sports and the Soviet addiction to sanatoria guaranteed Chimgan's growth.

The road from Tashkent follows the Chirchik river past hydroelectric dams and the modern city of Chirchik, famed for its chemical works. A right fork leads straight to Chimgan, or left to the town of Khodjakent, boasting Bronze Age rock carvings, tea

Conolly and Stoddart

When Colonel Charles Stoddart rode into Bukhara one week before Christmas 1838, on a mission to reassure the emir over British movements on his southern border, little did he know that he was to be kept in the foulest pit in Asia for over three years, tortured and tormented by a sadistic, paranoid madman, finally to be publicly beheaded in the central market square of the holy city, abandoned by the very country which had sent him there.

Things had not gone well from the start. Totally unsuited for the tasks ahead and unschooled in the essential subtleties of Eastern diplomacy, Stoddart rode up to the Ark when he should have dismounted, floored an attendant instead of offering the customary sign of submission and was equipped with neither gifts nor letters from the Queen. Earlier that day he had saluted the emir on horseback in the Registan and the offended emir had not responded, except to glare demonically at Stoddart for just a moment too long for the Englishman's good. Now his reponse was more emphatic. Stoddart was thrown into a six-metre deep vermin-infested hole, salubriously named the Bug Pit, a victim of his own ignorance and arrogance.

For the next three years the sadistic Nasrullah played with Stoddart like a cat with a mouse and his treatment yo-yoed with the rise and fall of the British Empire. He was eventually moved from the Bug Pit into the marginally less revolting Black Hole and when the British took Kabul in July 1839 he even lived for a time in the house of the Chief of Police. In the meantime the vermin were fed raw offal to tide them over until Stoddart's return. Only once, when an executioner climbed down a rope into the pit with orders to execute him on the spot, did Stoddart's nerve understandably crack. He became a Muslim and was rewarded with house arrest.

Then, in September 1840, light at the end of Stoddart's tunnel rode into town in the shape of Captain Arthur Conolly, of the sixth Bengal Light Cavalry. A quintessential Great Game player, Conolly had even invented the phrase. His mission impossible—to unite the perpetually warring khanates of Central Asia against Russia and to open up the Oxus to the dual benefits of God and British-made goods. Yet other factors motivated this complex one-man rescue mission. His zealotry hardened on a long sea passage to India with the Bishop of Calcutta and his heart broken by a jilting lover, Conolly had nothing to lose. Within weeks however, events had conspired against the two men and both were back in jail, their fate finally sealed by an unsolicited letter from the treacherous vizier of Herat, Yar Mohammed, describing Conolly (Khan Ali) as a spy, and a second missive from the Governor General of India, disowning him coldly as a 'private traveller'. The third long-awaited reply to the emir's personal letter to Queen Victoria never even arrived. All three confirmed the emir's most paranoid suspicions. When reports came of the British defeat in Kabul and their subsequent massacre in the Khyber Pass, Nasrullah knew he had no retribution to fear.

On 24 June 1842, the two men limped into a packed Registan, dug their own graves and knelt silently before them, their arms tied behind their backs. Eyewitness accounts state that Stoddart was the first to be beheaded (though it is more likely that he had his throat cut) and that Conolly was soon to follow (although some say that as a convinced infidel up until his death, he would have suffered a different fate than his converted compatriot). Their bodies were buried where they fell, forgotten and abandoned.

But not quite. Three years later the eccentric Bavarian clergymen Joseph Wolff arrived in Bukhara direct from Richmond, Surrey, his journey funded by a Conolly and Stoddart Society whip-round. Armed with little more than three dozen copies of *Robinson Crusoe* in Arabic and an array of cheap watches, Wolff had come to reason with the most brutal and unpredictable ruler in Asia. He had, at least, learned from Stoddart's mistakes. Dressed in full red canonicals, he prostrated himself before the emir, crying "Allah Akhbar" a full 30 times instead of the proscribed three. For, as Fitzroy Maclean wryly notes, Wolff may not have been prepared to become a Muslim, but he was prepared to go to considerable lengths to avoid being thrown in the Bug Pit. In the end the brave eccentric's demands were refused and he was soon sent packing as the band played *God Save the Queen* over the emir's hysterical laughter. Later, in his bedchamber, he was forced to fight off the advances of an unveiled beauty sent to tempt him in the night and as he slept he clasped a package of opium to numb the potential pain of sudden execution. Eventually however, Wolff was freed to leave Bukhara, his life saved by his own ludicrousness, and the last page was turned on the Conolly and Stoddart legend.

But not quite. Twenty years later, incredibly, Conolly's prayer book arrived through the post at his sister's house in London. The verses which had given him such relief in his darkest hours had become his final testament, the last of his diary entries ending abruptly in mid-sentence...

houses and juniper forests. A two-kilometre climb ends at Charvak dam, protected by a statue of Farkhad. Of multiple versions of the romantic Iranian legend **Farkhad and Shirin**, one account, doing little for inter-ethnic relations, describes Shirin as a beautiful queen living beyond the Syr Darya. To choose one of two suitors, an old woman bade Shirin set a difficult task and marry the winner. She commanded a canal be dug through the Hunger Steppe. The honest Uzbek Farkhad took his spade and began digging a channel through the mountains. The crafty Tajik Khosru laid a carpet of reeds upon the steppe to shine like water at dawn. Once the wind bore Farkhad the news of Shirin's marriage to his deceitful rival, his sorrow turned him into a rock (alternatively he tossed his spade into the air to decapitate himself). Shirin soon discovered the truth and melted into a river of tears. Dams, hydroelectric power stations and canals throughout the country bear the name of her martyred hero.

The dam holds back the stunning blue of **Charvak Reservoir**, built in 1982 at the mountain-girdled confluence of the Pskem, Koksu and Chatkal rivers. The road skirts high above the water until Bakachur, where villas and *chaikhana* attract weekend crowds. Russian windsurfers skim past Uzbek matriarchs swimming fully clothed as hang-gliders soar overhead. Ladas sprout tents and overnight on stony beaches smoky with grilling shashlik. Isolation, rather than scenic beauty, drew an early British visitor. Colonel F.M. Bailey hid in villages throughout the area while on the run from the Cheka (Secret Police) in 1918 and 1919. His first base was a bee farm in the hills above Brichmulla, a settlement on the Koksu now marooned on the other side of the reservoir. Despite constant threat of arrest and the trauma of dislocating his leg while hunting wild boar, Bailey showed Great Game pedigree by indulging his passion for butterfly collecting 'with a net issued by the Soviet authorities'. He finally escaped to Persia in 1920 and later had four species of butterfly named after him.

Twenty minutes' drive from Bakachur is **Chimgan** itself, Uzbekistan's winter-sports centre. The name originates in the Turkic for 'green slope', justified by the poplar, maple, acacia and countless fruit trees. When it whitens, skiers flock to the three-kilometre-long Kumbel track. Hire equipment is available for early arrivals. From January to April heli-skiers may drop onto virgin snow at 3,000-plus metres (10,000-plus feet) for 5–10 kilometre (3–6 mile) descents. Whatever the season, take the chair-lift part way up Great Chimgan, at 3,309 metres (10,850 feet) the highest summit in the region, for splendid views across to the reservoir. Hiking trails include Aksay and Kyzyldzhar peaks, the Marble river and Gulkamsay waterfall. Arab visitors are surprised to see their fellow Muslims revive the primitive tree worship of Zoroastrianism, for locals festoon railings and tree stumps with strips of cloth marking their wishes. Once fulfilled they should return and make an animal sacrifice of thanks.

Beyond Charvak stretch many adventurous possibilities in the Pskem, Chatkal and Ugam ridges. A drive up the Pskem valley reveals the rapids of the Pskem river. If they seem somewhat daunting, try rafting Chatkal's five canyons or canoeing Koksu to three Saryram lakes. Rafting the Ugam can include caving to underground lakes. Walking routes range from a few hours to a five-day trek to Sary Chelek lake in Kyrgyzstan. For a closer look at nature, pay a visit to UNESCO-protected Chatkal biosphere reserve, a haven for 35,000 hectares of juniper forest. Petroglyphs on the rocky banks of the Tereksay river confirm that the area's rich plant and wildlife attracted Stone Age man. Hidden among birch groves and deep gorges are Siberian goats, Bailey's boars, snow leopards and white-clawed bears. The spring blanket of tulips includes the fiery red Kaufmann, dedicated to the first governor-general of Turkestan. He is similarly honoured with an onion.

■ CHIMGAN PRACTICAL INFORMATION
Regular departures for Chirchik leave from Tashkent's Samarkand bus station, or you can catch one near Maxim Gorky metro. Change buses at Chirchik for occasional departures to Khodjakent or Chimgan. Taxis are available to both destinations, or even the *elektrichka* train from the North (Severnaay) station to the dam at Charvak. This is good tenting country; alternatively, try various complexes at Bakachur and elsewhere on Charvak reservoir. A *chaikhana* bed is ideal for stretching out one's sleeping bag under the clear night skies. In Chimgan there is a suitably Soviet Intourist giant with large suites, proletarian canteen and table-tennis. For inexpensive windsurfing, Tashkent contacts include Ludmilla (tel. 964617) or Sergei and Olga Snmornikov (tel. 673795/358254), who also offer hang-gliding, skiing and camping. Heli-skiing and longer treks are handled by Uzbektourism or Asia Travel.

Excursion to Kazakhstan: Turkestan

At the southern edge of the Kazakh steppe, in the town of Turkestan five hours northwest of Tashkent, stands the monumental memorial complex Tamerlane built for revered Sufi saint **Hazret Sultan Khodja Ahmed Yasawi**. The town began life as the caravan oasis of Shavgar in the tenth century. Under Karakhanid rule, the first Islamic Turkic dynasty, it grew into a religious centre and adopted a new name, Yasi, from that of a nearby Turkic tribe. Khodja Ahmed was later called Yasawi to denote where he had preached and died. He was born in Sairam near Chimkent in 1103, but moved to Yasi after losing his father at the age of seven. There his mentor was the famous Sheikh Arslanbob. Legend holds that when Mohammed was dying he called, 'Who will take my *amanat* [a persimmon stone, the symbol of Islam] and continue my ideas?' Arslanbob, already 300 years old and familiar with 33 religions but now recognizing Islam alone, volunteered and won Allah's approval. As he wandered the steppe 500 years later, Arslanbob met a boy of eleven, who demanded 'Aksakal [white beard], give me my *amanat* !' He was, of course, young Ahmed.
   After Arslanbob's death, Ahmed became a disciple of a renowned Sufic sheikh in

Bukhara, earning the right to explain 'the way to the understanding of the truth'. He succeeded his teacher in 1160, before returning to Yasi to develop his own concept of the *tariqat*, the path to God. Legend also enfolds the close of Yasawi's life, when, aged 63, out of mourning for Mohammed who died at that age, he retreated to a subterranean cell to preach out his days. The small mausoleum erected for him in 1166 drew many pilgrims as dervish disciples of the Yasawiya Sufic brotherhood spread his mystical doctrine and didactic poetry across the steppes, later reaching Persia and Anatolia. The strength of Sufism survived the Mongol onslaught to promote the conversion of Mongol rulers to Islam.

By Tamerlane's time, Yasi's population had expanded with pilgrims, priests, merchants and craftsmen, while the mausoleum's riches attracted frequent looting. The great conqueror ordered reconstruction work in 1394 and, on a 1397 visit, en route to receive a Mongol bride, gave exact instructions for a new building on the magnificent scale of the Ak Serai in Shakhrisabz or Bibi Khanum in Samarkand. His pious action not only won favour by increasing the splendour for pilgrims and revenue for residents, it also set forth a tangible proclamation of Timurid power at the imperial borders. Yasawi's reputation was such that a three-time pilgrimage equalled a trip to Mecca. He was called *Hazreti Turkestan*, the patron of the land of the Turks, and thus the town received its modern name. In the following centuries Turkestan was both seat and battleground of the would-be Genghis Khans that sparked the genesis of the Uzbek and Kazakh peoples. Many nomad notables joined Yasawi in his tomb.

Once the khan of Kokand took the town in the 19th century, the mausoleum was turned into a wall-wrapped fortress. Before his death, Yasawi is said to have predicted the invasion of an ill-defined enemy in 1864. Right on cue came the Russians and only the mullah's surrender saved the mausoleum from their artillery. Tsarist restoration often meant harmful whitewashing yet the complex still functioned, whereas Soviet methods bolstered the building, but desanctified it into a museum of anti-religious propaganda. Since Kazakhstan's independence, the new republic's major religious and tourist site has been undergoing its latest and greatest facelift from the foundations up, courtesy of the Turkish government, grateful beneficiary of Yasawi's teachings.

Madrassah pupils studying Arabic

SIGHTS

From a distance it is hard to appreciate the grandeur of the **Yasawi Mausoleum**, for the rest of the old city has mostly disappeared, yet on approach all doubts vanish. Flanked by massive corner towers, the south portal rises 37.5 metres (1,230 feet) and measures 50 metres (164 feet) across. The compact rectangular building it announces is enclosed by great façades of brick mosaic. Across these walls studded with carved windows spread dizzying geometric patterns in blue- and green-glazed tilework, tied together by continuous bands of Koranic inscription along the top and yellow limestone and majolica panel along the bottom. The north façade is a visual treat lifting the eye up to the crowning glory of the ribbed, melon-shaped dome over Yasawi's burial vault. Its beauty even challenges the central dome, with a diameter of 18.2 metres (60 feet) the largest in Central Asia.

With Tamerlane's death, work on the mausoleum stopped until the portal arch was completed by Bukhara's Abdullah Khan in the 16th century. Tiling was never added, leaving a framework of skeletal scaffolding to this day. Buy a ticket from the nearby booth and pass through the carved wooden doors into the main assembly hall beneath the giant dome. On proud display is Tamerlane's bronze cauldron or *kazan*, a Turkic symbol of harmony and hospitality. Weighing over two tonnes and measuring 2.45 metres (8 feet) in diameter, it held sacred water for worshippers at Friday prayer. From the hall, eight two-storey corridors divide the complex into eight independent sections, the secret of its seismic resistance. Over 35 rooms fill this warren, all for different uses. The southwest corner was a kitchen for preparing ritual dishes; north was a library beside cells for meditation. The mosque in the northwest features a beautiful mihrab and a cupola dripping with stalactites. North of the main hall is the burial vault itself, guarding Yasawi's finely wrought jasper tomb. Like commoners down the ages, you may only be permitted a glimpse through a wooden screen. Along the east side were the large and small palace rooms and a chamber with spring. Climb the spiral staircases to explore the second floor and continue up for a breathtaking rooftop encounter with the 52-ribbed dome over Yasawi's tomb. Introduced from Persia, it was the first of its kind in Transoxiana.

Work also proceeds on nearby monuments. Most striking is a replica of the 15th-century **Rabiya Sultan Begim mausoleum**, an octagon with portal topped by the Timurid trademark sky-blue dome. She was the daughter of Ulug Beg, given in marriage to adventurous Uzbek **Abul-Khair Khan** (1412–68), true founder of Uzbek power, whose tomb lies within the main complex. Close by is another reconstructed tomb, that of **Kasim Khan**, Kazakh ruler from 1509–18, when he took over Abul-Khair's territory, giving the Kazakh empire a strength that defined Kazakh as the tribes to the north of the Syr Darya. Other attractions include a 15th-century bathhouse museum, a 19th-century mosque museum and reconstructed subterranean prayer crypts.

TURKESTAN PRACTICAL INFORMATION

■ TRANSPORT

Train connections include Moscow, Almaty and Tashkent, but buses are more convenient. One direct bus to Turkestan leaves Tashkent long-distance bus station daily at 7am. Alternatively, take one of many Tashkent–Chimkent buses (3 hours) and change to a Chimkent–Turkestan bus (2–3 hours). The bus station in Turkestan is beside the bazaar a few kilometres north of the mausoleum and hotels, so ask the driver to let you off. Local buses ferry people in between.

■ KAZAKH IMMIGRATION

Under the inter-republic visa agreement, visitors with an Uzbek visa do not require a Kazakh visa for a stay of up to 72 hours. If you plan a longer stay, apply to the Kazakh consulate in Tashkent. At the Uzbek–Kazakh border the most obvious sign of customs is bus-boarding by men bristling with calculators and currencies, eager to change Uzbek sum to Kazakh tenge. Until banking becomes workable, it is worthwhile to follow the example of your fellow passengers.

■ ACCOMMODATION & FOOD

The basic **Hotel Turkestan** (tel. 51172) should function again, post-refit, by 1996. It stands to the north of the mausoleum. Diagonally across adjacent Lenin Square (still occupied by a statue of the revered Communist saint) and behind the Restaurant Navruz is the cosy **Hotel Saule** (tel. 31898), with only seven rooms but clean and friendly. The **Navruz** is well-meaning, offering mutton, vodka, dumplings and salad. Alternatively, find Central Asian standards at the bazaar.

Tashkent to Dzhizak

Christened the V.I. Lenin Great Uzbek Highway, the four-lane M-39 strikes out southwest from Tashkent to follow silken routes to Samarkand, Shakhrisabz and, far to the south, Termez on the Afghan border. Some 64 kilometres (40 miles) from Tashkent, the road reaches **Chinaz** on the right bank of the Syr Darya. Here, in the last century, ferrymen rowed passengers on the hour's crossing of the great expanse, while tsarist merchants pictured roaring river trade on Aral Sea steamships. The railway finally crossed the Syr Darya in 1895, linking Tashkent to Samarkand and the Transcaspian line. Poor navigation on the shallow river forced abandonment of trade plans and Chinaz was turned to intensive cotton production, draining precious water resources. Earlier travellers bound for Dzhizak then faced a perilous journey across an arid zone the Russians called the *Goldnaya*, or **Hunger Steppe**. The Buddhist monk

Xuan Zang encountered it on his classic Silk Road pilgrimage from China to India in the seventh century:

> *We enter on a great sandy desert, where there is neither water nor grass. The road is lost in the waste, which appears boundless, and only by looking in the direction of some great mountain, and following the guidance of the bones which lie scattered about, can we know the way in which we ought to go.*

Although irrigation and cultivation projects were underway in tsarist times, it took Soviet mass mobilization to effect the transformation one views today. Gulistan, capital of Syr Darya Province, has grown from a small 19th-century settlement into an industrial centre of construction and cotton-cleaning. In another new town, **Jangiyer**, tourists may visit the Development of the Virgin Lands Museum, a shrine to the Brezhnev-directed scheme that brought vast numbers of Russians and other republicans to Central Asia. The M-39 speeds through the fruits of their labour—villages, collective farms, grain fields and, above all, cotton plantations.

DZHIZAK

A welcome sight for those traversing the Hunger Steppe, Dzhizak was an important Silk Road crossroads, a junction on the road to Ferghana. The name has been described as 'Key', for it controlled the strategic Pass of Jilanuti in the nearby Turkestan range, gateway to the famed riches of the Zerafshan Valley, Samarkand and Bukhara. Others say it is Sogdian for 'small fort', since it was a large settlement in the medieval principality of Usrushana, whose chief town was based on the ancient Sogdian city Bunjikath, present-day Pendzhikent in Tajikistan.

The Islamic conquest gave Dzhizak a vital role in relations between the settled farmers and nomadic Turkic raiders. Each required the other's products, crops and clothing or meat and horses, but too often the nomads came for plunder rather than trade. The Muslim response was the building of *rabats* or blockhouses, guarded by volunteers known as *ghazis*, 'warriors for the faith'. Dzhizak was a rallying-point for these fighters of infidels, for whom many *rabats* were built. By the 19th century, the town was a major frontier fortress of the Bukharan khanate. In 1866, the Lion of Tashkent, General Chernaiev, was unable to take it at the first attempt, but the Russian advance was only delayed a few months. Tsarist troops lost six men and the natives 6,000 in a battle that destroyed the old town. Colonialism brought the railway and a slackening of caravan trade. In 1916 Dzhizak was involved in an anti-Russian uprising, which was bloodily repressed. The following year Dzhizak's greatest modern claim to fame was born, one Sharaf Rashidovich Rashidov, future guardian of the Uzbek nation.

Yasawi mausoleum, Turkestan

■ SIGHTS

Locals claim Dzhizak was merely earth and sky before the Rashidov era, when they say he even planned to make it the republican capital. Tree-lined avenues now mark a city devoid of antique appeal, but one which offers a quietly industrial picture of contemporary Uzbek life. From your balcony in the outsize Hotel Uzbekistan, gaze down upon President Rashidov's bust at the centre of **Rashidov Square**. Walk out from the hotel lobby under the gaze of Rashidov's portrait to adjacent Rashidov Garden, featuring a *chaikana* and a two-storeyed madrassah founded in 1890 but used as a theatre in Rashidov's time. Independence has brought Saudi Arabian money to restore it to religious use. Nearby is Rashidov's school and, a little further up Sharaf Rashidov Street, is the **Sharaf Rashidov Memorial Museum** (closed on Sundays), bursting with memorabilia from peasant childhood to Soviet statehood. Photos, paintings, embroideries and ceramics tell the official story. Pride of place goes to a stuffed crocodile presented by an admiring Fidel Castro.

Continue up Sharaf Rashidov Street for ten minutes to reach No. 33, where only a small plaque distinguishes his birthplace (closed to visitors) from the other traditional Uzbek homes. A few minutes away is the **Provincial Museum**. Models of the 1916 uprising and backward pre-Revolution life may not survive post-independence historical revision. The bust opposite is of Hamrakul Nosirov, decorated head of the local collective from 1940 to 1972. Next door is another memorial museum, to Dzhizak's second most famous son, the gifted Uzbek poet and writer **Hamid Alimjan** (1909–1944). His life and works are on display in photos, paintings and literature. In 1938 Alimjan wrote *Zaynab and Aman*, a story poem of love and women's liberation on a Soviet Uzbek collective farm. Promoting modernism over traditionalism, it was at heart a popular love story and the author's death six years later in a Tashkent traffic accident was much mourned. In 1958 his poetess widow turned the text into an opera. For an ethno-religious resurgence, and antidote to political cultism, pay a visit to the **Yasawi Turkestan Khalk Markazi** (People's Centre). Run by a remarkable Sufi and holistic healer, Saparboi Kushkarov, the centre can arrange herb-gathering trips and pilgrimages to holy shrines in the Turkestan range. Find it beside a spire-topped church, on the road towards Samarkand, at No. 3 ex-Karla Marxa Street, (tel. 37222/38937).

■ DZHIZAK PRACTICAL INFORMATION

Transport:
The regional bus station is ten kilometres from the city centre, along the M-39 Tashkent to Samarkand highway. Long-distance buses run all day in each direction and local bus no. 1 connects the station to the Hotel Uzbekistan. The train station is four kilometres from the hotel, and the airport seven.

Accommodation
Hotel Uzbekistan, Sharaf Rashidov Sq, 1 Dustlik St (tel. (37222) 31697, fax. 34232) Newly built and quickly deteriorating. Rooms range from $10 to $50 per person, with bathroom, air-conditioning, telephone and television. Uzbektourism live here so other hotels may be reluctant to accept foreigners. The adequate ground-floor restaurant has cold beer and a nearby café serves ice-cream. City bazaars are reliable providers of bread and fruit.
Sanzar Tourist Camp, Karasai Village (tel. 22502)
This holiday complex a few minutes east of Tamerlane's Gates, on the asphalt road to Samarkand, includes lodges, rose gardens, sauna, pool and Amir Timur restaurant.

Travel Agents
Uzbektourism at the Hotel Uzbekistan offer transport to, and accommodation at, Zaamin National Park, Nuratin Nature Reserve and Sanzar Tourist Camp. English speakers are rare, so try Rais, a local English teacher, on 42348.

TAMERLANE'S GATES
Beyond Dzhizak, road, rail and even flight paths follow the Dzhizak River along the Pass of Jilanuti, the strategic valley between the Nuratin and Turkestan hills. Where the defile narrows to a rocky portal stand *Timur Darwaza*, the **Gates of Tamerlane**. Scene of many a bloody struggle, this gateway to the Zerafshan recorded triumphant conquerors through the ages. Despite Soviet widening and modern graffiti, two inscriptions survive to the right on the way to Samarkand. The first tells of Tamer-

Wish cloth-wrapped stump, Chimgan

lane's grandson, Ulug Beg, returning victorious from eastern campaigns in 1425. The second describes Bukhara's Abdullah Khan, who in 1571 slew 400,000 enemy troops; he gave to death so many of them that, from the people who were killed in the fight and after being taken prisoner, during the course of one month blood ran on the surface of the water in the river to Dzhizak. Let this be known'.

ZAAMIN NATIONAL PARK

The district centre of Zaamin lies 75 kilometres (47 miles) southeast of Dzhizak, through dusty collective farm country where web-like wooden carts bump through barren fields. The second-largest town in the medieval principality of Usrushana, Zaamin stands at the edge of the parched steppe before the rolling slopes of the Turkestan range that leads to Tajikistan. The road to the mountains passes a number of Young Pioneer camps before climbing a ridge above a beautiful hill-ringed reservoir. At the park entrance, visitors must register and pay a small admission fee. Beyond stretch 47,000 hectares of national park, established in 1926 as the first nature reserve in the republic.

The road winds with the Zaamin river up through apricot orchards of Uryuklisai gorge, on towards juniper-green mountain slopes. The main visitor centre is based here—a monstrous sanatorium on the left, solar-roofed flats to the right and, at the head of the valley, the Sharshara Dacha, holiday home of the late, great Sharaf Rashidov. It nestles beside the 100-metre (330-foot) Sharillak waterfall, diverted to soothe presidential slumber with the sound of running water so cherished by Uzbeks as a fond reminder of rural idyll. For local day-trippers in hardy Ladas, the dacha and surroundings is Zaamin, but the real spectacle lies over nearby Suffa Pass, where alpine meadows climb to 4,000-metre (13,000-foot) peaks like Shaukartau and triple-headed Tokalichuk. Trail routes cover 150 kilometres (90 miles) of great diversity, from the river canyons of Kulsai and Guralash to mountain passes over 3,000 metres (10,000 feet).

Spring and summer boast the brightness of red tulips and white acacias, while autumnal gold shines from hazelnut and birch trees. Some 700 plant species and 30 medicinal herbs have been studied here, while there are 40 species of mammal and 150 types of bird, including the endangered Turkestan lynx, snow leopard and Asiatic black bear. Remote Chortangi gorge is home to the rare bearded vulture and the black stork, driven almost to extinction by superstitious belief regarding it the antithesis of the auspicious white stork. Visitors are more likely to spot a squirrel-like tree dormouse, a porcupine or badger at twilight, and hear the startled cries of a partridge, nuthatch or bluebird.

Part of the Suffa Plateau is giving way to a new observatory and workers' housing, but more traditional ways of life survive in the felt yurts of the Kyrgyz nomads who roam with age-old abandon over high national borders.

■ ZAAMIN PRACTICAL INFORMATION

Transport

Hired cars from Dzhizak (e.g. Uzbektourism) are the easiest, and most expensive, way to explore the park. Otherwise take a public bus from Dzhizak to Zaamin town and hitch from there to the park. Getting rides within the reserve is rewarding for the very patient.

Accommodation

Sharshara Dacha, Zaamin National Park (tel. 21550)

Sleep in the President's bed. Full board Uzbek fare is included in room rates of $30–50 per day. The shady garden and babbling brook become crowded at weekends.

Zaamin Sanatorium, Zaamin National Park 708120 (tel. 21735)

Cheaper and more proletarian is this remarkable structure dominating a hillside. Over 5,000 beds for the convalescent or merely pleasure-seeking. Standard (around $20) rooms and many facilities—cinema, video halls, disco, restaurants, bar, sauna and swimming pool.

Camping should be possible—bring supplies from Dzhizak and follow the nomads for a good site.

NURATIN NATURE RESERVE

This is one of Uzbekistan's newer reserves, established in 1975 to preserve the Kyzyl Kum ram (also called the Severtsov ram) and rare varieties of walnut and hazelnut. It lies in the Farish district, in the northwest of Dzhizak province on the northern slopes of the Nuratin Mountains south of Aidarkul lake. Ranging from 400–2,100 metres (1,300–6,900 feet) above sea level, the slopes fall steeply to the saline Aidar valley through canyons of willow, mulberry and poplar. Besides the rams, keen observers may encounter wild boar, rock martens and the poisonous Turkestan 'gurza' snake. Uzbektourism run tours here or take a local bus from Dzhizak to Yangi-kishlak and hitchhike the rest on a cotton truck. Self-sufficiency is advisable, though you may find room with reserve personnel who tend the animals year-round.

The Ferghana Valley

Just as Uzbekistan is the heart of Central Asia, the **Ferghana Valley** is the heart of Uzbekistan. Over seven million people, about a third of the population, live in this fertile flood plain of the Syr Darya. The river sweeps down from the Pamirs into a valley approximately 300 kilometres (190 miles) long and 170 kilometres (105 miles) wide, surrounded by spurs of the Tian Shan—the Chatkal range to the north, Ferghana to the east, and the Pamir-Alai to the south. The best approach for traders and conquerors was through the Khodjent Gates to the west, where the river leaves the valley before the Hunger Steppe. Stock-breeding tribes came this way in the Bronze Age, mixing with local farming peoples. Rock-carvings high in the mountains, such as Saimaly-Tash in the Ferghana range, reveal ancient scenes of hunting and agriculture.

The town of Khodjent dates back to the conquests of Alexander the Great in 329 BC, when the Macedonian founded his ninth Alexandria here, Alexandria Eskhate (the furthest). Two centuries later the Chinese envoy and Silk Road pioneer Zhang Qian reached the valley, after a decade spent detained by the nomads harrying China's borders. He welcomed Ferghana's more sophisticated civilization:

> *The people are settled on the land, plowing the fields and growing rice and wheat. They also make wine out of grapes. The region has many fine horses which sweat blood; their forebears are supposed to have been foaled from heavenly horses. The people live in houses in fortified cities . . . the population numbers several hundred thousand. They fight with bows and spears and can shoot from horseback.*

Descended from the legendary dragon-horses of the far west, the blood-sweating horses of Ferghana were coveted for their great size and speed by the Han emperor, Wudi. They formed the focus of Chinese campaigns that blasted open East–West trade routes, taking silk to Europe and wine to China. The blood was less celestial perspiration than the work of a busy parasite, but the door had been opened to commercial and cultural exchange. Sogdian merchants proved consummate Silk Road middlemen. Buddhist remains such as the temple near Kuva in Kyrgyzstan demonstrate the intellectual growth.

Arab invasion followed Turkic and Chinese as the valley became the Samanid empire's frontier against the heathen Turks. Leadership shifted from Kasansay to Aksiketh, Uzgen and Andijan, where Tamerlane's great-great-great grandson Babur, the last Timurid and the first Mogul, was born in 1483. His memoirs speak of great pride in a homeland he was forced to abandon by the triumphant Uzbek Shaybanid dynasty. From the early 19th century, the khanate of Kokand expanded beyond Ferghana into Central Asia's third power. Economic growth sponsored Islamic

Harvesting a rich crop of 'white gold'

learning and public works in traditional styles, while territorial gains sparked frequent warfare with Bukhara.

When Soviet aggression succeeded Tsarist colonization, the valley arose in the *basmachi* (bandit) movement, Central Asian mujaheddin versus Russian infidels. As the last resistance was eliminated, national delimitation from 1924 carved today's ethnic jigsaw, where pieces are shared by the republics of Uzbekistan, Kyrgyzstan and Tajikistan. Divide and rule tactics have left national islands adrift in foreign seas, like the Uzbek enclave of Shakhimardan inside Kyrgyzstan. Soviet overlordship promoted intensive agricultural and industrial development. Following the proverb 'it is not land but water which bears fruit', the 270 kilometre- (170-mile)- Great Ferghana Canal was dug in 1939 in only 45 days by 180,000 'volunteers'. Acclaimed as a grand example of the Uzbek *khoshar*, a collective undertaking for the common good, it typified efforts to extract the maximum from nature to placate cotton-hungry Moscow.

Independence has given internal borders a solidity never imagined by their devisors. In recent years petty disputes have occasionally exploded into pogroms between formerly 'fraternal peoples'. The valley, the most densely populated part of Central Asia, is not just a political but also a religious barometer for the region. Throughout the Soviet era, Islamic practices survived most strongly here. Foreign money now finds fertile ground for brands of Islam more extreme than local governments care for. With its overlapping cultures and hopefully interacting economies, Ferghana is a microcosm of Turkestan as it was and may be once more. Add to the intrinsic fascination stunning scenery, distinctive local architecture and traditional crafts, from silk-weaving and wood-carving to pottery and knife-making, and the result, at the very least, makes for a worthwhile side-trip from Tashkent, to the place locals proudly dub the 'Golden Valley'.

Tashkent to the Ferghana Valley

Public buses and trains enter the valley through the traditional invasion route, via Khodjent in Tajikistan. Founded in the fourth century BC by Alexander the Great some 3,500 miles east of Macedonia, Khodjent grew into a major city in Islamic times. Governor Timur Melik in the 13th century put up the most spirited resistance the Mongol invaders met in Transoxiana. Frequent sparring ground of the khanates of Kokand and Bukhara in the 19th century, the city was submerged in the Samarkand region of Russian Turkestan, then the Uzbek Soviet Socialist Republic and finally, in 1929, was ceded to Tajikistan. This enabled the mountainous republic to meet the one million-plus population requirement for full Union status, and perhaps compensated for the loss to Uzbekistan of Samarkand and Bukhara, historic centres of Tajik culture. After newly-independent Tajikistan slid into civil war in 1992, Khodjent was the base for pro-communist forces fighting clans from the more Islamic south. The town has shed its Soviet-era name of Leninabad, but thorough modernization has left nothing of antiquity to delay the traveller. Road and rail on to Kokand follow the great Karakul Reservoir, fed by the Syr Darya and fringed by the Kuramin hills, before crossing into Uzbekistan's Ferghana Province.

In the late fifties, Soviet might blasted a shorter connection between Tashkent and Ferghana through the southern slopes of the Chatkal range. Public buses fail the gradient, but private cars bump their way over. South from the capital, the road skirts the depressed mining towns of Almalik and Angren to climb above a beautiful reservoir and into the cleaner air of the Akhangaran river valley. A monument commemorates the workers: "Our fathers looked for paths; we are building roads". Each turn reveals more of the snow-capped Chatkal before the 2,268-metre (7,450-foot) Kamchik Pass leads down into Namangan Province and haze reclaims the mountains. On the flat valley floor, the power of irrigation is obvious; desert retains the left side of the road while the right groans under the weight of the fruits of socialism: orchards, cotton fields and mulberry trees for silkworm farms.

Kokand

Defined as the 'town of the boar' or the more enigmatic 'city of winds', Kokand lent its name to the powerful 19th-century khanate stretching from the Ferghana Valley to Tashkent and the southern Kazakh steppes. Though young compared to other Fer-

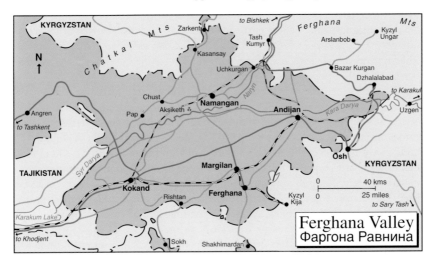

ghana towns, Kokand quickly blossomed into a prosperous trading and religious centre, contesting the spoils of Central Asia with the khanates of Bukhara and Khiva. Around 1710 the Shaybanid Shahrukh established his Uzbek Min tribe as an independent principality in the western part of Ferghana. He built a citadel in his capital, the village of Kokand, as did his son Abd al-Karim. In 1758 Shahrukh's grandson Irdana was forced to recognize Chinese suzerainty that extended into the rule of Abd al-Karim's grandson Narbuta Beg, from 1774 to 1798. Kokand's authority was still limited to western and central Ferghana when Narbuta's son Alim succeeded him. Combining great ambition with ruthless efficiency, Alim Khan hired a mercenary army of Tajik highlanders to curb hostile tribal chiefs and dissenting dervish orders. He secured the whole valley and took Khodjent and Tashkent, before his assassins set his brother Omar on the throne in 1809. A poet who fostered cultural and religious life, Omar Khan nevertheless pursued expansion, taking Turkestan in 1814 and building steppe fortresses against the Kazakh tribes.

Omar's son Mohammed Ali (Madali Khan) was only 12 at his accession in 1821. During his reign, the khanate reached its greatest power and extent, frequently interfering beyond the Pamirs in Chinese Turkestan. Great Game diplomacy acknowledged Kokand's importance, though Russian mishandling of envoys paved the way for open enmity. British Officer Captain Arthur Conolly stayed for two months in 1841 in a fruitless attempt to persuade Madali to resolve differences with the neighbouring khanates. He left for Bukhara on the ill-fated trip to rescue fellow officer Colonel Charles Stoddart [see page 100-1]. Despite the best efforts of Omar's widow, the poetess Nadira, their son chiefly excelled at cruelty and debauchery, giving Emir Nasrullah of Bukhara the excuse to take Kokand and their lives in 1842. Preferring their own despots, Ferghana's people soon expelled Nasrullah and established Madali's cousin Shir Ali, but the next two decades saw the khanate rived by bitter internecine warfare, worsened by Bukharan and Russian incursions. Shir Ali's son Khudayar ruled from 1845, amid the bloody conflicts of the Uzbek Kipchaks and the Persianized urban population. Towers of skulls marked the battlegrounds.

Nasrullah's second entrance into Kokand in 1858 replaced Khudayar with his brother, but once restored in 1865, Khudayar immediately came under the sway of Nasrullah's successor. The rivalry of the khanates fatally undermined resistance to the common enemy, tsarist Russia. Since 1850 Kokandi troops had fought the infidel invaders with greater zeal than their Bukharan or Khivan counterparts, but force of numbers and arms toppled their northern forts one by one. Appeals for British military assistance met no response. Tashkent fell the following year, Khodjent a year later. The khanate was reduced to the valley from which it had sprung. At this time Kokand's most infamous export, Yakub Beg, one-time lord of Tashkent, seized Kashgar from the Chinese to begin a decade of terror.

A commercial treaty in 1868 left Khudayar a Russian vassal, yet free to continue building his lavish palace by squeezing more taxes from a shrunken proletariat. Visitors were impressed with this city of 80,000 people, whose 600 mosques and 15 madrassah, teaching 15,000 students, bestowed a reputation second only to holy Bukhara. American diplomat Eugene Schulyer visited in 1873: "Everywhere around are clay roofs, half hidden in luxuriant verdure, and surrounding all the brilliant green of the gardens and orchards." The Russians had left native justice in place: "When a criminal is to be put to death—and executions are very frequent there—he is taken through the streets of the bazaar, the executioner following behind him, while the crowd hoot and pelt him with stones. Suddenly, without a word of warning, when the executioner thinks the spectacle has lasted long enough, he seizes him by the head, thrusts the knife into his throat and cuts it, and the body sinks to the ground, where it is left for some hours before it is carried away and the blood is covered with sand."

Insurrections against the puppet khan spread across the valley, forcing Khudayar into Russia's embrace in early 1875; first Tashkent, then Orenburg and death in exile. His kinsman Pulad Khan's anti-Russian stance provoked the annexation of Kokand in August by Generals Kaufmann and Skobelov. By March 1876, after fierce fighting, the khanate was declared the province of Ferghana in Russian Turkestan. Tsar Alexander II had "yielded to the wishes of the Kokandi people to become Russian subjects". Colonial rule added a Russian town of wide avenues and increased cotton and silk production, yet rebellion was never far away. In the wake of revolts against the World War I draft and the Russian Revolution, Mustafa Chokayev in late 1917 established in Kokand the Provisional Autonomous Government of Turkestan, a progressive, nationalist, Muslim alternative to the Tashkent Soviet. Branded counter-revolutionary by the Bolsheviks, this last hope for democratic self-governance was snuffed out by the Red Army. Breaching the walls of the old Muslim city on February 18, the attackers began a three-day rampage of rape, plunder and arson, leaving 14,000 slaughtered and old Kokand ablaze. Chokayev escaped to Bukhara and then Paris, as his armed chief Irgash Bey channelled Ferghana's outrage into Holy War. From their mountain strongholds *basmachi* groups harassed the Red Army throughout the early years of Soviet rule.

SIGHTS

■ KHUDAYAR KHAN'S PALACE

From 1863 to 1873, through upheaval and invasion, Khudayar, Khan of Kokand, erected his palace citadel, called an *urda* as opposed to a Bukharan *ark*. American diplomat Schulyer judged it on completion, "much larger and more magnificent than any other in Central Asia . . . glittering in all the brightness of its fresh tiles, blue, yellow and green". Ongoing restoration gives today's visitor a similar impression of vibrant, crowded colour glazed onto a long façade of arches and minarets. Besides

Ferghana Valley knives

satisfying his own extravagance and proclaiming his name in garish inscription, Khudayar also built the palace for his Kyrgyz mother, Hakim Ayin. Ashamed that she persisted in using a nomadic yurt, he installed her in style, only to watch her set up the felt tent in a courtyard. Mir Ubaidullah led the valley's finest architects on the project. Legend tells that when Khudayar asked how long his building would last, Ubaidullah placed a dish of millet on top of a minaret. Even in windless weather, millet spilled slowly down. The architect saved his life and the palace by identifying the cause—the vibrations from the paper factories for which Kokand was famous—whereupon Khudayar had them relocated.

A ramp leads through the entrance portal, studded with poles to ward off the evil eye, into the 19 rooms to survive from an original 113. To the right, the former chief secretary's office entertains a natural-history display of stuffed animals and cotton plants. Beyond is the redecorated office and mosque of Khudayar's war minister. The khan received his bowing guests in what is now a museum of jewellery, clothing and metalware. Russian troops later used the hall as a chapel, hanging an icon behind the throne. The works of Kokand's master woodcarver Khaidarov (1889–1984) fill an antechamber created for soldiers to change for prayer. Khudayar's 'second receiving room' was his opulent bedroom, where the top band of wall painting has been left unrestored. Wall niches house *objets d'art* including Japanese and Chinese vases. As the Koran permits only four official wives, so the lucky pick of Khudayar's 40-strong harem was sworn in by a mullah as a one-night stand. These teenage girls donated by subject lords lived and died in a two-storey complex of pavilions and swimming pools that stood at the palace rear. As with the last emir of Bukhara, rumour describes Khudayar watching his harem bathe from a poolside divan, before tossing an apple to the apple of his eye.

The palace is closed on Mondays. Formerly the focus of a 40-hectare park dense with a multitude of trees, it now shares the narrower confines of Mukimi Park with a mini-railway shunting past fountains, rusting fairground rides and an Aeroflot Yak 40 converted into a children's cinema. The Uzbek poet Mukimi (1851–1903) was a major contributor to Kokand's literary heritage. His life and works are detailed in a museum south of the Jummi mosque at 77 Mukimi St. West of the palace in Independence (ex-October) Square, the names of 74 Soviet martyrs have been scraped off a memorial to the 1918 massacre and Lenin has vacated his podium at the park's east gate.

■ JUMMI MOSQUE

South from Mukimi Park along Turkestan (ex-Lenin) Street, the road forks beside the Ghuldasta teahouse to cross the Kokand canal bridge that once divided old and new Kokand. Khamza Street runs through this former heart of Muslim learning. The chief survivor is the **Jummi Mosque**, the khanate's main mosque for Friday worship. Built by Omar Khan between 1809 and 1812 as a magnified version of the rural Ferghana design, it was shut in Soviet times and reopened after restoration in 1989. Non-Muslims may request a gateway glimpse of the vast courtyard beyond, a 22-metre minaret and the mosque's highlight, a 100-metre- (30-foot-) long *iwan*, supported by 98 wooden columns from India and decorated in the diverse colour and carving of traditional Ferghana architecture. Nearby is the **Amin Beg Madrassah**, built for one of Madali's sons in 1830, but often named after Khomol Khozi, the 1913 restorer responsible for the ornamental façade of coloured tiles. The madrassah accepts 40 students a year since its religious revival in 1991. Among a host of neighbours were madrassah built by Omar's mother, Modari Khan, and Khudayar's brother, Murad Beg. The ornate wooden gate to Hakim Ayin's madrassah lies within her son's palace.

■ KHAMZA MUSEUM

Opened in 1989 on the 100th anniversary of his birth, this museum regales the life story of **Hakim Hakimzade Niyazi**, Kokand's foremost Soviet hero, the first national poet of Uzbekistan and the founder of Uzbek Soviet literature. Born to a doctor's family, he attended an Uzbek school and madrassah before a mixed Russian school broadened his horizons. Early verses in the Uzbek classical style dealt with the social themes of a Turkestan slowly waking to progressive ideas. He opened schools in a lifelong push for public enlightenment and soon became an active Bolshevik propagandist. Throwing himself into theatre, he organized a drama company in Ferghana in 1918, performing plays like *The Bey* [landlord] *and the Farmhand*, in which, against a backdrop of social injustice meeting bold revolution, the Uzbek character Gafur welcomes his Russian comrades in good proletarian internationalism. For the next decade Khamza worked throughout the young republic, teaching and composing, "an ardent fighter for a new life and unappeasable enemy of obscurantism". Another play, *The Mysteries of the Paranja*, tackled female emancipation, just one of the sensitive topics behind Khamza's assassination and martyrdom in 1929.

The three-storey museum is at 2 Akbar Islam St, (tel. 40638), north of Khamza's statue in Furkata Park, and the striking Khamza Musical Comedy and Drama Theatre (tel. 22329). One of Khamza's Kokand residences is also a museum, near the Jummi Mosque, at 28 Matbyat St.

■ NARBUTABEY AND DASTURKHANCHI MADRASSAH

North from Khamza's museum, turn down Nabiyev St for the **Narbutabey Madrassah**, a plain but imposing seminary built under Khan Narbuta in 1796 and completed in 1799. Unique among Kokand's religious institutions, the madrassah functioned in the Soviet era. Teachers of Arabic and the Koran inhabit eight rooms in the main façade. Only male Muslim visitors may enter the inner courtyard of 36 study cells for up to 200 male students, aged from 15 to 25. Female tourists (even non-Muslim) can experience a girl's Islamic education at a nearby girl's madrassah, the **Dasturkhanchi**. Built (for men) in 1833, it was restored this century and in 1992 opened its doors to 60 girls aged from 15 to 20. Traditional textual studies are augmented with lessons in domesticity and embroidery. Take the lane opposite Nabiyev St to 20 Tinchlik St. Follow the twisting paths on past mud-walled houses and small parish mosques, to return to Mukimi Park.

■ ROYAL CEMETERY

From Narbutabey Madrassah continue along Nabiyev St to a cemetery thick with trees and tombs. Renovation work is restoring grand 17th-century entrance domes to this venerated retreat, patronized by holy men and those seeking their blessing. Two graves stand out from a whitewashed crowd. To the right is the **Modari Khan** mausoleum, built in 1825 for the mother of Omar Khan and other female royals. A small crypt and two minarets have survived from a larger mosque and grave complex, where Soviet archaeologists discovered the remains of Nadira Beg. Andijan poetess, Omar's wife and Madali's mother, she met a cruel death in 1842 at the hands of Bukhara's Emir Nasrullah, who resented her role in public life. Many of her poems focus on the government of society: 'If a king cares not for the poor man's life, his grand rule and sublimity are all in vain'. She was reburied beneath a white marble monument behind the **Dakhma-i-Shakhon**, the Grave of Kings. Nadira herself commissioned the tiled entrance portal holding wooden doors deeply carved with Omar's poetry. The inner hall boasts the decorative arts of all three khanates—Ferghanan painting, Bukharan ganch carving and Khivan woodcarving. Among the tombs beyond are those of Omar, brother Alim, son Madali and grandson Amin. (If the mausoleum is locked, ask for the key at 59 Nabiyev St.)

■ KHAIDAROV WORKSHOP

For a living museum of Kokand woodcraft, visit the family workshop run by Hassan-

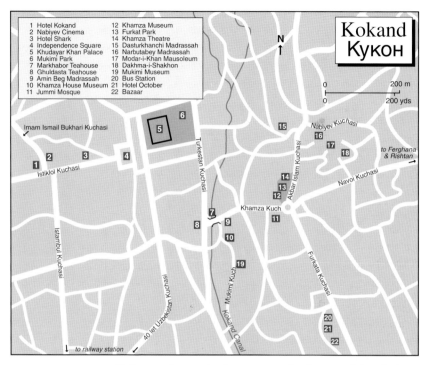

1 Hotel Kokand	12 Khamza Museum
2 Nabiyev Cinema	13 Furkat Park
3 Hotel Shark	14 Khamza Theatre
4 Independence Square	15 Dasturkhanchi Madrassah
5 Khudayar Khan Palace	16 Narbutabey Madrassah
6 Mukimi Park	17 Modar-i-Khan Mausoleum
7 Markhabor Teahouse	18 Dakhma-i-Shakhon
8 Ghuldasta Teahouse	19 Mukimi Museum
9 Amin Beg Madrassah	20 Bus Station
10 Khamza House Museum	21 Hotel October
11 Jummi Mosque	22 Bazaar

Kokand
Кукон

jon Umarov. His grandfather, Kodirjon Khaidarov, renewed a dying tradition during his long life, supplying gifts to Soviet leaders from Lenin to Brezhnev. On display are examples from chairs to Koran stands, both here and inside Khudayar's palace. Amid piles of timber, intricate columns, doors and sleep-inducing tea-beds, Umarov trains boys aged 10 and upwards in the arts of carving. The workshop is at 67 K. Khaidarov St, off Furkata St, one kilometre southeast of the bazaar (tel. 30610).

KOKAND PRACTICAL INFORMATION

■ TRANSPORT

There are two flights a day to Tashkent and daily services to the regional centres from Kokand airport ten kilometres (6 miles) from the city centre. The ticket office is near the Hotel Kokand at 3 Imam Ismail Bukhari St. The train station in the southwest of the city has slow and crowded departures to Tashkent Yuzhni twice a day. The long-distance bus station, for all valley destinations and beyond, is at 102 Furkata Kuchasi, beside the main bazaar. At least three buses a day run to/from Tashkent via Khodjent in Tajikistan. Bargain hard for private taxis taking the shorter Tashkent route over the mountains via Almalik and Angren. Useful city buses include: No. 14, airport–railway

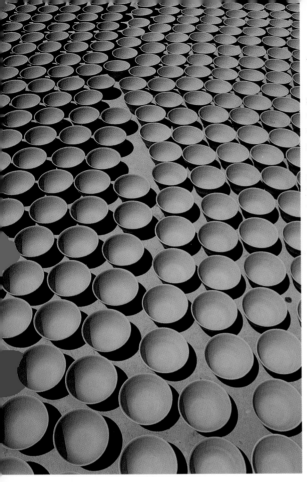

Rishtan ceramics dry before glazing

station–Hotel Kokand; Nos. 3 & 8 (and *marshrutnoe* taxis 1, 5 & 8) hotel–bus and railway stations.

■ ACCOMMODATION

The **Hotel Kokand** (ex-Intourist) has spartan doubles (under $10 per night), with uncertain plumbing, at 1 Imam Ismail Bukhari St (tel. 43400, 36403) opposite Abdullah Nabiyev Square, where Kokand's first Communist Youth League member survives in stone. East 200 metres at 16 Istiklol St is the simple **Hotel Shark**. Another cheap and basic option is the **Hotel October** near the bus station and bazaar at 94 Furkata St.

■ FOOD

The restaurant beside the Hotel Kokand can produce excellent Russian and Uzbek dishes, carefully sculpted salads and cold fruit juice. When it fails, try **Café Niluvar** over the road, **Café Dyshlod** in Independence Square or **Café Shark** opposite the Djumi Mosque. Kokand is renowned for its *chaikhana* (teahouses). For an authentic Uzbek afternoon, head to Turkestan Kuchasi south of Mukimi Park. First visit one of two restored bathhouses (*hammon*) for a long soak, then retire to one of two nearby *chaikhana*, either tea and kebabs in the carved alcoves of the Ghuldasta or draught beer and *plov* in shady pavilions over the Kokand canal at the Markhabor.

■ TRAVEL AGENCIES

Uzbektourism has a small branch opposite the Amin Bek madrassah on Khamza St (tel. 41782, fax. 22700). Individual travellers may be pounced upon to engage their services for city tours and ticket-buying, though neither is compulsory.

RISHTAN ART CERAMICS FACTORY

Halfway between Kokand and Ferghana is the town of Rishtan, famed for its bright blue and green ceramics. Legend claims the art is over 800 years old, passed down from father to son, using local red clay and natural pigments made from minerals and mountain grasses. In 1920, some 30 small workshops were collectivized onto the present site of the Rishtan Art Ceramics Factory. Two thousand craftsmen and women employ both modern machinery and time-honoured methods to produce over 5 million items each year. Tourists are welcome to watch as giant balls of clay are shaped down and decorated with elaborate floral designs before glazing and baking in vast furnaces. Around the factory halls survive private family workshops, marooned in a sea of bowls drying in the sun. A showroom sells (for dollars) various ceramic goods, including tea-sets, flower vases, water jugs and *lyagan*, decorative *plov* plates. Department stores near Rishtan bazaar offer some of the same products in local currency. The factory is one kilometre east of the town centre and bazaar at 6 Burkhaneddin Roshidoni St, Rishtan 713330 (tel. 37345/21549, fax. 22888).

Ferghana

As the regional centre of tsarist and Soviet rule, the town of Ferghana has grown into the valley's third-largest city, with a population of 220,000. Founded in 1876, 20 kilometres from the ancient town of Margilan, it was christened New Margilan, then in 1907 became Skobelov, after the first military governor, and in 1924 assumed the valley's name. Ferghana's wide avenues spread fan-like from the old military fortress, recalling the St Petersburg design of Tashkent. Parks, fountains, Russian architecture and industrial zones strengthen the similarity, and the contrast, with Uzbek Islamic Margilan.

SIGHTS

Proudly termed the greenest city in Central Asia by its citizens, Ferghana is usually just a stopover en route to the rest of the valley, yet its plane- and poplar-shaded streets of blue-washed houses deserve a walkabout. From the bazaar, follow pedestrian Mustakillik Kuchasi (Independence Street) to the verdant

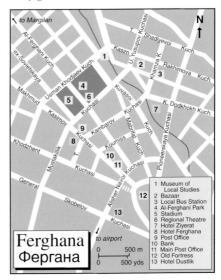

Ferghana
Фергана

1 Museum of Local Studies
2 Bazaar
3 Local Bus Station
4 Al-Ferghani Park
5 Stadium
6 Regional Theatre
7 Hotel Ziyerat
8 Hotel Ferghana
9 Post Office
10 Bank
11 Main Post Office
12 Old Fortress
13 Hotel Dustlik

central park, formerly named after Russian writer Gorky, now claimed by the ninth-century astronomer al-Ferghani. At the crossroads of Mustakillik and Al-Ferghani streets, stands the **Regional Theatre**, once the grand 1877 residence of General Mikhail Skobelov. His troops knew him as the 'White General', from his uniform and horse, but to the Turkomans he terrorized after subduing Ferghana he was 'Old Bloody Eyes', from his bloodshot post-battle appearance. Further up Al-Ferghani, north of the Oilworker Stadium, are the Deputy Governor's house and the 1902 men's gymnasium. Turn northwest up Uzman Khodzhaeva for the **Museum of Local Studies** (tel. 43191, open 9am–5pm, 9am–2pm Monday, closed Tuesday). A 3-D map puts the valley in revealing perspective before stuffed standards of natural-history give way to archaeological displays and pictures of remote carvings. Among other exhibits are a hall of colourful Rishtan ceramics, postcards of pre-revolutionary Turkestan and unconventional *tubiteika* embroidered with figures, poetry and even Soviet motifs. [for practical information see page 126-8]

Margilan

Long privy to the secrets of sericulture, Margilan was a major Silk Road stop by the ninth century, although local legend extends its history back to Alexander the Great.

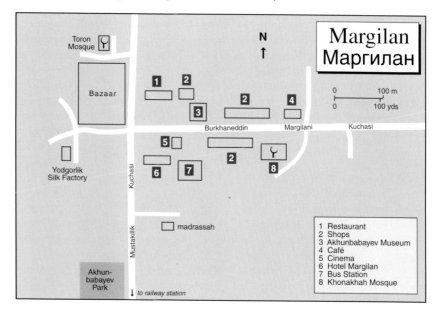

Toron Mosque

N ↑

Margilan
Маргилан

Bazaar

1 2

3

2   4

0   100 m
0   100 yds

Burkhaneddin   Margilani   Kuchasi

Yodgorlik
Silk Factory

Kuchasi

5

6   7

2

8

Mustakillik

madrassah

1 Restaurant
2 Shops
3 Akhunbabayev Museum
4 Café
5 Cinema
6 Hotel Margilan
7 Bus Station
8 Khonakhah Mosque

Akhun-
babayev
Park

↓ to railway station

On his arrival he was given chicken (*murgh*) and bread (*nan*), from which the town grew its name. In the late 15th century Babur found it 'a fine township full of good things. Its apricots and pomegranates are most excellent . . . the hunting and fowling are good', though he warned 'most of the noted bullies of Samarkand and Bukhara are Margilanis'. In recent times mass machinery has transformed the handicraft of sericulture to make Margilan the heart of Soviet silk production, rolling out millions of metres of iridescent rainbow every year. Like much of the valley, the town enjoys a reputation as a traditional stronghold of Islam, with deeper roots than further west. In the 19th century, Margilan had several madrassah and over 200 mosques, but many fell to rampaging Bolsheviks. Official atheism kept the faithful indoors, until independence released their savings into a flurry of mosque-building, making up for lost years.

SIGHTS

A stroll through the main **bazaar** reveals the full cacophony of Uzbek life, trading, greeting and tea drinking in a swirl of long gowns and local silk. Babur's apricots and pomegranates fill basins bordering melon carpets and cloth sacks pungent with spice. Bread-sellers push pram frames laden with baskets of freshly-baked *non*. Just north of the bazaar is the small **Toron mosque** (1840), an elegant example of the Ferghana style. Restoration has rejuvenated the multicoloured ceiling of the pillared *iwan* used for prayer in mild weather. Ten minutes east along Margilan's high street (where local Sheikh Burkhaneddin has supplanted Kirov) the **Khonakhah mosque** is well signposted by two 26-metre (85-foot) minarets and a two-storey entrance. Non-Muslims may request a look beyond, for a series of exquisitely carved and painted wooden buildings. First built in the 16th century, Khonakhah's rebirth since independence has restored its role as Margilan's leading mosque, attracting over 6,000 men for Friday prayers. The **Said Akhmad Khodja Madrassah**, 20 minutes south of the Hotel Margilan, is another example of religious resurgence. Its 19th-century sponsor was a wealthy philanthropist, tsarist advisor and factory owner, before he fled the revolution to Afghanistan and Saudi Arabia. After use as a jail and office, the madrassah reopened in 1992 for 300 students in two shifts, girls and boys. Visitors are welcome to view the beautiful decoration, mostly unrestored, for the ceilings were covered in Soviet times.

East of the central crossroads is the museum to Margilan's major revolutionary contribution, one-time president **Yuldush Akhunbabayev** (1885–1943). As a peasant's son he received only three years of education at a Margilan madrassah, but soon found his vocation and by 1916 was jailed for anti-tsarist activities. After the revolution, he organised rural collectivization in the valley. Illiteracy proved no barrier to promotion, as in 1923 he became President of the Executive of the Uzbek Communist Party and in 1938 replaced executed leader Khodjaev. Outside the museum, Islam rediscovers itself after a destructive experiment; inside lurks this unreconstructed time capsule, the life of one of its protagonists. Pay a visit to the store of socialist realist art, onward-marching workers and peasants, before silk displays edge out history. Across the road rears his statue. He has lost a neighbour, the Uzbek actress **Nurkhon Yuldasheva**, killed by her brother on their father's command, for performing unveiled in 1929. One of countless heroines in the struggle for female emancipation, her statue was judged unseemly for the post-Soviet era.

Silk Factories

To discover the silk secret for yourself, pay a visit to the **Yodgorlik** (Souvenir) **Factory**. In 1983, a group of Margilani silk workers bucked the mass production trend to establish a workshop pursuing and preserving traditional methods. Demand for their strictly handmade goods, even at thrice the price of the industrial competition, has expanded the labour force to 2,000, yet the original premise is maintained. Individual households feed silkworms with fresh mulberry leaves until the worms spin their cocoons of silk. Before the pupae mutate into moths, the cocoons are steamed and dispatched to the factory where they are plunged into boiling vats to soften and draw out the treasured thread. Follow the process as the entire thread is carefully unwound and woven into compact fabric. Only men perform the painstaking process of wrapping and unwrapping the silk for dyeing in various colours. Next door women fill a hall clattering to the sounds of their weaving. The result is the *khanatlas* 'king of satins' pattern; the shimmering blur walking every Uzbek street. Burning *isrik* grass is passed over workers and their looms to ward off the evil eye. Last stop is the exhibition hall and gift shop, at 138 Imam Sakhriddin St, south of the bazaar off the main street.

At the **Margilan Silk Factory**, the biggest in the CIS, annual output of silk materials tops 22 million metres (Yodgorlik manages 250,000 metres). Some 15,000 workers handle acres of machinery at 32 Burkhaneddin Margilani St (tel. 37333/33845). Another huge operation is the **Khanatlas Silk Factory**. Find its 10,000-strong workforce at 119 Mustakillik St, (tel. 33831).

Ferghana/Margilan Practical Information

■ TRANSPORT

Up to five daily flights connect Tashkent with Ferghana (and another four Moscow–Ferghana). The airport is 6 kilometres (4 miles) south of Ferghana centre; the ticket office is one block up Makhmud Kasimov Kuchasi from the Hotel Ferghana. Three trains per day from Tashkent take around 12 hours to reach the station in Margilan and continue on to Andijan. Buses from Tashkent (ten hours), Samarkand and throughout the valley use the Yermazar regional station north of Ferghana on the road to Margilan. Buses 3 & 4 run from the airport via the Hotel Ferghana to the local bus station beside the central bazaar. This station has frequent departures for Yermazar and Margilan.

■ ACCOMMODATION
Hotel Ziyerat, 2a Dodkhokh St, Ferghana 712000 (tel. (37322) 68600, fax. 68602)
Ferghana's newest hotel is Uzbektourism's eight-storey Chinese-built complex, well placed near the bazaar. Room rates for large, clean doubles with bathroom and air-conditioning range from $20 to $50 per night.
Hotel Ferghana, 29 Makhmud Kasimov St, Ferghana 712010 (tel. 49456)
The old Intourist establishment offers 100 rooms in various stages of dilapidation from $10 to $20 per night, with TV, phone, fridge and shower (some operable).
Hotel Dustlik, 30 General Skobelov St, Ferghana 712000 (tel. 68618, fax. 68602)
South of the city centre, the Dustlik sells expensive ($50 per night) and fairly stand-ard accommodation. Presently closed to foreigners, it should accept them again at a later date.
Hotel Margilan, 343 Mustakillik St, Margilan (tel. (37333) 64642)
Southeast of the bazaar, next to the bus station near the central crossroads, this basic guesthouse is the best budget option ($1–2 per night).

■ FOOD
The bazaars in both towns supply the essentials of Central Asian travel: tea, shashlik, *non* and fruit. Cafés near Al-Ferghani Park will prevent starvation, as will identical hotel fare—the Ziyerat's Chinese chefs left with the builders. When you feel *plov*-ed out, a saving grace is the splendid Korean *kuksi* restaurant at 84 Usman Yusupov St, (tel. 40720), 15 minutes' walk northeast from the bazaar. Set in the courtyard of an ordinary Korean home, it serves cheap, spicy and delicious cold noo-dles.

■ TRAVEL AGENTS
Uzbektourism, Hotel Ziyerat, (tel. 68600, fax. 68602, telex 166250 Epos)

Yodgorlik silk factory, Margilan

Even if you require no help, Deputy Manager Usmanov is a font of information and enthusiasm. Besides local trips to Shakhimardan, silk factories and silkworm nurseries, he can arrange itineraries throughout the valley.

■ OTHER
National Bank for Foreign Economic Activity, 150 Pakhlavan Makhmud St.
Post Office, 35 Mustakillik (Independence) St.

Shakhimardan

In summer, the Ferghana Valley's resemblance to a dusty cauldron helps many people renew latent nomadism and head for the hills. A popular resort is Shakhimardan, where the appeal of cool air, rushing rivers and mountain lakes is laced with the twin allures of political and religious pilgrimage. Half of the 55-kilometre (33-mile) drive south from Ferghana runs through Kyrgyz territory, for Shakhimardan is an isolated Uzbek enclave nestling in the Kyrgyz Alai range. The villages change little on the gradual climb, but Kyrgyz herdsmen stand out in their white *ak-kalpak*, felt hats trimmed in black. The road follows the luminous grey of the Shakhimardan River to its source in the town itself, where the clear Kok-su (blue river) collides with the bright Ok-su (white river).

In season, a holiday atmosphere pervades bazaars and fairgrounds; vendors ply strings of dried apricots as photographers offer souvenir snaps beside eagles and peacocks. A long escalator leads from the valley floor to the focal point of most visits, the hillside held in uneasy timeshare by Bolshevik and Islamic martyrs. The name Shakhimardan, King of Men, refers to **Hazrat Ali**, son-in-law of Mohammed and the fourth caliph of Islam. After Ali's assassination in Kufa (Iraq), the Ommayad clan wrested caliphal authority by killing his younger son, the Prophet's grandson Husain. This bloody coup gave rise to Islam's major divide: the Sunni follow the Ommayad line, while the Shi'ite venerate the stolen inheritance of Hazrat Ali. One of various legends claims Ali, nearing death, instructed seven graves be dug in different parts of the world. His body was put on a camel and after a few metres it multiplied into seven camels, each bearing holy remains. Uzbekistan claims three stopped on her territory; here, Khiva and Nurata. Other claimants include Iraq (most likely), Saudi Arabia and Afghanistan. Whatever the historical truth, Shakhimardan acquired a sacred spot.

For the Communists, it was a 'centre of double-dyed counter-revolutionaries', scene of fierce fighting against the *basmachi*. The Soviet version says local sheikhs torched Ali's mausoleum in 1919 to flush out Red Army soldiers. It was repaired in 1924, once more a 'nest of charlatans and parasites'. In March 1928, the poet **Khamza** [see Kokand page 119] spoke against the 'reactionary clergy', proclaimed the tomb's imminent destruction and was stoned to death by a 'crowd of fanatics'. Over the following decades the cult of Khamza claimed the town—renamed Khamzabad—as his tomb and an anti-religious museum claimed the hillside. Yet Ali's popularity bequeathed his mausoleum a stubborn cycle of death and rebirth. Today you can see the latest reconstruction, guarded by mullahs confident now in its future and visited by countless pilgrims, particularly childless women praying to end their barren curse.

In front of Ali's tomb there rears a monument to Soviet soldiers killed in the counter-revolution, a bold affront to local sensibilities and doubtless one with little time left to enjoy the view. As for Khamza, he rests nearby in a dramatic mausoleum hewn from the same Pamiri marble used for Lenin's blockhouse in Red Square. His future role is uncertain. Easier to predict are cosmetic changes to his museum, such as removing photos of the Khudjum 'Attack' movement, showing women killed for removing their veils. Four kilometres (2.5 miles) further up the valley visitors can take a creaking but spectacular cable-car ride to **Kuli Kulon**, the sky-blue lake. Encircled by rocky peaks, the 1,800-metre- (6,000-foot-) high lake provides good hiking terrain and a beautiful, if chilling, swim. Uzbektourism and Asia Travel in Tashkent offer a ten day 'Around Alai' trek beyond the lake into Kyrgyzstan, over 4,000-metre (13,000-foot) passes to the Koksu river valley, Abramov glacier, rock carvings and hot springs.

SHAKHIMARDAN PRACTICAL INFORMATION
Five buses a day run to Shakhimardan from Ferghana's local bus station near the bazaar. A Kyrgyz visa is unnecessary to transit that Republic's territory. In Shakhimardan you can choose from the simple Hotel Shakhimardan in the town itself, various Young Pioneer camps dotted around the valley or the holiday chalets of Uzbektourism's Turbaza Shakhimardan, one kilometre up the hill from Ali's tomb.

Andijan

Known in the tenth century as the village of Andugan, Andijan's steady growth ensured it the full force of Mongol destruction. Yet in the late 13th century Kaydu Khan, great-grandson of Genghis Khan, rebuilt the town into the capital of Ferghana. It remained so for the next three centuries, giving its name in Chagatai Turkish to the whole valley. As the eastern gate to Transoxiana, Andijan was the centre of lucrative trade with Kashgar. In 1483 Andijan's foremost son was born, one Zahiriddin Mohammed Babur, great-great-great-grandson of Tamerlane. Having lost his homeland, and Samarkand three times, Babur fought his way to India to found the Mogul empire. He recalled in his memoirs,

LAST TIMURID, FIRST MOGUL

"In the twelfth year of my age, I became ruler in the country of Ferghana." So does Zahir ud-Din Mohammed Babur begin his famous autobiography, the *Baburnama*, a lively account of a remarkable career as soldier of fortune, empire-builder and poet. Born in Andijan on 14 February 1483, Babur enjoyed distinguished ancestry, for on his father's side he was a fifth-generation descendent of Tamerlane and on his mother's side he claimed fifteenth degree descent from Genghis Khan. The death of his father, Umar Sheikh, in 1494 left Babur a troubled legacy of internecine struggle for the spoils of the Timurid empire. By late 1497 this gifted teenager had secured his Ferghana throne and occupied Samarkand, but trouble in his Andijan base soon forced him out. Caught up in fraternal squabbles, he was powerless to stop the rise of Uzbek Khan Mohammed Shaybani, lord of Mawarannahr by 1500. Babur's surprise offensive recovered Samarkand until Shaybani counter-attacked from Bukhara in 1501, starving Babur into life on the run. Gathering other refugees he made for Afghanistan, taking Kabul in 1504 and Kandahar in 1507.

Once the Persian Shah Ismail had crafted Shaybani's skull into a golden goblet, Babur joined forces with him for a triumphal re-entry into Samarkand in October 1511. The people rejoiced at the restoration of Timurid authority, yet the honeymoon dissolved after eight months for Babur's sponsors were Shi'ites, considered heretics by Sunni Samarkand, loyal to the rival sect of Islam. A crushing defeat by Shaybani's cousin Ubaydullah forced Babur out of Transoxiana for the last time. Wisely heeding the dictum 'Ten dervishes may sleep under one blanket, but two kings cannot share one country', he turned south from Kabul in pursuit of India. In 1526 he overcame the Sultan of Delhi to found the Mogul empire, over which his descendants ruled until 1857.

Babur himself combined the resilience and courage of an ambitious warrior with the humanity of a poet. The colourful literature of the *Baburnama* reveals his deep interest in people and art. He wrote fondly of the natural and architectural beauties of Ferghana, Samarkand and Kabul. In verses of Chagatai Turkish he ranks high after Alisher Navoi, for his songs of love and wine were borne of a life lived to the full: he married seven times, held drinking parties and was not averse to the catamites common at court. Several years after his death at Agra on 26 December 1530, his body was moved to a Kabul garden.

Zahiriddin Mohammed Babur (1483–1530)

Andijan produces much grain, fruits in abundance, excellent grapes and melons. In the melon season, they are usually given away at the beds . . . After Samarkand and Shakhrisabz, the fort of Andijan is the largest in Mawarannahr. It has three gates. Its citadel is on its south side. Into it water goes by nine channels; out of it, it is strange that none comes out at even a single place. Andijan has good hunting and fowling. Its pheasants grow so surprisingly fat that rumour has it four people could not finish one they were eating with its stew.

The khanate of Kokand pushed Andijan out of the limelight. Yet the Russians met stiff resistance on their first advance against the town, losing at least 50 men, until General Skobelov secured victory in January 1876. The rebel spirit resurfaced in May 1898 when Nakshbandi ishan Madali led a three-day revolt, put down after much bloodshed. The Transcaspian Railway, harbinger of Russification and modernization, arrived in 1899, three years before an earthquake took 4,500 lives and most of the old town. Today Andijan is an industrial city of over 300,000 people and capital of Uzbekistan's most densely populated province. The growth is founded on oil and cotton: the region is the premier oil producer in the republic and the most intensive cotton farmer in the CIS, with about 75 per cent of irrigated land turned over to 'white gold'.

SIGHTS

■ BAZAAR

On Sundays and Thursdays, the always interesting Andijan bazaar bursts its banks and floods the surrounding streets in a deluge of haggling, repartee and insults. Trucks deposit mountains of melons into the epicentre while fringes are devoted to pigeon fanciers, carpenters, blacksmiths, brush sellers, knife makers and skullcap embroiderers. Whatever you could want, be assured that somewhere it is for sale. Invest in a melon and a knife, settle down with a pot of green tea and enjoy the show.

■ BABUR LITERARY MUSEUM

A rose garden retreat from the pounding anvils of Bazernaya Street craftsmen is this former madrassah given over to one of its former pupils. Destroyed after Babur's departure, it was restored in the 18th century as the Ark Ichy, residence of the city's ruling family. Since 1990, it has housed a literary museum detailing Babur's poetry and prose, liberally sprinkled with reproductions of famous miniatures and paintings of chapters in his story. One entitled 'Babur feels ill' shows the conqueror in India, suffering the poison legend suggests was secretly administered by the mother of Delhi's defeated Sultan. He asked for one of his beloved Ferghana melons to ease his pain. Told three times it was Indian, he recognized at first bite the sweet taste and aroma of far-off Ferghana. One hall is devoted to Andijani poetess Nadira Beg (1792–

1842), wife of Omar, khan of Kokand, and long-time Babur fan. The museum is open 9am–4pm, closed Mondays, at 21 Bazernaya St.

■ JUMMI MADRASSAH & MOSQUE
Andijan's chief religious complex was built near the bazaar at the end of the 19th century. Extensive restoration followed the 1902 earthquake in order for a Soviet literature museum to be established. In 1990 the museum gave way to a resurgent madrassah, fuelled by Saudi Arabian-backed Wahabbism, a more extreme creed than everyday Sunni Islam. Vaulted halls span the corners of a monumental façade almost 123 metres long. In the centre rises a traditional Ferghana portal crowned by ornamented minarets. Non-Muslims are refused entry, but are permitted a glimpse of the inner courtyard, minaret and vast summer *iwan* from the mosque's north gate. Reach it via the road past the madrassah and behind the adjacent regional museum of local studies (open 9am–5pm).

■ NAVOI PARK
This green haven of trees and boating ponds lies east of Babur (ex-October) Square, where a horseback Babur has knocked Lenin off his podium. In the park's northeast corner rests the gently decaying splendour of the residence of Akhmed Beg Khodja. This capitalist factory owner fled the Bolsheviks to China, leaving his 1897 home to become a folk museum. Since independence its new role as office for Andijan Muslims does not prohibit visitors from wandering two storeys of living quarters and guest rooms. To the north is a brightly reconstructed mosque and madrassah complex, built on the site of the 1903 original. The sponsor is Khodja's nephew, now resident in Saudi Arabia and keen to help his hometown find the right path back to the future.

■ BABUR MEMORIAL PARK
Seven kilometres (four miles) southeast of Andijan is this park, opened in 1993 to celebrate the arrival of earth brought from Babur's Kabul grave. Entombed in marble,

the earth is the centrepiece of a large garden spread over a hillside Babur was fond of visiting. Before he left Andijan for the last time he is said to have come here for a final panorama of his hometown. There is a small museum devoted to Babur and a chairlift ride to a hilltop fairground. The best time for pilgrimage is a summer Sunday morning, when regional fairs light up the park with Uzbek life. Wrestling, singing and dancing take place against a backdrop of bazaars and craft displays. From Andijan's main bus station take one of the hourly departures to Bagishamal village.

ANDIJAN PRACTICAL INFORMATION
■ TRANSPORT
Andijan airport, ten kilometres (six miles) from the Hotel Zolotaya, is served up to five times daily from Tashkent, once a day from Bishkek and Almaty and twice a week from Moscow. The ticket office is at 1 Koltsevaya St. There are two trains per day to Tashkent, but the two bus departures (6am and 7pm) are a little quicker at around ten hours. The main bus station is close to the train station on Amir Timur St and runs services throughout the valley. City routes from the bus station to the Hotel Zolotaya and the central bazaar include buses nos. 1, 8 (also goes to airport), trolleybus no. 2 and *marshrutnoe* taxi no 1.

■ ACCOMMODATION & FOOD
Hotel Zolotaya Dolina, 19 Mashrabi St, Andijan 710033 (tel. (37422) 68708, fax. 61025).
The proud name, 'Golden Valley', conceals a cliché of dys-

Ferghana woodcraft, Khonakhah mosque, Margilan

functional service, dirty rooms and bad food. Doubles range from $15–$30 per night. Uzbektourism are based here (tel. 61004, fax. 61022), but don't expect too much.

Hotel Andijan, 241 Ralaba St
Cheaper than the above and better located near the bazaar. An Andijan stamp on your visa will help persuade reception staff to let you stay.

No particular restaurant deserves a mention; choose one of the *chaikhana* near the bazaar.

■ OTHER
National Bank for Foreign Economic Activity, 37 Mashrabi St.

Namangan

The city of Namangan ranks third largest in Uzbekistan, after Tashkent and Samarkand, yet it appears a relative newcomer to this eastern cradle of Ferghana civilization. Nearby are the ancient graves of Munchak Tepe and the ruined towns of Kasan and Aksiketh, capitals of the valley from the 7th to 11th centuries. By the 17th century Namangan had emerged as a large settlement close to the confluence of the Naryn and Kara Darya rivers, source of the Syr Darya. It takes its name from local salt mines, *namak kan*, longtime suppliers to the kitchens of Tashkent. At the time of the Russian occupation, the Namangan district had developed into a bastion of Islam, with over 20 madrassah and 600 mosques. The tsarist and Soviet eras Russified the centre and industrialized the suburbs, spawning a rise in population to 330,000, but never tamed the people.

Since independence Namangan has made headlines as a major player in the religious half of the Great Game mark II. The Saudi Arabian Ahle Sunnah movement has funded the growth of Wahabbism, a 'fundamentalist' creed within mainstream Sunni Islam. Local Muslim organizations include Adalat (Justice) and Sawad Azam (Big Group). Periodic crackdowns reveal government displeasure, but the signs on the street suggest secular authority is waning; mosques and madrassah mushroom at every turn; countless loudspeakers relay the call to prayer while the majority of women have discarded colourful headscarves for large white veils and some return to the black horsehair *paranja*, the traditional veil attacked and publicly burnt in female liberation campaigns of the 1920s.

SIGHTS
In common tsarist style, the streets of the Russian town lead to the **central park**, founded in 1884 as the governor's garden. Later renamed Pushkin Park and installed

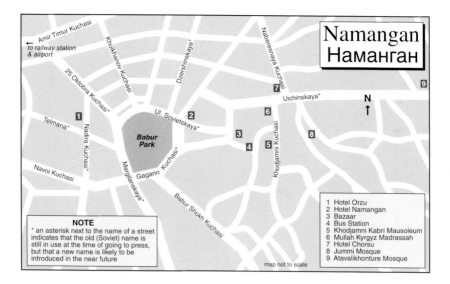

with requisite Lenin statue, it now enjoys Babur's sponsorship and the uninterrupted patronage of Uzbek patriarchs tea-drinking and chess-playing in the shady calm of heavy *chinar* trees. The Square to the northwest has dropped Lenin for Independence and a carved display of provincial monuments. Nearby at 25 ex-October Street, the **Namangan Natural History Museum** houses many archaeological discoveries, but poor presentation hampers understanding. To the east is the pedestrian avenue Uichinskaya, lined with cigarette kiosks disguised as giant cans of western beer, a bizarre prelude to the heart of the Uzbek town, the crowded **bazaar**. Beside stalls of meat, fruit and vegetables, craftsmen offer brightly painted wooden cradles, complete with convenience hole, while thickly-veiled women sell embroidered skullcaps and woollen shawls.

Just east of the bazaar is the **Mullah Kyrgyz madrassah**, built in 1910 by a local cotton magnate. Having served time as a Soviet literature museum, it reopened in 1992 after Namangan residents donated funds for restoration of the façade, domed corners, tiled portal and minarets. Unlike other Namangan holy places, non-Muslims are welcome to view the inner courtyard, shaded *hauz* and 35 cells for 150 students. Five minutes south along a lane famous for metal workshops is the **Khodjamni Kabri mausoleum**. Only men may request a look at this 18th-century imitation of earlier portal and dome tombs. The ornate carved terracotta façade is a striking example of Ferghana decoration. Extensive reconstruction will restore the adjacent Soviet anti-religious museum into the mosque and madrassah Khojamni built.

East and south of Uichinskaya is Namangan's Jummi Mosque (off limits to visi-

tors), proudly announced by towering Turkish-style minarets. Further east along
Uichinskaya is the **Atavalikhonture mosque**, easily recognizable by its immense
dome, 14.1 metres (46 feet) in diameter, one of the largest in Central Asia. First built
in 1915, it is presently home to Namangan's Wahabbi fraternity and does not entertain outsiders. For a look inside a newly restored mosque, try the more open **Mullah
Bozor Akhun** on Akhunbabaev St. Behind a flurry of fresh domes and minarets is a
shady courtyard, *hauz* and the mausoleum tower of Mullah Akhun, the 17th century
teacher of Sufic poet Mashrab. The poet himself has been commemorated in a theme
park six kilometres (four miles) west of the city centre. **Babarakhim Mashrab Na-
mangani** was born in Namangan in 1640. By 16 he was a dervish heading for Kashgar
and a life of creative itinerancy. He was hanged in Afghanistan in 1711, either for
inciting the people to revolt against illiteracy or for being the object of desire of a
prominent imam's wife. His heartfelt poetry has survived Soviet censorship to enjoy
contemporary revival:

> *In my dream I saw the candle of thy elegance,*
> *Circling around it, I became distraught.*
> *This body of mine died away for the wine of thy love,*
> *Both the cupbearer and goblet did I become.*

> *Allworth, Edward: from* The Holy Fool

A small museum at the park displays his poetry, philosophy and travels. Besides
the lake and obligatory big wheel are various *chaikhana* designed in the style of
regions Mashrab visited, such as Turkey, Iran, Afghanistan and China.

NAMANGAN PRACTICAL INFORMATION

■ TRANSPORT

From the airport 15 kilometres (9 miles) west of the centre there are three daily departures to Tashkent and weekly flights to Moscow, Bishkek and Almaty. The ticket
office is at 41 Mashrab St. The train station is on Amir Timur Street four kilometres
(2.5 miles) west of the Hotel Orzu. Twice-daily trains to Tashkent take about 12
hours. The long distance bus station is off Dustlik Street, two kilometres (1.2 miles)
north of the train station. Buses run to Tashkent and throughout the valley (for the
quicker mountain route to Tashkent, bargain with a taxi driver). The local bus station
is opposite the central bazaar. Bus 1 runs east–west from Atavalikhonture to Mashrab,
buses 7 and 15 connect bus station and bazaar and most buses east from the train
station also head for the bazaar.

■ ACCOMMODATION

Hotel Orzu, 1 Nadira St, Namangan (tel. 36922-65545, fax. 64547)

Uzbektourism's 'Dream' Hotel offers 150 rooms for $10–40 per night. Some have air-con, many have fridge/TV/phone and most have bathrooms. It is west of Babur Park.

More basic are the **Hotel Namangan**, northeast of Babur Park, and the **Hotel Chorsu** (tel. 67301), cheap and well-placed near the Mullah Kyrgyz Madrassah. More modern options far to the west include Hotels **Parvuz** and **Fazo**.

■ FOOD

The Hotel Orzu restaurant serves filling *dimnama*, a meat and vegetable stew, plus *dymbul shurpa*, a sweetcorn, potato and stuffed pepper soup. Otherwise, try the Besh (Five) Chinor *chaikhana* in Babur Park, various bazaar teahouses or the municipal railway workers' zone of rest, the Oromgokh *chaikhana*, an elegant imitation of traditional design on a hill above Mashrab Park.

■ TRAVEL AGENCIES

Uzbektourism, Hotel Orzu (tel. 64382, fax. 64547, telex 116248 PTB SU)
In 1994 enthusiastic staff here organized an international tourist festival, Namangan Olmasi, named after the local apples, to introduce the city to a wider audience. Besides providing guides, transport and accommodation for trips around the province, Uzbektourism also plans helicopter rides to Kyrgyzstan's Sary Chelek Lake and trekking in mountains near the Kok Serai *turbaza*.

■ OTHER

National Bank for Foreign Economic Activity, 2 Mashrab St.

AROUND NAMANGAN

■ AKSIKETH

On the right bank of the Syr Darya, 25 kilometres (15 miles) southwest of Namangan near Shakhand *kishlak* are the ruins of ancient Aksiketh, first occupied in the first century AD. It recovered from Arab destruction to become the Ferghana Valley's main city under Samanid rule in the ninth and tenth centuries. Arab geographers describe a metropolis of mosques, bazaars and craftsmen, with the tripartite division common in Central Asia; citadel, *shakhristan* (inner city) and *rabad* (large suburb). The Mongolian steamroller pushed Aksiketh downstream, where the Timurids restored it to importance. Omar Sheikh ruled here, sparking claims that his son Babur was not born in Andijan. An earthquake in the 17th century forced survivors to leave for Namangan. The remains are impressive in extent and for views across the river, though little can be distinguished beyond the ghosts of city walls and houses.

■ PAP

Further southwest the old Silk Road town of Pap has no extant architecture to prove

its credentials, but does boast a new archaeological museum of finds from the
UNESCO-protected graves six kilometres
(four miles) away at **Munchak** and **Balyand
Tepe**. Thirty reed-wrapped sarcophagi were
discovered, dating from the first to the
seventh centuries. The museum also displays Zoroastrian ossuaries and personal
items buried with the dead.

■ CHUST

North of Pap, Chust claims even earlier
settlement, for Soviet archaeologists found
here a series of crouching corpses dating
back to 1000 BC. The site itself reveals little
to the non-specialist, but the town remains
a lively one, where only ten per cent of the
population is Uzbek. The rest are mostly
Tajik, in relaxed mood at the **Mavlono
Lutfullo Park**, named after a local 16th-
century scientist whose irrigation works met
the approval of Soviet mythologists. Having
visited Mavlono's mosque and minaret,
Tajik pilgrims taste the springwater before
retiring to separate male and female
chaikhana. Choose the latter for impromptu
song and dance among women temporarily
free of family pressures and responsibilities.

Chust is long-renowned for knife and
skullcap production. Uzbek national knives,
pichok, date back to the early Stone Age,
since when their decorative and symbolic
value has outweighed their military use. In
addition to being ideal melon cutters,
knives are worn as amulets against injury
and evil. To watch the production process,
visit the **National Knife Factory** at 46
Chusti St (tel. 36942 31025), where halls of
young men smash and grind a wide variety
of blades—carved or stamped and curling at

Cotton harvest

Boiling silk cocoons

the tip—and handles, plated with horn or inlaid with mother-of-pearl.

The **Skullcap Factory** at 7 Istiklol St (tel. 33510), makes the famous Chust *tubeteika*, prototype of most Uzbek skullcaps. The black tetrahedral shape bears a pattern of white embroidery resembling burning capsicums or almonds. Four arches decorate each side of the cap band. Traditionally the *tubeteika* was worn only by men, but by the beginning of this century women joined the fashion and it is they who make up the factory's 1,200 needlework force. Other products include colourful embroidered panels known collectively as *suzyane* and considered essential to a bride's dowry.

■ UCHKURGAN MARKET

Northeast of Namangan, the town of Uchkurgan rests on the Naryn River dividing Uzbekistan and Kyrgyzstan. A day trip to the market brings the valley's ethnic mix into clear focus, for a bridge connects the two worlds: on one side the skullcaps and gowns of Uzbek cloth merchants; on the other, the animals and dairy products of Kyrgyz herdsmen. Uchkurgan buses leave from Namangan's local bus station opposite the bazaar.

■ KASANSAY

North of Namangan on the Kyrgyz border is the old town of Kasan, lord of the valley in the seventh and eighth centuries, when Turkic tribes (and briefly a Chinese force) ruled from the fortress of **Mug Tepe**. The surviving mound of isolated wall fragments affords a fine panorama across to the Chatkal foothills. Like Chust, Kasansay is a predominantly Tajik place, where leafy *chaikhana* line the busy river. The main attraction is the remarkable **Jummi mosque**, a one-time Soviet museum but now one of the largest mosques in Central Asia. Only the gate remains from the 13th-century original, but through the donations and labour of every *malhalla* in the district, this artefact is now attached to a religious complex breathtaking in wealth and expanse of detail. Five silver domes proclaim the building, but the heart is the cavernous prayer hall seating 8,000 worshippers on two storeys. Revived and revamped traditions of Ferghanan decorative art fill every inch with precision colour and carving. Kasansay buses leave from Namangan's main station.

■ SHAH FASIL MAZAR

Northeast of Kasansay take the first left after Zarkent for the mausoleum of Shah Fasil. A characteristic of Central Asian Islam is the cult of saints, combining the veneration of genuine Islamic figures and historically more hazy Sufic saints with pre-Islamic beliefs such as ancestral cults and Zoroastrianism. Holy places representative of such beliefs are particularly common in the Ferghana Valley; Shah Fasil provides a 12th-century example. Folk tales maintain the legend that 2,700 Companions of the

Prophet invaded the valley in the mid-seventh century, only to fall in battle with infidels at Ispid Bulan. History prefers to credit Qutaiba ibn Muslim with the invasion of Ferghana in 712, but legend continues to hold sway. The sacred spot later earned the mausoleum of Shah Fasil, a distant descendent of Mohammed. The Mongols left the mausoleum untouched, so today's pilgrims can enjoy the buttressed original. They arrive in segregated buses disgorging men and women at separate areas for washing and prayer. Latent Zoroastrianism resurfaces in the fervent smearing of dust on faces and the atavistic tree-worship inherent in the wish-making practice of tying cloth strips to bushes. Inside the conical mausoleum, Koranic slabs worn smooth by the faithful rest on Fasil's whitewashed tomb. The tiled interior shines in many-coloured motifs. Finally, pilgrims tramp the path to the hilltop beyond where the holy warriors are said to be buried. To hitch on a pilgrim bus enquire in Namangan or Kasansay.

■ SARY CHELEK
North of Zarkent is Nanay village on the southern slopes of the Chatkal, 70 kilometres (45 miles) north of Namangan. Uzbektourism runs a holiday complex here, the Kok Serai turbaza, a chalet base for trips into the mountains to places such as Padshaata stream and Kapchugai gorge. A further 30 kilometres (20 miles) north, inside Kyrgyzstan, is Sary Chelek (yellow cup), a lake reserve more than justifying the oft-quoted Kyrgyz claim to be the Switzerland of Central Asia. At 1,872 metres (6,150 feet) it sits among rocky, fir-clad hills still teeming with wildlife. Kyrgyz visas and permits for the reserve are required—in Tashkent, Uzbektourism and Asia Travel can organize these for a 12-day trek from Charvak Reservoir to Sary Chelek. In Namangan, Uzbektourism handles tour arrangements, including helicopter rides. Individuals will need their help for paperwork, but can then make their own way to the lake; take a bus to Karavan, just east of Nanay, and try to hitch to the lake from there.

Excursions to Kyrgyzstan

Travel less than an hour eastwards out of Andijan into the republic of Kyrgyzstan and gradually, imperceptibly, things begin to change. The Ferghana Valley's uncompromising monopoly of skullcaps is broken by the appearance of curious white felt hats resembling miniature yurts and men with Mongol cheekbones ride the village streets confidently on nomadic steeds. The eastern edges of the Ferghana Valley rise like a curved scimitar over the valley floor; beyond rises an amphitheatre of awesome mountains opening on China, Afghanistan and India. The traveller has reached the edge of the Uzbek world and approaches the gateway to a distinct and rival tradition. The fumbling modern boundary between the republics of Kyrgyzstan and Uzbekistan masks a more ancient geographical, ethnic and cultural transition zone, dividing settler and nomad, lowland and highland, Uzbek and Kyrgyz, east and west Turkestan.

OSH

Perched on the fringes of the Ferghana Valley, the border town of Osh is situated only five kilometres (three miles) from the Uzbek border, yet is already physically and spiritually closer to Kashgar than to Tashkent.

Although the town is one of the oldest in the Ferghana Valley (the three thousandth anniversary of the founding of Osh was celebrated on the dubiously specific date of 9 October 1994), little remains of the original Arab citadel, palace, prison, city walls or *rabat* fortress, built to defend the frontiers of Islam from nomadic incursions. Nevertheless, Osh is a pleasant place and, as Kyrgyzstan's second city, its busy market acts as a regional centre for the whole of southern Kyrgyzstan.

■ SIGHTS

The town lies at the foot of the **Tacht-i-Suleiman (Throne of Solomon)** hill and is dominated by its auspicious shadow. The huge splinter of rock some 150 metres (500 feet) high is one of the holiest sites in Central Asia and a second pilgrimage to this very physical metaphor of Islamic endurance ranks alongside Turkestan in Kazakhstan [see page 103-5] as a substitute for Mecca. A more strenuous walk than at first seems likely brings you to the mythical resting place of the biblical Solomon who is said to have ruled from his throne here. A more tangible visitor to the shrine was Babur, last of the Timurids, who retired here during the late 15th century to carry out his *chilla*, the annual 40-day retreat performed by all Sufis. Babur describes the town in his famous autobiography, the *Baburname*, recalling how local scallywags would open the nearby town canals, drenching unsuspecting travellers. Closed in 1961, a victim of its own success (after a mysterious explosion boosted a Soviet drive for atheism), the recently rebuilt tomb now attracts a stream of believers praying at its attractive, white ganch grill. A more prosaic reward for the unbeliever is the commanding, albeit hazily toxic, view of the Ferghana Valley floor to the west and the high road to the Pamirs to the east.

A slippery slope, worn smooth by pilgrim piety, continues downwards, above a scorched cemetery of crescents and stars, to the local museum. The rather space-age entrance bores sacrilegiously into the holy mountain, carving out a bizarre fairy grotto of a museum, whose lonely exhibits range from anonymous bits of pottery to an exhausted-looking stuffed bear. Upstairs houses a fully functional yurt, displayed by the Soviets as a relic of a lost ethnic trait.

Back in the town, the large sprawling bazaar is the beating heart of post-independence Osh. Local produce and Kyrgyz *kalpaks* compete with Western chocolate bars, as elderly Russian women crouch in the dust with their belongings strewn around them, hoping to raise the cash for a train ticket to Moscow. The progressive economic reforms of President Akaev have revitalized the market and made Kyrgyzstan the Central Asian darling of the United States, even though the early instability of the new IMF-backed currency has led some economists to wryly dub Kyrgyzstan the 'land of the rising som'. Cool in the summer and warm in the winter, a felt *kalpak* makes a good souvenir and retails at around five dollars.

A novelty for visitors coming from Uzbekistan is the continued persistence of icons of Lenin that are strewn around Osh in various guises. Whereas Uzbekistan's Soviet icons quietly disappeared into the dead of night, only to be replaced by a new variant on a familiar theme, in Kyrgyzstan financial considerations have outweighed ideological statements. A metal cutout Lenin still spies down on Lenin Street from the rooftops, while a silver statue of Lenin in Lenin Square seems to be waving goodbye—to Moscow, at least. A bust takes shade just off Navoi St and a profile is embossed on the side of an apartment block. However, the largest Lenin in town takes centre stage in the main square at the southern end of town. The statue once stood in the capital, Bishkek, in the days when it was known as Frunze, but when the

Baiga, or Kyrgyz polo, at Osh Hippodrome

capital followed suit with other regional cities and disposed of its communist monuments, the great leader was bussed unceremoniously over the mountains to adorn the republic's second city. Not far from the statue lies the forsaken Russian Orthodox church.

The Kyrgyz have traditionally enjoyed the nomad's somewhat relaxed interpretation of Islam and this is reflected in the secondary position mosques are accorded in Osh. Until the new *jummi* mosque in the northeast of town is finished with Turkish money, local *guzar* mosques such as the Bakhi (Mohammed Yusuf Baihadji Ogli) on Navoi St or the older Rabag Abdullah Khan, at the base of the Tacht-i-Suleiman, will continue to fulfill the needs of the faithful. The uninspiring Asaf ibn Burchiya Mausoleum is also situated at the base of the hill in the marvellously juxtaposed shadow of the Fifty Years of Kyrgyzstan Monument.

A ten-minute bus or taxi ride out of Osh towards the village of Tuleyken brings you to the **Hippodrome**, the location for the irregular, but highly spectacular, traditional Kyrgyz sports staged on festivals or anniversaries. The fun and games include *Kyz Kum* (a form of kiss chase where if the woman catches the man she gets to ride behind him, whipping him across the field), *Udaresh* horseback wrestling, *At Chabysh* horse racing and even Kyrgyz eagle hunting. However, the highlight is without doubt *Baiga* (or *Ulag*), an intense, frenzied game of polo played with the corpse of a decapitated goat. When the rules are observed it will seem to the outsider that there are no rules. When, up in the hills, there really are no rules, injuries and even fatalities are par for the course. Swirling clouds of heavy dust, Mongoloid faces framed in old flying helmets, yurts overflowing with vodka and mutton, frequent half time *plov* breaks and solo recitals of the *Manas*, the Kyrgyz national epic, combine to make the event a photographer's dream and an occasion to remember.

■ OSH PRACTICAL INFORMATION
Transport, visas, money
Regular buses from Andijan cross the border with no immigration formalities, arriving at the new bus station several kilometres west of the town. Local buses serve the city centre from here. Buses also leave from the new bus station to such other destinations as Bishkek, Karakul and Dzhalalabad. Buses to Uzgen, however, depart from the old bus station a few hundred metres from the bazaar. There are flights to Bishkek and Moscow as long as fuel lasts.

Foreigners are officially allowed 72 hours in Kyrgyzstan without needing a Kyrgyz visa, as long as they have a valid Uzbek visa. However, a letter from your embassy stating this could be useful, especially in hotels, as regulations do not always filter down to ground level.

Kyrgyz money is the *som*, as opposed to the Uzbek *sum*, and is exchanged at a different rate from its Uzbek counterpart, at present worth approximately three times the *sum*. Money can be exchanged on the bus or at official booths in the bazaar, which exchange cash dollars at practically the same rate as the black market. Som can also be bought in the Andijan bazaar.

Accommodation
The **Hotel Osh**, Ulitsa Babalinov (tel. 33222-24717), a ten-minute walk from the centre, is the old Intourist hotel with the best facilities in town.
The **Hotel Alai**, Ulitsa Navoi, 400 metres from old bus station, is more rough and ready, but has a better location and sometimes accepts som.
The **Turbaza Ak Bura** is inconveniently situated in the eastern suburbs.

Travel Agencies
Alptreksport, 3 Ul. Gogol, Osh 714018 (tel. 33222-77906 or 23001)
Owner Yuri Lavruschin has links with the Association of Mountain Guides and Sovintersport in Moscow and can organize caving in nearby Aravan, horseriding in Arslanbob or Sary Chelek and treks/helicopter trips to Peak Lenin. He needs at least one week's notice. Prices are reasonable and flexible with a trip to Peak Lenin working out at about $35–45 dollars a day, depending upon the itinerary.

UZGEN
Situated on the banks of the Jaxartes tributary, the Kara Darya (Black River), less than an hour's drive northeast of Osh, is the small town of Uzgen, former capital of the Turkic Karakhanid dynasty. Uzgen's position ensured that it profited from the side shoots of the Silk Road, for the town marked the passage into the Turkic world, a place for pause. Traders would tally up profits and swap their animals here, bracing themselves for the rigours ahead or recuperating from a completed journey. Its position at the head of a narrow valley also made the town a centre for Silk Road taxation.

Uzgen reached its zenith under the Karakhanids, when it was the capital of a loosely knit empire that stretched over both sides of the Tian Shan and incorporated most of the lands of Transoxiana. It is said that the great Ismael Samani was imprisoned in Uzgen before he managed to escape, disguised in women's clothes. After the Ilek Khan had secured a sufficient power base, the capital was transferred to the centralized town of Samarkand and Uzgen slipped a rung to become the residence of the ruler of Ferghana. In 1141 the infidel Kara Khitai Gurkhan defeated the Muslim Karakhanid khan and Uzgen became the home of their dynastic treasury. News of the Turk's defeat by a non-Muslim elder (or Presbyter) called Gurkhan (translated as John) was to filter back to the Levant as Chinese whispers, passing into beleaguered Crusader imagination as the legend of the Christian leader Prester John who, it was said, was en route to Jerusalem to rout the Muslim empire.

■ SIGHTS

The isolated relics of Uzgen's hazy past glories lie a five-minute walk from the bus station and bazaar, one hundred metres from a strident silver Lenin. The small minaret and three mausoleums that remain are mainly notable because of the rarity of pre-Mongol architecture in Central Asia and for the exquisite quality of the tilework. The complex is said to represent an important step in Islamic art, denoting a shift of emphasis from the interior to the exterior, and is the forerunner of such later architectural high points as the Kalon minaret in Bukhara and the Shah-i-Zindah complex in Samarkand.

The tenth-century Uzgen **minaret** stands divorced from its long-destroyed mosque to the north of the mausoleums. The structure rises 20 metres (65 feet) from an octagonal base of fired brick, through five main bands of decorative brick, to a crenellated top crowned with a brick hat, indicating that in the past a second section continued on from here. The bands are broken by thin rings of brick circles and embroidery designs. Elements of the design can be traced through to the later Karakhanid minaret masterpieces in Bukhara and Vabkent. The raised entrance to the minaret is locked, but the local *hakkim* (mayor) has the key.

Of the three mausoleums, the central **Mazar of Nasr ibn Ali** predates the others by over a century. The portal has been largely restored, but a section of melted *girikh* to the left still points to its original glory. Tradition associates the tomb with the resting places of the first Karakhanid khan who died in 1012 and also of the great Seljuk leader Sultan Sanjar. The first story is true. The second, however, is not; Sultan Sanjar's impressive mazar still stands in Merv, Turkmenistan.

To the left is the **Jalal Ad Din Al Hussein mausoleum**, built in 1152. Beautiful foliated Nakhshi calligraphy above the arch contrasts with the less ebullient plaited Kufic above the door and the two are separated by a fine incised terracotta *girikh* design underneath the arch. The circles to either side of the arch may be an echo of earlier Zoroastrian beliefs.

The most obviously beautiful and eye-catching designs, however, are reserved for the **southern mausoleum** (1186), whose incised terracotta plaques and inscriptions cover every arch and concave of the façade like some monotone trial run of the Shah-i-Zindah, which it predates by over 200 years.

All three buildings are visited by pilgrims, especially women, who use the tombs as mosques, touching the walls and rubbing their faces as they leave. Mostly, however, the tombs lie deserted, quietly reflecting the pinkish hue of the ground whence they came.

■ PRACTICAL INFORMATION

Buses run from both Andijan and Dzhalabad to Uzgen although the most frequent connections are from Osh. The cheap and basic **Hotel Uzgen** is only a few minutes' walk from the mausoleums, but the sights are best visited as a day trip from Osh or Andijan. The bus station is right next to the photogenic main bazaar.

ARSLANBOB

Three hours and a million miles from Andijan, the high mountains and verdant valleys of Arslanbob are a quite literal breath of fresh air for any traveller jaded by the rigours of the Ferghana Valley. Clear rushing waterfalls, subdued silvers, autumnal reds and dense groves of ancient walnut trees all lead up to the towering rock wall of the Bagbash Ata Mountains, sheer and gnarled, capped by snow and ice. Uzbek farmers tend grids of beehives, Kyrgyz shepherds lead their flocks up to high, lonely pastures and grazing horses roam the hills freely. Arslanbob is indeed one of the few places still able to realize the ideal of an untouched, utopian, turn-of-the-century rural Turkestan, as depicted by Paul Nazarrof in his book *Hunted* :

> *The red tint of the soil harmonises with the green of the fields and the forest, and the deep blue of the sky with the white fleecy clouds. The whole scene offers an enchanting picture of nature unspoilt, and this escape into the depths of the mountain country, away from communist experiments, brought peace and consolation to my aching soul.*

Local gastronomic specialities include wonderful blueberries and honey (*assal* in Kyrgyz), as well as the famous walnuts from which the valley gets its Kyrgyz name, 'King of the Forests'.

■ PRACTICAL INFORMATION

In the summer buses serve Arslanbob daily from Andijan. If, however, these are not running catch a local bus to Bazar Kurgan, from where regular buses ply the two hour, boneshaking ride to Arslanbob. The only way to know when you have crossed the extremely porous border is to check the colour of people's money as they board the bus.

The ramshackle hotel in the centre of town may be open in season, although a better bet is the *turbaza*, a

Mountain lake high in the Pamirs

two-kilometre (1.2-mile) walk uphill, where semi-detached chalets (or rather bar-racks) attract summer school and tour groups. Out of season the caretaker can often find visitors a place to stay.

The village and *turbaza* only stir from their winter hibernation from around June to September when they erupt into mad activity, as Andijanis escape the summer heat. Spring and autumn are, however, the most beautiful seasons to visit Arslanbob, although you should be prepared to be self-sufficient at these times. In winter the entire region is blanketed in a metre of snow. Many local tour agencies offer walking or horse-riding trips to Arslanbob.

KYZYL UNGAR

Kyzyl Ungar is another valley of startling beauty further into the foothills of the Fer-ganski Mountains. The valley is deeper and more dramatic than Arslanbob's and its mountains rise sheer from the churning Kara Ungar River.

The quiet village spreads lethargically over the valley contours and is in itself worth a visit. Any traveller who makes it this far off the beaten track can be assured of a humbling barrage of hospitality and curiosity. Yet the village is poor and the traveller should bring everything he needs with him.

The road leads through the village and continues the three kilometres up the valley to the *turbaza* and beyond, to the beginning of the network of hiking trails which lead up endless pristine side valleys. Approximately six kilometres from the *turbaza* the narrow valley is studded by a beautiful trout-filled lake. The region offers outstanding trekking potential.

■ PRACTICAL INFORMATION

The only place to stay or eat in Kyzyl Ungar is the *turbaza,* which is much smaller than its affiliated partner in Arslanbob. Outside the main summer season it is, unlike Arslanbob, most definitely closed. Daily buses go to and from Bazar Kurgan, but without your own transport you will need to spend the night. From Arslanbob drive down to the crossroads at Chorvak to join the bus route up to Kyzyl Ungar. Hitching is a distinct possibility, but be aware that there is more livestock on the road than traffic. To kill time in Chorvak try a visit to the 16th-century mausoleum perched on a hill above the crossroads.

Samarkand

Sweet to ride forth at evening from the wells
When shadows pass gigantic on the sand,
And softly through the silence beat the bells
Along the Golden Road to Samarkand.

We travel not for trafficking alone:
By hotter winds our fiery hearts are fanned:
For lust of knowing what should not be known
We make the Golden Journey to Samarkand.

James Elroy Flecker, Hassan (1913)

The Mirror of the World, the Garden of the Soul, the Jewel of Islam, the Pearl of the East, the Centre of the Universe. Lying in the river valley of the Zerafshan (gold-strewer) and flanked by Pamir-Altai mountain spurs, this fabled oasis at the fringes of the Kyzyl Kum desert has never lacked breathless admirers. Another name, City of Famous Shadows, reveals Samarkand as witness to the full sweep of Central Asian history. Up to 40,000 years ago, natural bounty drew Palaeolithic man to the area. The city proper claims equity with Rome and Babylon, for archaeologists date urban settlement at least to the sixth century BC. Until the 16th century, Samarkand was always the first city of Transoxiana in population, commerce and culture, for fertile earth rewards the farmer and trade routes west to Persia, east to China and south to India met here to form a major Silk Road crossroads and emporium. Among conquerors to cast their shadows were the Macedonian Alexander the Great, the Mongol Genghis Khan and, above all, Tamerlane, whose capital of fluted domes and sky-blue mosaic excites the traveller even today.

History

Like the city's early history, the very word Samarkand, so resonant with enigma and romantic legend, still eludes the scholar's grasp. Did a King Samar lost in hoary antiquity found this town (*kand*), or rather King Afrosiab, mythical founder of Turan in millenniums past, who later lent his name to the ancient ruins in the northeast? When Alexander arrived in 329 BC, those ruins comprised Marakanda, the rich, fortified centre of Sogdiana, a satrapy of the Achaemenid empire peopled by a cultured Iranian race. Despite a 13-kilometre (8-mile) wall, he took the city without resistance to find 'Everything I have heard about the beauty of the city is indeed true,

except that it is much more beautiful than I imagined.' As soon as the Greeks moved east to Ferghana, Sogdian rebel Spitamenes inspired guerilla warfare so effective that Alexander was forced to use scorched-earth policies. He finally secured the citadel over a year later.

Excavations reveal the Hellenic influence of his successors and the arrival of Kushan power, but by the first centuries of the Christian era Samarkand had faded into disrepair, as merchants and craftsmen left for elsewhere. It took the re-routing of world trade from the third century to effect the city's recovery. Though plundered by Hun tribes in the fifth century and engulfed by the Turkic khanate in the sixth, the indomitable Sogdians of Samarkand seized the opportunities of the Silk Road. In 630 Buddhist pilgrim Xuan Zang, on his odyssey from China to India, visited a flourishing city extending far beyond its walls: "The precious merchandise of many foreign countries is stored up here. The soil is rich and productive, and yields abundant harvests. The forest and trees afford thick vegetation, and flowers and fruits are plentiful . . . The inhabitants are skilful in the arts and trades beyond those of other countries . . . They are copied by all surrounding people in point of politeness and propriety". His disciple recorded, "The king and the people do not believe in Buddhism but worship fire. There are two monastery buildings but no monks dwell in them, and if an occasional wandering monk seeks shelter there, the barbarians follow them with burning firebrands and drive them away."

Xuan Zang's description of a Zoroastrian society was confirmed by ossuaries excavated at Afrosiab. The greatest discoveries were wall paintings rich in colour and pageantry, for this was the Sogdian heyday, when her colonists swarmed to China taking glass and wine-making among diverse new skills. Like the West centuries later, the Tang Chinese were charmed by the exotic glamour of remote Samarkand, nurtured by gifts to Chang'an (Xi'an) of flute players, twirling girls, pygmies, leopards and golden peaches. However, Chinese hopes of joining Sogdiana to her western empire were dashed by the Arab invasion. Where Xuan Zang had tried to reason with the pagans, the sword of Islam came to devastate. After besieging and taking Samarkand in 712, Arab commander Qutaiba ibn Muslim erected the town's first mosque and deported much of the population. In the chaos that followed, Samarkand acquired a valuable skill, for the Battle of Talas in 751 supplied Chinese prisoners to teach its people the art of paper-making. In time, trade routes carried the secret west to replace parchment and papyrus.

Only in the ninth century, under Samanid rule, did Samarkand enjoy a renaissance. Like Bukhara it grew in the tripartite formation of Persian towns: a citadel with prison, the *shakhristan* (town proper) containing government offices and a great Friday mosque, and *rabad* (suburbs) for bazaars and warehouses. Protecting the *shakhristan* were a moat and wall with four main gates: Bukhara (north), Kesh (south), Chinese (east) and Iron (west). The streets were paved with stone and

Bibi Khanum mosque, Samarkand

benefactors supplied iced water for free at some 2,000 locations. Surviving Zoroastrians were made exempt from the poll tax to maintain the ingenious irrigation system of lead-covered pipes that fed every house and garden. The tenth-century traveller Abdul Kasim ibn Hakal climbed the citadel for "one of the most beautiful views that man has ever gazed upon: the fresh greenness of the trees, the glittering castles, the canals . . . large market places, blocks of dwellings, bathhouses, caravanserai."

Transition of power during the tenth, eleventh and twelfth centuries from the Samanids to the Karakhanids, Seljuks and Karakhitai, steadily wore down Samarkand's lustre. After the invasions of Khorezmshah Mohammed from 1207–12, the population declined from around 400,000 to 100,000. Yet the worst was still to come. Like the Arabs in the eighth century and the Russians in the 19th, Genghis Khan in March 1220 first dammed the canals, lifeblood of Samarkand. When the city capitulated, the Mongols fell to plunder, driving the people beyond the walls where many were slaughtered. A thousand brave men attempted a sortie from the citadel, but Genghis trapped them in the Friday mosque. According to contemporary historian Juvaini, a volley of naptha pots ensured "all that were in it were burnt with the fire of this world and washed with the water of the hereafter." The 30,000-strong Turkic garrison was "drowned in the ocean of destruction and consumed by the fire of perdition." A similar number of craftsmen were deported to Mongolia, leaving barely enough people to occupy a single neighbourhood.

When Taoist monk Chang Chun arrived in 1221, en route from China to enlighten the Great Khan with his philosophy (and disappoint his quest for eternal life), he stayed in the shah's abandoned palace, scorning the threat of brigandage brought on by famine. Outlying areas remained cultivated—he thought the gardens and melons surpassed even those of China—and Islam still held sway: "whoever neglects their religious duties is executed". Chang Chun also noted, "If a man becomes poor, his wife takes another husband; when a husband goes off on a journey and does not return within three months, his wife can marry another man. But there is one thing very strange about these people; some of the women have beards and moustaches." Marco Polo, travelling far to the south of Samarkand in the late 13th century, reported it was a "very large and splendid city". In 1333, the Moroccan ibn-Battuta, dubbed the greatest traveller of pre-modern times, for his wanderings outdistanced the Venetian, found much in wall-less ruin, yet was moved to call it "one of the largest and most perfectly beautiful cities in the world."

After the Turco-Mongol Tamerlane, sheep rustler turned empire builder, achieved supremacy in Transoxiana in 1370, his choice of capital was obvious. Samarkand's history, fertility and potential for rebirth far outweighed the claims of his nearby birthplace Shakhrisabz. The city had shifted south since the Mongol destruction and the new monarch cemented the move with moats, walls and gates. The list of master craftsmen imported to embellish his imperial dream reads like the history of the next 35 years of near-constant campaigning. For in addition to treasure and slave-levy, the lands of Persia, Syria, Asia Minor and India yielded their finest minds—scholars, historians, theologians—and hands—architects, masons, painters, calligraphers, tile-glaziers, silk-weavers, glass-blowers, silversmiths, gunsmiths, bow-makers and armourers. Tamerlane derisively named outlying villages after the great cities of Baghdad, Damascus, Sultaniya, Shiraz and Cairo.

Six main streets led from the gates through squares opening on fountains, mosques, madrassah, mausoleums and caravanserai, to the domed trade gallery at Samarkand's centre, the Registan. Tamerlane's four-storey Kok Serai (Blue Palace) stood within the citadel bordering the western wall, yet on his brief visits he preferred his suburban palaces, gardens and fabulously ornate tents hung with silks and tapestries. In 1404, visiting Spanish envoy Ruy Gonzalez de Clavijo marvelled at Samarkand's green belt: 'a traveller who approaches the city sees only a mountainous height of trees and the houses embowered among them remain invisible'. In the sumptuous surroundings of the Garden of Heart's Delight and other such Edens, Clavijo observed the Conqueror of the World receiving foreign tribute or playing chess, but chiefly feasting and drinking with spectacular abandon. He witnessed Tamerlane's creative power too, as the despot ordered the immediate construction of a vaulted bazaar street running across the city, or the two noblemen in charge would answer with their heads: "the tumult was such that it seemed all the devils of hell were at work here. Thus in the course of twenty days the whole new street was carried through: a wonder indeed to behold; but those whose houses had been thus demolished had good cause to complain."

Tamerlane's death prompted internecine struggle and the reduction of his realm, but for half a century Samarkand continued to blossom under his grandson Ulug Beg, the astronomer-king. However, the rise of nomadic Uzbeks spelt the end of Timurid power and Samarkand's prosperity. Tamerlane's great-great-great-grandson, Babur, seized Samarkand for the third time in 1512, but the Uzbeks quickly recovered to chase this last Timurid towards India, where he would later found the Mogul empire. His autobiography, the *Baburnama*, rich in praise for Samarkand's buildings, bazaars, gardens, fruit, paper and crimson velvet, serves as an epitaph to a golden age.

From the 16th century onwards, Bukhara grew at Samarkand's expense under the Shaybanid and Astrakhanid dynasties, although the whole region was suffering the death of Silk Road trade. Grand works were few, save for those of Uzbek governor Yalangtush Bakhadur in the mid-17th century. Earthquake damage, looting and in-fighting left the city a virtual ghost town in the 18th century, until the Bukharan emir repopulated it in the 1770s by repairing the houses, citadel and 13 kilometre (8-mile) city wall.

For the tsarist general Kaufmann, Samarkand held as much symbolic as military significance, for Tamerlane once plundered Russia to within a stone's throw of

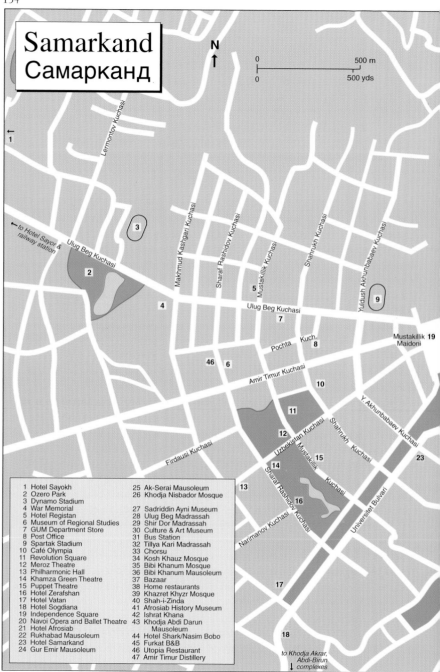

Samarkand
Самарканд

N

0 .... 500 m
0 .... 500 yds

Lermontov Kuchasi

← to Hotel Sayor &
railway station

Ulug Beg Kuchasi

Makhmud Kashgari Kuchasi

Sharaf Rashidov Kuchasi

Mustakillik Kuchasi

Shahrukh Kuchasi

Yuldush Akhunbabaev Kuchasi

Ulug Beg Kuchasi

Pochta Kuch.

Mustakillik **19** Maidoni

Amir Timur Kuchasi

Y. Akhunbabaev Kuchasi

Firdausi Kuchasi

Uzbekistan Kuchasi

Shahrukh Kuchasi

Mustakillik Kuchasi

Narimanov Kuchasi

Sharaf Rashidov Kuchasi

Universitet Bulvari

to Khodja Akrar,
Abdi-Birun
↓ complexes

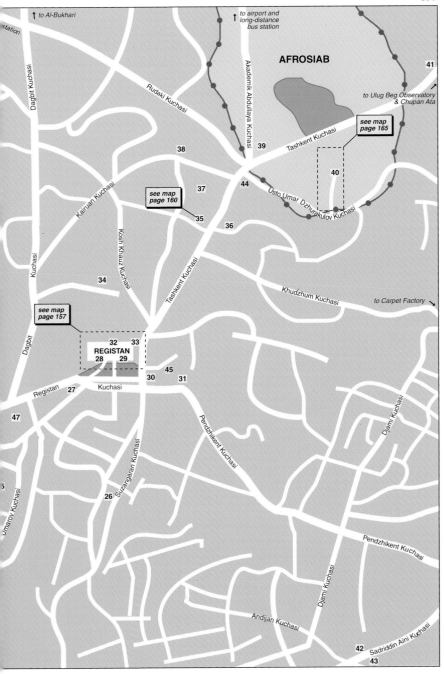

to Al-Bukhari

to airport and
long-distance
bus station

AFROSIAB

41

to Ulug Beg Observatory
& Chupan Ata

station

Dagbit Kuchasi

Rudaki Kuchasi

Akademik Abdullaya Kuchasi

Tashkent Kuchasi

see map
page 165

38

39

40

44

Usto Umar Dzhurakulov Kuchasi

Kairuan Kuchasi

see map
page 160

37

35

36

Kosh Khauz Kuchasi

Kuchasi

34

Khudzhum Kuchasi

to Carpet Factory

Tashkent Kuchasi

see map
page 157

Dagbit

32 33
REGISTAN
28   29

45

30   31

Registan

27

Kuchasi

47

Djami Kuchasi

Umarov Kuchasi

Pendzhikent Kuchasi

Suzangaran Kuchasi

26

Pendzhikent Kuchasi

Djami Kuchasi

Andijan Kuchasi

42   Sadriddin Aini Kuchasi

43

Moscow. Despite leading only 3,500 men, Kaufmann lost but two of them, before the city surrendered to avert destruction in May 1868. Leaving a garrison of under 800 able-bodied men, Kaufmann pushed on, giving 20,000 hostile troops from Shakhrisabz the chance to reverse his gain. For five days the beleaguered garrison was trapped in the citadel as the citizens of Samarkand joined this purge of the infidels. Nearly 200 Russians were killed before Kaufmann's speedy return drove the attackers away.

Tsarist colonization changed the look of the city: the walls were demolished, the citadel became a military fortress and to the west fanned the Russian town in wide, tree-lined streets. The arrival of the Transcaspian Railway in 1888 brought development, a nascent working class, anti-tsarist sentiments and Western dreamers, as Samarkand was released from an isolation broken by only two European visitors between 1404 and 1841. Explorer Douglas Carruthers in 1907 caught a common reaction: 'Even in its decline, Samarkand is like some fair lady looking out from the seclusion of her garden on to the wilderness around her.'

In late 1917, the red banner of revolution hung over the Registan; in 1920 Bolshevik general Frunze gathered his troops here for the assault on Bukhara; in 1925 a mass rally declared Samarkand the capital of the Uzbek Soviet Socialist Republic, leaving its predominantly Tajik citizens somewhat at a loss. Industrial progress boosted the population to today's figure of 372,000, second only to Tashkent, as the ancient city was stamped with all the hallmarks of a Soviet metropolis—factories, institutes, apartment blocks and public transport. Lenin Square, a House of Soviets and an Opera and Ballet Theatre consumed the site of Tamerlane's Blue Palace, yet where extant glories were concerned, the new landlords reversed centuries of neglect. Whatever one's views on the ethics or quality of restoration, these ongoing efforts afford the traveller a spectacular glimpse of Tamerlane's Centre of the Universe.

Sights

Registan

The Registan of Samarkand was originally, and is still even in its ruin, the noblest public square in the world. I know of nothing in the East approaching it in massive simplicity and grandeur; and nothing in Europe . . . which can even aspire to enter the competition. No European spectacle indeed can adequately be compared to it, in our inability to point to an open space in any western city that is commanded on three of its four sides by Gothic cathedrals of the finest order.

(George Curzon, Russia in Central Asia, 1899)

The Registan ensemble at the heart of Samarkand, restored to its original splendour, ranks first in Central Asia and among the greatest of all the grandiose and magnificent works of the Islamic world. Its meaning, sandy place, after a stream that washed sand over the earth, does little justice to the architectural and decorative wealth on show. Like the Shah-i-Zinda necropolis, repeated visits are necessary to grasp the depth of detail as changing light explores multiple shades of mosaic radiance.

Here lay the crossroads of Tamerlane's capital, where six arteries met under a domed bazaar, yet his grandson Ulug Beg envisaged a more cultural and political role. From 1417–20 he built a beautiful madrassah (Islamic college) on the west side of the square. Opposite, he replaced the headgear bazaar of Tuman Aka, Tamerlane's youngest wife, with a lofty-domed *khanagha*, a hospice for dervishes. To the north arose the Mirza Caravanserai and to the south the huge Alike Kukeldash Mosque, alongside the elegant Carved Mosque and a bathhouse bright with mosaic. The square itself was the scene of military parades and public executions. Tamerlane's great-great-great-grandson Babur placed his command post on top of Ulug Beg's madrassah as he repelled Uzbek hordes early in the 16th century.

Just a century later only the madrassah remained in good repair. Uzbek governor Yalangtush Bakhadur made a bid for immortality by dismantling the *khanagha* and caravanserai in favour of two new madrassah of complementary size and ornamentation, thus completing today's layout. Eighteenth century troubles emptied the Registan; Ulug Beg's madrassah lost its second storey and "owls instead of students housed in its cells, while the doors were hung with spiders' webs instead of silk curtains". All three were used as grain warehouses until a slow religious recovery in the 19th century. The Bolsheviks revived the square's political potential with party rallies, mass veil-burnings and trials of counter-revolutionaries. They also revived its appearance: straightening minarets, rebuilding domes, restoring tilework and removing the detritus of centuries—over two metres of earth—leaving Ulug Beg's madrassah slightly over-shadowed by its near replica, the later Shir Dor.

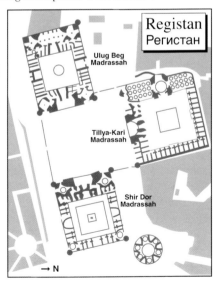

Registan
Регистан

Ulug Beg Madrassah

Tillya-Kari Madrassah

Shir Dor Madrassah

→ N

■ ULUG BEG MADRASSAH

While his grandfather is remembered for monumental mosques and mausoleums, Ulug Beg's legacy is appropriately educa-

The Registan ensemble, Samarkand

tional. The madrassah housed at least 100 students under the tutelage of the finest scholars of the age both in Islamic and secular sciences. Legend claims the ruler himself lectured here on astronomy, his greatest passion, reflected in the panoply of azure-blue stars on the 35-metre *pishtak* (portal). A Kufic inscription reads: "This magnificent façade is of such a height it is twice the heavens and of such weight that the spine of the earth is about to crumble". Yet its size is more than balanced by the sheer elegance of its design and ceramic tile coating. A yellow-brown background, the colour of the earth, highlights glazed green, turquoise, yellow and light and dark blue. Mosaic and majolica panels shine with floral motifs and Kufic calligraphy, but dominant are geometric *girikh* patterns stretching across the walls and up the minarets flanking the façade. These 33-metre columns, still flouting the perpendicular, terminate in *muqarna* honeycomb decoration. Ulug Beg's 600th anniversary in 1994 accelerated the pace of restoration, so that the interior too resembles the building of Samarkand's heyday. Through the *pishtak* entrance is a square courtyard, from which four large *iwans* (vaulted arches) give onto 50 *hujra* (student cells) on two storeys. Under the corner domes lie spacious *darskhana* (lecture halls), while the western axis conceals a five-bayed mosque.

■ SHIR DOR MADRASSAH
"The skilled acrobat of thought climbing the rope of imagination will never reach the

summits of its forbidden minarets." Such is the inscription extolling the Registan's second madrassah, built by Governor Yalangtush between 1619 and 1636. His architects strove to match the first in scale and nobility, though Koranic prohibition against symmetry forbade an exact mirror-image. Façade length is identical, 51 metres from minaret to minaret, and the tall, fluted domes flanking the *pishtak* suggest the Ulug Beg once bore the same over its front *darskhana*. Structural differences include the lack of mosque, rear *darskhana* and auxiliary entrances in the lateral façades. Every inch seems covered with richly coloured geometric, floral and epigraphic patterns. While experts detect proportional and decorative decline since the Timurid period, the stylized representation of animal life is a striking development. Above the *pishtak* arch, in hot pursuit of two startled white does, through spiralling shoots and flowers, run the lions that give the madrassah its name, Shir Dor—'lion-bearing'. The striped beasts resemble tigers and from their backs rise beam-fringed suns with human faces. Various theories explain this break with Islamic taboo on figurative art. The powerful lion-tiger is perhaps Yalangtush himself, swallowing his neighbours as the sun radiates his glory, or rather the animal-sun shows the tenacity of pre-Islamic Zoroastrian solar symbolism. Legend claims the architect responsible died for his heresy, yet other 17th-century madrassah are similarly adorned—see those built by Nadir Divanbegi in Samarkand and Bukhara. The choice of colours, blue, white, yellow and green, also reflects Bukharan influence.

Shir Dor madrassah, Registan, Samarkand

■ TILLYA KARI MADRASSAH

To enclose the square in pleasing harmony, Yalangtush had his architects stretch the façades of the third madrassah to 75 metres (245 feet), built between 1646 and 1660. Smaller corner turrets are preferred to minarets, but the mosaic feast is just as lavish—sprightly solar symbols and interlacing floral motifs in similar colours to the Shir Dor. Where the other madrassah feature façade wings of shallow niches without openings, the Tillya Kari declares its religious purpose with two storeys of *hujra*, ventilated by *panjara*, carved plaster windows. The single floor of cells on the other axes emphasizes the great turquoise dome and portal on the west side. They announce the city's congregational mosque, for Tamerlane's Bibi Khanum was already in ruins and the Kukeldash had disappeared. Its magnificent interior is swathed in *kundal* style gold leaf—hence the title Tillya Kari, 'gilded'—from Koranic inscriptions and stalactites above the marble *mihrab*, to carpet-like wall panels and trompe l'oeil ceiling of delicate leaves and flowers circling to infinity.

The domed prayer galleries to either side display exhibitions of terracotta and restoration work such as the dome—never previously completed—and mosque decoration, now falling prey to Samarkand's rising water table. Like the Shir Dor, some of the *hujra* have become gift shops, whose owners may direct you to rooftop access.

Soviet restorers placed beside Tillya Kari's southeastern turret the 16th-century

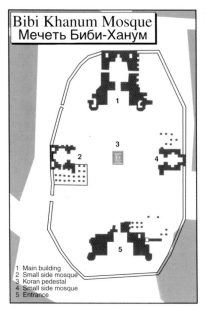

Bibi Khanum Mosque
Мечеть Биби-Ханум

1 Main building
2 Small side mosque
3 Koran pedestal
4 Small side mosque
5 Entrance

dakhma of the Uzbek Shaybanid dynasty, a burial platform topped with carved marble tombstones. Nearby is the domed, 18th-century skullcap bazaar **Chorsu** ('four ways', literally 'four waters'), constructed with materials from the rapidly disintegrating Bibi Khanum at the request of the emir of Bukhara.

BIBI KHANUM MOSQUE

Flush with plunder from the sack of Delhi in December 1398, Tamerlane vowed to create a mosque without parallel in grandeur or decor throughout the Muslim world. Despite the ravages of time on one of his foremost expressions of power, the remains still captivate the visitor by their fantastic scale and romantic legend. The best slave-artisans in the realm laboured to realize the emperor's plan. Ninety-five elephants imported from India hauled wagons laden with marble. In October 1404, Spanish ambassador Clavijo judged it "the noblest of all", yet Tamerlane, believing the portal too low, had it rebuilt at great haste: "in his litter every morning he had himself brought to the place, and he would stay there the best part of the day urging on the work. He would arrange for much meat to be cooked and brought, and then he would order them to throw portions down to the workmen in the foundations, as though one should cast bones to dogs in a pit . . . and at times he would have coins thrown to the masons when especially they worked to his satisfaction."

As at Tamerlane's palace in Shakhrisabz, courtyard activity was paramount and the *pishtak* (portals) leading onto these magnificent arenas were considered just as important as the buildings themselves. Bibi Khanum's soared over 35 metres (115 feet) around an arch 18 metres (60 feet) in diameter with flanking minarets 50 metres (165 feet) high. It led to a rectangular court (167 by 109 metres/550 by 360 feet) paved with marble, cornered by minarets and fringed by a gallery of 400 cupolas supported by 400 marble columns. North and south were side mosques with fluted domes and to the east the portal of the main sanctuary topped 40 metres (130 feet). Ornamentation was suitably magnificent—carved marble and terracotta, glazed mosaic in multiple form, blue-gold frescoes and gilt papier-mâché. The court historian declared; "The dome would have been unique but for the sky being its copy; the arch would have been singular but for the Milky Way matching it."

Yet soon after consecration of the mosque, worshippers were already dodging falling bricks. Debate continues on the reasons why—unsound foundations, ambition outpacing contemporary possibilities or simply undue haste. Later earthquakes accelerated the decay. Bukharan emirs stripped it for building supplies and in the early 19th century one melted down the gates of seven metals into coinage. Tsarist officers used the mosque as a stable and cotton market before Soviet preservation became reconstruction in 1974.

Today a rusting crane and scaffolding appear moulded to the heavy entrance pylons still dwarfing the neighbourhood. All three mosque domes have been reappeared, retiled in turquoise-blue on yellow-brown brick, the classical Samarkand contrast of sky and earth. Below the spheri-conical main dome, sheathed in smooth blue, runs a Koranic phrase so vertical as to seem geometric rather than epigraphic. Such a design complemented the upward sweep of the complex, achieved by tapering portal towers and slender corner minarets. At the centre of the courtyard stands a great lectern of grey Mongolian marble donated by Ulug Beg. Once it held the one-metre-square Osman Koran, a seventh-century treasure brought here by Tamerlane, taken to St Petersburg in 1875 (when the Russians removed the lectern from the dangerous prayer hall) and subsequently returned to Tashkent by the Bolsheviks. Legend promises children to barren women who crawl three times between the lectern's nine legs.

Opposite the entrance to Bibi Khanum is the blue-domed **Bibi Khanum Mausoleum** (1397), also named after the famous Chinese princess, Tamerlane's favourite wife, Khanum. Historians disappoint the romantic by denying her existence and naming Tamerlane's chief wife, involved in building both mosque and mausoleum, as Saray Mulk Khanum, daughter of a Mongol khan, and so advanced in age as to be unlikely to tempt the architect. Three female burials were discovered in the crypt beneath the octagonal chamber.

BAZAAR

In the shadow of Bibi Khanum lies Samarkand's main bazaar, focus of the old town. While officially it is the Siab collective farm market, and melons come by truck not camel, the bustle of people and trading is faithful to centuries-old tradition. Early mornings and Sundays offer the most activity. Beside cloth sacks of exotic spices, the famous Samarkand *non* fills barrows and pushchairs. These roundels of unleavened bread include some 20 varieties with individual pattern and name. When Tamerlane left on his first campaign, he took the best wheat and bakers the city could offer, plus salt, water and firewood, yet the *non* were not up to standard and the bakers paid with their heads. He later concluded that the superior flavour was in fact due to Samarkand's pure air and from then on ate only *non* delivered from the capital of his empire. Fruit stalls are piled high with apricots, peaches, figs and pomegranates; in autumn melons carpet much of the bazaar. Samarkand could boast over 100 kinds of grape by the tenth century—look for the popular *kishmish*, sweet and seedless. When you tire of bargaining, relax at *chaikhana* on the western perimeter.

On the southwestern edge of Afrosiab, opposite the bazaar, rears the **Khazret Khyzr Mosque**, a must for any traveller as Khyzr is the patron of wayfarers and possesses the water of life. However, he appears only to the devout who perform *namaz bamdad* prayers 40 Mondays in succession. Like Chupan Ata, this figure of legend predates Islam and this spot may have seen an ancient temple before the Arabs built the city's first mosque here. The present building, dating from the mid-19th century but reworked ever since, has an asymmetrical composition of minaret, entrance lobby, indoor and outdoor premises. From under its beautiful wooden *iwan*, enjoy the view across bazaar traffic to Bibi Khanum and east to Shah-i-Zinda.

SHAH-I-ZINDA

The holiest site in Samarkand is a necropolis of mausoleums climbing back in time from the northeast fringe of Tamerlane's capital over the old city wall and onto the southern slope of ancient Afrosiab. In the 14th and 15th centuries, it developed into an architectural testing ground whose celebration of ceramic art, unrivalled in Central Asia, makes this street of the dead perhaps the most visually stunning sight in a city of superlatives.

THE FATAL KISS

As Tamerlane devastated northern India, his favourite wife, Chinese princess Bibi Khanum, ordered the construction of a giant mosque to surprise the conqueror on his return to Samarkand. Its towering minarets and vast dome soon challenged the heavens, with just a single arch remaining unfinished. When she questioned the chief architect, a young captive from Persia, she found him so enraptured with her beauty he refused to continue until she granted him a kiss. "But all women are the same," she replied, "take one of my slave girls. Look at this dish of coloured eggs, every shade of the rainbow, yet break open the shell and all difference disappears." Her suitor brought forth two *piala* bowls, filling one with spring water, the other with white wine. "Their colour and shape are the same," he reasoned, "but one leaves me cold and the other is intoxicating." Fearful of Tamerlane's imminent return, she finally agreed to a kiss through her hand. Alas! The ardour of his passion burnt an imprint on her cheek. The arch was finished, but her master's joy at the spectacular present turned quickly to rage at this mark of infidelity. The luckless princess was cast to her death from the top of a minaret, while the architect fled up another with a squadron at his heels, sprouted wings and flew off to Mecca. From that day forward, Tamerlane commanded all the women in his empire cover their faces with veils, lest they tempt men to covet their neighbours' property.

Bibi Khanum portal and South Mosque

Legend traces its history back to 676, when Kussam-ibn-Abbas, a cousin of the Prophet Mohammed, arrived to convert Zoroastrian Sogdiana to Islam. The success of his preaching provoked a gang of fire-worshippers to behead him whilst he was at prayer. It appears the Arabs established Kussam, who probably never saw Samarkand, into the cult of Shah-i-Zinda (the Living King) by adapting a pre-Islamic mythical ruler, maybe Afrosiab himself, reigning beyond death beneath the earth. The Mongol conquest flattened the surrounding complex but left Kussam's grave alone, as Moroccan traveller ibn-Battuta reported in 1333: "The inhabitants of Samarkand come out to visit it every Sunday and Thursday night. The Tartars also come to visit it, pay vows to it and bring cows, sheep, dirhams, and dinars; all this is used for the benefit of the hospital and the blessed tomb."

The Timurid aristocracy continued the tradition of building mausoleums near the sacred site, often on earlier remains. These works display the creative wealth of the empire in surprising harmony, for no mausoleum repeats another. Their modest size permits an intimacy impossible in more grandiose projects. When American diplomat Schulyer visited the saint's grave in 1876 he heard of "a prophecy that he was to appear in 1868 to defeat the Russians; but Samarkand was occupied, and Shah Zindeh appeared not, so that his fame has of late somewhat fallen off." Worshippers still flocked to the necropolis until Soviet conversion into an anti-religious museum forced visitors to cloak their beliefs with secular trappings. Independence has restored sanctity to the street, holy men to its mosques and pilgrims to its tombs.

■ THE ENSEMBLE

In 1434–35 Ulug Beg built the grand *pishtak* (entrance portal) as a finishing touch to the southern end of Shah-i-Zinda. Behind it is the first of three *chortak*, domed transit halls, here flanked by a mosque and prayer halls, leading to the 1910 wooden *iwan* of a 19th-century mosque opposite the **Davlet Kushbegi** madrassah (1813). Halfway up the steep Staircase of Sinners ahead rise the twin blue domes of the **Qazi Zadeh Rumi** mausoleum (1420–25), the largest in the complex, though the skeleton beneath was female, perhaps Tamerlane's wet nurse, rather than his grandson Ulug Beg's astronomer-tutor. Through the second *chortak* at the top are the brick-ribbed domes of the **Emir Hussein** mausoleum (1376) to the right and opposite the **Emir Zade** (1386). The former is also called Tuglu-Tekin, after the mother of Tamerlane's general Hussein, while the latter commemorates an unknown emir's son, yet their finely worked façades bright with colour pale beside the adjacent pair of mausoleums—the Shadi Mulk Aka and the Shirin Bika Aka.

The left-hand **Shadi Mulk Aka** (1372) was the first Timurid structure in Samarkand and takes pride of place in Shah-i-Zinda. The inscription "This is a tomb in which a precious pearl has been lost" describes Tamerlane's beautiful young niece, buried and later joined by his eldest sister Turkhan Aka. The plain brickwork on its melon-shaped dome and three external façades highlights the brilliance of its lace-like portal. From the stalactite vault over the entrance to the filigree corner columns run panels of carved and glazed terracotta and majolica, exhausting the turquoise-blues and floral motifs of the age. An octagonal star crowning the tiled interior divides the dome into eight sections pierced by a teardrop medallion, a jewel in the cosmos of the cupola, for each tear conceals a sun and six planets.

Opposite, the **Shirin Bika Aka** mausoleum (1385), ascribed to another sister of Tamerlane, also boasts its original decor. The later date explains the first appearance of true mosaic tilework in Samarkand, for the conqueror had abducted craftsmen from Iran and Azerbaijan. Instead of relief carving, the entire portal is faced with incised majolica mosaic in calligraphic inscription and scrolling floral patterns. Other innovations include a tall, 16-sided drum, tiled cupola and interior murals in gold paint. *Panjera* windows with coloured glass illuminate traces of landscapes and mythical beasts suggesting

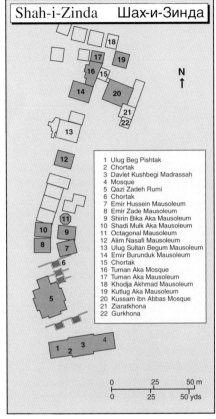

Shah-i-Zinda   Шах-и-Зинда

N ↑

1 Ulug Beg Pishtak
2 Chortak
3 Davlet Kushbegi Madrassah
4 Mosque
5 Qazi Zadeh Rumi
6 Chortak
7 Emir Hussein Mausoleum
8 Emir Zade Mausoleum
9 Shirin Bika Aka Mausoleum
10 Shadi Mulk Aka Mausoleum
11 Octagonal Mausoleum
12 Alim Nasafi Mausoleum
13 Ulug Sultan Begum Mausoleum
14 Emir Burunduk Mausoleum
15 Chortak
16 Tuman Aka Mosque
17 Tuman Aka Mausoleum
18 Khodja Akhmad Mausoleum
19 Kutlug Aka Mausoleum
20 Kussam ibn Abbas Mosque
21 Ziaratkhona
22 Gurkhona

0   25   50 m
0   25   50 yds

chinoiserie. The nearby 15th-century **octagonal mausoleum**, an open-air rotunda faced in glazed brick, remains anonymous to history, as do the next four mausoleums on the left. The second preserves the name of architect **Ustad Alim Nasafi**, creator (c.1385) of a vibrantly coloured star design tightly bound in epigraphic straps, such as "There is no creation that does not disappear; there is no friendship except in sleep". Stalactites and multicoloured majolica coat the interior. The portal fragment of the third mausoleum, named after an **Ulug Sultan Begum** (c.1385), shows stellar patterns in blue, red and gold. Last is the large, unfinished mausoleum (c.1390) attributed to Tamerlane's general **Emir Burunduk**.

The final *chortak* connects Kussam's shrine on the east with the northern courtyard. To the left is the mosque and mausoleum complex (1404–5) built by and for Tamerlane's favourite young wife **Tuman Aka**. Beneath a sky-blue dome the chamber portal carries lavish mosaic faïence resembling Shirin Bika, though the geometric designs and violet-blue are new. Calligraphy above the finely carved door reads "The tomb is a door and everybody enters it". The inner cupola paints a blue night with golden stars above delicate landscape murals. Closing the street is the **Khodja Akhmad** mausoleum (c.1350), second oldest in the ensemble and prototype for the rest—a domed cube with elaborate façade. Samarkand master Fakhri Ali signed its carved and glazed terracotta portal. The adjoining mausoleum (1361), popularly linked to Tamerlane's wife **Kutlug Aka**, reveals similar decoration and motifs, while features like the stalactite hood serve as a model for the later Shadi Mulk.

The *chortak*'s eastern door (1405), though stripped of gold, silver and ivory,

Khodja Akhmad mausoleum

retains exquisite carving framed by calligraphy welcoming the true believer to paradise, for three pilgrimages here equal one to Mecca. Just inside is a section of 11th-century minaret whose top peers out of the roof. Built in brick reminiscent of the Samanid mausoleum in Bukhara, it is Samarkand's only fully preserved pre-Mongol structure. A vaulted corridor leads to the **Kussam-ibn-Abbas** mosque (1460), a three-domed rectangle with blue-tiled *mihrab*, before the brightly tiled *ziaratkhona* (room for pilgrimage), rebuilt in 1334 on 11th-century foundations—an original wooden frieze of grapes and Arabic nestles beside the doorway and underground lie *chillyakhona* cells for 40-day fasts. Visible through a wooden trellis is the focus of every visit, the *gurkhona* (grave chamber) housing Kussam's four-tier tombstone (c.1380), a blaze of majolica richly coloured and gilded in floral styles and Koranic inscription: "Those who were killed on the way of Allah are not to be considered dead: indeed they are alive."

A walk around the adjacent cemetery provides a panorama of Shah-i-Zinda's varied cupolas and proof of the popularity of sacred proximity, from simple Muslim graves to striking Soviet memorials. Count the steps on your way down the Staircase of Sinners. If the number differs from your ascent, your penance is to climb them a further 40 times on your knees. That is the step total, a holy number for many religions, expressed locally by hair plaits and mourning schedules.

AFROSIAB HISTORY MUSEUM
From the sixth century BC to 1220 AD, Samarkand weathered the pattern of invasion and renewal from the hill-fort Afrosiab in the northeast of the modern city. The most

popular derivation of the name is from a legendary king of Turan, portrayed as treacherous yet brave and wise in Firdausi's Persian epic *Shah Nama*. Behind defensive ramparts with corridors and arrow slits, built of unbaked brick, waterproof reeds and anti-seismic juniper, lived the Sogdians, famed go-betweens of East–West commercial and cultural relations. They were lost to history until Russian archaeologists began probing the ruins in the 1880s. Their finds and those of later Soviet experts are gathered in this marble museum on Afrosiab's southeastern slopes.

The first hall contains excavation photos and relief maps showing the city's expansion south of the ruler's citadel. The exhibits and reconstructions of the following halls enable the visitor to see Afrosiab's evolution through the centuries. Early ceramics and architecture received an aesthetic boost from the Graeco-Bactrian period; other souvenirs of Alexander's visit include silver coins, swords and knives. Zoroastrianism in the Kushan period is evident from altars for fire offerings, bricks with solar symbols and ornamental ossuaries for the bones of the dead, once picked clean of flesh by birds and beasts of prey. Local cults also prospered—find terracotta statuettes of Anahita, goddess of the waters (divinity of the Amu Darya) and of fertility (she holds a seed-packed pomegranate).

Silk Road profits from the fifth century onwards are reflected in jewellery, cosmetics, coins and bone-carved chessmen, but chiefly in wall paintings on public buildings and gentry dwellings. In 1965 the royal palace yielded the museum's highlight, a series of seventh-century murals over two metres (6.5 feet) high, displayed in their original layout like an epic narration of courtly splendour. Even with the decay of time and Arab mutilation—the Prophet's prohibition on idols led the Arabs to scratch out the eyes—the paintings survive in colourful testimony to the skilled artists at the peak of Sogdian cultural activity. Leading a bridal procession from Surkhandarya to the ruler of Samarkand is a princess atop a white elephant before an entourage of maids on horseback, bearded camel-riders holding the rods of ambassadorship, a cavalcade of horsemen and a file of sacred swans. The central mural depicts the ruler himself, magnificently clad in robes and jewellery, receiving the gifts of foreign envoys: silk-bearing Chinese, long-haired Turks, Pamiri nomads and pigtailed Koreans. The last scene suggests a Chinese princess in a boat, perhaps being rowed to the royal harem, while on the shore horsemen chase a leaping leopard. The museum is open daily from 9am to 5pm, on Tashkent St, 10–15 minutes' walk north from the bazaar, or take *marshrutnoe* taxis 17 or 45 from the Hotel Samarkand or the bazaar.

The actual ruins sprawl over 300 acres of dry loess cut by ravines and excavations. Most impressive are the remains of the ruler's citadel to the northeast, overlooking the River Siab, a tributary of the Zerafshan. Thick walls extend two storeys deep into the earth, dividing the palace complex of halls, rooms and corridors. Fifteen minutes' walk from the museum, hugging the southern bank of the Siab and the northern wall of Afrosiab is the legendary **Tomb of Daniel** (Doniyor) of the lion's den, the Hebrew saint allegedly brought back from Persia by Tamerlane. Beneath five domes is a giant sarcophagus, 18 metres long, for mullahs believed that even in death Daniel grew half an inch every year (he will rise again when he reaches a certain size) and thus his grave was enlarged annually. The flow of Muslim, Jewish and Orthodox pilgrims has translated into a new road connecting Daniel to Tashkent Kuchasi (turn left before the bridge over the Siab).

ULUG BEG OBSERVATORY

In the foothills overlooking Afrosiab to the northeast are the remains of a remarkable 15th-century observatory, the crowning achievement and path to disaster of Tamerlane's grandson, astronomer-king Ulug Beg [see p170–1]. In 1908, the mystery of its whereabouts was solved after years of painstaking research by Russian archaeologist Viyatkin. Today visitors can view his discovery, the underground section of a vast meridian arc, ignored by the fanatics who destroyed the building in 1449. It was the largest 90° quadrant the world had ever seen, though it is called a sextant as only 60° were used. Deeply embedded in the rock to lessen seismic disturbance, the surviving 11-metre (36-foot) arc sweeps upwards in two marble parapets cut with minute and degree calibrations for the astrolabe that ran its length. The arc completed its radius at the top of a three-storey building. Above ground floor service rooms were arcades designed as astronomical instruments. A witness described the planetarium-like decoration: 'Inside the rooms he had painted and written the image of the nine celestial orbits and the shapes of the nine heavenly bodies, and the degrees, minutes and seconds of the epicycles; the seven planets and pictures of the fixed stars, the image of the terrestrial globe, pictures of the climes with mountains, seas and deserts . . .'

The sextant is now covered by a portal and vault at the centre of the observatory's foundations. Viyatkin's grave lies nearby, as he had requested. A **memorial museum** (open 9am–6pm daily) details the careers of Tamerlane and his grandson. Ulug Beg's scientific success, the culmination of a Central Asian tradition including al-Khorezmi, al-Beruni and Avicenna, is set alongside the political failures that cost him his life. The observatory lies a further ten minutes' walk northeast from Afrosiab Museum—the same *marshrutnoe* apply.

CHUPAN ATA SHRINE

On the hilltop around and beyond the observatory, in the pleasure garden Tamerlane had planted for his infant grandson, Ulug Beg erected a hall of Chinese porcelain and a two-storey summer palace, Chihil Sutun (Forty Pillars), a marvel of fluted, twisted stone columns. The only survivor is a shrine to Chupan Ata (Father of Shepherds), a pre-Islamic figure of legend adopted as patron both by nomads and the city of Samarkand. Built for pilgrims in the 1440s, its high, cylindrical drum still bears a Kufic inscription in coloured tiles, but the tombstone in the mausoleum chamber has no grave below it. A legend connects Chupan Ata with the arrival of Islam. When the first three Arab missionaries reached the city, they rested on this hill to determine their future journeys by cutting up and boiling a sheep. Chupan Ata put his hand in the pot and drew out the head, which gave him first choice; he chose to remain in Samarkand. Another drew the heart and decided to return to Mecca, while the third got the hindquarters and elected Baghdad. Thus Samarkand was called the head and Mecca the heart of Islam (Baghdad wisely ignores the legend). The shrine, visible from the Tashkent–Samarkand road, lies a 45-minute walk from the observatory beside a military installation, so maps omit its location and visitors are discouraged.

On the Tashkent side of the hill, bus passengers may also spot the **Zerafshan Arches** crumbling into the river downstream of the railway bridge. While popularly ascribed to Tamerlane or Abdullah Khan, another energetic builder, they probably formed part of a chain of water channelling bridges erected by the latter's ancestor Shaybani at the beginning of the 16th century.

GUR EMIR

'Should the sky disappear, the dome will replace it' enthused a poet on glimpsing the peerless cupola atop Tamerlane's mausoleum Gur Emir, the Tomb of the Ruler, a few minutes' walk from the Hotel Samarkand. Between 1400 and 1401 his favourite grandson, Mohammed Sultan, erected a madrassah and *khanagha* complex here. Mohammed's death in 1403 prompted Tamerlane to complete the ensemble with a mausoleum. Spanish envoy Clavijo reported how the ageing emir, carried to the site in late 1404, had demanded it rebuilt with added grandeur in only ten days 'under threat of a terrible forfeit to the workmen'. Although he intended burial in his home-town Shakhrisabz, Tamerlane was soon laid to rest beside his grandson and followed by descendents down to Ulug Beg, whose presence has spurred recent restoration.

Mohammed Sultan's blue-tiled portal opens onto a courtyard once cornered with minarets and flanked by madrassah and *khanagha*, but today only the foundations survive. Their absence emphasizes the simple monumentality of the Gur Emir itself, based on an octagonal chamber decorated with geometric *girikh*. Above it, belting the tall, cylindrical drum, the inscription 'God is Immortal' thunders in white Kufic script three metres (ten feet) high. Crowning the building in fluted majesty is the sky-blue dome, gently swelling to a height of over 32 metres. Across its 64 ribs spreads a skin of coloured glazed tile in a continuous lozenge pattern. Yellow and green offset turquoise-blue as light and shade play with mosaic hue. Just as spectacular is the mausoleum interior, reached via the eastern gallery added by Ulug Beg. Hexagonal onyx tiles lend the lower walls a greenish translucence, topped by Koranic inscriptions carved in marble and painted on jasper. Geometric panels shine with radiating stars, beside niches hung with stalactites moulded from papier-mâché painted blue and gold. The inner dome drips an intricate gilded coating around high lattice windows. Enclosed by a marble rail, seven marble tombstones encircle a dark-green slab 1.8

ULUG BEG, THE ASTRONOMER KING

Perhaps the heavens determined his enquiring nature by birthing Mohammed Taragai on March 22, 1394, during the vernal equinox. Tamerlane soon
recognized his grandson's talents, for he named him Ulug Beg, 'grand duke',
and took him on campaigns to the Caucasus and India. In 1404 Spanish
ambassador Clavijo attended the ten-year-old's wedding feast; five years
later, his father Shahrukh made him viceroy of Samarkand, lord of Transoxiana, while he ruled Persia from Herat. The young man's love of mathematics,
history, theology, medicine, poetry and music gave the city a reputation for
learning and culture that drew the Turkish astronomer Qazi Zadeh Rumi.
Under this tutor Ulug Beg found his favourite science.

From 1424 to 1429 he ordered the construction of an observatory without
equal in East or West, on a scale to ensure unprecedented accuracy and make
Samarkand the stargazing capital of the 15th century. With a circle of experts
Ulug Beg plotted the coordinates of 1,018 stars (the first such undertaking
since Ptolemy), devised rules for predicting eclipses and measured the stellar
year to within one minute of modern electronic calculations. Ever alert for
flattery, he accepted no observations until honest debate secured agreement.
His memory was exceptional—when a librarian reported his hunting logbook
lost, Ulug Beg instantly dictated the full list of kills, almost to perfection, as
the logbook proved when rediscovered.

Like Galileo two centuries later, he challenged religious orthodoxy with
statements of bold secularity, even heresy: "Religions dissipate like fog,
kingdoms vanish, but the works of scientists remain for eternity." Shahrukh
ruled Herat as an ideal Muslim monarch, devout and strong, whereas his
son's court revelled in the feasting, song and dance of Tamerlane's day. Ulug
Beg was supported by the official clergy and built various madrassahs and
mosques, but he failed to diffuse the growing hostility and power of Sufic
dervishes. On his father's death in 1447 events simply overtook the new head
of the troubled Timurid realm, exposing him as lettered scholar, not decisive
ruler.

Blamed for the unruly behaviour of his son Abdulaziz and defeated several
times in battle, Ulug Beg was seized in October 1449 by his other son, Abd
al-Latif. A secret court of dervishes dispatched him on a redeeming pilgrimage to Mecca. He had only reached a village outside Samarkand when he was

beheaded with Abd al-Latif's connivance. The observatory was raised to the ground as the "cemetery of forty evil spirits", yet just six months later the severed head of the parricide was displayed on his father's madrassah.

Ulug Beg's fellow scientist Ali Kushji fled to Constantinople, where the martyred ruler's star atlas was published to great acclaim throughout the Muslim world. Although these tables became known in Europe only in the mid-17th century, superceded by Tycho Brahe's discoveries around 1600, the observatory was still being imitated in India in the 18th century. In 1994, Uzbekistan proudly celebrated the 600th anniversary of the birth of Mirza (learned) Ulug Beg by restoring the beautiful buildings that survive him.

Ulug Beg Observatory

metres (6 feet) long, once the largest piece of jade in the world. Ulug Beg brought it back from Mongolia in 1425 to cover his grandfather's grave. The split is blamed on Persian invader Nadir Shah who tried to remove it in 1740. Tamerlane lies as requested at the feet of his spiritual adviser Mir Sayid Barakah. In clockwise order are Mohammed Sultan, Ulug Beg, Tamerlane's sons Shahrukh and Miranshah, and two unnamed children. The horsehair pole marks the grave of a holy man, whose remains were discovered when the mausoleum was under construction. The emblem was a common sight on the hard pilgrimage to Mecca. These tombstones are actually cenotaphs matching the layout of the real graves in the vaulted crypt below, which is usually closed to visitors.

In the courtyard stands a great marble block carved in arabesques and known as the **Kok Tash**. Historians discredit the belief that this was Tamerlane's throne, but from the 17th century it was certainly used as coronation stone by the Bukharan emirs. Prisoners of noble birth served as footstools. Stories claim the nearby bowl was Tamerlane's bath for pre-prayer ablutions or even a gauge of military loss: before battle each soldier squeezed pomegranate juice into it; once the survivors had drunk, the residue determined the number of fallen.

Buried in back yards just southeast of Gur Emir is another Timurid mausoleum, known as **Ak Serai** (White Palace), built around 1470. Still elegant even in ruin, the building's cruciform chamber, arch design, glazed mosaic and *kundal* gold leaf resembled the larger Ishrat Khana. Stalactites pepper the inner dome and some wall paintings also survive. Archaeologists removed a headless skeleton from the open crypt, possibly that of Abd al-Latif, son and murderer of Ulug Beg.

A paved path once led north from the Gur Emir to the **Rukhabad Mausoleum** off Registan Street, built by Tamerlane at the same time to honour Sheikh Burhan al-Din Sagarji. The grave of this mystic lent the mausoleum its popular name Rukhabad, "Abode of the Spirit". Legend claims a casket of the Prophet Mohammed's hair was buried with him. The classical plan—cubic chamber, octagonal drum, conical dome hairy with grass—plus lack of portal and decorless brickwork give the monument an archaistic look. Only the grand dimensions remind one of its Timurid origin.

KHODJA ABDI DARUN AND BIRUN MAUSOLEUMS

For a picturesque scene from Samarkand's Islamic revival, visit the charming shrine complex **Khodja Abdi Darun** in the southeast of the city. It is associated with the name of ninth-century Arab jurist Abd al-Mazeddin (Khodja denotes one who has made the pilgrimage to Mecca). Seljuk Sultan Sanjar erected a mausoleum for him in the 12th century, rebuilt by Ulug Beg in the 15th century behind a *khanagha* with portal and dome. In the 19th century a mosque and madrassah completed the ensemble set around a large *hauz* (pool). Four ancient *chinor* trees throw dappled light onto the water as young boys attend Koran classes and old men pray beneath the colourful wooden *iwan*. The complex stands in a cemetery where a new madrassah is under construction. Nearby are fragments of the city wall, hence the mausoleum's title Abdi Darun, (the inner *Abd*), compared to al-Mazeddin's other shrine **Abdi Birun**, (the outer *Abd*), far beyond the walls in a southern suburb. Bukharan vizier Nadir Divanbegi is credited with building the latter in 1633 and, as in his other works, the tiling borrows from earlier floral and geometric styles. Ongoing restoration is refreshing these patterns on the portal and dome above the mausoleum chamber, while the donations of the faithful rebuild the adjacent mosque complex. Tell the taxi driver Lenin Byrogi Kolkhoz (Lenin's Flag Collective Farm). To reach Abdi Darun, take bus 14 or *marshrutnoe* taxi 32, from University Blvd or Registan St, to the Andijan/Sadriddin Ayni junction.

ISHRAT KHANA MAUSOLEUM

Over the road from Abdi Darun lies the noble desolation of the Ishrat Khana, or House of Joy. Legend suggests a wife of Tamerlane built it as her tomb, but it became a pleasure palace once the ruler embraced her in awe at its beauty. The vanished opulence of its interior decor explains the joyous epithet—gold leaf, multicolour mosaic and stained glass—yet it was built as a mausoleum in 1464 by the wife of Tamerlane's great-grandson Abu Said for their favourite daughter. Over 20 tombstones of Timurid women and children occupy the crypt. Above ground the impressive portal, a survivor of the 1904 earthquake that claimed the high turquoise dome, leads to a cruciform hall once flanked by two-storey galleries. Two of four spiral staircases still permit a rooftop panorama.

KHODJA AKRAR COMPLEX

Four kilometres (2.5 miles) south of the Registan stands the ensemble built around the grave of Sheikh Khodja Akrar (1404–1490), leader of the Nakhshbandi dervish order and dominant political figure in Transoxiana following Ulug Beg's death. Acclaimed by the people as a religious ascetic and miracle-worker, he yielded great wealth and influence over Tamerlane's great-grandson Abu Said and his sons. Between 1630 and 1635 Bukharan vizier **Nadir Divanbegi** incorporated the funerary mosque built by Akrar's sons into a large madrassah. The mosaic tiling has been fully restored so the portal shines again with heretical art—the Persian heraldic emblem of lion-tigers chasing does, similar to those on the Shir Dor madrassah. Around the courtyard, faced with solar and floral motifs similar to Tillya Kari, runs a gallery of student cells, lecture halls and a domed mosque, all functioning again in the wake of independence. South of the madrassah is the ornate **Khodja Akrar mosque** (17th–20th centuries), a row of summer and winter premises featuring tiled and doubled *mihrab*, wooden *iwan* embedded with star shapes and columns finishing in *muqarna* stalactite capitals. The Sheikh's burial platform lies to the south of the *chinor*-shaded octagonal *hauz*. Reach the complex by bus 9 or *marshrutnoe* taxi 31 from the bazaar and Hotel Samarkand.

HISTORICAL MUSEUM OF UZBEK CULTURE AND ART

The monumentalist designs of the Registan dwarf this Soviet effort at its southeastern corner. Try to find time for a visit, however, as the collection, established in 1874, is extensive and well-displayed. The ground floor houses modern paintings and early Soviet posters, when anti-feudal propaganda was still conducted in Arabic. Archaeological exhibits on the first floor include vessels and ossuaries from Afrosiab, plus fully painted copies of its fragmented murals and replicas of finds from ancient Bactria, such as the Kushan Ayrtam frieze, a graceful limestone sculpture of an Indo-European culture. Among later treasures are Tamerlane's wooden coffin and the immense 19th-century Koran that replaced the Osman Koran on Bibi Khanum's lectern. Traditional crafts are set out in bazaar workshops: skullcaps, jewellery, instruments, embroideries and bizarre animal ceramics. Address: 1 Tashkent St, (tel.353958) open 9am–5pm, Tuesday 9am–3pm, closed Wednesday.

MUSEUM OF REGIONAL STUDIES

This fascinating museum deep in the old Russian town inhabits the eclectic mansion of Bukharan Jewish millionaire Abraham Kolontarov, evicted by the Bolsheviks in 1917. His synagogue houses archaeological exhibits from Palaeolithic to Timurid, before a revealing collection of 19th-century photographs—see the Registan crumbling yet bustling with traders. After tsarist colonization comes the rise of progressives like Social Democrat Morozov, whose illegal printing press published the revolutionary paper *Samarkand* from 1905–7. The highlight is a richly coloured reception hall decorated after Islamic fashion. The ganch carving on the balcony incorporates the Star of David and the Russian eagle, for Kolontarov hoped to entertain the tsar. Instead he got the Central Committee of the Uzbek Communist Party from 1925–30, forging the Sovietization of Uzbek life from this hybrid of feudal tradition.

Their period lies upstairs, closed for 'revision', though the exhibition on Samarkand's role in World War II remains open, and another hall displays dried flora and stuffed fauna. Address: 59 Sharaf Rashidov St, (tel. 330352) open 9am–5pm, Wednesday 9am–2pm, closed Thursday.

SADRIDDIN AYNI HOUSE MUSEUM

As Khamza is acclaimed the father of Soviet Uzbek literature, so Ayni (1878–1954) is his Tajik counterpart. Behind the white bust near Registan square is his Samarkand residence, restored with modest traditional furnishings, where the poet, writer and later president of Tajikistan described from personal experience the sufferings of the bad old days. Works on display in various languages include the novels *Bukharan* and *Slaves*, the inspiration of a mock-up house inside the Museum of Regional Studies. Address: 7b Registan St, (open daily 9am–5pm).

Samarkand Practical Information

TRANSPORT

■ AIR

Two planes a day arrive from Tashkent, as well as intermittent regional and international flights. The airport, renovated in 1998, is located six kilometres (four miles) north of the city centre at the end of Akademik Abdullaev St. Uzbekistan Airways ticket office (open daily 9am–8pm) is beside the Hotel Sayokh at 84 Gagarin St.

■ TRAIN

The railway station is seven kilometres (4.5 miles) to the northwest of the city at the end of Al-Biruni St near Titovar Bazaar. Expect stiff competition for seats as the daily trains east to Tashkent and west to Bukhara do not start from Samarkand. Express trains pass through only very late at night.

Dome of South Mosque, Bibi Khanum, Samarkand

■ BUS

The tarmac road to Samarkand is the most convenient option. From the long-distance bus station, to the east of the airport, there are half-hourly departures to Tashkent (3–4 hours by minibus, 5–6 hours by bus); hourly departures to Bukhara (5 hours); 2 daily to Shakhrisabz (3–4 hours); and 2 to Urgench (14 hours). Night buses to Tashkent and the Ferghana Valley wait outside the railway station. For local connections, (e.g. Urgut), use the bus station south of the Samarkand museum. Nearby on Suzangaran St are taxis to Shakhrisabz and Pendzhikent.

City Transport

A ramshackle fleet of taxis and private cars supplement an extensive network of buses, trolleybuses and *marshrutnoe* taxis. Find a city map with marked routes—useful numbers include bus 10, connecting the bus station, airport, bazaar, hotels Samarkand, Zerafshan, Registan and Sayokh; buses 21 and 52 between the bus station and the Hotel Sayor via the bazaar; trolleybuses 1 and 3 between the railway station and the Registan; *marshrutnoe* taxis 17, 19, 23 and 45 between the Hotel Samarkand and the bazaar.

Accommodation

Hotel Afrosiab, 2 Registan St (tel. (3662) 311341, fax. 311044)
Samarkand's newest hotel (formerly the Kok Serai) is Indian-built, Uzbektourism-run, and stands on the hilltop west of the Registan, once occupied by Tamerlane's Blue Palace—view the foundations in the Museum Bar. Facilities are the best in town; travel agency, air tickets, pool, sauna, gym, shop, bar and two restaurants. Adequate singles/doubles US$90/140.

Hotel Samarkand, 1 University Blvd (tel. 351864, fax. 358812)
West of the Gur Emir, beside the new Tamerlane statue staring regally towards the Registan, the Samarkand offers clean, air-con singles/doubles with bathroom for US$48–95/60–140. Postal desk, shop, gallery, restaurant and bar.

Hotel Vatan, 20 University Blvd (north of Navoi Statue) (tel. 337214)
This splendid budget option of tsarist origin houses 20 heavily draped chambers. Singles/doubles for US$20/40.

Hotel Sogdiana, 33 Usman Yusupov St (south of Navoi Statue) (old building tel. 352426, new building tel. 351476)
Once the exclusive Dacha Khokimiyat (Mayor's Office), this business complex has opened 30 standard doubles at US$60 per night.

Hotel Zerafshan, 65 Sharaf Rashidov St (tel. 333372)
Near the heart of the Russian town, the recently renovated Zerafshan has been reincarnated as one of the best value options in town at US$30 per room.

Hotel Registan, 36 Mustakillik St (tel. 335225)
A no-frills choice for up to US$6 a night.
Hotel Sayokh (formerly Turist), 85B Gagarin St (tel. 240704)
Disintegrating rooms, deep in the Russian northwest, between US$14–44.
Hotel Sayor, 148A Ulug Beg St (three bus stops north) (tel. 214916)
Bargaining buys a clean single/double from US$20–40 and the restaurant pounds with nightly belly dancing.
Furkat B&B, 32 & 105 Mullokandov St, just east of Registan (tel. 353261)
Unbeatable location, two courtyard complexes housing 50 people in singles/doubles for US$35/50.
Ikbol Opa's B&B, 3 Uvisy St (off Samarkandskayar and U. Yusupov St) (tel. 352574)
Lovely Tajik courtyard home, great hospitality, US$10-15 per bed plus breakfast.
Hotel Shark, 27 Tashkent St (opposite Afrosiab Bazaar) (tel. 356442)
Until the police evict you, rub shoulders with bazaar-goers at this collective farmers hostel, under US$1 per bed. Good *chaikhana* next door.

Food

Chaikhana on the west side of the bazaar serve pot after pot of hot green tea to accompany your choice of fruit and freshly baked *non*. On the east, head upstairs at Nasim Bobo Oksakol, 32 Tashkent St, beside the Hotel Shark on the Khazret Khyyzr crossroads. For a good, home-cooked Uzbek meal, head north onto Kairuan St, walk behind the car park, pick up a jar of beer from a mobile tanker and accept an invitation into a local house. Prices are cheap and the menu varied, from favourites like *plov*, shashlik, *laghman* and *manty*, to the chick-pea stew *nakhot shurak* and the cold soup *chalop*. Lively *chaikhana* at the south end of pedestrian Tashkent St, near Chorsu market, also offer fried fish and ice-cream, though be wary of hygiene and pickpockets. The Hotel Afrosiab has the best hotel fare. Try the Hotel Samarkand's rooftop shashlik, ice-cream and Registan/Gur Emir views. The restaurant scene is highly fluid; best bet in 1998 was the excellent Utopia, European cuisine at 62 Sharaf Rashidov, tel. 335372, opposite the Museum of Regional Studies. A few minutes' walk south at no. 86 are the cheeseburgers of Café Boris (tel. 333378).

Money & Communications

Hotels Afrosiab and Samarkand have exchange counters, or try the National Bank for Foreign Economic Activity, 7 Firdausi St (tel. 335750).

The new Business Centre Samarkand at 1 Kok Serai St offers international phone and fax plus other services, though the cheapest connections are at the 24-hour telegraph office on Pochtovaya St, south of GUM department store. A counter in the Hotel Samarkand has stamps and postcards; for parcels and telegrams, the main post office, south of GUM at 5 Pochtovaya St, is open 8am–8pm.

The Trial of the Basmachi

I'll risk it. I manage to squeeze through to the foot of the dais where three judges are gossiping as they wait for the accused to be brought. I show them my camera, tell them I have a permit to use it, and ask if I may stand near them. They hesitate a little, then acquiesce. One of them is wearing a grey mackintosh, and a white cloth cap whose peak overshadows the aquiline Armenian nose. The two others wear the Uzbek "tiubiteka", and chapans striped with green and lilac. Beyond them, on the alcove wall, are the twin portraits of Marx and Lenin. From the vault of enamelled bricks a scarlet velvet banner hangs, on which is embroidered a man standing in front of a counter and holding the scales of Justice up to an interested onlooker. On the ground, at the foot of the great ogival arch, I see the enormous head of Stalin soaring in the sky of a "Five Year Plan" photomontage.

A big carpet has been spread over the dais, in the middle of which is a table behind which the President of the Court sits: a spare man with his head jammed into a black fur bonnet, and wrapped in a black overcoat that makes him stand out sharply. On one corner of the table, covered with a length of red cotton, is a bronze bust of Lenin, the salient features, knitted brows, and bossy forehead, emphasised by the white light of the rain-washed sky.

Then come the accused, brought in under escort, some forty in all, all natives, wrapped in their padded coats, patched and variegated. One man has bare feet, and his hands are crossed over his chapan *covered with a design of roses. He sets down a kettle in front of him.*

"There's Amrista," my neighbour says, "their chief!"

"Which ?"

"The smallest of them, with the green skull cap."

Drooping shoulders, round spare skull, deep-sunken eyes, thin lips: his mantle wraps him round like a marionette, as he jokes with the crowd.

"He has been imprisoned twelve times already," says my neighbour with the splendid, casually bound turban. "He has always managed to escape, and cares nothing for the police. He said to them, 'Well, kill me; why should I worry? There are scores more ready to make my place.'"

"That big chap, near you, is a tailor by trade, but he has killed eight people already."

During the day each of them worked at his trade: goldsmith, journeyman, street sweeper, café proprietor. But at night they came together, discussed the new laws, criticised the Government, created malcontents and organised raids against the farms which had accepted Bolshevism, sabotaging wherever possible.

On the dais, the man is still reading: an endless succession of syllables that follow on each other, muffled, guttural, strangely commingled, and terminating with sudden emphasis...

A cry, a prolonged howl... The women rush forward, passing under the cord. The nineteen prisoners whose names have been read are sentenced to death. The confusion is heart-rending.

Their swords drawn, the militiamen force a passage through the khalats and turbans, and again the little trees are mown down by the turmoil, and the women, forcibly torn away, are removed to a distance from their men.

Violently buffeted about, it is impossible for me to see what is happening, and I have to use all my strength not to be swept away. Impossible to get back to my place. A little after and the crowd begins to melt. For the last time I get a glimpse of the Basmachi with bare feet, his chipped blue enamel kettle tucked under an arm: yes, to the very moment of death the human carcase demands to be fed.

In the empty courtyard the little trees miraculously stand erect once more; the chairs lie scattered about.

When I wake next morning, Lenin still mediates alone upon the table. The chairs are being piled up prepatory to being taken away. An Uzbek passes dressed in a thick black winter mantle, a white earthern teapot in his hand. His boots re-echo through the courtyard, now void and silent again.

In the newspapers I can find no slightest detail about the trial of the Basmachi.

Ella Maillart, Turkestan Solo, 1934

SHOPPING

The Hotel Afrosiab has a well-stocked souvenir shop, as does the SamArt Gallery, ten minutes' walk down the street at 21 University Blvd. For the widest choice of embroideries, ceramics and paintings, be enticed into the former student cells of all three Registan madrassah (bargaining essential). In the Shir Dor's left-hand façade find 'Afghan Bukhara Samarkand', Abdul Badghisi's remarkable project to resurrect traditional carpet-making, and visit his factory ('Fabrika Hudjum') at 12, Hudjum St east of the Registan. On pedestrian Mustakillik St are various boutiques, a book shop and nearby is the State Department Store, GUM, at 17 Ulug Beg St. The Meros Artisans' Association of Samarkand at 43A Tashkent St is the place to watch quality handicrafts being produced (see their shop inside the History Museum).

TRAVEL AGENCIES

Uzbektourism, 10 Kemal Ataturk St (tel. 335594)
Runs city tours and excursions to Shakhrisabz, Pendzhikent and Al-Bukhari Mausoleum. A good guide can bring the glories to life, so consider hiring an expert like Ludmilla Kosogorskaya.
Asia Travel International, 2nd floor, Hotel Samarkand (tel. 358676, fax. 330686)
A private company offering reasonably priced Silk Road tours from Tashkent to Khiva, camel-trekking in the Kyzyl Kum desert and homestays with Uzbek families.
Afrosiab Travel Agency, 2nd floor, Hotel Samarkand, tel./fax. 358250, e-mail: bugsy@hotsam.samuni.silk.org
Avesta-N inside Zerafshan Hotel, tel. 333373, fax. 332363
Sairam Tourism, 2 Kok Sarai, tel./fax. 351032
Optimist Travel, SBC, 1 Kok Serai St, tel. 353502, fax. 311179, e-mail: optimist@sam.silk.org

ENTERTAINMENT

Ask Uzbektourism about theatre performances at the following: Alisher Navoi Opera & Ballet Theatre, 3 Mustakillik Sq; Samarkand Puppet Theatre, 51 Mustakillik St; Khamza Green Theatre, 57 Sharaf Rashidov St, beside an open-air cinema; Philharmonic Hall, 68 Makhmud Kashgari St. Uzbek song and dance sometimes enliven the Shir Dor Madrassah. Summer evenings can also bring a *son et lumière* display to the dignified Registan itself. The Meroz Theatre offers another cultural clash: a folk costume show in the Tsarist Officers Club (58 Mustakillik St), where Bolshevik power was proclaimed in 1917. Relieve sightseeing tensions on the in/outdoor tennis courts of clubs Samarkandtrans and Dynamo (tel. 334249/335801), behind swimming lake Park Ozero, 52 Ulug Beg St, the very park where archaeologists discovered the flint tools and campfires of Palaeolithic man.

Around Samarkand

AL-BUKHARI MAUSOLEUM

After the Koran, the book most revered by Muslims is the collection of Hadith (sayings of the Prophet Mohammed) selected by, among others, Abu Abdullah Mohammed ibn Ismail Imam Al-Bukhari. Born in Bukhara in 810, the young boy showed a precocious talent for memorizing the traditions of Mohammed. At 16 he accompanied his mother and brother on the hajj pilgrimage to Mecca. They returned home without him, for Al-Bukhari was set on his chosen task of roaming the Islamic world in search of Hadith. His 97-book masterpiece took 16 years to compile from over 600,000 traditions, gathered from over 1,000 sheikhs. He would not insert a text without first washing and praying. In addition to Mohammed's life, Al-Bukhari explained the creation of heaven and hell.

Though his veracity and peerless knowledge were recognized in his lifetime, his popularity and independent spirit drew enemies in Persia that forced him back to Bukhara. Al-Bukhari wished to keep learning open to all who attended his mosque, so he refused private tuition for the Bukharan governor's children. His subsequent expulsion brought him to the village of Hartang outside Samarkand. Depressed by his treatment, the old master was heard one night in 870 to pray for God to release him. Within a month he was dead.

Centuries of research have confirmed Al-Bukhari's work as the most reliable and respected collection of Hadith. As he never attached himself to a particular school, his mausoleum attracts pilgrims from around the world. Today one sees a complex dating back at most 200 years. Ongoing renovation expands this place of worship into a centre for international scholarship. All visitors must dress conservatively (women must cover their heads) and request permission at the entrance. Reception and prayer rooms are spread around a *hauz* shaded by *chinor* trees. Through an archway beside the minaret is Al-Bukhari's tomb, beneath a blue-domed mausoleum. Throughout the complex are fine examples of Koranic carving and colourful mosaic tiling.

The mausoleum is 25 kilometres (15 miles) north of Samarkand in Khodja Ismail Kishlak. To reach it take an Uzbektourism tour, hire a taxi or enquire about pilgrim buses at the station. En route, between the Black and White rivers, is the **Machtumi Azam complex** in Dagbit village. The name is an alternative for Sheikh Khodja Mohammed Kasani, a devout follower of Bukhara's Naqshbandi, who died here in 1542 aged 81. The large mosque, now heavily restored, was first built in 1613 by Yalangtush Bahadur, the Shaybanid ruler of Samarkand, said to rest in the raised *dakhma* of marble gravestones in the cemetery behind.

URGUT

The fresh hills of Urgut offer a welcome break from the city heat of Samarkand. Fast-flowing mountain streams refresh a dense network of shady pools and *chaikhanas*, which in turn refresh thirsty bands of relaxed whitebeards. The centre is spiritually served by the restored Chubin Mosque, while the layered shelves of the valley behind conceal the sublime Chor Chinor Mosque. The cool stone chambers of the mosque are dwarfed by a grove of huge sycamore and *karagacha* trees that line the lime-green shade of a freshwater spring. The hills around Urgut beckon with rich hiking potential, but be aware that the region is rumoured to be one of Uzbekistan's main drug growing centres. Alimbank, Uzbekistan's first private bank, was set up in the sleepy town by four men, who supplied the necessary one million sum capital between them without breaking into a sweat. Urgut's Sunday and Thursday bazaar is also famed as the region's busiest, dealing mostly in modern goods, but old handicrafts are sometimes available. The Urgut Hotel offers basic accommodation at basic prices.

Sogdian ruins, Pendzhikent

Excursion to Tajikistan: Pendzhikent

Sixty-five kilometres (forty miles) east of Samarkand, up the Zerafshan River, is the town of Pendzhikent, inside the Republic of Tajikistan. Visitors come for a culture that predates political boundaries and lies at the ethnic foundation of both the Tajik and Uzbek peoples. In the fifth century **Bunjikath** (five villages), to the east of the modern town, merged from five small settlements to form an important part of the Sogdian confederacy, which included Samarkand's Afrosiab. On a loess plateau above the Zerafshan River, there developed a prosperous civilization of warriors, noblemen and artists thriving on Silk Road commerce. Yet this society of great tolerance and cultural diversity could not withstand the sword of Islam and fell to the Arabs in the eighth century.

It was lost to the world until 1933, when a shepherd on Mount Mug, about 130 kilometres (80 miles) east of Pendzhikent, discovered a willow twig basket of Sogdian manuscripts. Experts found more and the ruined castle of Divastich, the last ruler of Bunjikath. He had fled his princedom after an unsuccessful rising against the Arabs, only to be caught, executed and his castle sacked. Excavation of his city began in 1946, exciting archaeological circles, since no later development had sullied the ruins. The greatest finds were wall paintings, monumental murals expressing, even in fragmentation, a lettered culture of grand legends, court feasts and dynamic battles. In the remote Yagnob valley further east, a Sogdian dialect has survived Persian and Turkic waves, giving philologists a tenuous link to a bygone age.

SIGHTS

Framed by the Turkestan range to the north and the Zerafshan to the south, **Bunjikath** enjoys a beautiful, breezy setting high above the river. The destruction wrought over 1,200 years ago and the subsequent ravages of nature require the visitor to bring some imagination to the excavation itself. You can wander 45 acres of battered walls of clay and adobe brick, discerning houses and doorways along ancient avenues, but a guide is necessary for deeper appreciation.

If you stand at the map display, near the small museum off the main road, four sections divide as follows: the ruler's fortified citadel far to the left; the *shakhristan* (inner walled city) in front; the suburban settlement to the right, surrounded by an outer wall; and the necropolis behind you. The *shakhristan* contained two temple complexes of buildings, courtyards and closed chambers for Zoroastrian priests and the worship of fire. Paintings revealed ritual meals and dances, yet Buddhists, Manichaeans and Nestorians also thrived. Residential housing was two or three-storeyed, boasting grand reception rooms, carved doors, spiral staircases and decorated façades. Zoroastrianism dictated that a corpse could not foul the four sacred elements, i.e. be burnt (fire), buried (earth), sunk (water) or abandoned (air). Once beasts of prey had devoured the flesh, Sogdians placed the bones in ossuaries (ornamental clay boxes) and finally in vaulted tombs.

A small museum at Bunjikath offers reproductions of some of the frescoes long spirited away to the Hermitage museum in St Petersburg and original wooden columns, bowls, jewellery and ossuaries. For a more extensive collection, don't miss the **Rudaki Republican Museum of Local Lore** in Pendzhikent itself, on Ulitsa Rudaki. Rudaki is acclaimed as the father of Persian and Tajik poetry for his long, versatile and prolific career at the courts of Samarkand and Bukhara. After his death in 940, he was buried near Pendzhikent. The museum explains the excavation process, displays material finds and contains more reproductions of this last flowering of pre-Muslim Sogdian art, where cultural traditions met and thrived. They include a sequence recognized as a Sogdian version of the Iranian epic hero Rustam, celebrated two centuries later in Firdausi's *Shah Nama* (The Book of Kings). There are Chinese themes, illustrations to Indian fables and mythic tales as if by Aesop, like the goose that lays golden eggs. A painting of a young prince being mourned in a palace recalls the Central Asian cult of the seasonal death and rebirth of nature. Sogdian and Turkic mourners are shown tearing out their hair and cutting their ear lobes in grief.

Pendzhikent Practical Information

■ TRANSPORT

Uzbektourism and other travel agencies in Samarkand offer day trips to Pendzhikent. If going independently, try a private taxi from southeast of the Registan on Pendzhikent Kuchasi or a public bus from the Kaftarkhana bus station at the end of that street. This journey once took under an hour, but independence and the legacy of civil war make delays likely, particularly for public bus users, who must alight, walk across no-man's-land and wait for a Tajik bus. To reach the ancient city, take a taxi from the centre of Pendzhikent or walk half an hour asking for '*drevniy gorod*'.

■ TAJIK IMMIGRATION

While Tajikistan is, in theory, part of the 72-hour visa-free agreement, if you have an Uzbek visa, Tajik officials prefer some additional documentation. Travel agencies can get a Pendzhikent travel permit in Samarkand, which suffices for border guards and day trips, but be warned that an overnight stay may require a proper visa from the Tajik consulate in Tashkent. City police have little hesitation in deporting stray foreigners. The new Tajik rouble can be acquired in Uzbek banks and bazaars or from entrepreneurs boarding the Pendzhikent bus once it enters Tajik territory.

■ ACCOMMODATION & FOOD

The **Hotel Pendzhikent**, 22 Mirnaya Ulitsa, off Ulitsa Rudaki in the south of town, is a solid Soviet-Oriental hybrid commanding a fair view of the valley. Double rooms with air-con and bathroom are around $10 per night. A cheaper alternative, if you are allowed in, stands nearby at the junction of Rudaki and Mirnaya. Intourist's successor will someday reopen at the Hotel Pendzhikent. English speakers are unlikely, so try instead Pamiri English teacher Aziz (tel. 242468). Eating options are basically the cavernous restaurant **Dusti** (friendship), near the Lenin statue 15 minutes' walk from the hotels, or bazaar teahouses further up Ulitsa Rudaki.

The Road South

Beyond Samarkand, the M-39 continues its odyssey from Tashkent to Termez by climbing into the Zerafshan Range, a Pamiri spur, towards the Takhtakaracha Pass. Along this major Silk Road branch marched the armies of the Greats, Alexander and Tamerlane, en route to India. Soviet tanks bound for Afghanistan also came this way. In 1395 Tamerlane ordered a palace and garden built here, between his imperial capital and his birthplace Shakhrisabz, 80 kilometres (50 miles) south. The finished park was typically Timurid in extent—when a builder lost his horse, it was only discovered six months later. Nearby stone quarries fuelled the tyrant's lust for construction. The road passes the village of Amankutan, resting in the shade of white acacias, Persian walnut, pine and plane; a legacy not of Tamerlane but of General Abramov, first Russian ruler of Samarkand. Nearby, past the Mologaya Gvardia Young Pioneers Camp, is an 80-metre-(260-foot-) deep cave, the deepest in Central Asia, where Russian scientist Lev found remains of a Palaeolithic settlement, now on display in Samarkand's Museum of Regional Studies. The road winds up to the 1,675-metre (5,500-foot) pass for a fine panorama of the Kashkadarya river valley and the ancient town of Shakhrisabz.

Shakhrisabz

The home town of Central Asia's foremost conqueror was the Sogdian town of Kesh when Chinese Buddhist traveller Xuan Zang passed through in the early seventh century. After the Arab invasion, it assumed the Muslim urban pattern, but fell into semi-dereliction during the Samanid period as Bukhara and Samarkand prospered. The Mongols faced little resistance here in 1220. By 1336, the year of Tamerlane's birth, Kesh and its dependencies were ruled by the Barlas clan, Mongols of the Chaghatai khanate, turkicised by their long sojourn in the fertile Kashkadarya valley. Tamerlane used his Barlas lineage to gather a band of followers with whom he progressed from sheep-rustler to lord of the valley by the age of 25. A decade of struggle later and he was lord of Transoxiana. While Samarkand was better suited to become the jewel of his empire, Tamerlane paid great effort to strengthen and beautify Kesh. The inner town was surrounded by high walls and a deep moat, crossed by drawbridge. The family cemetery was enlarged and, towering on a scale all its own, Tamerlane's White Palace took shape. Though Tamerlane's dynasty would crumble like the buildings he commissioned, Kesh took from its golden age a new appellation, Shakhrisabz, Green Town, after the spring verdure of its many gardens.

Abdullah Khan of Bukhara destroyed much of the Timurid legacy in the late 16th century—local stories claim he was furious at losing his favourite horse from exhaustion on the approach to the city. Yet Shakhrisabz retained semi-independence from Bukhara into the 19th century, when it resisted Emir Nasrullah for over thirty years. On the ruler's surrender in 1856, Nasrullah abducted his recently married sister, only to have her executed beside his deathbed four years later. The city won a last decade of autonomy before General Abramov stormed it in 1870, to avenge an attack on a tsarist tax collector. The American diplomat Schulyer, visiting in 1873, found the city comprised two towns surrounded by one wall: Kitab and the larger Shaar, with 90 mosques and three madrassah. He noted his reception warmer than elsewhere; unlike Bukhara, slavery was never allowed and "from motives of humanity, they usually cut a man's throat before hanging him". While the Soviet era brought great change to the people and appearance of Shakhrisabz, the town preserves a rich store of history in legend and architecture and enjoys a relaxed, thoroughly Uzbek atmosphere in its mosques, teahouses and winding mud lanes of traditional homes.

Though Tamerlane built lavish mausoleums for his relatives, in Shakhrisabz he made himself but a simple crypt and, with his last breaths, requested: 'only a stone, and my name upon it.' Instead he lies beneath Samarkand's sumptuous Gur Emir and a giant slab of jade. His wish for simplicity is fulfilled only at his birthplace, Khodja Ilgar village, 13 kilometres (8 miles) south of Shakhrisabz, where a small brick kern quietly marks the entrance of the Terror of the World.

SIGHTS

■ AK SERAI PALACE

"Let he who doubt our power and munificence look upon our buildings." Like the rest of Tamerlane's most grandiose project, this inscription survives only in part, yet the ruined entrance towers stand in monumental testimony to an age of power writ large on tiled canvas. Following his capture of Kunya Urgench in 1379, Tamerlane dispatched its craftsmen to his home town to build his greatest palace, similar in structure to Samarkand's Bibi Khanum Mosque, begun twenty years later, but unparalleled in size and decoration. The name Ak-Serai (White Palace) symbolizes his noble descent, not the dominant colour, for blue, green and gold patterned the vast mosaics.

The slave artisans of Khorezm and Azerbaijan were still at work in 1404 when Spanish ambassador Clavijo passed, wide-eyed, between 65-metre-(215-foot-) high towers, flanking a portal arch 40 metres (130 feet) high and 22 metres (70 feet) wide, into a marble-paved courtyard 100 metres (330 feet) wide, enclosed by two-storeyed arcades. Beyond another ornate gateway was Tamerlane's domed reception hall, "where the walls are panelled with gold and blue tiles, and the ceiling is entirely of gold work". Clavijo's tour continued through "marvellously wrought" chambers and a banqueting hall for Tamerlane's wives to a garden of fruit trees and water pools, ideal

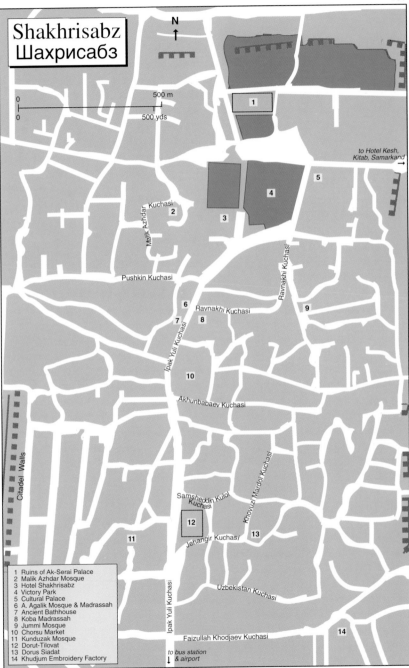

Shakhrisabz
Шахрисабз

N
↑

0 —————— 500 m
0 —————— 500 yds

to Hotel Kesh,
Kitab, Samarkand
→

1

4

5

3

2

Malik Azhdar Kuchasi

Pushkin Kuchasi

Ravnakhi Kuchasi

6
7   8

Ravnakhi Kuchasi

9

Ipak Yuli Kuchasi

10

Akhunbabaev Kuchasi

Samsheddin Kulol Kuchasi

Khovuzi Mardoi Kuchasi

12

13

11

Jehangir Kuchasi

Citadel Walls

Uzbekistan Kuchasi

Ipak Yuli Kuchasi

14

Faizullah Khodjaev Kuchasi

to bus station
& airport

1 Ruins of Ak-Serai Palace
2 Malik Azhdar Mosque
3 Hotel Shakhrisabz
4 Victory Park
5 Cultural Palace
6 A. Agalik Mosque & Madrassah
7 Ancient Bathhouse
8 Koba Madrassah
9 Jummi Mosque
10 Chorsu Market
11 Kunduzak Mosque
12 Dorut-Tilovat
13 Dorus Siadat
14 Khudjum Embroidery Factory

for summer days of mutton, horse flesh and wine. "It is the custom with the Tartars to drink their wine before eating, and they are wont to partake of it then so copiously and quaffing it at such intervals that the men soon get very drunk. No feast we were told is considered a real festival unless the guests have drunk themselves silly."

The complex extended past the modern war memorial up to the Hotel Shakhrisabz. Today visitors must conjure the whole from 38-metre- (125-foot-) high entrance towers and dazzling façades at the base of the arch. Local boys climb perilous staircases to golden tiles and swallows' nests. The band of Kufic inscription on the east flank reads "The Sultan is the shadow of Allah [on earth]", while the west abbreviates to "The Sultan is a shadow". Perhaps the craftsman intentionally avoided symmetry—prohibited by the Koran—but legend has the easily insulted Tamerlane pushing him from the top of the masterpiece he had created.

■ A WALK THROUGH SHAKHRISABZ

West of the Hotel Shakhrisabz is the 14th-century Malik Azhdar Khanagha, former home to wandering Sufic dervishes. The working mosque beneath its large brick dome (1904) served briefly as the city's Jummi Mosque for Friday prayers, until Soviet atheism made it a museum. A more popular secular role as a *chaikhana* was the fate of the Abdushukur Agalik Mosque and madrassah (1914), previously called the Khodja Mirkhamid, south along Shakhrisabz's main street. Since independence it has resumed Islamic teaching for 200 boys and girls. Nearby a 15th-century bathhouse is under renovation, to prolong over 500 years of public service. The Koba madrassah opposite is of equal age, though later use as a caravanserai determined its new life as shopping mall rather than seminary. A five-minute walk east of the madrassah brings you to Shakhrisabz's current Jummi Mosque (1915). Back on main street, approach the Chorsu (four ways) domed bazaar, a classic Silk Road structure first built on the trade crossroads of the 15th century. The road that now skirts it has dumped Lenin for the more appropriate Ipak Yuli (Silk Road). Beside the covered market is the open-air version, crowded with people, fruit and vegetables.

Dorut Tilovat

After walking ten minutes south, the Kok Gumbaz Mosque (1435-6) is obvious from the blue dome after which it is named. Tamerlane's grandson Ulug Beg built it as Shakhrisabz's Jummi Mosque and centrepiece of the madrassah Dorut Tilovat, Seat of Respect and Consideration. The impetus of his 600th anniversary in 1994 brought teams of restorers to refresh the mosaic tiling on the portal and 10-metre arch, though critics consider he matched the monumentality but not the elegance of his grandfather's works. The madrassah's porticos are also reappearing, once more to flank two surviving mausoleums from the Barlas cemetery. The earlier was constructed by Tamerlane in 1373–4 for Sheikh Shamseddin Kulyal, a Sufic leader and spiritual advisor of Tamerlane's father, Taraghay. Tradition says both men lie beneath the tombstones, shorn of tiling but retaining some onyx carving. Under the tall blue dome of the chamber and portal Ulug Beg built next door, in 1437–38, are four tombstones of his kinsmen. The Kok Tash (blue stone) on the left bears a hollow worn by parents pouring water for sick children to drink—scientists confirm the stone contains medicinal salts. Other tombstones belong to Termezi *sayyids* (those claiming descent from Mohammed's grandson, Husain); their presence explains its local name Gumbazi-Sayyidan, Dome of the Sayyids. Renovation brightened the richly painted designs on the plaster interior, now falling prey to a rising water table.

Dorus Siadat
The other Barlas ensemble, Seat of Power and Might, lies a few minutes' walk east of Dorut Tilovat. Lacking an Ulug Beg connection, restoration is more leisurely on this once imposing dynastic mausoleum. The original complex, stretching 50 by 70 (165–230 feet) metres, was on a par with Tamerlane's greatest projects. It arose on the death of his eldest and favourite son Jehangir, killed in 1375, aged only 22, falling from his horse. When another son, Umar Sheikh, joined Jehangir in 1394, Tamerlane even built himself a crypt. In 1404 Clavijo observed: "here daily by the special order of Timur the meat of twenty sheep is cooked and distributed in alms, this being done in memory of his father and of his son." Jehangir's mausoleum, crumbling yet impressive, is all that remains above ground. A tiled corner tower reveals the mausoleum as left pylon of a grand entrance facing the street, while the unusual conical dome, 27 metres high on a 16-sided drum, shows the hand of captured Khorezmian craftsmen. (Beware that visitors, like Jehangir's white tombstone, make ready targets for roosting pigeons.)

Tamerlane's crypt was rediscovered in 1943 when a child playing football fell through the ground 35 metres behind the mausoleum. Uzbektourism guides can unlock the green door leading down to a small room faced in white limestone and sandstone slabs. The marble *sunduq* (casket) waited in vain for Tamerlane, though the crypt later received two anonymous bodies. Entry to Jehangir's mosque is through the adjacent Khazreti Imam Mosque, marked by a wide silver-coloured dome. It was attached to Dorus Siadad in the 16th century, but drew its name from an eighth-century holy man, whose corpse legend says Tamerlane brought back from Baghdad. Such imported sanctity gave local mullahs weight to prevent Abdullah Khan and other purgers of the Timurid legacy from destroying the whole complex. Old men in turbans, long *maksi* boots and flowing *chupans* come through the mosque's courtyard, shady with chinor trees, to drink at the well before prayer under the high wooden *iwan*.

Khudjum Embroidery Factory
The traditional motifs of Shakhrisabz carpets and embroidery are popular throughout

Ak Serai entrance tower, Shakhrisabz

Uzbekistan. Shops around town stock brightly patterned examples, but the greatest range is on show and loom at the Khudjum Embroidery Factory, 39 Faizullah Khodjaev St, 20 minutes' walk southeast of Dar-al Tilavah. The factory name refers to the Attack (feudal traditions) movement of the 1920s, when women were encouraged to discard their veils and take their handicraft skills into the workplace. Founded in 1928 with just 16 women, Khudjum now employs 1,600 to produce carpets, Tamerlane mats, *suzaine* wall hangings, gowns and *tubeiteka*, notably the carpet skullcap embroidered with *iroki* cross-stitch.

SHAKHRISABZ PRACTICAL INFORMATION

■ TRANSPORT

There are twice-weekly flights from Tashkent to Shakhrisabz airport, seven kilometres from the town centre. The train station is four kilometres (2.5 miles) out, but most travellers arrive by road from Samarkand; either the twice daily 3- to 4-hour lowland route by public bus, skirting the mountains, or the 1- to 2-hour ride by tour bus or taxi over the Takhtakaracha Pass. Shakhrisabz taxis congregate on the road leading south of Samarkand's Museum of History and Culture and taxis for Samarkand leave from Kitab bus station. Local buses connect with the Samarkand bus terminal in Kitab, ten kilometres (six miles) to the north, with the main bus station on Ipak Yuli Street in the south of Shakhrisabz.

■ ACCOMMODATION

Hotel Shakhrisabz, 26 Ipak Yuli St (tel. (37522) 33861, fax. 35709)
Clean, air-conditioned doubles cost from $10-40 at this friendly and relaxed hotel. The restaurant is easily the best in town—good service and above average Uzbek/ Russian fare.
Hotel Kesh, 112 Amir Timur St (tel. 42031)
A cheaper, simpler alternative, three kilometres (two miles) north on the road to Kitab.
Ming Chinor, 17 kilometres (11 miles) north in the foothills of the Zerafshan, up a track 300 metres south of the 'Welcome to Kashkadarya' gateway straddling the M-39

from Samarkand. Holiday chalets, mountain breezes, sauna and indoor/outdoor swimming pools.

■ TRAVEL AGENCIES

Uzbektourism, at the Hotel Shakhrisabz, offer standard city tours and wine-tasting trips.

Sogdiana Adventure Tourism Club, at 9 Ipak Yuli St (tel./fax. 41852), not far from the Hotel Kesh, produce a splendid map of the little-known attractions of southeastern Uzbekistan. To explore them, join one of the Club's expeditions: horse-riding along the Hissar range; trekking up the holy mountain of Khazreti Sultan; caving in the vast grotto that hid Timur and his robber band; heli-fishing in glacial lakes; hunting for rock paintings and Jurassic tracks.

AROUND SHAKHRISABZ

■ KHODJA OLIM KHAN ENSEMBLE

A beautiful setting on the windswept foothills of the Zerafshan range, overlooking the Kashkadarya valley across to the Hissar and Turkestan ranges, makes this the most worthwhile side trip from Shakhrisabz. Amid an overgrown cemetery stands a grand, plain brick *khanagha*, a hostel for Sufic dervishes, topped by a broad dome shining with steel protection. The burial here of holy man Khodja Olim Khan (1510–1600) sanctified the building of the *khanagha*. Its portal faces his *dakhma*, a raised platform bearing the tombstones of Khodja and his son. White flags and bells hanging from wooden frames mark the deep reverence in which they are held. A five-minute walk beyond the *dakhma* brings one to a hilltop dotted with twelve giant wells—locals claim they appeared at a mere touch from Khodja's walking stick. To reach the ensemble by public transport, take a bus to Kitab and transfer to any Sivas bus for 12 kilometres (seven miles). From the Khodja Olim Khan stop, opposite a mourning-mother war memorial, walk for 20 minutes uphill through a quiet Uzbek village.

Khazreti Imam mosque, Shakhrisabz

■ KATTA LANGAR

High up the Langar valley, withdrawn into the protective foothills of the Hissar range and isolated by the Langar Gorge, lies one of the few towns in Uzbekistan which the long arm of Soviet transformation never quite reached. The traditional town of Langar spills down the hillside in horizontals of clay brick, its fall broken only by its remarkable **Friday Mosque**. The plain exterior of the mosque (1520, 1562, restored 1807) masks an inner world of blue, black and gold mosaic tilework created by Samarkandi and Bukharan masters. Flowered grills of alabaster punctuate a ceiling band of tiled calligraphy.

Perched on a mountain spur, overshadowing the town, stretches the high Timurid drum of the **Langar Ata Mazar**. The mausoleum marks the beautiful tomb of the most famous local sheikh, Mohammed Sadik (d.1545), his father Abul Hasan, son Hudaykel and an unknown Timurid noble, thought to be the seven year old daughter of Tamerlane.

Buses run from the town of Kamashi to Kyzyl Kishlak, from where Katta Langar lies a six-kilometre (four-mile) hitchhike away and buses return to Kamashi in the afternoon. By car, follow the Langar River east from the junction at Kyzyl Tepe. From Katta Langar the road continues into the mountains to the dinosaur footprints and the Cave of Tamerlane at remote Tashkurgan.

Karshi

Strategically situated on the main 11-day trade route from Balkh to Bukhara, Karshi has transcended previous incarnations as the Sogdian city of Nakhshab, the Arab city of Nasaf and the second city of the Bukharan emirate to become the innocuous capital of a neglected soviet oblast.

Karshi ('palace' in Mongolian) gets its modern name from the twin palaces built here in the 1320s by the Chagatai Khans Kabak and Kazanby on the site of Genghis Khan's old summer pastures. In 1364 another Mongol, Tamerlane, wintered in Karshi and ordered the construction of a citadel and moat in what is now the southern part of Karshi. It was into this citadel that most of the town later fled, under siege from the successive campaigns of Shaybani and Abdullah Khan.

The 18th century saw the city's importance grow as Shakhrisabsz declined and before long Karshi was to become the second city of the Bukharan emirate and the begship of the emir's heir designate. By this time the double set of city walls had expanded to encompass four madrassahs, ten caravanserais, public baths, gardens, a prison and even a secret tunnel which, in times of nomadic incursions or domestic revolt, would provide the palace of the beg with an escape route to the outside world. The city even had the occasional pane of glass—the truest indicator of ostentatious wealth.

In 1868 the Russians annexed the fertile Zerafshan Valley, turning the Kashgar Darya valley around Karshi into the main granary for the entire emirate and, in 1873, the main document that relegated Bukhara to a dependency of Russia was signed in the city, much to the gall of the emir's son, Abdul Malik, who led a brief rebellion here before fleeing to Peshawar.

SIGHTS

At the top of the bazaar square and within earshot of its endless thumping pop music is the attractive, turn-of-the-century Bekmir or **Rabiya Madrassah**. As a once again functioning female madrassah, curious visitors will most probably be politely shooed away by the embarrassed eyes of a black-veiled beauty. Four hundred yards behind the Rabiya on Nasaf St, the **Khoja Abdul Aziz Madrassah** is the largest in town and now houses the obligatory **Regional Museum**. The right half of the museum is crammed with endless black-and-white photographs of heroic Soviet labour construction, but the left has some interesting exhibits on the history of the Bukharan emirate, including a photograph of the emir's personal army on parade. The army enjoyed a wide repertoire of marching songs, one of which was entitled 'Our general is a brave man and does not fear the Bolsheviks'.

A story runs that before a battle the emir's troops would dumbfound the enemy by falling to the ground for several seconds, waving their legs wildly in the air, as if in some mass epileptic fit, before resuming the fight. This strange custom apparently dates back to an early massacre by the Russian forces which took place on the banks of a river. At the end of the rout the Russian troops proceeded to lay on the ground to shake the water out of their knee length boots. The astonished Bukharans naturally attributed some dastardly magic to the victors' bizarre convulsions and the manoeuvre passed swiftly into official military training.

One hundred yards from the museum is the crumbling **Khoja Kurban Madrassah**. From here cross to the far side of the bazaar, past the 16th century baths on the right, to the **Kurgancha Mosque**, one of the best attended on Fridays with turbaned believers filing past its deep *hauz* and intricately carved pillars. Also hidden in the maze of old town alleys lurk the revived Chakar local mosque and the now defunct, miniature 18th-century **Sharafbai Madrassah** (Ramazan Ibragimov St).

A five-minute walk east of the bazaar along Nasaf St brings you to the **Kok Gumbaz Mosque**, a pale reflection of its better restored architectural forefather in Shakhrisabz. This very Timurid-looking *namazgokh* mosque was actually built at the end of the 16th century as part of a whole series of architectural buildings given impetus by the great Abdullah Khan, which include the still-standing public baths and bridge over the Kashkadarya. The faithful originally spilled out of side chambers into the courtyard in front of the mosque, but now only the main hall and right hand chamber are used for weekly Friday *namaz* prayer.

At the other end of Karshi a monolithic ensemble of monumental squares, anonymous Orwellian ministry buildings and bizarre and striking relics of the soviet era

Miniature of the birth of Ulug Beg

comprise the alter ego of this rather schizophrenic town. For the bizarre, try the Soviet fighter plane stuck on a metal stand as if about to blast off into space. But for the truly monumental, pay homage to what is, without doubt, Central Asia's most epic **World War II Memorial**. A series of plaques along Lomonosov St remember the major Soviet casualties of the war (Leningrad, Volgograd, Sevastapol etc.) and lead up via a 100-metre (330-foot) walkway to an eternal flame, above which stands a 30-metre (100-foot) tower topped with a huge red star. On the inside of the tower a series of stained glass windows depict Soviet soldiers leaving their mothers and wives as old Uzbek men and young children harvest wheat and cotton to support the front line.

KARSHI PRACTICAL INFORMATION

■ TRANSPORT
Karshi has excellent bus connections to Bukhara (3 hours), Shakhrisabsz (2 hours), Termez (5 hours) and almost everywhere else in Uzbekistan.

■ ACCOMMODATION
Hotel Tong (formerly the Hotel Zarai), 245 Uzbekistan St (tel. (37522) 51903).
Marginally the best hotel in town but still relatively basic, the Tong hums with resident East European businessmen who hustle in the nearby bazaar. Single room with hot shower $20. Uzbektourism management. The restaurant serves some of the better food in town.
Hotel Karshi, Mustikallik Prospekt (formerly Karl Marx) (tel. 32849)
The former Hotel Leningrad, this huge Soviet block has erratic water and negligible service but, as it is mostly empty, it is at least quiet. Single room $20 or perhaps $2 in sum.
Dom Dikhanlaya, Nasaf St
The cheapest place in town, this hostel also has the best location opposite the main bazaar. Lodgings are basic and dormitory style with outside toilets. Less than $1.

AROUND KARSHI

The area around Karshi is dense in holy sites and littered with archaeological settlements, any number of which can be combined into an enjoyable half or full day exploring a very untouristed part of rural Uzbekistan. Friday is a good day to visit.

Halfway between Karshi and Kasan, in the village of Fudina (or Pudina), lies the functioning mosque, tomb complex, *ziaratkhanah* and *takharatkhanah* (place for ablutions) of the **Khasim Ata Ensemble**. The complex originally grew up around the tomb of the 11th-century holy man Khazreti Khusam Ata and was subsequently added to by the 13th- and 14th-century graves of several Mongol noblemen, including Ogotai, Sagatai and Masrati Khan, and 19th-century Uzbek tombs to form an architectural time span of about one thousand years, linking the Samanid era to the khanate. Decoration is now concentrated in one tile of ornate carved terracotta inscription, but jigsaw pieces to the past in the form of shards of coloured, glazed tiles lie in neglected piles at the entrance. An old tree to the left of the mosque stands graffitied with coloured rags and pilgrims add a contemporary feel to a place so deeply rooted in the past.

A few kilometres nearer to Karshi, the unflinching road and railway lines suddenly come crashing through the walls of the **Erkurgan Fortress**, throwing the fourth and 20th centuries together in a perfect example of the unstoppable confidence of Soviet technology. Erkurgan was a Hephalite and Sogdian city fortress built around a large fire-worshipping temple complex, but today only the double set of city walls and corner bastions stand to forcibly remind one of the rigours of medieval life, turned in against desert storms and nomadic raids.

The town of Kasbi, located approximately thirty kilometres (20 miles) southeast of Karshi, gets its name from the nearby medieval city of Kasba. At the time of the Arab conquest the town lay on the trade route to Bukhara and was easily the largest in the region, but past glory is today only dimly reflected in the **Sultan Mir Haidor architectural complex**. The complex is centred upon a local religious dynasty of sayyids, the Mir Haidor, and spans the 11th to 16th centuries. The façade of the complex is made up of the arches of an open-air summer mosque and a small minaret made from the bricks of ruined Kasba. The heart of the complex consists of three 14th- and 15th-century mausoleums grouped around two northern courtyards. The fine collection of carved headstones is covered in a web of spellbindingly intricate calligraphy and constitutes some of the most beautiful work in Central Asia. The complex is set in the post-apocalyptic wasteland that was once Kasba and is attended by a merry band of *aksakal,* to be found perpetually drinking tea among the flies.

Two hundred metres from the complex is an ancient brick *sardoba,* once as regular a sight as caravanserais along the trade routes and desert settlements of Central Asia. Also visible one or two kilometres from the complex is the 400 year-old *namazgokh* mosque which marks the suburbs of the old town.

Other less active holy sites in the region include the **Imam Mohammed Sadir Islam Kabristani mazaar and mosque** on the road to Kasbi near the village of Khoja Kharlik. Set in a heather-filled cemetery, the crumbling 4-domed mosque has a very exotic, almost Indian air and the mausoleum is attended by a mass of white flags and melted candles. The **Khazrati Sultan mazaar** in Beshkent itself barely warrants a visit, but the nearby, formerly innocuous, statue of Lenin has now gained some novelty value as one of the few such statues left standing on Uzbek soil.

■ IRON GATES

The road to Afghanistan passes the 19th-century Afghanabat Madrassah and 18th-century Gulshan mosque and minaret (1730) of the former beglick of Guzar and rises through the southern spurs of the Hissar mountain range, past the traditional mountain *kishlaks* of Dekhanabad and Gumbulak, into the narrow valley of the Buzgala Defile. For over two millenniums this narrow gorge has funnelled, channelled, taxed and regulated the flow of traffic through the strategic gateway of the Timur Darvaza or 'Iron Gates', assuring its masters a steady flow of revenue, security and prosperity.

The pass gets its name from the double set of wooden doors, strengthened by iron and furnished with bells, that the Buddhist monk Xuan Zang saw on his journey to Termez in 629 AD. References to the gates are, however, shrouded in an air of ambiguity due to the existence of another set of iron gates in the Caucasus (also located in a village called Derbent), but it was a confusion happily tolerated by Tamerlane when the two gates, spaced some 1,500 miles apart, grew to symbolize the might of his empire, lauding him with the epithet 'master of all between the iron gates'. By the time of Clavijo's visit in 1404 the original gates had long since gone, but the pass was still strictly controlled and complemented the Oxus crossing at Termez to form a double system of immigration and taxation control.

Under the centralized strength of Tamerlane's empire the pass linked the two halves of empire, but in times of greater fragmentation the mountain road east marked a transition from Sogdian to Bactrian or a gradual descent into the lawlessness and semi-autonomy of eastern Bukhara.

Derbent, Baisun and Sairob

Pass through the Iron Gates and one approaches a triangle of secluded mountain villages offering access to the isolated mountains and river gorges beyond. The geology of the area lies open for all to see and is ripe for exploration. **Derbent** is the first of the three towns to be reached from the west and nestles at the foot of a large cliff just off the main M-39. The town marks the gateway to the Machai River gorge and cave complexes, the *archa* juniper forests and remote Tajik valleys beyond. There are even said to be mummified bear remains in the Berloga caves. Both Uzbektourism and Sogdiana Travel are able to organize trips to this remote region.

Described as a Wild West town with teahouses, **Baisun** is the largest settlement in the triangle and the only one to boast an official hotel. The main attractions are again natural and the Gur Gur Ata massif and Ketmanchapt Mountains, which tower above the town, attract walkers from the whole oblast.

For the day-tripper, however, the most picturesque of the three is the village of **Sairob**. The small village spills over the narrow valley, sheltered to the west by a deeply etched mountain ridge and to the east by a splintered spine of rock which curls protectively around the town in a giant paternal embrace. Layers of stone cottages tumble down from the hills, separated by bands of deep, earthy reds and whitewashed walls to make the area reminiscent both physically and culturally of Turkey's mountain hinterland. The two *chinor* trees in the centre of town are also its greatest pride and joy, each said to be over 1,000 years old.

From Sairob the M-39 follows ancient paths down to Shirabad and the Oxus.

PRACTICAL INFORMATION

The only hotel in the region is the **Gastinitsa Dustlik** in Baisun and is worth avoiding if possible. If you get stuck in Sairob late at night, the local Russian-speaking school-teacher Tura Dijumakuluv may be able to help.

All buses that run west from Termez (ie to Samarkand, Tashkent, Bukhara) pass through Sairob and the turn off to Derbent. Buses to Baisun go most regularly from Termez and can be caught from the turn off just to the south of Sairob. Some taxis ply the route, but (paid) hitchhiking is the most convenient mode of transport.

Shirabad

The town of Shirabad marks the last echoes of the fading Gissar range as the hills finally cede to the hot and arid plains of the southern border. The Kungrat emir, Shir Ali, is said to have founded the modern town and its royal connection was continued by many subsequent emirs of Bukhara, who were wont to use the local beg's palace as a summer residence. Even the last emir, Alim Khan, stopped here to catch his breath as he fled the Bolsheviks en route to Afghanistan in 1920. Today, however, all that remains is the stepped *kurgan* upon which the fortress once stood.

SIGHTS

The two pilgrimage sites of Hazrati Akhtam Mara and Suleiman Ata ride the crest of the Shirabad ridge, which overshadows the town. Of greater historical and religious importance, however, is the **Mausoleum of Khoja Abu Isa Mohammed Imam Terme-zi**, one of the seven collectors of the Hadiths, or Traditions, situated some six kilometres (4 miles) out of town on the road to Denau. Originally from Merv, Isa divided his youth between Shirabad and the religious centre of Termez before embarking on a 30-year itinerant search for wisdom that would take him to Khorasan, Merv and Medina. He eventually returned to found a madrassah in Shirabad and to collate the many Hadiths that he had collected in the course of his wanderings. The Hadith is a varied collection of sayings attributed to the Prophet Mohammed which form the second holiest book of Islam, after the Koran.

The rather austere 20-metre (65-foot) long building consists of two prayer chambers and the tomb itself and is attended by a gracious and timeless imam.

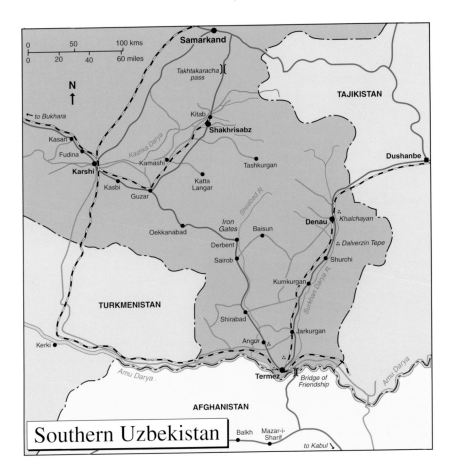

Southern Uzbekistan

Termez

Throughout its illustrious and epic history, Termez has played the role of political and cultural chameleon, switching roles, religions, allegiances and even locations with the consummate ease of a circus performer. Gather its faded stars under one roof and sit back and enjoy as Buddhist monks discuss philosophy with Mongol invaders, Greek garrison guards ogle Soviet tanks and Bactrian Silk Road traders talk shop with modern Afghan entrepreneurs. Bridges become borders which become bridges again, heartlands fade to backwaters and cosmopolitan Silk Road junctions shrivel into a forgotten corner of a neglected republic. Termez is nothing but a survivor.

THE SILK ROAD

It is said that silk was first discovered by the Chinese when the wife of the Yellow Emperor watched a silk cocoon fall from a mulberry tree into her cup and unravel in the hot tea before her very eyes. Years later a Chinese princess, unable to face married life in the barbarian lands of Turkestan without one concession to civilization, hid quantities of silkworms in her extravagant coiffure and China's secret was led innocuously out through the Jade Gates. The 'marvellous vegetable' was traded to the Parthians for an ostrich egg and soon the sensuous Romans, captivated by their new 'glass' togas, were clamouring for the quality that only China could provide. The Silk Road was born.

Traversing the Silk Road has never been easy. The physical dangers of crossing the world's greatest deserts and mountains—thirst, heat, cold, altitude sickness, avalanches, blizzards, snow blindness—were rivalled only by the brigands, thieves and slave raiders encountered en route. Merchants would thus gather safety in numbers, often travelling at night to avoid the heat, in caravans of up to 1,000 camels. Remote caravanserais dotted the route at about 25-kilometre intervals, the average daily distance travelled, and offered living quarters under the stars, stables for the animals and secure storage for valuable cargo. Larger city caravanserais grew to become luxuriant points of transit where goods changed hands, fresh animals were procured and guides, mercenaries and resident craftsmen were hired.

Yet the very phrase 'Silk Road' is a misnomer (albeit an admirably romantic one) coined in the 19th century by the German geographer and uncle to the Red Baron, Ferdinand von Richthofen. There was never a single, static Silk Road, but rather a network of routes cast over the continent which evolved over the centuries. Central Asia hosted the key stretch of this long haul and the language of its omnipresent Sogdian middlemen soon became the lingua franca of the commercial world. The two main routes came from Kashgar (for nearby was the Stone Tower, scene of the greatest transfer of goods in the region) via the Ferghana Valley or Balkh to Samarkand or alternatively skirted the northern Tian Shan through the Dzungarian Gap to Tashkent. Routes westwards converged on Bukhara or Merv and then split west to Persia and the Mediterranean, south to Kabul and India or north to Gurganj and the Volga. Routes were carefully chosen allowing for the time of year, snowfall, conditions of passes, political considerations and the regional differences in rates of tax, piracy or both. The fragile threads of the Silk Road were always changing, waxing and waning at the mercy of history. Roles changed as well as routes, as traders were joined by a motley crew of diplomats, invaders, refugees, pilgrims and proselytizers en route to outrageous new lands.

The eponymous silk was in reality a mere fraction of the goods carried on the Silk Road. Gold, textiles, saffron, cucumbers, pomegranates, peaches, melons, wine and coloured glass were all carried into China along with the most alluring exotica—golden peaches from Samarkand, blood-sweating heavenly horses from Ferghana, dwarf jugglers from Persia and the prized, magical 'camel bird' (ostrich). From the East came not only ceramics, cinnamon, rhubarb and bronze but also paper, printing and gunpowder, as secrets were swapped alongside goods.

For the Silk Road's greatest achievements transcended mere trade. Like an ancient information highway, it enabled men of different cultures to meet in a fertile exchange of ideas and philosophy and then to carry these new art forms and religious doctrines back home. Manichaeism and Nestorian Christianity both fled along the Silk Road to claim sanctuary in China, but Buddhism took the firmest root, flourishing like a distant echo as it died in the heartlands of India. Art forms were no different. Indian art merged with Greek and Persian to form Gandaharan; a synthesis of styles which consequently spread westwards under the Kushans to confront Roman influences and eastwards to China to become the Serindian art of Chinese Turkestan.

By the 13th century, however, the Silk Road that had been forged by the Han and that had crescendoed under the Tang, had been sentenced to death by the Ming as China retreated behind its Great Wall. Its *raison d'être*, silk, was now in full production in Europe, secreted to Byzantium in the staff of a Nestorian monk, and a maritime spice route had shown itself cost-effective, wiping out as it did the numerous middle-men whose rapaciousness had made Silk Road goods so expensive. The Silk Road withered to leave entire cities marooned in the desert sands, as Central Asia was transformed from the shop window of Asia into an isolated and neglected wasteland.

The Silk Road connected the two ends of the known world, China and Rome, at a time when each was only a faint glimmer in the imagination of the other. Now, in an age when direct flights from Rome to Beijing take a magical ten hours, a Silk Road renaissance is underway and a near-complete route is open again. An Iron Road leads from Moscow to Samarkand, Urumqi and Beijing and final connections to Iran and beyond are imminent.

For the last 80 years Termez has been one of the furthest and most sensitively sealed outposts of the Soviet empire, enforcing an unnatural religious cutoff point between Islam and atheism. The modern traveller who comes to taste the sheer variety of its Islamic and especially pre-Islamic sights, the wealth of its local history and the *frisson* of excitement that comes from such proximity to the Oxus and Afghan border can rest assured that he is one of the first.

HISTORY

As with half the cities of Central Asia, the founding of the ancient city of Termez is traditionally attributed to the ubiquitous Alexander the Great. Greek troops did indeed conquer this former Achaemenid satrapy in 330-327 BC and soon set about building a line of fortresses to defend their distant and tenuous outposts, but there is little hard evidence to show that Alexander himself ever set foot in Termez. The settlement's more prosaic origins are more likely to lie instead on the banks of the Oxus, where a large island and shallows offered a convenient crossing of the mile-wide river. After 306 BC Termez became part of the Selucid empire which, some fifty years later, evolved into the elusive Graeco-Bactrian kingdom, a territory now thought to have straddled the Oxus with its capital at Balkh. The kingdom, which was to last for more than a century, was underpinned by the material and spiritual culture of Hellenism. The ensuing centuries were to see Termez thrive at the crossroads of an intense material, spiritual and artistic melange, where the afterglow of Mediterranean classicism collided with the nomadic Turkic and the Buddhist Indian worlds to shape a new Bactrian identity which would reach a peak under the Kushan empire. The subsequent Bactrian collapse was the first such event in history to be recorded in both Greek and Chinese histories; eloquent testament to the extent to which Bactria had managed to fuse the Eastern and Western worlds. The succeeding Kushan ruled an empire that stretched from Delhi to Khorezm, an empire every bit as powerful as its contemporaries in Rome, Parthia and Xi'an, but which is today still largely anonymous. Under the unified empire, the former suicide routes leading from the Indus to the Oxus began to fuel a boom in the new Silk Road traffic between Sogdiana, Balkh and India and Tarmita (Termez) provided a perfectly placed point of transit. Indian trade brought Gandaharan art and the errant threads of Buddhism, both of which found fertile ground in Termez under the state sponsorship of King Kanishka I in the second half of second century. When the Chinese monk Xuan Zang arrived in Tarmita in 679 AD he counted over 12 monasteries within the 20-li (11-kilometre/seven-mile) city walls alone, housing some 1,100 monks.

By the seventh century, however, Buddhism was in decline and the political landscape looked altogether different. The golden age of Bactria had fractured into 27 feudal and feuding principalities, known collectively as Tokharistan, who paid nominal lip service to a succession of shadowy nomads: the Tokhari, the Hephalite

Hakkim al Termezi mausoleum, Termez

White Huns, Khidarites and Turks. Any attempt at controlling this maze of semi-independent, clan-based states was akin to grabbing handfuls of sand, only to watch them slip between one's fingers; a pattern that would endure the centuries, only to find itself reinterpreted in the recent conflicts in Afghanistan and Tajikistan. The more powerful of these local principalities were Chaghanian (modern day Denau), Gupthan (modern day Shirabad) and, most importantly, the Termezshah, whose strong fortress soon became the a facto capital of the region.

By the mid-seventh century the first rumblings of the Arab invasion began to be felt in Termez. In 689 the breakaway Arab commander Musa ibn Khazim conquered Termez and ruled as king for 15 years. But it was to be only a question of time before he was brought back into line and in 704 the Abassid leader Uthman converged on the island opposite Termez with a force of over 15,000 men. The inevitable conquest marked the integration of Termez with the rest of Transoxiana.

The tenth and 11th centuries saw another high point in the development of Termez, this time under the nominal rule of the Bukharan Samanids and local rule of the Taharid and Mukhtajid local dynasties. Deep in the landlocked and mountainous heart of a continent, the rather incongruous port of Termez had reached its zenith. Boats were built, exported and employed up and down the Oxus as far as Gurganj in Khorezm. Rapid urbanization supplied a new Friday Mosque, a large bazaar and the

remarkably ornate palace of the Termez shah, all strongly fortified within two city walls. The Sultan Saodat complex was commissioned and the Hakkim Al Termezi Mausoleum at the time ranked as one of the greatest architectural monuments in the Islamic world, all of which served to confirm Termez's position as the region's spiritual and artistic centre.

The 12th century was a bewildering time for Termez. Karakhanids were replaced by Seljuk Turks, Afghan Ghaznavids, obscure Karluks, even more ignominious Gurids and finally the Khorezmshah, as nomad empires toppled like dominoes. The latter briefly thrust Termez into the Islamic spotlight when Khorezmshah Mohammed proclaimed a local sayyid, Allah al Mulk, the true descendent of Mohammed in the latest move in his theological and political struggle with the Abassid rulers in Baghdad. The bemused Termezi thus suddenly found himself temporary caliph of the entire Islamic world before slipping back into ignominity. The Khorezmshah's ambitions, however, were spread too thinly and in 1220 the Mongols took Termez after an 11-day siege and proceeded to raze the city to dust. A census was taken, the population divided up amongst the Mongol soldiers and massacred. Historians tell the story of a woman who pleaded for mercy, saying that she had swallowed a valuable pearl and would give it the soldier in question. The impatient Mongol merely ripped open her stomach to find the pearl and the order was given to follow suite with all the other corpses. Half of the city walls were hurled into the depths of the Oxus and the restless Genghis summoned his sons to the carnage to plan the next assault in Khorezm. After the Mongol destruction, the curtain closed on Old Termez. The city was marginally rebuilt here later in the 15th century, but the barely beating heart of the city was transplanted to the area around the Sultan Saodat Complex.

■ NEW TERMEZ

In 1333 the Arab traveller ibn-Battuta visited new Termez and the burgeoning city he saw had a palace, canal, prison, city wall with nine gates and a famous river market where Termez's famous soaps, perfume, clothes and metalwork were in high demand. Soap however seemed destined for export only, for Battuta describes how the local women washed their hair only in sour milk, kept in plentiful supply in all good Termez bathhouses. Tamerlane rested here in 1399 on his Indian campaign and, not content with control of the Iron Gates, he set up a series of pontoons across the Oxus to control and tax the human and mercantile traffic entering and exiting his glittering capital. The city's reconstruction continued apace, so much so that in 1404 the Spanish envoy Clavijo complained that the city was so noisy that it could be heard in Balkh 100 kilometres (60 miles) away.

Timurid squabbling turned Termez into a strategic front line between the two rival camps of Tamerlane's nephew Khalil Sultan at Samarkand and Shahrukh at Balkh and in 1449 Ulug Beg and his son Abdullatif found themselves glaring at each other from opposite sides of the Oxus, with no love lost in the waters in between. The next few centuries saw an endless series of local power struggles that even saw the fugitive descendents of Babur return as brief invaders in 1646 and the town repeatedly destroyed. During this period of weakness, Balkh and Mazar-i-Sharif seceded from the emirate of Bukhara.

By the 19th century the third town of Termez grew up around the village of Patta Hissar. The shift in location indicated not only shift in focus but also a shift in the balance of political power as Termez gradually became the Russian border gate of the Great Game. For it was here, as the British and Russian empires crept perilously close to each other, that the Russians found the permanent, defendable border for which it had been searching so long. By 1888 regular Russian steamers and military boats plied the river from the naval base at Chardzhou to the newly built Russian fortress at Patta Hissar and ten years later the region was formally ceded by the Bukharan emirate. In 1914 the first electric light was switched on in Termez and two years later the railway arrived finally to tie Termez irrevocably to Tashkent.

Little is known about Soviet Termez and Fitzroy Maclean, in 1937, was one of only very few travellers to penetrate this far. He had wanted to cross the Oxus into Afghanistan, as so many illustrious travellers had done before him, but when cryptically informed by the Soviets that the border was, well, not exactly closed, just 'not working', and furthermore that he would find it considerably more comfortable to return several thousand kilometres overland to Moscow and then fly to Kabul, rather than attempt the one kilometre wide river crossing, Maclean knew that he was in for a tough trip. The first two boats he unearthed lay beyond redemption and the third "which rejoiced in the name of *The Seventeenth Party Congress*, though, to judge by her antiquated appearance, she must have been built long before the Communist Party was ever heard of, was handicapped by the absence of an engine or motor of any kind". Not the type of man to let such mere details perturb him, Maclean commandeered the third and set off across the Oxus with a captain who claimed to be learning English from a book entitled *London From The Top of an Omnibus:*

"For purposes of conversation, however, his knowledge of the English language seemed to be limited to the one cryptic expression: "Very well by us" of which he was inordinately proud, and it was to repeated shouts of "Very well by us!", heartily reciprocated by myself, that some time later I embarked on *The Seventeenth Party Congress*".

The Soviet boat managed the Oxus crossing admirably and, after the crew were counted and recounted in case any had escaped, "the remarkable craft started off stern first for the Soviet Union as if the whole capitalist world was infected with the plague."

Modern Termez is Uzbekistan's only international border crossing and, as Russia's de facto border, still has a relatively high proportion of fair-haired slavs on its streets.

Train Party

My intention had been to get some sleep on the way in order to be fresh for my impending struggle with the frontier authorities in the early hours of next morning and so I stretched myself on one of the hard wooden shelves, from which the "hard" carriage gets its name. But this was not to be. "Hard" carriages are always lively places. This was the liveliest I had ever experienced. My immediate neighbours were two dark-skinned, almond-eyed characters in khalats and skullcaps. I had no sooner got to sleep than they dug me in the ribs and introduced themselves as Tajiks. They had been in Kirghizstan, they said, and were going back to their native Tajikistan, which was a much better place and they were sorry they had left it. Where had I come from and where was I going to? I explained that I had come from Frengistan (roughly Europe) and was going to Afghanistan and possibly Hindustan.

Having found out all they wanted to know about me, and having observed that "anyone with so many belongings" (I had a kitbag and a rather disreputable bundle) must be a rich man, the two Tajiks now proceeded to regale me with an account of their own affairs.

They next proceeded, still laughing loudly (for they were irrepressibly cheerful), to pass round a bottle of bright pink vodka and then to take off the elaborate system of wrappings swathed round their feet in the place of socks. This, they explained to me somewhat superfluously, was a thing they only very rarely did, but they thought it might interest me as a Frengi. I could not help wishing that they had postponed the operation a little longer.

Then we all went to sleep for a time, one of the Tajiks occasionally waking me, in order to tell me of some amusing thought which had occured to him. This happy state of affairs did not last long. Soon, a Russian with a basket of vodka bottles and another basket of pink Soviet sausages appeared and announced that the shelves on which we were lying were reserved for refreshments. We said that we had never heard of such a thing, but the consensus of opinion in the carriage seemed to be definitely on the side of the sausage seller, who had all the demagogic attributes of his classical prototype, and we eventually suffered ourselves to be moved, protesting, to some other shelves further up.

I now gave up all hope of sleep and spent the rest of the daylight looking out of the window. We were travelling through typical Central Asian country, occasional oases and stretches of pale, yellowish desert, broken by ranges of low, red hills, across which the pilgrims used to make their Golden Journey.

Meanwhile, the sausages and vodka had begun to have their effect. A little further up the carriage a group of travellers had formed themselves into what is known in the Soviet Union as an ansambl or concert party, and were giving spirited renditions of various folk songs and dances. Vodka flowed more and more freely and soon pandemonium was let loose. Even the elderly couple's benevolent smile broadened into a bleary grin. Several members of the party were entirely overcome by their exertions and we had to hoist them like sacks on to the top shelves, from which at intervals they crashed ten feet to the floor, without any apparent ill effects. When we reached my destination, Termez, an hour or two before dawn, the party was at his height.

Fitzroy Maclean, Eastern Approaches, 1949

The city is much quieter than the 1980s, when it served as the major command centre for the Soviet invasion of Afghanistan, but its hotels now hum with Afghan entrepreneurs as Soviet era adversaries become Islamic brothers.

SIGHTS

The further back in time you travel, dislocated in both time and space, the more interesting Termez becomes. The Soviet city merges into the tsarist town to provide some points of interest, but the two previous incarnations of the city, grouped around Old Termez (six kilometres/four miles northwest of the city) and the Sultan Saodat complex (nine kilometres/5.5 miles east), constitute the region's star attractions.

■ MODERN TERMEZ

As most of the hotels are situated in the Soviet city, it is to here that the traveller constantly returns. The cold heart of the town is the central square, surveyed by a large statue of Hakkim al Termezi (former Lenin) and the scene of many an epic bypass of Soviet war machinery. To get a closer look at the machinery, walk a few minutes southeast to the old Russian **military fort**. For here, stuffed and mounted in timeless parade, is a disciplined line of tanks, rocket launchers, armoured vehicles, troop transporters and even a fighter plane, displayed in front of the fort like the open page of a Soviet cold-war military manual.

To the south of the Soviet centre, grouped around the Festival Square, is the heart of the Russian settlement of Patta Hissar and the site of the local **museum**. The museum is closed for renovation at the time of writing, but is said to hold a good collection of artefacts recovered from the oblast's dense scattering of archaeological sites. Further south is Termez's main place of worship, the **Murch Bobo Mosque**, completed in the same year as the railway line (1916). The thriving Friday mosque and religious school boasts no remarkable architectural interest, but the random visitor can be assured of a confused, but essentially friendly, reception from a hardcore of mullahs with shaved heads and bushy beards worthy of any Afghan mujaheddin.

■ OLD TERMEZ

Six kilometres northwest of the modern city, along a side road that leads off the main M-39, rests the original, pre-Mongol city of Old Termez. The best preserved walls, now broached by the road leading to the Hakkim al Termezi mausoleum, are those of the *shakhristan* or *medina*. Within these walls lay the citadel of the Tokhar and Termez shahs, the mint, main bazaars and prison, all strongly defended against both local and foreign invaders. Around the *shakhristan* radiated the *rabad* or suburbs, home to merchants and craftsmen, comprising a site of over 500 hectares. This *rabad* was then surrounded by a second city wall, whose main gatehouse still survives in the far northeast corner of the site, and further east lay a walled orchard area (*suradikat*) which sheltered the intensely decorated stucco walls of the shah's ornate country palace. Scattered around the site are the archaeological remains of houses, caravanserais, a network of *aryk* canals which brought water from the Oxus and even a Nestorian Christian church, but the professionalism of the Mongol destruction has left the site largely incomprehensible to the casual visitor.

Outside the *shakhristan* is the spiritual centre that unites Old and New Termez, the **Hakkim al Termezi Mausoleum**. The complex commands a superbly romantic location on the raised northern bank of the Oxus, with a view across the waters to the shores of Afghanistan. The realities of international geopolitics and modern history have, however, conspired to make the region an extremely sensitive one and the electrified border, army barracks and radar station which lie only fifty metres from the Sufic saint charge the air with tangible tension. The undeterred faithful regularly descend upon the site every Wednesday lunchtime to offer prayers to the patron saint of Termez and boil up huge cauldrons of mutton in the communal cooking area set aside for pilgrims. The food is all donated by a rota of rich local businessmen atoning for their sins and the rare visitor will be received with open arms and a liberal helping of mutton and tea.

Sufi Abu Abdullah Mohammed ibn Ali al Termezi, nicknamed 'al Hakkim' (the wise), was a ninth-century Sufic, jurist, mystic and author who lived and received his pupils in Old Termez. After an education in Balkh and a hajj to Mecca at the tender age of 27, Termezi began to write his theories on the terminology for sainthood; the very titles which he himself would soon enjoy. Upon his death in 869 AD, he was buried where he had worked and in the ensuing centuries a mausoleum (10th century), mosque (12th century) and Timurid *khanagha* (15th century) grew up around his name. The impressive carved marble *sunduk* tombstone chronicles the life of the saint and was added to the complex in the early fifteenth century by Tamerlane's son Shakh Rukh. The theft of the missing section of the tomb is attributed to British archeologists, accused of having seconded the marble back to the British Museum at the turn of the century. The building provided a point of focus for local philosophers and thinkers, a place where holy men could provide counsel, and broke with the *khanagha*'s more customary role of providing dervish living accommodation.

Between the mausoleum and the Oxus are the archaeological remains of the old port of Termez, which include the wharf, customs house and port hotel. West of the site is the large island that gave Termez so much of its strategic and commercial importance. Originally named after the Arab leader Uthman, who led his attack of the city from here, the island is now called Aral Paigambar, or Island of the Prophet, after the prophet Dhul Kifl, contemporary of Mohammed, who is said to have died here. The island is also the exotic but forbidden location of the 12th century Zul Kifl Mausoleum.

Bronze age rock carvings, Sarmysh

■ BUDDHIST TERMEZ

So pervasive has Islam's hold been on Central Asia for over a millennium that it is difficult for the modern-day traveller to envisage a time when nomadic shamanism, Persian Zoroastrianism and Indian Buddhism predated the monopoly of belief. A visit to the archeological remains of Kara Tepe and Fayaz Tepe, however, requires from the visitor just such a leap of faith.

The Buddhist monastery complex of **Kara Tepe** is unique in Central Asia. Not only is it the only rock-hewn Buddhist cave complex in the region, and thus the main connecting thread between the Afghan sites of Haibak and Bamian and the sites of the far side of the Oxus, it is also the only monastery to lie behind an electrified fence in international no-man's-land, access thus necessitating official permission.

The **Fayaz Tepe** site, two kilometres north of the Termezi mausoleum consists of the archaeological remains of a two-millenniums old Buddhist temple and monastery complex, whose impact is perhaps more intellectual than visual. The large central courtyard, the heart of the Buddhist temple, is flanked to the west by the main living quarters of the monastery and to the east by the main refectory. The brick stupa to the north of the temple dates from the first century BC and is only the inner section of a much larger construction that rose from the cross shaped foundations. Clay and gypsum statues of Buddha, a series of murals depicting various adorants in Kushan dress and fragments of pottery containing Brahmi, Punjabi, Kharoshti and Bactrian scripts have all been found on the site, underlining its essentially Eastern orientation. Remains have also been discovered of a two-kilometre aqueduct that supplied the monastery with water from the Amu Darya.

The monastery was looted in the 5th century by Sassanid troops and later used as a burial ground and retreat for Sufic mystics of a rather different religious persuasion. Today the whole site is set in marvellous juxtaposition to a modern radar system, silently scanning the Afghan skyline for any signs of the rising tide of Islam.

The trio of Buddhist archaeological memorabilia is completed by the sixteen metre high **Zurmala Tower**, situated three kilometres southeast of Old Termez and visible from the main M-39. This sixteen-metre-high brick tower is the remnant of the largest Buddhist stupa in the area and is possibly the oldest construction still standing in Uzbekistan. Back in the third and fourth centuries AD, at the height of Buddhist influence, the base of the stupa would have been covered with white lime-stone slabs below red brick decoration and would have housed a collection of sacred Buddhist relics. Today, this former religious magnet lies lost in a deserted cotton field, torn by a huge, heart-rending crack.

PRACTICAL INFORMATION

It is advisable to avoid Termez in summer when temperatures can reach a blistering 50°C (122°F). Winters are the mildest in Uzbekistan and spring and autumn are bearable.

■ ACCOMMODATION

Hotel Surkhan Hakkim Al Termezi Street (tel. (37622) 46545)
Centrally placed, clean, with warm water, air conditioning and a good, if uninspired, restaurant, the Surkhan is the best hotel in town, used by businessmen and the rare group. Single $10. Uzbektourism managed.
Hotel Shark Khodjaev Street, next to Uzbektourism. (tel. 31352)
Friendly but basic, with a good location and a café. $3 for a single with bath.
Hotel Termez 21 Akmal Ikramov Street (former Oktobraskaya Street), corner of Safar Sakibov Street. (tel. 31753)
On a par with the Shark, noisy but clean, mostly used as a modern caravanserai for Afghan traders. $3-6
Hotel Uzbekistan Khodjaev Street. (tel. 31514)
The cheapest hotel in town with basic dormitory rooms and few facilities. Less than $1. Close to the Shark.
UN Hotel (tel. 43375 or 42317)
For UN workers, guests and friends.

■ TRANSPORT

There are daily flights to Tashkent and weekly flights to Moscow. Termez is on the railway line to Dushanbe, Urgench (am), Moscow and Tashkent (overnight) and has regular bus connections to almost everywhere. Occasional buses go to Afghanistan but very rarely carry foreigners. City bus and *marshrutnoe* minibus number 6 goes from the bus station to the Surkhan and other hotels and number 4 goes to and from the train station. The sights of Termez are easiest seen by renting a taxi for a day.

■ TRAVEL AGENCIES

Uzbektourism, 17 Khodjaev St, Termez 732008. Tel. (37622) 26420 Fax. 25850
The office cheerfully admits to possessing no English-speaking guides, no transport, no tour itineraries and no tourists, but may be able to mobilize support if financial persuasion is forthcoming.

AROUND TERMEZ

■ SULTAN SAODAT COMPLEX AND ENVIRONS

An eight-kilometre (five-mile) car, taxi or public bus ride northeast of modern Termez, past the airport, to the village of Namuna, provides an enjoyable half-day itinerary to the varied remains of post-Mongol Termez.

The **Sultan Saodat Ensemble** is a collection of seventeen mausoleums that comprise the family burial place of the Termez sayyids, a family dynasty claiming descent from Ali, whose considerable political and religious power reached a peak during the 13th and 14th centuries. It is said that even Tamerlane numbered among their followers. The founder of the dynasty, Sayyid Hasan al Emir, grandson and fifth in line from the prophet Mohammed, was buried here in the ninth century and set a precedent that his descendents were to follow for the next nine centuries. The two original mausoleums are widely attributed to be the magnet that attracted the settlement of post-Mongol Termez.

The mausoleums form a long, rectangular street of plain-brick tombs, turned in upon themselves and dominated at the western end by the two earliest tombs, of which the larger northern building is the earlier. The 11th- and 12th-century structures are connected by a memorial mosque whose high *iwan* was raised in the 15th century (1405-1409) by Khalil Sultan, after whom the ensemble is said to be named. Traces of cobalt blue tilework still cling tenaciously to the Timurid façade and the subdued brick khakis of its arches, columns and patterned designs supply a sombre smudge of decoration. In the second half of the 15th century a burst of architectural energy added another two adjoining mausoleums, expanding but not upsetting the artistic equilibrium, and a three-sided portal façade was created. The southern mausoleum is characterized by the 32-pointed star on its inner dome.

Steps lead up from the other mausoleums to give a fine aerial view of the complex and scattered ruins beyond. The modern descendents of the sayyids still live in the local village of Namuna.

A few minutes' walk from the Sultan Saodat complex stands the imposing façade of the 16th-century **Kokil Dara Khanagha**. This complicated and unusual memorial building, with sweeping side wings and complex vaulting, owes much of its design to Afghan influence and is, in many ways, closer to the architecture of Balkh than Bukhara. Yet this is hardly surprising, since the Timurid empire at the time spread all the way to Delhi and Tamerlane's architects were sequestered from all over his empire.

Throughout Central Asia legends based around a shadowy '40 girls' are endemic. Whether describing the 40 Amazonian daughters of a local Mongol warlord, the exploits of the poor Central Asian soul held captive in his fortress by his 40 nubile young serving girls or even the original 40 girls held responsible for the progeneration of the entire Kyrgyz race, the kernel of truth at the core of the legend of the 40 girls, or *Kyrk Kyz,* has long since passed into popular imagination and been lost.

Subsequently, clues to the origins of the **Kyrk Kyz fortress** are easier to find in the region's local name, the *Shakhri Saman* or Town of the Samanids. For it is now believed that this fascinating, self-contained bastion of 50 rooms was the country residence of the ruling Samanid dynasty in the ninth and tenth centuries. The fortress is a typical example of the type of *kushk,* or castle, that came to dominate the Sogdian and post-Sogdian feudal periods as a fusion of both pre- and post-Islamic architectural styles.

The 55-metre (180-foot) long square walls of the fortified castle rise out of the dusty ground like bleached bones and envelop a maze of twisting hallways, arched corridors and individually shaped rooms. The rooms included bedrooms, storage rooms and a large six-domed guest room or mosque, all arranged on two floors around the food and water of a central domed courtyard. The two floors have melted into one in places and the roof has long since disappeared, but in general the dwelling has survived in excellent condition and offers a unique chance to wander around the inside of a Central Asian feudal castle. Kyrk Kyz is situated only a few hundred metres away from the Kokil Dara. Its main entrance faces north.

■ THE AFGHAN BORDER

Sixteen kilometres east of Termez, the rather ironically named **Bridge of Friendship** straddles the Oxus and provides the international border crossing between Uzbekistan and the turbulent fiefdoms of Afghanistan beyond.

The bridge was the major entry point for the Soviet troops who poured into Afghanistan in 1979 and also the exit point for the remnants who limped home ten years later under the leadership of General Gramov. Local Uzbeks and Tajiks were initially targeted for conscription into the war, often called the Soviet Union's Vietnam, in a move designed to win over the ethnic Uzbeks and Tajiks who make up the dominant ethnic groups in Northern Afghanistan. But when confronted with their ethnic and religious brothers, many Soviet Uzbeks felt fundamentally torn allegiances and, after a few years, the policy was scrapped. The asphalt square above the border crossing was the former parade ground of the Soviet troops and several nearby graves remember young Russians buried far from home.

Close to the border crossing lie the famous archeological sites of **Ayrtam** and **Kobadiyen**, site of the famed Achaemenid **Oxus Treasure** which now resides in the British Museum.

■ JARKURGAN MINARET

Situated in the village of Minor (Kommunizm Kolkhoz), seven kilometres from the pleasant town of Jarkurgan and 38 kilometres (24 miles) from Termez, this unique minaret can be visited as a day trip from Termez or as a stopover on the way to Denau. Either way, it is well worth the visit.

The main trunk of the minaret is composed of 16 herringboned crimps or semicolumns, reminiscent of traditional castle architecture, which continue through a band of sixteen arches and foliated Kufic, Koranic inscriptions to suggest that the minaret was double or even triple linked and that the present 22-metre (72-foot) construction originally reached a estimated height over 50 metres (165 feet).

Jarkurgan minaret

Considerable skill must have gone into applying the herringbone brickwork, set not only in curved ribs, but also in ever-decreasing diameters in order to narrow the minaret. A vertical inscription given pride of place on one of the ribs names the architect as one Ali ibn Mohammed of Serakhs (in modern-day Turkmenistan), while another dates the construction to 1108–1109 AD and the rule of Sultan Sanjar.

The pleasant village of Jarkurgan is refreshed by the waters of the Surkhan River and has a traditional Sunday market.

Denau

Denau is set between a rock and a hard place. With the magnificent snow-dusted Hissar Mountains to the north, Chulbair Range to the west and turbulent Tajik border to the east, Denau and the traditional rural *kishlaks* surrounding it constitute one of the farthest-flung and most untouched mountain cul-de-sacs of the Uzbek republic.

As the semi-independent land of Chaghanian, Denau ('New Town') enjoyed relative freedom over the centuries and even at the beginning of this century it maintained only nominal relations with the emirate, via the east Bukharan capital at Hissar (in present-day Tajikistan). It provided taxes, soldiers and beautiful women for the emir's harem, as did all the other 26 begships of the emirate, but rebellions were commonplace and bandits rife. In the 1880s Denau was partly destroyed by a punitive force sent from Bukhara to pacify the rebellious beg. The mountains that provided such effective cover for bandits also concealed the later *basmachi* and Denau merged with the lands to the east to provide the dramatic backdrop for the last stand of these early *mujahedeen* and also the final fall of Enver Pasha, the Turk who had briefly united them.

Sights

The colourful and kinetic **bazaar**, fuelled by cross-border trade with Tajikistan, forms the vibrant heart of modern Denau and, in this region where *chapans* heavily outnumber tracksuits, is a good place to invest in some traditional Central Asian garb. Close to the bazaar and the central bus station, lies the **Sayyid Attalik Madrassah**, vestige of Denau's past and auspice to its future. The 16th-century madrassah, one of the biggest in Central Asia, has reopened its doors since independence and at present tutors some 70 students in classes of Russian, English and Arabic. Also in the town centre is the impressive, circular **fortress** of the Beg of Denau, set high above the Sangardak River as silent testament not only to the power of the local rulers but moreover to the distant, and sometimes uncertain, hold of the emirate.

Just outside Denau in the small *kishlak* of **Yurchi** lies another feudal fortress, dating from the tenth century. Colin Thubron visits the ruined fort in his book *The Lost Heart of Asia*, in an attempt to get to the root of the myth surrounding the death of Enver Pasha, but Pasha was most probably killed further east in present-day Tajikistan. *Marshrutnoe* taxis ply the road to Yurchi. Ask for the *"stary krepast"*, 100 metres (330 feet) from the town *chaikhana*.

Thirty kilometres (twenty miles) east of Denau lies the village of **Vakhshivar** and the Sufi Allah Yar Mosque (1713), named after the celebrated Uzbek poet buried here in 1724.

Outside Denau

The Surkhan River valley around Denau/Chaganian was one of the main cradles of Kushan urbanization. The Graeco-Bactrian and Kushan city of **Khalchayan** (fourth century BC to third century AD) lies ten kilometres (six miles) northeast of Denau, but its remains are faint and its fascinating past is better tasted through the remarkable collection of Parthian-, Greek- and Kushan-influenced sculptures today housed in the State Art Museum, Tashkent. The slightly better-preserved site of **Dalverzin Tepe** was once one of the most glorious Kushan cities of the age and an early capital for the Yue Chi Turkic tribes. Today only the sunken remains of a Buddhist temple, Bactrian shrine and Zoroastrian altar remain, encased in a five-sided city wall between the modern towns of Denau and Shurchi.

Denau Practical Information

Public buses run regularly to and from Termez, Shirabad and Jarkurgan from the new bus station. There are also daily buses to Baisun and Tashkent. At present buses for Dushanbe only run to the border, from where onward buses can be caught. The only hotel in Denau is situated on the corner of Rashidov and Mustakillik (Lenin) Streets, some 400 metres (1,300 feet) east of the bazaar. Double rooms cost less than a dollar, but its toilets will make a grown man run screaming. There is an even more basic hotel at the bus station for late arrivals and early departures.

The Royal Road

The *Shah Rah*, or Royal Road, was a major Silk Road thoroughfare uniting the foremost cities of Transoxiana, Samarkand and Bukhara. Merchants faced a six- or seven-day journey to cover the 270-kilometre (170-mile) stretch along the Zerafshan Valley. Today, most travellers rush through in their enthusiasm to reach Bukhara, but the intervening sites are rich in history, well worth a couple of leisurely breaks.

Tim

This tiny and remote village, hidden deep in the hills behind Katta Kurgan, is the surprise location of one of Central Asia's oldest and most influential architectural prototypes, the Arab Ata Mausoleum

The tomb is best known as Central Asia's earliest surviving example of a domed tomb with a monumental *pishtak* (portal) and interior trilobe squinch, and has influenced the construction of generations of local mausoleums. Also in the quiet village lies the 15th-century White Mosque. Tim is not easy get to, as buses only run once a day from Katta Kurgan. Frequent buses run to nearby Ingichna, from where it is possible to hitch.

Karmana

Along the Zerafshan Valley one reaches Karmana, the old Silk Road town of Karminiya and favoured place of rest for Bukharan emirs. Local legend claims the Arabs named it so, finding fertile land and plentiful water 'similar to Armenia' (ka Arminiya). Merchant-caravans broke their journeys here and elsewhere at a network of rabats or caravanserais—safe haven against robbers or the elements. Beacons fired warning of trouble up and down the line. Outside Karmana, 26 kilometres (16 miles) on the route to Bukhara, stands the impressive portal of the Rabat-i-Malik, the royal caravanserai, for this is the royal desert steppe and the building's sponsor was a royal himself.

Karakhanid Khan Shams al Mulk Nasr ruled much of Transoxiana from 1068 to 1080 as an ideal Muslim prince, focusing on Islamic expansion, court splendour, patronage of scholars and public building. The surviving 12-metre (40-foot) portal held a mighty gate opening on a large courtyard surrounded by high walls and corner towers. Ground floor stalls housed the horses, camels and bales of silk, while weary travellers retired upstairs for food, rest and prayer. An elegant wall of columns and arches reached this century but has since dissolved underfoot, leaving a lone façade of polished brick and carved ganch. Beside a *chaikhana* beyond the modern highway a brick dome covers the caravanserai's great well, part of the medieval irrigation system still supplying Karmana with mountain meltwater.

Trucks from Tehran flash past **Rabat-i-Malik**, for the 70 year hiatus is complete and overland traffic pursues the ancient traditions. Not all travellers were driven by commerce, however. By the 16th century, when Karmana had recovered from the numerous sackings so common to towns on the major paths of invasion, the Sufic brotherhoods were in their heyday. Wandering dervishes met, prayed and stayed at special hostels called *khanagha*. The **Kasim Sheikh Khanagha** in Karmana is a striking example of the size and importance these hostels acquired. Without one a town had no right to city status. In the late 16th century, Bukharan emir Abdullah Khan, a native of Karmana, commemorated it with a *khanagha*, built as was customary near the tomb of a holy man, marked by the usual white flag. Beneath the blue dome raised on a high drum is the central hall of the *khanagha* where dervishes joined in services of religious fervour. Now a working mosque, its two antechambers boast marvellous resonance for the muezzin's call to prayer.

In a park near the busy Uzbek bazaar is the **Mir Said Bakhrom Mausoleum**. Like Arab Ata in Tim, this 11th-century portal and dome composition marked the birth of a style that would dominate architecture for the next few centuries. The ornamental portal wrought solely in trimmed brick is a foretaste of the more ambitious Samanid mausoleum in Bukhara.

Navoi

A few kilometres south, the Silk Road turns Socialist along a wide highway dividing the Uzbek mud walled houses of Karmana and the high-rise workers' blocks of Navoi. Named after the Uzbek national hero, this 30-something city has replaced desert with urban sprawl. Guides point proudly to the streets, offices and parks of progress, while an industrial zone of electrochemical works chokes out the environmental cost. For the visitor, Navoi is an accessible example of a Soviet Uzbek new town, conjured from nothing into the capital of the republic's largest and newest province. Population density is the lowest in the country, as the territory falls within the vast Kyzyl Kum (Red Sands)—the biggest desert plain in Central Asia at around 300,000 square kilometres (116,000 square miles). This ancient scourge of travellers and invaders remains both a challenge to development and a tempting treasury of precious resources. Nomadic herdsmen share the steppeland with state cotton farms and new towns like Zerafshan built around the gold mining centre of Muruntau. Soviet engineers are but the latest to leave their mark on the desert. Three thousand years earlier, men were engraving scenes in stone that survive today. The Sarmysh gorge north of Navoi offers a rich taste of this most ancient Central Asian art. Over 3,000 petroglyphs from the Bronze Age to the Early Middle Ages lie on a dramatic canvas of dark shale rock in the Karatau (Black) hills. For over ten kilometres (6.25 miles) one can scramble among the rocks to find remarkable images of primitive man and the animals so central to his existence. Beside bulls, deer, goats, dogs and horses, human figures hunt with weapons or perform ritual dances. In common with early cultures elsewhere, fertility is depicted by extremely well-endowed men. Research on the petroglyphs continues to look for clues into the remote society that produced them. Tourists should visit for the sheer vitality of antiquity on show, plus some surreal surprises such as a lifelike spaceman, perhaps presaging Soviet cosmonaut hero Yuri Gagarin. The road to Nurata leaves the scrubby desertscape to wind through the Karatau range, over Black Crow Pass and down to the ruined fort of Debaland, once a link in the fire message chain. Next to it is a 16th-century memorial complex for the venerated, renovated tombs of two brothers, Imam Hasan (625–669) and Imam Husein (626–680), sons of Hazrat Ali, husband of the prophet Mohammed's fourth daughter. Their tombs rest in identical halls separated by a small mosque. Long poles bearing white flags and a hand shape on top denote their holy status.

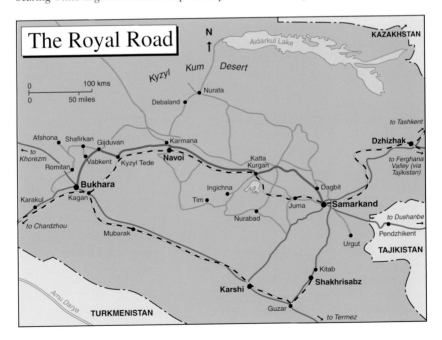

PRACTICAL INFORMATION

■ TRANSPORT

Daily Tashkent–Navoi flights arrive at the airport 25 kilometres (15 miles) along the road west to Bukhara (one short of Rabat-i-Malik). Uzbektourism can arrange tickets. Navoi has the main train station and Karmana the bus station. At least four trains a day pass through towards Bukhara/Urgench and Samarkand/Tashkent/ Ferghana Valley, but buses are preferable for greater frequency and ticket availability. Many buses run Karmana–Nurata, but reaching Sarmysh gorge or Aidarkul Lake is difficult without hired transport. Sarmysh is sign posted on the road to Nurata, where a track leads 25 kilometres through the desert into the Karatau hills. The petroglyphs begin shortly after a Young Pioneers camp.

■ ACCOMMODATION & FOOD

Hotel Yunust (Youth), 138 Khalklar Dustligi Kuchasi, No. 7, Microraion (tel. (43622) 44021). Best choice in Navoi. Reasonably priced apartments.
Hotel Navoi, Khalklar Dustligi, Navoi Centre 706800 (tel. 31164). Standard rooms, failing facilities, hostile management and outrageous prices. Avoid if possible. Another possibility is the basic Hotel/Cafe **Zerafshan**, near the central department store–TSUM. The major restaurant in town is the above average **Vetcherni**, behind the Hotel Navoi. Go for Russian meat/aubergine salads and cold champagne.

In Karmana, bazaar teahouses provide solid Uzbek fare during the day. Near Sarmysh, the Gorniya (Mountains) Young Pioneers camp of playgrounds and swimming pools may well offer a bed and a school meal to tired travellers. Nurata's simple guesthouse is located near the bazaar.

■ TRAVEL AGENTS

Uzbektourism, 29 Severnaya Street, Navoi, tel. (43622) 35471, fax. 34749. Keen assistance for a range of activities from sightseeing to camel trekking.

Nurata

Once known as Nur, this ancient town held a strategic position on the frontier between the cultivated lands and the steppe. It lends its name to the nearby mountain range, the westernmost spur of the Gissaro Alai, soon expiring in Kyzyl Kum wasteland. Today, home to 25,000 people and renowned for marble and astrakhan fur production, Nurata has retained some of the holy sites that attracted pilgrims from all over Central Asia. The ruins of a hilltop citadel in the town centre near the bazaar mark Nurata's history. Said to have stood before the arrival of Alexander the Great, his soldiers rebuilt it in the stronger design of the celestial plough, as they prepared for the siege of Samarkand. Later the fortress was involved in the struggles of the last Samanid ruler Muntasir. Below is the chief pilgrimage site, the Chashma spring, miraculously formed when Hazrat Ali—Mohammed's son in law—struck the ground with his staff. Hundreds of holy (unfishable) fish swim in mineral packed water. Parents anoint their children, while others fill bottles for ailing relatives. A grave nearby may be that of one of Alexander's generals. The mosque for visiting pilgrims dates back to the tenth century and subsequent reconstructions have preserved the roof of 25 cupolas. An adjacent museum details local history and culture through tools, clothes and ceramics.

CAMEL TREKKING

Camel farms to the north of Nurata supply the mounts for anyone wishing to experience desert life in proper Silk Road style, aboard the stubborn and enigmatic ships of the desert. Kazakh families dominate the pasturelands of the Kyzyl Kum. Unlike the Uzbeks, they remained nomads into the 20th century and, despite Stalin's enforced collectivization in the 1930s, many traditions survive. Kazakh yurts, round felt tents set on a wooden framework, stand next to modern shacks and are preferred for summer use. However drab the exterior, inside you will often find a blaze of colourful scarves, blankets and embroideries. Guests are quickly made welcome with a refreshing bowl of *koumiss*, fermented mare's milk. Central Asia's sharply continental climate is at its most extreme in the desert, with bitter winters and summer air temperatures over 45°C (113°F). Timing is of paramount importance: March to May and September to October are best for trekking, particularly spring after the first rains have fallen to carpet the plains in poppies and tulips. The Central Asian tortoise is only active for the three spring months and hibernates once the ephemeral plants have withered away. Birds, lizards and beetles busy about the sands, disappearing at the first sign of the devastating hot winds, *garmsil*, that sweep up from the south engulfing land, sky and travellers through the ages in terrible sandstorms. Most itineraries offer a range of scenery, from flat wastes to rolling *barkhan* sand hills.

Leaving Nurata there are the ancient *karyz* wells, a system of irrigation from Alexander the Great's time. Camping is in Kazakh yurts, wherever water can be found, burning *saxaul* bushes for fuel. Good sites include Usen's Well and Sentyabsai, an ancient gold digger's fortress.

Aidarkul Lake is the favourite destination for camel trekkers to swim off the dust of the saddle and fish for a welcome change of diet. For over 200 kilometres (125 miles) the lake stretches through the desert within sight of the Nuratin mountains. Once the winter ice has melted, it becomes a breeding site for migrating birds. Euphrates poplars and pink tamarisk bushes bend under the weight of cormorant nests heavy with young. Islands on the lake take their name from the cackling colonies of pelicans, gulls, terns and herons that gather at this remote sanctuary.

Gijduvan

ULUG BEG MADRASSAH

The former prominence of Gijduvan is shown by Ulug Beg's choice of the city as site for his third, though least impressive, madrassah built in 1433. Eighty years later the last Timurid, Babur, met humbling defeat here at the hands of the Uzbeks. He escaped, never to return to Transoxiana. A majolica frieze running along its portal wall announces the madrassah as "a sacred place, a cloister equal to the gardens of Paradise". The building is thought to have served as more of a *khanagha* than madrassah, offering shelter to hopeful pilgrims who still come to pay homage and receive blessings from the forecourt.

TOMB OF KHOJA ABDUL KHALIQ

Khaliq (1103–1179) was a holy Sufic master of royal Turkish descent who taught pupils, including Nakhshbandi, to "speak little, eat little, sleep little . . . postpone marriage as long as you can" and that "ornament is a mark of inner poverty": Khaliq, went on: "Place no trust in this world and do not rely on worldly people. Let your heart be filled with melancholy and disillusion, let your body suffer and your eyes weep. Let your conduct be upright and your prayers sincere. Wear old clothes and choose a poor man as your companion."

POTTERY WORKSHOP

Hidden in the Gijduvan backstreets is the family ceramics workshop of Alisher and Abdullah. The brothers are fifth generation potters who continue to make *pialas*, bowls and dishes in traditional floral designs of local browns and yellows. The brothers are happy to give a demonstration of their art, highlighting the techniques of needle-fine *kharosh* work, colour glazing and firing in huge *tandyr* kilns, but speak only Russian or Uzbek. Address: 42 Navoi Street, tel. (8267) 22412.

Vabkent Minaret

This thin, fragile minaret, tapering through ten decorative bands of bricks and bows to an impressive 39 metres (128 feet), is another creation of the Karakhanids, the unsung heroes of Central Asian architecture. Its lower Kufic and upper divani inscriptions decree that it was commissioned by local ruler Bukhari Ad din Ayud al Aziz II in 1196, making it just 70 years younger than Kalon Minaret in nearby Bukhara. The minaret lies just two kilometres north of the modern Royal Road, but is missed by many travellers eager to reach the delights of Bukhara, 20 kilometres (12 miles) away. From Bukhara public buses to Vabkent are sadistically irregular and absurdly full, but almost all buses to Gijduvan, Shafirkan or Samarkand go via Vabkent.

Bukhara

Samarkand is the beauty of the earth, but Bukhara is the beauty of the spirit
Traditional

Bokhara, the most shameless sink of iniquity that I know in the East
Armenius Vambery 1868

Bukhara! For centuries it had glimmered remote in the Western consciousness: the most secretive and fanatical of the great caravan cities, shored up in its desert fastness against time and change.
Colin Thubron 1994

Bukhara the Holy, Bukhara the Noble, the Dome of Islam, the Pillar of Religion, the most intact city in the hoary East, the most interesting city in the world.

History

The traditional founder of the city has always been the Persian prince Siyavush who built a citadel here shortly after marrying the daughter of Afrosiab in Samarkand, but its growth has for centuries depended largely upon its strategic location, uniquely placed on the crossroads to Merv, Gurganj, Herat, Kabul and Samarkand.

The early town was taken by the Persian Achaemenids in the sixth century BC, by Alexander the Great in 329 BC and by the empires of the Hephalite and the Kushan. By Sogdian times the town was known as Numijent, later to be renamed after the Sanskrit word for monastery, *vikhara* and was a major city in the Sogdian confederation but it was still merely a younger brother to the thriving merchant towns of Paikend, Romitan and Varakhsha (home to the ruling dynasty of Bukhar Khudats) until the storm of Islam arose.

THE ARAB INVASION

After the fall of Merv (641) and Paikend (672), Bukhara managed to keep the Arab fighting machine at bay with an annual tribute. Relations grew strained when 80 Bukharan hostages were abducted to Medina, only to rebel en route and commit mass suicide. But Bukhara was left largely unmolested until the fire-worshipping city was taken by Qutaiba in 709 in the first leg of his *jihad* against the lands beyond the Oxus. Three times the city was taken and three times the city rebelled, but ruling Queen Khatum finally fled the city, leaving behind a slipper worth 200,000 dihrem, and the city was taken.

The Arabs were assiduous and thorough in their Islamification of the town. Whole districts of the city were evicted to make room for Arab troops and an Arab soldier was posted in every household. Non-Arabs were conscripted into the ruling elite and Qutaiba offered two dihrem as an incentive to attend the makeshift Friday mosque. Islam flourished; grafted onto existing beliefs.

Revolts persisted whenever the Arabs turned their backs and terrible punitive campaigns were regularly unleashed, but the roots of Islam took hold and the essence of the city was transformed.

SAMANID BUKHARA

By the late ninth century internal dissent in the heart of the Ummayad Arab empire had translated into a weakening of power on its fringes. The local Iranian governors broke with the caliphate and, after a fratricidal struggle between Bukhara and Samarkand, Ismael ibn Ahmed founded the Samanid dynasty and ushered in a golden age whose commercial and cultural vitality soon attracted the finest intellectuals of the time. Ismael and his dynasty ruled as ideal Muslim rulers, offering patronage to the most talented men of letters in the land. Ibn-Sina, al-Beruni, the historian Narshaki and poet Rudaki all served to turn Bukhara into the centre of a Persian renaissance and of Islamic science. Persian poetry fused with court Arabic as Bukhara's library expanded to become the most famous in the Islamic world. Irrigation networks were expanded and rapid urbanization swelled the population to over 300,000, larger indeed than the soviet city. The city became "embellished with the rarest of high attainments . . . the meeting place of the highest intellectuals of the age, the horizon of the literary stars of the world".

By the 11th century the urban Persian yielded to the nomadic Turkoman. In 999 the Samanids fell to the Karakhanids, the Karakhitai in 1141 and Khorezmshah in 1206. The Chashma Ayub, Kalon Minaret and Namazgokh Mosque were all added to the city, but in general it was a period of decline and uncertainty.

THE MONGOL INVASION

In March 1220 the Mongol tide of calamity was spotted outside Bukhara's gates, its troops more numerous than locusts, each detachment like a billowing sea. Thirty thousand defensive troops sped to meet them and were slaughtered to a man. "From the reflection of the sun the plain seemed to be a tray filled with blood." Their leader Genghis Khan, The Wind of God's Omnipotence, rode to the Namazgokh Mosque, and proclaimed himself the Scourge of God. "If you had not committed great sins," he said, "God would not have sent a punishment like me". The citadel was taken, the city put to the torch and razed to a level plain. No man was spared who stood higher than the butt of a whip. Soon cartloads of booty and trains of slaves were seen snaking away from the charred remains of the holy town, to be employed as human

Kasim Sheikh Khanagha, Karmana

shields in the forthcoming assault on Samarkand. A refugee who finally managed to escape to Khorasan said of the massacre: "They came, they sapped, they burnt, they slew, they plundered and they departed."

Years later the Khan's grandson Hulaku again arrived at the city gates intent on plunder. He was met by a young boy, a camel and a goat. When he demanded to know why the city's envoy was a mere baby, the precocious boy replied, "If you want someone larger then talk to the camel and if you want someone with a beard then talk to the goat. If you desire reason then talk to me." Hulaku listened to the boy and the city was saved.

The city took a century to recover from the trauma and when it had, it was taken, destroyed and depopulated by the Persian Khan Abaqa II. By 1366 ibn-Battuta recorded that "all but a few of its mosques, academies and bazaars are lying in ruins". The once holy city had a "reputation for fanaticism, falsehood and denial of the truth". The town glimmered again under the Timurids, but was never more than a faint shadow of Tamerlane's capital at Samarkand.

SHAYBANID BUKHARA

In 1500 the Uzbek clan leader Mohammed Shaybani Khan entered Bukhara and murdered its ruler Ali, thus supplanting the squabbling Timurid line with his Uzbek dynasty. The Timurids rallied briefly under the return of Babur to Bukhara in 1511, but on 12 December 1512 Babur and his Shi'ite Persian allies were routed in the pivotal battle of Gijduvan and the Timurid leader fled Transoxiana for ever. The Uzbeks were undisputed champions of Transoxiana and Bukhara was its capital again, with the Oxus a fragile border with Shi'ite Safavid Persia. Abdullah Khan reunited the Uzbek clans in a reign of ruthless public order that must have come as a pleasant change from decades of prevailing anarchy. Abdullah's reign prepared the ground for Bukhara's second golden age and his name grew to near-legendary proportions. Craftsmen abducted from conquered Herat fuelled a flowering of decorative and miniature art and the city began to take its present shape under a programme of religious and secular construction spurred on by a rising trade with Russia. The clergy and the khan's spiritual adviser, the Sheikh al-Islam, in particular grew in power and Bukhara grew to boast 150 madrassahs and 200 district mosques.

In 1558 Anthony Jenkinson, the first Englishman to stagger into Central Asia, spent two and a half months in Bukhara in his search for new markets and a route to Cathay. His journey was unsuccessful, but he managed to teach Abdullah how to shoot a gun, a kindness the khan repaid by absconding to Samarkand owing Jenkinson money for nineteen bolts of cloth—the only merchandise he managed to sell during his stay.

In 1552 Russia annexed Astrakhan and the Mongol leader Yar Mohammed and his son Jan fled to Bukhara to eventually found a new Uzbek family dynasty, the Janids or

Astrakhanids, who ruled for the next 150 years. As overland continental trade routes withered and wars with Shi'ite Persia intensified Sunni Bukhara's religious isolation, the khanate sank into obscure barbarism, economic stagnation and religious fanaticism. There were brief recoveries under Imam Kuli Khan and Abdul Aziz Khan, but even a change of dynasty to the Mangit in 1785 could do nothing to halt Bukhara's slippery decline as the city shrunk from an international to a regional player.

PLAYING THE GAME

The 19th century thrust Bukhara into the limelight on the world political stage after centuries of obscurity. As Anglo-Russian rivalries, mutual suspicions and ignorance grew more marked, a series of disguised pilgrims, traders, clergymen and tourists crept, rode and stumbled into Bukhara's palaces and caravanserais to find out just what was going on in this suddenly crucial desert oasis, half way towards the ends of the earth. Bukhara remained an apple of discord between the British and the Russians and the emirate played the two off each other, whilst keeping a close eye on which had the upper hand and acted accordingly.

In 1825 William Moorcroft arrived in Bukhara in an attempt to open up the city to trade and pre-empt Russian influence, meeting with "as much kindness from the emir as could be expected from a selfish, narrow-minded bigot". Moorcroft's mission lasted five months, but was soon overshadowed by the classic trip to Bukhara executed by Alexander "Bokhara" Burnes in 1832. Burnes, a captain in the Indian Army, relative of Scottish poet Robert Burnes, audacious and charming polyglot and rising star of the Great Game, entered Bukhara on 27 June 1832 with a shaved head, Afghan dress and a hidden agenda to glean as much strategic and military information on the city as possible. Almost immediately, he was summoned to see the Kosh Begi (grand vizier) and early in the interview had to sidestep a barrage of tricky questions, one of which concerned the relative taste of pork. He rather riskily revealed that amongst his belongings he carried certain cartographic instruments, but soon realized he had little to fear. When he saw Burnes' sextant the Vizier merely asked what it said about the price of grain in the following year and on sight of a compass, he merely proceeded to haggle over it. Burnes stayed a month in Bukhara and although he never managed to see the emir he left the Holy City with a wealth of valuable information and blockbuster material for his classic account of Bukharan life, *Travels into Bokhara*. He returned to England to a Gold Medal from the Royal Geographical Society, a private audience with the king of England and a subsequent knighthood.

In retrospect it was probably for the best that Burnes never managed to obtain an audience with the emir, for the newly enthroned emir was none other than Nasrullah, one of the most viciously and violently deranged rulers the East has ever seen:

One must be able to form to oneself an idea of the society of the Bukhara of the day, crippled by boundless hiprocrosy, crass ignorance, and unscrupulous tyranny, and sunk in the swamp of immorality in order to imagine the mixture of cunning and stupidity, of pride, of vain-glory and profligacy, of blind fanaticism and loathsome vices which make up the character of Nasrullah Khan.

Armenius Vambery 1873

Nasrullah has attained near mythic notoriety in the West as the ultimate bogey-men of Bukhara. Described by Conolly as <u>mad</u> (with the word underlined twice) and affectionately referred to by his subjects as 'The Butcher', Nasrullah's official title was the only marginally less spine-tingling 'The Shadow of God Upon Earth'. As an

ambitious young man, he initiated a bloody scramble for succession, ordering 28 of his close relatives murdered in cold blood and three younger brothers beheaded on the banks of the Oxus. When, 20 years later, in a moment of blind rage he reputedly cut his closest adviser in half with an axe, it seemed that middle-age had failed to mellow the emir. Not even on his deathbed did the monster relent,

Kalon mosque, Bukhara

only content to pass away after he had witnessed the bloody execution of his wife and three daughters in front of his fading eyes, in order it seems to ensure their continued chastity in his absence.

Nasrullah had little to fear. A series of campaigns had secured his eastern borders with Afghanistan and the triangular balance of power between Bukhara, Kokand and Khiva had finally shifted his way with the capture of Merv and Kokand and the death of its khan, Mohammed Ali. Bukhara was in its ascendency and in Nasrullah's world he reigned as king of kings, a vanity which Russian and British one-upmanship only served to confirm. A shadowy Azeri adviser fanned the flames of Nasrullah's paranoia, but Russian diplomats "tickled the haughty Nasrullah behind the ear with pompous titles" so seductively that he paid scant attention to the distant sounds of Russian cannon fire echoing from the far side of the Syr Darya. Yet, even if he were a different type of man, there was little that could be done. The Central Asian khanates were exhausted from an endless cycle of squabbling, war and retribution and stood as divided as they would soon fall.

THE RUSSIANS

Bukhara's sandcastle finally crumbled in the rising tide of tsarist military might. With its forces routed at the battle of Zerabulak near Katta Kurgan by Kaufmann's more professional troops, Bukhara lost control over the Zerafshan and the water supply that kept the city alive. In 1868, in the emirate's second city of Karshi, the emir signed the document that ceded Samarkand, Dzhizak and Katta Kurgan to the territory of Russian Turkestan, allowed Russians free trading concessions in the city and finally acknowledged Bukhara as a Russian protectorate. It received in return the rebellious city of Shakhrisabsz and some of the territory of the khanate of Khiva. For the next 40 years Russia gradually subsumed the surrounding lands like an army of antibodies envelops a malignant cell. In 1886 a decree was signed outlawing slavery in the emirate and two years later the Trans Caucasian Railway finally connected the Russian cantonment of Kagan with the large scale Russian trade and military centre that already existed in Tashkent.

Nadir Divanbegi Khanagha, Bukhara

But Bukhara was never formally incorporated into the Russian empire and the emir still held the power of life and death inside the city. Eventually and inevitably, faint echoes of distant revolutions permeated the closed city walls "like the faint murmur in the hollow of a sea shell" and a medley of ideas ranging from Islamic *jadid* reformism and Istanbul inspired pan-Turkism to Bolshevik-supported communism fermented in the desert heat, finally to find a voice in the shape of the Young Bukharans and their leader Faizullah Khodjaev and focus in a series of reforms that included a public printing press.

In March 1918 the Bolshevik governor of Tashkent, Kolesov, arrived outside the city gates and demanded the city be handed over to the Young Bukharans. The emir played for time, local mullahs called for a jihad against the infidel invaders and reinforcements were rushed in. Local Bukharans might have been excused a questionable loyalty to their vicious emir but, following a theme that ran through the entire Soviet period, they preferred to follow their own Islamic tyrant rather than a godless foreign invader. The Bolshevik delegation inside the city was massacred to a man and several hundred Russian residents of Bukhara were later executed. The Bolshevik reinforcements turned tail (a retreat variously attributed to a lack of ammunition or divine intervention) and limped back to Tashkent, forced to relay the pieces of track they had just passed over in front of them—their western technology mutilated by holy guerillas. Bukhara had secured a two year reprieve from the Bolshevik advance and remained a closed oasis of a past era, riddled with a dangerous cocktail of fleeing White Russians, young revolutionaries and an increasingly desperate emir.

During the next two years the Bolsheviks sent a total of 15 spies to Bukhara to investigate rumoured existence of British Army advisers, each one of whom was caught by the emir's network of informers, tortured and strangled. The 16th was Fred Bailey, a British spy who had somehow managed to get himself hired by the Bolshevik secret police and then issued with instructions to hunt himself down. This master of double deals and disguises entered Bukhara in 1919 with a visa and two letters of introduction hidden respectively in the back of his watch and a box of matches. In his breast pocket was the developer needed to decipher the invisible ink. Bailey had initially planned to stay in Bukhara and set up a British listening-post to complement the one in Kashgar, but after one month he crept out of the city at dawn disguised as a Turkoman nomad. It was a good piece of timing—nine months later, on 2 September 1920, Soviet troops arrived at the city gates, this time under the able command of General Mikhail Frunze.

After four days of bitter fighting, the Ark was largely destroyed, a mass revolutionary meeting was held in the Registan and the red flag was raised from the Kalon Minaret. The Emir Alim Khan had fled his summer palace for Afghanistan, desperately dropping his favourite dancing boys one by one in a vain effort to slow down the Red Army, in hot pursuit. On 6 September 1920 the first people's congress was convened in the courtyard of the Sitorai Makhi Khosa and the People's Republic of Bukhara was proclaimed.

SOVIET BUKHARA

During the first few years of the republic the Soviets followed Lenin's blueprint policy of encouraging local revolution under the aegis of a local national bourgeoisie, in an attempt to win over the local Muslim population. Two weeks after the fall of Bukhara the ranks of the Communist Party swelled to over 14,000 as the local inhabitants rushed to pledge allegiance to the city's new emir. As the Soviet state grew in stability so its confidence in Bukhara grew. By 1922 a series of purges stripped the numbers to just over 1,000 and on 10 February 1924 the Bukharan Republic, seized by a moment of revolutionary martyrdom, voted itself out of existence. Uzbekistan was born.

In Bukhara the Soviet transformation took a passive form. Conjuring up class consciousness in a city of merchants and mullahs was not easy and women formed a surrogate proletariat. The Soviets decided against a radical overhaul of Bukhara, preferring to ignore it and wait for it to fall apart. The town was sanitized and secularized. Bukhara the Holy became Bukhara the Noble. Canals were drained, mosques converted to working men's clubs or local offices and occasional Western visitors decried "the soft and heavy oppression of a city and a life disintegrating". In

1959 the last veil in Central Asia was burned in a public ceremony, fittingly in Bukhara's Registan. Revolution by attrition continued in Bukhara for over 70 years, but it never managed to capture the city's soul. Today old town shrines are dusted off anew and a pantheon of local saints and holy men stir from their slumber. The hibernation is over.

While in Tashkent and Samarkand East and West lie side by side and often intermingle in the most disconcerting way, Bokhara has remained, and I think, cannot but remain, so long as it survives at all, a wholly Eastern city.

Fitzroy Maclean, 1946

Sights: The Old Town

The majority of sights lie scattered around the old town and are thus most easily reached on foot. The following itinerary starts at the Registan and proceeds through the heart of the old bazaar quarter to the area around the Lyab-i Hauz square. Bukhara's range of interesting sights requires at least two or three days to do the city justice and is perhaps the Central Asian city that most rewards the inquisitive traveller prepared to veer off the main Intourist itineraries and immerse himself in the old town.

THE ARK FORTRESS

The dark heart of the Bukharan emirate rises sheer from the Registan Square, a symbol of the Mangit dynasty reign of terror, described by tsarists as 'a disgusting ulcer on the body of the Russian Empire'.

Home to the rulers of Bukhara for over a millenium, the Ark is as old as Bukhara itself. The founding of the original fortress is blurred in antiquity, but it was certainly the focus around which developed the medieval town. The first fortress to be documented by local historians was built in the seventh century by the Bukhar Khudat Bidun, but after repeated collapse it was remodelled, on the advice of local soothsayers, to reflect the Great Bear constellation, only then to stand firm. Arabs built the first ever Bukharan mosque here in 713 on the smouldering ashes of a Zoroastrian temple. Samanids and Karakhanids fortified it from the ninth to the 12th centuries with a series of ramparts, the Karakhitai and Khorezmshah destroyed and rebuilt it three times between them and finally, and indeed rather predictably, the Mongols pulverized it in 1220. The Ark finally began to take its present form in the 16th century under the Uzbek Shaybanids and all its present buildings date from the last three centuries. By this time, the Ark had grown to house not only the emir, his family and retinue, but also the whole range of government accessories, in a complex of over 3,000 inhabitants providing a palace, harem, throne room, reception hall, office block, treasury, mosque, gold mint, dungeon and slave quarters.

The Ark was 80 per cent destroyed in September 1920 by a fire, sparked either by a vindictive and fugitive emir or a merciless Bolshevik bombardment, depending upon your politics. What survived soon became a natural target for waves of Soviet propaganda campaigns and was finally emasculated and pacified into the town's main history museum and archive. But to this day, hidden behind the cluster of restored museum buildings, lie the hearts and bones of the Ark, left to rot in a secret, derelict wasteland.

Today the Ark is entered from the austere and forbidding western façade. Originally a second, southern Kalon Gate gave direct access to the Friday Mosque and it is here that the mythical Iranian hero of the Shah Nameh, Siyawush, is said to lie buried. The present gateway built by Nadir Shah in 1742 consists of two towering bastions linked by a balcony of six porticoed windows. Up to the turn of this century Bukhara's only mechanical Arabic clock hung from the gateway, the desperate work of captive Italian clockmaker Giovanni Orlandi. Orlandi had been abducted to Bukhara from Orenburg in 1851 by a band of Turkoman slave traders, but had temporarily managed to buy his life by offering to make a customized clock and telescope for the gadget-crazy emir. When, however, the emir dropped his favourite telescope from the top of the Bakhauddin Minaret and the infidel Orlandi was discovered drunk with an Armenian acquaintance, he was again sentenced to death. The skin of his neck was cut as a final incentive to embrace Islam and the next day he was beheaded; the final European victim of the mad Nasrullah. To the left of the clock hung a huge six-stranded *khamcha* whip, symbol of the emir's punitive powers, and to the left was a valuable scimitar, carried off by the Red troops in 1920.

From the stone ramp entrance a narrow, winding arcade known as the *dolom* leads past a raised booth where the commander of the fortress, the *Tupchi Bashi*, received the reports of his spies, and climbs alongside the infamous row of cells and torture chambers known as the *khanah khaneh*, up into the heart of the Ark. Here, it is only the thin veil of time that separates the visitor's footsteps from the ghosts of Burnes, Conolly, Stoddart, Wolff and others lured by the bait of the Game.

At the top of the walkway one reaches the deeply carved 'mushroom' topped stalactite pillars of the **court mosque**, now a small museum of the calligrapher's art. Exhibits include two pages of a tenth-century Koran and examples of the divan poetry of Navoi and Jami. The red subscript of the manuscripts provides a Persian translation of Arabic texts.

Next to the mosque stands the *elchi khanah* or embassy of the Kosh Begi, which currently houses the World War II and Soviet History Museums. Mixed in with the more staple fare of photographed Uzbeks surveying the harmonious growth of heavy

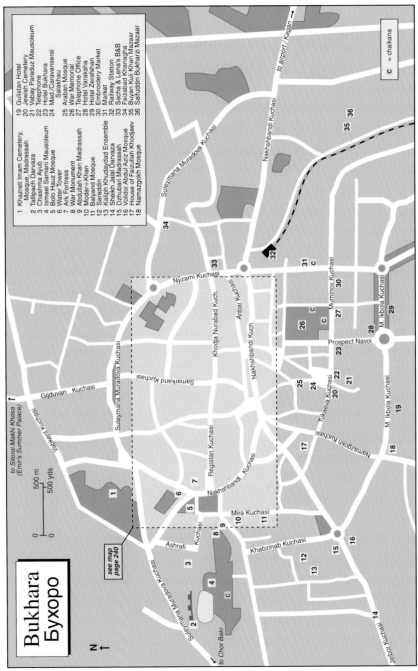

Bukhara
Бухоро

N

0 500 m
0 500 yds

to Sitorai Makhi Khosa (Emir's Summer Palace)

to Chor Bakr

to airport / Kagan

1 Khazreti Imam Cemetery, Mosque, Madrassah
2 Talipach Darvaza
3 Chashma Ayub
4 Ismael Samani Mausoleum
5 Bolo Hauz Mosque
6 Water Tower
7 Ark Fortress
8 War Monument
9 Abdullah Khan Madrassah
10 Modari-Khan
11 Balyand Mosque
12 Saraddin
13 Kaliph Khudaydad Ensemble
14 Sheikh Jalal Darvaza
15 Dzhubari Madrassah
16 Voldor Abdul Aziz Mosque
17 House of Faizullah Khodjaev
18 Namazgokh Mosque
19 Gulistan Hotel
20 Jewish Cemetery
21 Yabay Paraduz Mausoleum
22 Telephone
23 Hotel Bukhara
24 Mad./Caravanserai Salakhau
25 Araban Mosque
26 War Memorial
27 Telephone Office
28 Hotel Varaksha
29 Hotel Zerafshan
30 Embroidery Market
31 Market
32 Railway Station
33 Sacha & Lena's B&B
34 Faizabad Khanagha
35 Buyan Kuli Khan Mazaar
36 Saifuddin Bukharzi Mazaar

C = chaikana

see map page 240

Vapkent Kuchasi
Suleymana Muradova Kuchasi
Gijduvan Kuchasi
Nyzami Kuchasi
Samarkand Kuchasi
Khodja Nurabad Kuch.
Anbat Kuchasi
Nakhshbandi Kuch.
Suleymana Muradova Kuchasi
Registan Kuchasi
Nakhshbandi Kuchasi
Mira Kuchasi
Ashrafi
Kuchasi
Khabzinab Kuchasi
Suleymana Muradova Kuchasi
Namazgokh Kuchasi
Tukaeva Kuchasi
Prospect Navoi
Muminov Kuchasi
M. Ikbola Kuchasi
M. Ikbola Kuchasi
Jelbor Kuchasi
Nakhshbandi Kuchasi

industry are a 3D model of *paranjas* being burnt in front of the Ark, a copy of the *Bukharan Proletariat* weekly in Arabic and a series of papers that highlight the U-turn development of Uzbek script changes from Arabic to Latin and Cyrillic. Created in the service of propaganda, these museums may soon, unfortunately, suffer a similar master, in the latest independent rewrite of Bukharan history. A Soviet display depicting the horrors of Bukharan torture has already disappeared from the Ark following a complaint lodged by the Birlik political party and these two museums may soon follow suit. The *elchi khana* also houses the memorial plaque and mass grave of the 20-strong Kolesov Bolshevik delegation, massacred here on orders from the emir in 1918.

Just next to the *chorsu* crossroads on the left is the seventeenth century **kurinesh khana** or throne room. Largely destroyed by fire, this three-sided wooden *iwan* has witnessed a series of royal coronations, with new emirs traditionally lifted into the marble throne on a carpet, in a conscious throwback to the golden age of Tamerlane. Court astronomers would determine an auspicious day for the coronation and prisoners were extravagantly released in a fleeting mood of clemency. The screen in front of the entrance was to ensure that no attendant would ever have to show his back to the emir. Underneath the present restoration work is the old mint and treasury of the emirate and present-day museum storehouse.

Through the *chorsu* lies the main museum courtyard where an old *kori khana* on the left has been transformed into an **Archaeological and Numismatic Museum**. Beyond this ranged the countless harem bedrooms that the emir would have made up at any one time to minimize the risk of assassination. Paranoia also spread to dining habits it seems; water was brought in from outside the Ark in skins guarded by armed officers, tasted twice by the *afta bachi* and only then resealed and despatched to the emir. Food was likewise tasted by the *kosh begi* and his officers and, after more than an hour of close scrutiny, placed in a sealed box (to which only the prime minister and emir had keys) and despatched to the emir, with the result that "we shall hardly suppose the king of the Uzbeks ever enjoys a hot meal or a fresh cooked dinner" (Burnes). It is perhaps here, buried deep behind two city walls, wrapped in the imposing bastions of a fortress and concealed in a maze of bedrooms, that the root of the emirate's introspection and isolation is most tangible.

The **salaam khana** or reception hall was where the emir granted his daily public audience. It was also where Conolly committed his tragic error of etiquette and where Wolff's overzealous deferences soon had the court in stitches. The emir soon grew tired of the countless daily 'salaam aleikum' directed at him and an officer was therefore specifically and solely employed to provide the 'aleikum salaam' reply that religious protocol demanded.

The courtyard is now a revealing **local history Museum**. The mesmerizing robe in the first room was the seventh and final robe worn during the coronation ceremony and was worn with the 20-metre (65-foot) turban that traditionally doubled as a shroud, were the emir to die on a journey. Other quirky exhibits include a rare Jewish/Russian/Uzbek dictionary, an excellent 1938 propaganda poster declaiming the emir's pyramid of power, a water melon spoon with serrated edges, a series of turn of the century dervish robes and a photograph of the first doctor in Bukhara placed above a collection of his gruesome tools of the trade.

The final courtyard looks onto the two-storey *nagora khana*, or orchestra, where the Bukharan state orchestra broke into a spirited version of *God Save The Queen* in honour of the Reverend Wolff and also from where a drumbeat would regularly herald the dark spectacle of impending execution. The main courtyard also housed the royal stables and whenever horses were washed down, water would flow down the still visible channel to drench the wretched souls in the torture cells below. Finally, to the left of the courtyard stands the emir's domed viewing pavilion, from where he and his closely screened-off female retinue would gaze coldly down onto the packed Registan and perhaps even from where they took delight in the last living moments of Conolly and Stoddart.

The Ark is open every day except Wednesday and there is a small entrance charge. The souvenir booths offer some of Bukhara's better-quality books and handicrafts. A guided tour of the Ark is inexpensive and strongly recommended, as the resident guide (Noila Kasijanova) is probably the best guide in Bukhara. An excellent aerial view of the Ark rewards anyone brave enough to ascend the rather unstable lift of the nearby water tower/bar.

ZINDAN

The *zindan* or city jail, epicentre of Bukharan 19th-century notoriety, lurks hidden behind the Ark, next to the former Shakhristan Gate. The heavy, sombre building was home to debtors, murderers, political prisoners, courtiers fallen from grace and 19th-century European guests all held in three diabolical cells, the most infamous of which was the Black Hole—a deep pit covered with an iron grill, accessible only via a long six metre rope—the true horror of which can only truly be appreciated from the bottom. The English missionary Henry Landsell was given a guided tour of the jail by his terrified guide in 1882 and observed how the wretched prisoners, manacled and chained at the neck, went largely unfed, with those whose families were too poor to bribe the murderous jailers forced to beg for food every holy Friday through an exterior grating.

Today the cells hold hostage only a few unconvincing dummies (from whose ranks Conolly and Stoddart have mysteriously disappeared) and an abridged collection of dungeon memorabilia displayed in the old torture chamber. There is a famous photograph of the bloody back of Sadreddin Ayni, future president of Tajikistan, who was publicly whipped in 1917 for his revolutionary ideas.

Registan

A stranger has only to seat himself on a bench in the Registan, to know the Uz-beks and the people of Bukhara.

Alexander 'Bokhara' Burnes. 1832

The leafy square lying at the foot of the Ark fortress is the Registan. This now desert-ed island of green was, until the Soviet era, the pulsating heart of the *shakhristan*, serving multiple roles as market place, public square and execution ground.

Up until the end of the century the Registan resembled far more closely its coun-terpart in Samarkand. The square was enclosed to the north by the Poyenda Beg Atligh Mosque, Daru i-Shifa (House of Healing) madrassah and clinic, and to the west by the Sodhim Beg and Bazar i-Gusfand madrassah. At the foot of the fortress walls lay the residence of the *tupchi bashi*, commander in chief of the emir's forces, equipped with a small arsenal and cannons captured from the rival khanate at Kokand. Spokes led out from the Registan to the four corners of the globe and a seething mass of hawkers, barbers, beggars, butchers, bakers, dervishes and courtiers thronged the bustling square. Vambery even recollects a Chinese tea merchant with a stall in the Registan who could distinguish by touch all 27 varieties of his tea.

Never was the Registan more jam-packed than when the chain which normally closed the gatehouse of the Ark was withdrawn to a slow and heavy drumbeat, the signal for yet another in the macabre series of executions, floggings and torture that took place in the shadow of the Ark. Beyond the blood-stained square lay the equally nefarious slave market, where mostly Persian, but also occasional Russian, slaves were traded at dawn every Monday and Thursday.

It was thus natural that the Soviets should choose this medieval bastion as the location to sweep away the old and usher in the new. In September 1920 the Red Flag was raised from the Ark and a meeting convened in the Registan to proclaim the fall of the emirate. Four years later, when news of Lenin's death filtered through to Bukhara, a mass meeting of mourning was also held here and the following year a statue of the dead revolutionary was unveiled in the heart of the square. By 1992 the fallen idol had disappeared. Nothing has since taken his place.

Bolo Hauz Mosque

Every Friday, an exquisite spread of deep red Bukharan rugs would embellish the ground leading from the Ark to the 'Mosque Near the Pool' and the splendidly attired emir would venture out from behind his fortress protection to atone for his sins un-der the splendid dome of the Bolo Hauz.

Today, the carved stalactites of its elegant wooden pillars still carry echoes from the royal court mosque in the Ark and the high carved and painted decoration of the

Kalon Minaret, the 'Tower of Death', Bukhara

Bolo Hauz (1712) still draws an admiring faithful after its brief Soviet interlude as a proletarian worker's club. The mosque's façade again attracts the eye with a veritable riot of restored primary colour and its 12-metre (39-foot) high *iwan* still stands as one of the highest, most graceful and most beautifully decorated in Central Asia.

Also bordering the Registan is the **Sadriddin Ayni Theatre** (1930), an early victim of the post-independence Russian exodus and economic hardships. Here in 1925 Mikhail Kalinin, first President of the Soviet Union, chaired the first congress of the Uzbekistan SSR. Today, its fusion of Russian columns and Arabic calligraphy plays host only to the occasional renegade martial-arts video.

CHASHMA AYUB

In the days before Bukhara even existed, a millenium before Islam was even a glimmer in the Prophet's eye, the prophet Job came to the Zerafshan Valley and witnessed a great and terrible drought. As people perished of thirst around him, Job struck the dusty earth with his staff and a cool source of sweet spring water brought liquid salvation. The Chashma Ayub, the Spring of Job, commemorates this site.

The present day mausoleum stands in fortress-like austerity, almost devoid of decoration, a few hundred metres from the Ismael Samani Mausoleum. It consists of four domed chambers, each built during a different epoch and topped in a different style of cupola to form a remarkable visual spread of architectural history. Although the original construction dates from the 12th-century rule of Karakhanid Arslan Khan, the earliest surviving dome was raised by Tamerlane in 1380 over the existing tomb chamber. This unusual conical cupola, rare for Transoxiana, has its roots in the nomadic tent designs of Khorezm and was most probably designed by architects forcibly repatriated by Tamerlane in the wake of his 1379 campaign to Gurganj (Kunya Urgench). Suspended underneath the conical cupola is a concealed second dome, so that from the inside the cupola looks much the same as its three later 16th-century additions.

The commemorative complex is underscored by the almost cultish respect given to water in these harsh and arid climes, a theme adopted by the modern order into the present day **Museum of Water Supply**. Displays range from the time of the emirate, when professional water carriers sold inflatable skins of worm riddled water in the bazaars, to the ecologically overambitious schemes of the Soviet era, such as the Amu-Bukhara Canal and the soon to be completed Samarkand-Bukhara Canal. For most local Uzbeks and Tajik visitors, however, these soviet schemes stand dismissed as mere drops in the ocean and their object of admiration and veneration lies in the deep, sweet spring water of Job.

Just opposite the Chashma Ayub is the main **produce market** where on summer Sundays a traditional **Uzbek circus** plies the high wire in the shadow of the spring. The bazaar is most active on Sundays and Thursdays.

CITY WALLS

Just beyond the Chashma Ayub, the weathered remnants of Bukhara's broken city walls encase the bazaar in a series of Morse-code dots and dashes. Sand castle remains are all that is left of the original 25 kilometre (15 mile) bastioned wall—ten metres high, five metres thick and wide enough to sit a cannon on its ramparts—that encompassed the Shakhristan and kept the hostile desert and its nomads at bay.

The first set of walls were raised as early as 850, when the medieval *shakhristan* was linked to the expanding suburb *rabad*. During the tenth century Samanid expansion a second set of walls was built, only to be subsequently fortified during the turbulent 12th and 13th centuries. Later still, a much larger oasis wall nicknamed the Kampirak or 'Old Woman' snaked all the way to Karmana and completed the Bukharan fortifications.

The seven original gates were expanded to 11 and named after the outlying suburbs. The Mazar Gate led to the shrine of Bakhauddin Nakhshbandi, the Karakul Gate led to Khorasan and the Tallipach Gate pointed the long march to Khorezm. From the outbreak of World War I until 1920 these gates were continually locked, sealing the city against Bolshevik agents and British spies, and permission to enter the city was granted only by the Bukharan consulate in Kagan. By this time, however, the walls performed more of a policing than a defensive role and they were no match for the Soviet artillery when the Red Army stormed the gates and entered the city through the Sheikh Jalal Gate on 2 September 1920.

Today the walls look like they have simply melted in the desert heat, but the **Tallipach Gate** still stands next to Pioneer Lake and the **Sheikh Jalal Gate** is still preserved to the southwest in the middle of Jeibor Street (ex-Oktyabrskya). Both date from 16th-century renovation.

ISMAEL SAMANI MAUSOLEUM

The mesmerizing tomb of Ismael Samani is an architectural bolt from the blue. It is also the oldest, best preserved and most breathtakingly original building in Bukhara and, without doubt, one of the architectural highlights of any visit to Uzbekistan.

The almost perfect brick cube was built at the beginning of the tenth century and belongs to the great cultural resurgence of the Samanid dynasty (875-999). The tomb derives its name from the founder of the dynasty, Ismael, and contains not only his tomb but also that of his father Ahmed, his nephew Nasr and others of the Samanid line.

The mausoleum draws elements from early Sogdian architecture (such as the heavy corner buttresses) and Sassanid fire worship (witness the circular brick suns and canopy shape of sacred Zoroastrian temples). Combining these with the recent arithmetic and geometrical advances made by al-Khorezmi, al-Fergani and ibn-Sina

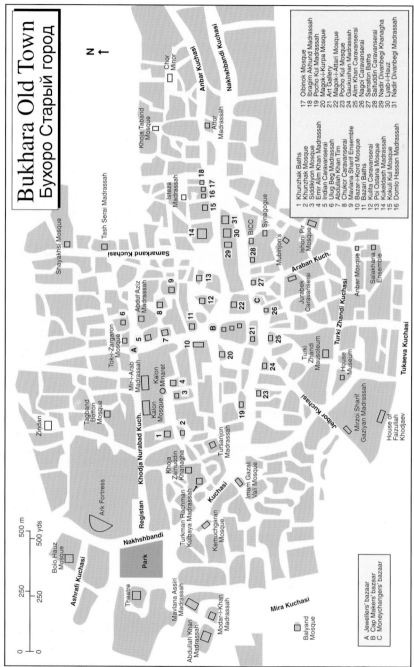

and the latest squinch technology, to forge an artistic style, the monumental *mazar*, would serve as an architectural formula for centuries to come.

The construction is of a 10.8-metre (35-foot) cube with four identical façades, all of which slope slightly inward and upon which sits a hemispherical cupola ringed with four domelets. Four internal arches supported by corner pillars form the squinch upon which rests the eight and 16-sided transition to the drum. This *chortak* ('four arch') system was revolutionary for the time and came to dominate countless subsequent memorial tombs in Transoxiana. From the outside the zone of transition is masked by a gallery of ten windows which provide light and ventilation for the cool inner tombs. The mausoleum is also rich in symbolism. Its cube not only refers back to the sacred *kaaba* stone at Mecca, but furthermore symbolizes the earth and complements its dome, symbol of the heavens, to create a metaphor of the universe.

The true majesty of the building lies in the vivacity and textured richness of its basket-woven brickwork, set in a series of absorbingly complex patterns after the completion of the main skeleton structure. Such is the skill of the brickwork that its mood is at once sombre and spectacular, subdued yet dynamic, shifting emphasis with the angle of the sun. Its corner buttresses stand as Herculean support, its two-metre (6.5-foot) thick walls woven in weightless delicacy. If time allows, try to visit the building at different hours, even at night.

The tomb is a sacred site for locals for several reasons. Originally, the tombstone had two openings, one where anxious pilgrims would place their questions, dilemmas and donations and another where a hidden mullah would leave the orthodox/considered solution. The site was also originally one of the holiest cemeteries in Bukhara, where even emirs were laid to rest. However, when in 1934 the mausoleum was discovered by the Soviet archaeologist Shishkin, buried under several metres of accumulated sand and earth, the graves were relocated wholesale and the area desanctified into the Kirov public park. The accumulation of earth accounts also its survival during the Mongol destruction. A more assiduous contemporary threat to the 1000-year-old tomb can be seen in the white salt marks left by the rising water table.

The Samani Mausoleum is situated in Samani Park, five minutes' walk due west of the Registan.

KOSH MADRASSAH

Kosh means 'double' and is a general architectural term that can refer to any two opposing or facing halves of an ensemble. In Bukhara, it refers more specifically to the Modar-i-Khan and Abdullah Khan madrassah, situated a few hundred metres from the southwest corner of the Registan towards the old Shirgaron Gate (present-day Ul Sverdlova). Both were built on the orders of Abdullah Shaybani Khan (1533–1597), one of the greatest sponsors of religious and especially secular buildings Bukhara has ever seen.

The smaller and less ambitious of the madrassah is the **Modar-i-Khan** (1566–7), built in two brief years at the beginning of Abdullah's reign, in honour of his mother (*modar* in Persian). The madrassah has an orthodox layout with restrained façade tilework and reflects the uncertainty of Abdullah's early few years as ruler.

It takes one look at the **Abdullah Khan Madrassah** opposite, built 23 years later, to realize that Abdullah probably loved himself more than he did his mother. The *girikh* designs of the façade are more complicated, the violets, greens and whites more vibrant and the portal more impressive than his mother's opposite. In fact Abdullah probably even loved himself more than he did Allah. For here, in a bold break with tradition, the artistic took precedent over the spiritual and the personal transcended the religious. The maverick madrassah and mosques were orientated not towards Mecca but rather to the cardinal points, partly so that the line of the façade reflected the symmetry of its *kosh* partner, but mostly so that Abdullah's future tomb could follow the customary north-south axis. At a time when the omnipotent clergy frowned upon lavish memorial mausoleums, it seems that Abdullah planned all along to be laid to rest in his smokescreen madrassah.

In another bold break with tradition, a two-storeyed octagonal chamber known as 'Abdullah's Lantern' bulges out of the northern wall to give the madrassah a unique plan. Narrow stairs access second floor cells to give an intriguing look behind the scenes at the bare bones of a madrassah and continue up to the roof to reveal piles of neglected 16th-century tiles scattered around bubbled domes and hujra chimney vents. The madrassah is a veritable architectural adventure-playground, unfettered by museum attendants or nannying Intourist guides. Unexpected access is gained through the neighbouring building site/lorry park.

BALYAND MOSQUE

Hidden on the fringes of the old town, some 400 metres (440 yards) south of the Kosh Madrassahs on Mira Street, the Balyand (High) Mosque is a frequently overlooked 16th-century gem.

Upon initial inspection, its façade is unimposing, notable only for the slender columns of the *iwan* which gives the mosque its name, devoid of the monumentality inherent in so much of Bukharan architecture. But beneath its anonymous exterior revels undisturbed some of the most opulent decoration to be found in Bukhara.

This architectural schizophrenia is buried deep in the mosque's *raison d'être*. For, as a local *guzar* mosque, its style is personal rather than public, introspective rather than ostentatious—a place of contemplation and refuge rather than ceremony or formality. Yet at the same time its district was a rich one and a district traditionally reflected its social standing and religious piety through its mosque.

The interior of the mosque is small and intimate and prayer mats quilt the floor in comfortable familiarity. The artistic and spiritual focus of the mosque, the glittering

Ismael Samani mausoleum, Bukhara

mihrab wall and niche, is an intense burst of polychrome mosaic and tilework, decorated with vegetable motifs and *thulth* Koranic inscriptions, and the beautifully carved wooden ceiling is remarkable for its unrestored *kundal* paintwork, suspended on chains from the cross beams above.

The Balyand now functions again as a working mosque and should be left in peace during *namaz* prayer.

Poi Kalon Ensemble

From the Registan, stroll five minutes east through the ghosts of Bukhara's old eastern bazaar (now semi-resurrected into a row of empty shops lining Khodja Nurabad Street), into the religious heart of Holy Bukhara, the Poi Kalon or Pedestal of the Great. Today the square that separates the Mir-i-Arab Madrassah from the Kalon Jummi Mosque echoes only to the muffled footprints of madrassah students and the fleeting bustle of foreign tour groups, but only a generation ago the square provided a chaotic home to the city's bustling cotton bazaar, where huge bundles of cloth listed dangerously atop swaying camels and where a man had to keep his wits about him:

> *When a large caravan of camels or creaking arbas sets out like a detachment of cavalry or artillery, everybody runs away in all directions to save life and limbs to which not much regard is paid and nor is much claimed either.*

> O. Olufsen, 1911.

■ THE KALON MINARET

The Kalon Minaret is one of the defining symbols of Bukhara. Towering over the city at over 48 metres (155 feet) high, this 'javelin thrust into the heart of the old town' has dominated the Bukharan skyline for over eight and a half centuries; the initial augur to exhausted caravans that they had, at last, arrived at a truly great city.

A minaret has stood here since 919, for after all, every Friday mosque needs its Friday minaret. The original minaret was destroyed by an act of God in 1068 and the subsequent wooden minaret built by the Karakhanid Arslan Khan collapsed within a fragile few years onto the packed Friday mosque with an equally inauspicious, and it seems quite devastating, loss of life. Thus in 1127, when the impatient khan rather ambitiously ordered the construction of the greatest minaret the world had hitherto seen, the architect wisely decided not to rush the job. Foundations were dug to a depth of 13 metres (45 feet), a base measuring nine metres (30 feet) in diameter was sketched out and a special mortar mixed, using camel's milk, egg yoke and bull's blood for that little something extra. The architect then promptly disappeared. Two years later he reappeared, claiming that the mortar had sufficiently hardened and raised the tallest free-standing tower in the world at that time. The khan was delighted and the status of the city was raised to the pinnacle of the Islamic world. However, the perfectionist architect was still dissatisfied and died not long after with the words "The flight of my fantasy was greater than the minaret I built". He was finally laid to rest in the shadow of his work, as far from the minaret as it was tall.

If the architect was not impressed then Genghis Khan certainly was. To this steppe nomad the vertical minaret explored a dimension his environment rarely provided. As he gazed up in wonder, historians recount how, in a rare gesture of humility, he bowed at the foot of the Great Minaret to pick up his fallen hat and quietly ordered the minaret spared the ensuing orgy of destruction.

The minaret did indeed survive the test of the ages, but only to see its skylight shattered by a Soviet shell during the 1920 civil skirmishes. It was subsequently repaired in 1924 and adorned with a bold red flag until excavated in 1964, when centuries of accumulated earth and sand where removed from its base and another two metres added to its official height. The minaret was further damaged in the 1976 Gazli earthquake, but has since been restored and is now under UNESCO protection.

The minaret was, of course, built to provide the call to prayer, a giant Islamic exclamation mark to overshadow the faithful. Four fit muezzins would sound the call and a forest of over 200 minarets would echo the call to outlying suburbs. But the outsize tower could be commandeered for an array of unholy causes. In times of war, its crow's nest provided an essential early warning system against the rival khanate armies which would regularly rise like mist from the sandy horizon and, in times of peace, beacons lit in its skylight created a lighthouse to guide lonely trade caravans through the desperate desert wastes of the Kara Kum. The minaret's most diabolically inspired variant was the twisted work of the degenerate Mangit Uzbeks. For here, on market days, particularly outrageous criminals were led up the 105 steps of this 'Tower of Death', whereupon their crimes would be enumerated to the transfixed crowd, the omniscient justice of the emir praised to the heavens and the accursed criminal tied in a sack and thrown off the top to hurtle to certain oblivion below. The gruesome spectacle was current well into the second half of the 19th century and only added to Bukhara's already widespread infamy, moving a young George Curzon to write in characteristic style:

> This mode of punishment, whose publicity and horror are well calculated to act as a deterrent to the Oriental population, is not the only surviving proof that the nineteenth century can scarcely be considered as yet to have got a firm hold on Bukhara.

The minaret rises golden from an octagonal base and tapers elegantly through ten individual bands of lacy brickwork up to a 16-windowed rotunda gallery. A band of blue tiles underneath the stalactite lantern stands out as probably the first usage of coloured majolica tilework to be seen in Transoxiana and a brick inscription dates it to 1127. The geometric brick designs would first have been laid out on the ground onto a grid and then added onto the bare trunk of the minaret. The conical stump that crowns the minaret is all that remains of an original extension which pushed the minaret even higher than it stands today. The honey bricks glow in the late afternoon light, when the ensemble is at it most bewitching.

In 1832 'Bokhara' Burnes noted that access to the minaret was tightly restricted to prevent lecherous local Uzbeks or Tajiks spying down into the female courtyards of local houses. Today the height of the minaret is equally out of bounds to the infidel tourist, but the key is kept in the Kalon Mosque and the right kind of persuasion may find doors miraculously opened.

■ KALON MOSQUE

The Kalon (Great) Mosque is the *Jummi*, or Friday, mosque of Bukhara, built to house the entire male population of the city during its main weekly *namaz* prayer. Not only is it one of the most ancient mosques in Central Asia, it is also the second biggest, with a stadium-like open-air capacity of 10–12,000 souls. Only the Bibi Khanum held a larger capacity and that was just a bit too large, collapsing around its congregation soon after completion.

It was the Kalon Mosque into which Genghis Khan rode defiantly in 1219, believing it to be the palace of the sultan. When informed that he was in the house of God, Genghis scornfully ordered the Koran holders be overturned into mangers for his horses and the pages of the Koran trampled in the dirt beneath their feet. He as-

BUKHARAN LIFE ON THE EVE OF THE TWENTIETH CENTURY

The physical layout of the city of Bukhara and life on its streets had hardly changed in over one thousand years. The town was a cramped and claustrophobic labyrinth of blind alleys, introspective courtyards and narrow streets flooded by a steady stream of laden camels, tottering *arba* carts, nobility on horseback and turbanned merchants. The walls, streets and tombs merged to resemble a "loess plateau where the rain has furrowed narrow drains" and the flat roofs were so dense that it seemed one could cross the city walking from roof to roof.

The city contained 20 caravanserais, over 50 madrassahs and around 100 pools, criss-crossing the city in a web of canals, but Bukhara's boast to have a mosque for every day of the year was, by this time, already an anachronistic echo from a holier, more devout past. While it was still said of the city that "in all other parts of the globe light descends upon the earth, from holy Bukhara it ascends", by now the reality on the streets was slightly more squalid. In the dry summer months the city's irregular water supply could be cut off for months at a time, with local Bukharans drinking, washing and cleaning in canals alive with skin disease and guinea worm. Visitors to the city soon became acquainted only too well with the horrors of the *reshta*, a parasite that entered the bloodstream only to emerge from the host's leg as a two foot white worm which had to be slowly wound around a match over a period of days. If the worm broke, it would split into a dozen pieces only to reemerge days later amidst the host's agonized cries. Bukhara's sanitation system was set afloat in a sea of its own filth and in an attempt to control its regular epidemics, those with serious skin diseases were quarantined in a closed section in the north of the city and any Bukharan was empowered to slay on sight a leper found outside his quarter.

The city was ruled with a despotic rod of iron. As darkness fell on the domed city a slow drumbeat began to eminate from the bowels of the Ark, signalling the evening curfew. All eleven city gates were barred and locked and the eleven keys taken to the chief of police, or *mirsab*, as night watchmen set off to prowl the deserted streets. Any man caught roaming the city after dark without a torch was assumed a thief and immediately brought before the *mirsab* for confession. As late as 1919, religious police would also regularly patrol the religious heart of the emirate, pausing only to grill a random passer-by over some aspect of Islamic law or to quiz him on an uncompleted *surah* from the Koran. Any man deemed ignorant of his faith was carried off, beaten and fined as a warning to all around. Mullahs were also empowered to search without warning any man's house for traces of alcohol, while anyone caught asleep during prayers or smoking in public was subject to arrest and fines. The city swarmed with the emir's spies and all seditious activity was carefully noted under cover of the outsize sleeves of the informers' cloaks.

Punishments were fiendish in the extreme. A convicted murderer could expect anything from decapitation (often onto a red-hot tray, after which, it was grimly reported, the corpseless head would move and wince upon the searing metal for several seconds) to mutilation (eyelids were cut off and eyes gouged out) to jaculation (thrown from the top of the Kalon Minaret, sewn in a cloth sack). A heavy cloud of violence permeated the holy City. But it seems that some Bukharans were in need of a certain extra moral guidance. A Russian trade delegate to the city in 1820 was flabbergasted by the "sexual enormities" of the local inhabitants, the sordid details of which he felt constrained by shame from divulging. Even the emir was said to have kept a bunch of 40 dancing boys in his court where "all the horrors and abhominations of Sodom and Gomorrah were practised".

Against this soiled backdrop of licentious depravity, Bukhara sought its salvation in Islam. On Fridays, all shops, without exception, were barred and shut before lunchtime prayers and the streets were crowded with the faithful streaming to the Jummi Mosque, decked in mountains of rustling silk and high-heeled boots with turbans set in the traditional 40 folds and *khalats* of such richness that George Curzon felt moved to quip that "in Bukhara, Joseph would have been looked upon as the recipient of no particular favour in the gift of a coat of many colours". Women on the other hand wore a darker shadow and were rarely seen. Girls over the age of puberty were hidded behind a black horsehair veil and long, loose *paranja* robe with "empty sleeves hanging suspended behind their backs, so that observed from behind, the fair ones of Bukhara may be mistaken for clothes wandering about" (Vambery, 1864). Women walking in the streets were never to be addressed and if any of the Emir's harem were to pass by, men were admonished to look in the opposite direction, upon pain of a swift clubbing from the emir's guard.

In spite of its vicious introspection, Bukhara was still a suprisingly cosmopolitan city and it counted among its population Jews, Afghans, Armenians,

Russians, Persians, Chinese and Hindus and even a shadowy European pharmacist named Reinhardt, the only Westerner ever granted Bukharan domocile. Teahouses and bazaars were social magnets where friends and acquaintances greeted each other with a hand over the heart, a stroke of the beard and a line from the Koran, and also open stage for dancing boys, professional storytellers and even dentists, whose victims would kneel with their heads between an assistant's knees as he used his body weight to lever out offending teeth. Bloodletting, the only real medicine thought to rival a visit to a saint's tomb as the most effective remedy for sickness, was also a teahouse profession. When executions and gutter dentistry failed to provide free entertainment, ram fighting, juggling and a melancholy quatrain from the *rubbab* filled the void. Tea was continually brewed in every dwelling but it seems the favourite drink in summer was a concoction of grape syrup poured over crushed ice, the latter buried in the winter months and stored underground to be dispensed almost free during the scorching summer heat. Life was a hedonistic blend of innocent charm and cynical depravity.

By the turn of the 20th century, Bukhara was sunk in a pool of bottomless vice, wore a halo of departed glory, and was heavy with an air of immutability. But its nefarious days were numbered and the medieval would slowly and inexorably yield to the modern.

For my own part, on leaving the city I could not help rejoicing at having seen it in what might be described as the twilight epoch of its glory. Were I to go again in later years it might be to find electric light in the highways. It might be to see window-panes in the houses, and to meet with trousered figures in the streets. It might be to eat zakuska in a Russian restaurant and to sleep in a Russian hotel; to be ushered by a tchinovnik into the palace of the Ark, and to climb for fifty kopecks the Minor-i-Kalian. Civilisation may ride in the Devil's Wagon but the Devil has a habit of exacting his toll. What could be said for a Bukhara without a Kosh Begi, a Divan Begi, and an Inak—without its Mullahs and kalanders, its toksabas and its mirzabashi, its shabraques and chupans and khalats? Already the mist of ages is beginning to rise and to dissolve. The lineaments are losing their beautiful vague mystery of outline. It is something, in the short interval between the old order and the new, to have seen Bukhara, while it may still be called the Noble, and before it has ceased to be the most interesting city in the world.

George Curzon, 1889

cended the pulpit, cried out "The hay is cut! Give your horses fodder!" and his troops burst out of the mosque, with the knowledge that they had the khan's tacit permission to decimate the city. The mosque was burnt to cinders and the city razed to the ground. Thus the present mosque is simply the latest in a series of Friday mosques to be grafted onto the dead remains of the past. The original mosque, built in 795 by the city's Arab governor was enlarged by Ismael Samani, suffered collapse twice during his nephew Nasr's reign, burnt to the ground in 1068 and then suffered the Mongol wrath in 1219. The present structure was finished in 1514 (witness an inscription on the mosque's façade) and the *mihrab* was embellished in 1541 under the Shaybani Ubaydullah.

The plan of the mosque forms a 127- by 78-metre (415- by 255-foot) open rectangle with four *iwans* on its axis and seven entrance gates drawing in all corners of the city. The main entrance lies through the beautiful eastern portal and steps descend through time from 1970s restoration to the original 15th-century ground level. The huge central open-air plaza opens like a rectangular burst of white heat and is encased in a colonnaded arcade of 208 pillars and 288 domes which rise from the roof in cool bubbles of shade. To the west the turquoise swell of the Kok Gumbaz (Blue Dome) gives the mosque its popular nickname and shelters the brilliant, gilded tilework of the *mihrab* niche, an opulence financed by Ubaydullah's victorious campaign to Gijduvan and signed by the architect Buyazid Purani. The white Kufic inscription running around the dome reads 'al-baqa' lillah' (Immortality Belongs To God).

The 19th century octagonal pavilion set in front of the *mihrab* is an intriguing late addition to the mosque. Some say it marks the ancient well used for centuries for ritual ablution, others that it was built to shade the emir during his weekly visits. Most probably, it served as an early tannoy system, from where a second imam would echo the words and motions of the first for the benefit of the congregation.

Today the mosque is a relic from a more devout age. Its doors have re-opened to embrace Islam, but its irregular and ageing cluster of a congregation huddles disconsolately in what is only a tiny corner of its deep cloister, themselves a remnant from a past age.

■ MIR-I-ARAB MADRASSAH

The Mir-i-Arab Madrassah has ranked as the most prestigious educational establishment in Bukhara for centuries. Today it stands at the forefront of Uzbekistan's Islamic renaissance, a place where the past, the present and the future blur into one and where, as the Soviet century recedes to dim memory, the 16th century looms on the near horizon.

In 1535 the Shaybani Ubaydullah Khan sold his share of a consignment of 3,000 Persian slaves for a profit that apparently lay heavy on his soul, for almost immedi-

Mir-i-Arab Madrassah, Bukhara

ately afterwards he commissioned a madrassah to face his newly-built Kalon Mosque. Responsibility for its construction fell to his close friend and spiritual adviser Sheikh Abdullah of Yemen, the Prince of the Arabs (Mir-i-Arab), at whose feet the khan was eventually buried in the northern domed *darskhana* of the madrassah. Even today the tombs are marked on the northern wall of the madrassah with a goat's tail and white flag, the customary symbols of sainthood.

The life of a madrassah student has changed little over the years. Up to the end of the 19th century, students received a religious stipend from the state and could freely marry, as long as their wives did not cross the holy threshold of the college. Tuition was solely in Arabic, writing and mathematics were deeply frowned upon and any student caught in the heinous study of literature, history or poetry was expelled on the spot. As Bukharan isolation intensified, the madrassah slid into a bastion of religious obscurantism and dogmatic fanaticism.

At present approximately 250 resident students study a five-year course of Arabic, theology and the Koran at the madrassah and its spill-over classrooms in the Kalon Mosque, on the first step to becoming fully fledged *imams*. Thus the madrassah is formally closed to tourists, who can only squint through the entrance grill at the intense tilework of its inner court. The two storey façade alone is reward enough though, with its fortress-like buttresses (*guldasta*) and twin domes which rise from lecture room and mosque like jade balloons. At night warm pin pricks of light diffuse from the alabaster grills of student cells.

The madrassah was closed from 1925–1946, after which it was re-opened as part of Stalin's post-war package of concessions to the region. These years were a time of startling juxtapositions and Gustav Krist recounts in his 1937 book *Alone Through the Forbidden Land* how, as he was ushered into the *hujra* cell of the madrassah's holiest *imam*, he found himself opposite a wall laden with sacred books titled in Kufic Arabic, above which hung a poster in Uzbek screaming "PROLETARIANS OF ALL LANDS UNITE!" in a distinctly unholy shade of red.

The southern steps of the Poi Kalon square relay the traveller back to the 20th century and the façade of the **Emir Alim Khan Madrassah**. The madrassah was built with a unique triple courtyard by the last emir towards the end of his rule (1914) and has been used as the city's children's library since 1924.

The library or *kitab khanah* is heir to an ancient and illustrious tradition of Bukharan libraries. During the tenth century the state library, the Treasury of Wisdom, was rivalled only by Baghdad and the great philosopher and physician Avicenna availed himself of its archives as his reward for curing the sick sultan. Calligraphers, miniaturists and scribes copied texts which were then categorized by their field of study and stored in great rows of wooden chests in madrassah storehouses. The library unfortunately could not survive the fires which regularly gutted the city.

A quick diversion west from the Poi Kalon square into the old town reveals the marvellously decorated **Khodja Zainuddin Ensemble**, consisting of functioning district mosque, *khanagha* hostel with five cells, the *mazaar* tomb of Zainuddin himself, concealed in a niche in the western façade, and a *hauz* water supply. The unexpected highlight of the early 16th-century building is the interior decoration of the dome, rising from majolica panelling, through a band of stalactite niches to the exuberant gold, blue and red paintwork set on the inside of the dome to represent the heavens. The painting is *kundal*, a technique used to create ornamental relief by the multiple application of sticky mineral paints by brush capped by a coat of gold leaf and is similar to that seen in the Balyand Mosque.

Mosque ceiling detail

Outside the *iwan*-fringed mosque oozes one of Bukhara's earliest water pools, sunk next to the mosque not only for ablutions but also to persuade locals to combine two daily necessities, water and prayer, into one social centre. Note the dragon-mouthed, inscribed water pipes that line and feed the pool.

ULUG BEG AND ABDUL AZIZ MADRASSAHS

A few hundred yards east from the Poi Kalon, beyond the Tok-i-Zargaron bazaar, lies the second of Bukhara's *kosh* madrassahs, separated by Khodja Nurabad Street and two hundred years of Bukharan history.

The **Ulug Beg Madrassah** (1417) was the earliest of three commissioned by the enlightened Timurid ruler (the other two stand in Samarkand and Gijduvan) and his secular influence dominates the exterior design of the religious college. Star motifs reflect Ulug's fascination with astronomy, *girikh* designs reflect the already established synthesis of science and art and an inscription on the entrance panel proclaims "It is the sacred duty of every Muslim man and woman to seek after knowledge". An earlier inscription on the door knocker further blessed the pursuit of wisdom; "Above the circle of people well schooled in the wisdom of books, let the doors of Allah's blessing be open every instant."

The name of the architect "Ismael, son of Tahir, son of the master craftsman Mahmud of Isfahan" is crammed into a star-shaped inscription above the main portal, but subsequent reconstruction work in 1586 under Khan Abdullah II added a darker majolica tint to the Timurid façade. Present day whitewashed *remont* was clumsily added in the rush to celebrate Ulug Beg's 500th birthday in October 1994 and much of its charm has sadly been lost in the dust.

Through the twisted border of the balanced façade lie a lecture hall on the left, mosque on the right and hidden library on the second floor. The mosque now plays host to an **Exhibition on the History of Renovation**, which includes examples of original tilework and interesting photographs of the Kalon Minaret with its crown blasted off and a band of old turbaned men plotting ceramic designs. The compact central courtyard, with what Ella Maillart described as its "high walls framing the silence", now houses fledgling Uzbek entrepreneurs keen to lure foreign tourists into their rented cells crammed with crafted memorabilia. Quality is generally high, as is the black market exchange rate.

Facing the Ulug Beg is the **Abdul Aziz Madrassah** (1652), glittering in mercifully unrestored 17th century glory. The soul of the madrassah lies in its decoration which bursts out of the artistic straightjackets of the age in an attempt "to break free onto the path of progress by rejecting the restricting traditions of the past", but which "could not find enough strength for such an active step" (G.A. Pugachenkova).

Colourful mosaic vases of eternal happiness lead up to richly starred stalactites and access the Chinese-influenced landscape decoration of the left-hand lecture hall and stunning interior decoration of the right-hand mosque. Inside the main courtyard look out for the twin-level *hujra* cell equipped with fireplace left on display in the far right corner, the rich ganch *iroki* stalactites of the southern portal, the three dimensional vases of the eastern portal and the Iranian-influenced yellows of the northern portal. The right-hand side of the courtyard and the left side of the main façade stand undecorated and unfinished, victims like their master of a successful coup.

BUKHARAN BAZAARS
From the Tok-i-Zargaron, the bustling commercial heart of the city snaked south-

wards through a street of shaded stalls, fortress caravanserais and domed bazaars to form one of the most colourful and cosmopolitan trading grounds in the Islamic world. From dawn to dusk an endless procession of supercilious camels, heavily-laden donkeys and creaking *arbas* crashed through bursting streets in a chaotic exchange of insult and barter. Turbaned Tajiks crouched in the dust, sparks flew from open workshops, deals were struck by secret handshake under outsized sleeves and agreements were sealed in wax by the rings of robed merchants. Saddles, ropes, gourds, skins, metal ewers, tobacco, tea and spices spilled out indiscriminately from dimly lit and cavernous stalls, melons hung individually from roofs and a small army of barbers, bakers, blacksmiths, tea boys and shashlik sellers hustled to serve myriad local needs.

Yet behind the commercial chaos lay a tightly organized system of control, for taxation was a serious business in Bukhara, especially after the 16th-century boom in Bukharan-Russian trade. A sliding scale ranged from the traditional one-fortieth tax rate proscribed by the clergy for Muslim traders to an almost 20 per cent rate for Christian Russians. Emergency war taxes were regularly imposed, lastly by Mozaffar to fight off the Russian invasion, and under Subkhan Kuli Khan (1681-1702) taxes were even demanded seven years in advance.

Five main vaulted and domed bazaars (*toks*), covered busy road intersections, each monopolizing a separate trade to facilitate tax collection and each referred to simply by number. The structures were utilitarian but complex as they straddled convergent trade arteries and all were accessed by entrance arches high enough for a laden pack camel. The northernmost and largest of the three remaining *toks* is the **Tok-i-Zargaron** (1570), or Jeweller's Bazaar, where gold, coral (especially valuable so far from the sea) and precious metals changed hands. At the northern end of the bazaar stands the affiliated Zargaron Mosque, positioned so that busy merchants were forced to waste as little valuable haggling time as possible en route to prayer.

South of the bazaar lay the huge Indian Caravanserai (now an empty square to the left) which sheltered a ghetto of resident Hindu money-lenders, forbidden to live with their families or other Muslims, and led onto a closed street of stalls or *dukkans* and caravanserais, constructed and rented out by rich merchants with a vested interest in the prime sites. Goods changed hands in over 40 bazaars, 24 caravanserais and also six *tims* (shopping arcade with only one entrance), of which only one, the **Abdullah Khan Tim**, remains. The Abdullah Khan was built in 1577 and was one of the most elegant trade halls in Bukhara where silk and wool was sold by Afghan traders, instantly recognizable by the tail of silk trailing from the left side of their turbans, in 50 stalls ranged around the cool central dome. Other *tims* dealt in killims, velvets and cotton. Continuing south down the main Shah Restan thoroughfare, the road was hemmed in on both sides by a wall of stalls shaded by mat coverings to produce a dark cool tunnel of trade.

The second main bazaar to have survived is the **Tok-i-Tilpak Furushon**, or Cap Maker's Bazaar, where gold embroidered skull-caps and karakul fur hats were displayed out of the heat of the sun and where Bukhara's most valuable books and manuscripts were sold in a series of 26 stalls. The bazaar, an especially complicated structure due to the irregular layout of its five main spokes, shelters the tomb of the holy man Khoja Ahmed I Paran.

Bukharan trade was serviced by a wide array of auxiliary buildings eager to profit from the densely assembled crowd of potential punters and included craft shops, hotels and baths, examples of which are all located next to the Tok-i-Tilpak. The 16th century **bathhouse** (*hammam* or *hambom* in Bukharan dialect) just to the north of the bazaar, one of an original 18 in the city, is at present under renovation but has for centuries provided its essential social service. Even Avicenna in his *Qanun* expounds the medicinal values of regular bathing and aromatherapy massage, a theme later expanded into an eleventh century code of public etiquette, the *Kabus Name*. The baths are sunk deep into the ground to preserve heat and form a series of halls clustered around a central skylit chamber.

Just opposite the baths lies the 16th-century **Bazar-i-kord Mosque**, whose High Tech logo highlights the spurious transition from place of prayer to free-market

Skullcap sellers

boutique, and the **Museum of the Blacksmith's Art**, a family of blacksmiths who have plied their ancient trade on this site for generations. At the back of the small museum do not miss the small door that leads off to the courtyard of the tiny **Kulita Caravanserai**. This unassuming bazaar ensemble is completed by the **Magok-i-Kurpa Mosque** (1637), the two-storeyed prayer halls of which now function as a Tajik Cultural Centre, whose role in a mood of rising Uzbek assertiveness must now be under question.

From the Capmaker's Bazaar continue south along the old bazaar road to the soviet square formerly named after Mikhail Frunze (he addressed a mass rally here), past the row of four battered caravanserais and Magok-i-Attari Mosque to the right to reach the **Tok-i-Sarrafon** or Moneychanger's Bazaar. Here resided the Punjabi moneychangers, dwarfed in their stalls behind huge piles of coins and notes, who would exchange Persian, Russian, Afghan and local currencies into the bronze *pul*, silver *tenge* and gold *tilla* that circulated as legal tender in Bukhara's bazaars. It seems they had a busy life—under the rule of Imam Kuli Khan (1611-1641) alone Bukharan currency was devalued 57 times. The bazaar was also home to Afghan and Armenian moneylenders armed with traditional tallysticks who, when left unpaid for too long, were wont to carve the embarrassing figure on a debtor's doorpost.

Also located around the bazaar is the Sarrafon Mosque (now an irregular *chaikhana*), Sarrafon Baths (presently under reconstruction as architects puzzle over how to drain excess water that has been continually drained for the last four centuries), Nagoi Caravanserai (under conversion into a new French hotel) and Shah Rud canal. The southern end of the bazaar street continues south to peter out around the ruined Jurabek Caravanserai and east to the Saifuddin Caravanserai.

Today modern entrepreneurial businessmen echo the call of ancestral traditions: metal chasers haunt the Jeweller's Bazaar; a lacklustre state cloth shop has commandeered the Abdullah Khan Tim; booksellers, embroiderers and Karakul milliners have set up shop in the Capmaker's Bazaar and free marketeers in the Moneychanger's Bazaar are more than happy to convert crisp, new dollars into crisp, new sum.

MAGOK-I-ATTARI MOSQUE.

Descend the six-metre (19-foot) deep cultural layers of the Magok-i-Attari Mosque and you will find heathen shrines, the remains of a Buddhist monastery, a Zoroastrian temple and the mosque of the Arab invaders, all sharing the same space, jostling as uneasy bedfellows. At least this is what the Soviet archaeologist V A Shishkin found during his 1935 excavations, unveiling as he worked a unique vertical spread of 2,000 years of Bukharan history.

By the Samanid tenth century the mosque began to be known by its present name, partly from the medicinal herb sellers (*Attars*) who displayed their spices in the busy bazaar here, partly from the name of the name of the square (*Mokh* meaning either moon or the name of a mythological prince) and the twice yearly religious fair convened here, and also in part from the depth of its cultural layers (*magok* meaning pit). In 937 the four-pillared mosque was burnt to the ground in a city-wide fire and in the 12th century the present mosque was erected, from which the focus of the mosque, the original southern portal, remains.

The absorbing portal draws the entire range of decorative techniques— ganch carving, polished brick, terracotta plaques and glazed tile work—into its richly receding façade. Two Sogdian-influenced quarter columns lead the eye to complex *girikh* panels, reminiscent of those in Uzgen, and fine filigree carved columns support a graceful arch still traced in turquoise majolica tilework.

In 1547 an eastern entrance façade was added with its skullcap dome, but today the mosque is still approached from the south. The mosque is today used as a **Museum of Carpets** whose highlights include a falcon holder and carpet bag for storing dead game, a heretic Christian Armenian carpet depicting figures and faces and a selection of Turkoman Ersari and Tekke carpets. Zoroastrian remains can be seen in the eastern pit, below a huge mass prayer carpet.

BUKHARAN ART GALLERY

In the southwest corner of former Frunze Square lies the shell of the first tsarist Central Asian Bank in Bukhara, designed by the same architects that worked in the emir's Summer Palace, and which now houses a two-floored gallery of Bukharan art, with works by both native Bukharans and painters from other parts of the former Soviet Union who spent formative years painting here.

Among the most evocative paintings are those of Pavel Benkov (1888-1949) who spent two years working in Bukhara from 1928-1930 and a series of local artisan portraits by Michael Kurzin (1888-1957) who, although born in the Altai region of Siberia, spent much of the 1940s here, often painting on disused cardboard when materials grew short. Look out also for one of the museum's most famous works, *The Fall of the Bukharan Emirate*, by Tashkent artist Ruzi Chariev which depicts a cowering procession of rich merchants and beys in front of the "victorious masses" and which took ten years to complete.

Many of the newer paintings are for sale in a ground floor shop, with prices cheaper and quality higher than most other bazaars.

GAUKUSHAN MADRASSAH

A few metres from the gallery, this 16th-century maverick is unusual for its lopsided arrangement, created by the awkward layout of the road junction, and subsequent merger of its classroom and mosque together into the right-hand chamber. Its two-storey façade also gives way, rather unusually, to a one-storey courtyard. The Gaukushan was originally built on the site of an old slaughterhouse (*Gaukushan* means 'one who kills bulls'), but today houses a workshop of metal-chasers whose plates and ewers sell for dollars or sum.

The affiliated **Gaukushan Minaret** opposite actually serves the Khoja Mosque, a large cloistered mosque built in 1598 by the Juibar Sheikh Khodja Kalon for Friday prayers but now firmly locked up. Also nearby is the **Alim Khan Caravanserai**, home to the vaguely defined 'Society for Booklovers', which occasionally sells Uzbek musical instruments such as the *tambur* or *rubab* in its front courtyard.

LYAB-I-HAUZ ENSEMBLE

And yet those ponds of Bukhara are wonderfully beautiful. In the evening,
after the muezzin has sounded from the minaret the call to prayer, the men of the
city gather around the ponds, which are bordered by tall, silver poplars and mag-
nificent black elms, to enjoy a period of ease and leisure. Carpets are spread, the
ever burning chilim is passed from mouth to mouth, the samovar steams away,
and lightfooted boys hand round the shallow bowls of green tea. Here the med-
dahs, or story-tellers, the musicians and the dancing boys assemble to display
their craft. And perhaps a conjuror or a juggler comes, performing the most
amazing and incredible feats of skill. An Indian snake charmer joins the throng
and sets his poisonous snakes to dance, while over all reigns the peace of a Bukha-
ran evening. No loud speech breaks the spell; items of scandal and the news of the
day are exchanged in discreet whispers. So it was centuries ago in Bukhara; so it
is today. There are things which not even the Soviets can alter.

Gustav Krist, Alone Through the Forbidden Land, *(1937).*

The pool and *chaikhana* of the Lyab-i-Hauz is the modern centre of traditional Uzbekistan. A place where the very soul of Central Asia lies mirrored in a *piala* of steaming green tea or in the reflected symmetry of a resplendent portal, where cloudy eyed
white-beards contemplate the march of time and take shelter from a land in turmoil.

The *chaikhana* is not only a way of life in Central Asia, it is also an escape and an
antidote to life in Central Asia. It is the essential lubricant to friendship, trade and
travel. Its professionals are a hard core of regular nine to fivers, equipped with
personal teapots, *pialas* and backgammon sets and brandishing gleaming arrays of
heroic Soviet medals. Many took part in the World War II and are a wonderful source
of local oral history. In few places does the name Churchill elicit such mad affection.

During the early years of Soviet transformation red posters adorned the walls of
the Lyab-i-Hauz *chaikhana*, one of a series of Red Chaikhanas which Anna Louise
Strong noticed on her 1932 trip to Central Asia, wondering with some concern
whether it was possible "that the East may lose its leisure, and drink its tea with one
lump or two of propaganda?"

The cool waters and bevelled steps of the *hauz,* or pool, date from 1620. It was the
largest of the city reservoirs, fed directly from the main canal or Shah Rud (Royal
Canal) which still bisects the old town. From here professional water-carriers would
deliver large leather bags of water to wealthy clients. Today the *hauz* lies idyllic, but
during the time of the emirate it was an idyll afloat on a sea of its own filth. Reshta
worms, 'blue sickness', water fleas and dead dogs infested the stagnant water supply
until the Soviets drained, restored and refilled it in the 1960s. The mulberry trees that
line its shore date from 1477.

Nasreddin

Nasreddin decided to express his loyalty to Timur the Great, who had just finished conquering his country. He asked his wife to cook a goose, and took it to the palace. It was quite a long way, and he got hungry, so he stopped and ate one of the goose legs. When he came to the palace, Timur accepted the humble present, but he laughed when he saw that there was only one leg. "Why are you laughing?" asked Nasreddin, offended, "All the geese in this area have only one leg. Look out of the window if you don't believe me." It was getting dark, and all the geese outside were sleeping standing on one leg.

Timur ordered his prized harquebus to be brought and mounted it on a tripod near the window. The crowd of courtiers and guests stood still. Timur quietly loaded the weapon, took aim, and fired at the geese. They cackled and flapped their wings, scattering in different directions. "Can you see now?" the satisfied commander asked. "They all have two legs." Everybody smiled with relief. "If they fired at you with such a terrible weapon, you too would have run away on all fours!" the wise man quickly replied.

Murat Akchurin, Red Odyssey, 1991

The building reflected in the waters of the *hauz* is the **Nadir Divanbegi Khanagha**. Commissioned at the same time as the pool by Nadir Divanbegi (Divanbegi was a government post equivalent to Finance Minister or Grand Vizier), the two are compositely linked. The *khanagha* consists of a central cruciform local mosque surrounded by a series of four *hujra* cells set on two floors which would offer accommodation to mendicant holy men. Today the high portal sparkles and the richly decorated *mihrab* is surrounded by an 'exhibition' of hard-currency souvenirs.

The **Nadir Divanbegi Madrassah** closes the eastern side of the ensemble and dates from the 1630s. When the Imam Kuli Khan passed the newly-built splendour of its façade, he commended the Divanbegi upon the madrassah and his religious propriety. The minister bit his lip, for he had actually built it as a caravanserai and lucrative source of personal income, but the khan had spoken and no-one could recind the words of Allah's chosen deputy. The portal was rebuilt and corner towers added, as befitted a religious seminary, but to this day the madrassah still lacks a traditional layout, equipped with neither mosque nor lecture hall. The famous tympanum mosaic depicts two fantastic but irreligious *simurgh* birds with two white does clasped in their talons, flying up a Mongol-faced sun in a heretic frieze, perhaps commissioned in a fit of secularism by a bitter Divanbegi. The madrassah cells today hold several craft and jewellery workshops, a first rate barber and a soft drinks/juice bar.

Between the madrassah and *khanagha* stands the statue of Khodja Nasreddin on his donkey.

The **Kukeldash Madrassah** (1568), lying to the north of the *hauz,* is the largest in Central Asia (60 by 80 metres/196 by 262 feet) and the religious magnet that spurred the construction of the ensemble. Its construction is linked to the general and statesman Kulbaba Kukeldash who sponsored many civic projects during the rule of Abdullah Khan II. Its heavy brick façade conceals some elegant interior tilework and complicated vaulting systems.

The madrassah today functions as a cheap hotel (entered from the west), but in the past has housed the local records office and was even at one time partly remodelled as a women's centre, the ultimate Soviet sacrilege for such a male-only bastion.

To the south of the Lyab-i-Hauz Square spreads the **Jewish Quarter** of the old town. Jews have been an important minority in Bukhara since their forced migration from Merv and Shiraz in the 14th century, representing one of the farthest-flung corners of the diaspora. Their pivotal role in the growth of international trade, especially with the Russian Volga, and their domination of certain industries such as cold silk dyeing belied their relatively small numbers, but unfortunately for the Bukharan Jews economic prosperity was rarely converted into political or social influence. Compelled to wear square caps of fur and pieces of rope around their waists to remind them that they could be hanged at any moment, Jews were also forbidden to ride within the city walls—a prohibition that even extended to one of the first of the city's rich merchants to buy a motor car, only to find himself compelled by law to leave it parked outside the city gates. Jewish evidence was inadmissible in court (as was women's) and as non-Muslims Jews were subject to an extra infidel tax. But there were few forced conversions and although some Jews, known as *chalas*, found it expedient to embrace Islam, most kept their distinct cultural integrity. In 1832 Burnes estimated the Jewish population at about 4,000 and described them as a remarkably handsome race, admitting that he had seen 'more than one Rebecca in his peregrinations'.

The main **synagogue** lies only 300 metres (330 yards) south of the Lyab-i-Hauz in an unassuming, almost underground location that enabled it to escape major Soviet repression. Its Hebrew Torah and seven-branched menorah are decorated by Uzbek *khanatlas* silk and almost all local Jews today speak Tajik and Russian. Those, that is, who have not already taken advantage of Israeli financial support and left for Israel. Further south on the edge of town lies the **Jewish Cemetery**, where chiselled Hebrew gravestones reflect a lost people and where the stars of Lenin and David mix uneasily.

CHOR MINOR

The Chor Minor (Four Minarets) is one of the most charming and quirky buildings in Bukhara, all the more surprising because, built in 1807, it dates from a period of suffocating cultural stagnation. The building, resembling an upside-down chair thrust deep into the ground, is merely the *darvazakhana* gatehouse of a madrassah (90 by 40 metres/292 by 130 feet) built by the rich Turkoman merchant Khalif Niyazkul. If you view the building from the south you are standing in the madrassah courtyard with its former summer mosque to your left and *hauz* to your right. The only remains of the madrassah lie crumbling to the sides of the Chor Minor.

The three-domed minarets (following the sad collapse of one in 1995) that sprout from gatehouse are not strictly speaking minarets and never have been. None of the structures has a gallery, precluding any call to prayer, and three out of the four were purely auxiliary, only the fourth providing access to a first-floor library. The 17-metre (55-foot) minarets are capped with sky-blue domes and up until this century small spikes provided regular nest support for generations of migratory storks.

BUKHARAN BACKSTREETS

At the turn of the century Bukhara boasted 127 working madrassahs and a mosque for every day of the year. Many are still standing, in varying states of disrepair and disregard, hardly touched since they were locked up after the fall of the emirate. Most are unfortunately still locked and the best views you will get of them is through padlocked wooden doors. Many are hidden deep in Bukharan backstreets where, unlike Khiva, Central Asian life reveals itself. Dogs yap, goats wander, children play in the dust and a whirling dervish lies hidden behind every corner.

None of the sights compare to the grandeur of the more famous monuments of Bukhara, all are on a far more personal scale, but the timeless alleyways offer a valuable insight into the character of the city and the life of its people. You will get lost— that is part of the fun—but recognisable sights are never far away and you might even get invited to dinner.

The following is divided into four sections arranged purely by geography, each starting from the Lyab-i-Hauz for convenience.

East from the Kukeldash Madrassah lies a collection of religious buildings with secular functions. The bristling dome of the Kokuli Kul Mosque rises over a dress shop, while the next-door Domlo Hassan Madrassah (18th century) sells a curious mix of holy texts and car parts. Next door are two perpetually-shut museums, but if your timing or persistence is good enough you may gain access to the Bronze Museum in the Oibinok Mosque (1894) and the Varakhsha Museum in the Ibraghim Okhund Madrassah (1854). The 19th-century Isteza Madrassah lurks surreptitiously behind. Further east, former Lenin Street has been transformed into Nakhshbandi Street, from Godless revolutionary to Sufic mystic, but still leads to the tiny Attor Madrassah, whose student cells now house an architect's office. Cross over to Anbar Street (ex-Pushkin) and continue further east to the small Imam Kazikhan shrine, then north to the Chor Minor and west to the local Khoja Taband Mosque. This thriving local mosque is the centre of the *makhallya* neighbourhood council and on Fridays is awash with striped cloaks and pampered beards.

North from the Lyab-i-Hauz, following Samarkand Street, leads to the dilapidated but refreshingly unrestored Poi Ostana Mosque and Madrassah, whose faded paintwork points to a past beauty and to a Bukhara before the renovation teams moved in. Just before the mosque turn left and left again to a madrassah courtyard, whose saint's tomb is one of the most popular places in the city for young women to pray for plentiful children. Two hundred metres (656 feet) north along Khorezm Street lies the concealed madrassah, mosque and tomb of the Mavlana Sharif ensemble and behind it the ruined Chukor Caravanserai, whose name means 'deep' and refers to the sunken ground level of its courtyard. Both are tricky to find, but are visible from behind the Abdul Aziz Madrassah. Close by is the Tok-i-Zargaron and the Mir Kemal Madrassah (1707) to the north. This part of the old town is one of the oldest in the city and the site of the original core *shakhristan*. Return eastwards to Samarkand Street and further north lies the fortress-like Tash Serai (Stone Palace) Madrassah and the recently re-opened Sheikh Aksavi (Shayakhsi) Mosque.

South from the Lyab-i-Hauz, past the Jewish Synagogue and Mubinjon homestay, turn right into the heart of the Ishoni Pir district and the Ishoni Pir local mosque and madrassah. Nearby on a triangular crossroads is the shrine of a local saint adorned with pre-Islamic motifs such as silver hand and sun and Islamic crescent and star. From here continue south down Araban Street to the local Araban Mosque and Sala-khana Complex, where rich merchants from India and Persia would set up shop, working out of caravanserai hotel rooms, much the same as modern foreign business-es do today in Tashkent. Further south, outside the city walls, lies the Jewish ceme-tery and the Vabayi Paraduz Mausoleum, a well-attended tomb under a high dome and holy white flag. From here, follow Tukaeva Street westwards. At the crossroads with Namazgokh (ex-Kirov) Street, turn right for the beautifully inscribed entrance to a rich merchant's house on the left and the high dome of the popular Turki Zhandi Mausoleum on the right, where the local imam will say a brief prayer for you before you take a deep breath and dive back into the town labyrinth. Retrace your steps and continue along Tukaeva Street, skirting the edge of the old town, to reach the House of Faizullah Khodjaev, Uzbekistan's first president, or Museum of the Daily Life of a Bukharan Merchant as it is officially known (see p264). At the next junction turn right up Jeibor (ex-Oktyabriskaya) Street to the 17th-century Mirzoi Sharif Gaziyon Madrassah, with its impressive main recessed *iwan* and the modern but functioning mixed baths opposite. Jeibor St finally emerges into central Bukhara by the Gaukush-an Madrassah.

The Ark Fortress, Bukhara

West from here, Nakhshbandi Street passes the 19th-century Pocho Kul Khoja Mosque on the left, now a floundering state food store, and a madrassah of the same name to the right, now a bureau with an anachronistic picture of Lenin plastering its hallway. The large madrassah further up the street to the right with the characteristic green pillar tilework is the Tursanjon Madrassah (1796), presently used by potters who make huge *tandyr* ovens here out of straw and clay. The madrassah is in good condition and lies open for exploration. Behind it lies the Khodja Zainuddin Mosque and also the functioning 16th-century Khunjak women's baths, where women can receive a cheap massage in the diffused natural light of a warm, sunken chamber and enjoy a rare opportunity to meet Uzbek and Tajik women away from family and male pressures.

Sights Outside the Old Town

Scattered outside the *shakhristan* lie a series of monuments marooned in Soviet socialist suburbia. The following tour follows an arc clockwise from the northeast to the northwest, but the monuments described can just as easily be visited individually.

The huge **Faizabad Khanagha** (1598–99) dervish hostel to the northeast of the old town follows the established *khanagha* design with a cruciform hall open on all sides and *hujra* cells arranged on several floors. Its stepped façade and side porticos lend it a grace and symmetry left largely undisturbed by visitors. The building is normally locked. The next door *chaikhana* offers refreshment for flagging tourists.

Further south is the old Fathabad suburb of the town, a centre of pilgrimage and festivals up until the turn-of-the-century which was once dense with shrines and hostels. In the days of the Uzbek SSR, the district was prosaically renamed Shark II (East II) and played host to the local railway station which had eventually crept its way into the old town after decades spent loitering ten kilometres outside the city walls at Kagan. In the midst of the railway shunting yards stand two 600-year-old mausoleums.

The **Saifuddin Bukharzi Mazaar** is the larger and older of the two buildings and honours the tomb of local poet and holy man Saif-ad-din (1190–1262). Shortly after the saint's death a *gurkhana* (tomb) was raised over the richly carved wooden cenotaph and a subsequent 14th-century *ziaratkhana* (prayer hall) and 15th-century portico added a monumental austerity to the construction. In 1978 an earth tremor damaged the dome and the building had to be reinforced with iron braces.

The smaller and more intimate **Buyan Kuli Khan Mazaar** (1358) honours neither poet nor holy man, but rather a Mongol nobleman and descendent of Genghis Khan killed in battle in Samarkand in 1358. Its eastern portal is a saturated web of floral ornamentation and inscriptive calligraphy older than the Shah-i-Zindah in

Samarkand, and the intense flashes of its violet and white majolica merely serve to highlight its neighbour's modesty. Structurally, it also marks an early development from the single-(e.g. Ismael Samani) to the double-roomed monumental *mazar*. The mausoleum is normally locked, but if your guide can get hold of a key it will open doors to a beautifully tiled chamber and secret passage.

The aggressively modern Hotel Bukhara marks the Soviet centre of the town, whose fallout takes control wherever the huddled and cramped old town peters out. To the north lies the **World War II Memorial** and eternal flame with a huge plaque detailing the names of Bukhara's 18,000 fallen. To the northwest lies the former site of a similarly fallen **Lenin**, now replaced with the Uzbek national insignia. For an illicit peek at the dismembered Lenin, sneak yourself into the garden of the city library, next to the hotel, where the butchered parts of the leader rust in shunned neglect like just another victim of the emir.

A few hundred metres due east of the Hotel Bukhara lies the **Bukhara Gold Embroidery Factory** at 14, Muminov Kuchasi (tel. 33502), where Uzbek women perform, and sell examples of, this once exclusively male craft.

From the hotel follow Tukaeva Street west for five minutes, skirting the edge of the old town, to the **House of Faizullah Khodjaev**, or **Museum of the Daily Life of a Bukharan Merchant** as it is officially known. It was deemed politically unsafe to name the museum after a man condemned to death by Stalin in the 1930s as a class enemy and doubly reviled by locals as the man who let the Russians into Bukhara. Khodjaev was a founder of the Young Bukharans, an early communist chief and the Uzbek SSR's first president, yet one look at his family house, fourth of six in the city and the one where Faizullah was born, shows that the young Bolshevik's class background was far from proletarian. It was said the Karakul fleece empire of Khodjaev's father was so lucrative that the emir himself would regularly came to the house in search of a loan.

The house is divided into male and female courtyards. The latter is best restored, with winter quarters and stove on the left and summer quarters, cooled by a high *iwan*, on the right. There is little furniture to clutter the small rooms, as all ornaments were kept in niches in the wall and the family slept on mattresses, as they do today. Only Khodjaev's table and mirror stand out. During the Soviet invasion the rich ganch ornamentation of the walls was covered in clay, partly to protect the decoration and partly to protect the family, but today the walls again shine. Both Uzbektourism and Sacha organize tea-drinking ceremonies and dinners here where the visitor can try on some traditional local Uzbek cloaks, including, for women, a real horsehair *paranja* veil. There are also ambitious plans to convert the house into a small hotel, but as we speak the idea is still being quietly mulled over in some *chaikhana* and probably will be for some time. A sign marks the museum, but you must knock hard on the door if you are unexpected.

To the south, M. Ikbola St runs east–west past the Gulistan Hotel and the

Namaz-gokh Mosque (1119), located deep in the heart of the former Shemsabad gardens. The mosque is a holiday mosque, used during the great Muslim festivals of Bayram Kurgan and Rosaheid, when men from both the city and its surrounding *kishlaks* would congregate for mass celebration and prayer, and thus its construction is quite different from the normal mosque design. Because of the large numbers of faithful involved a *namazgokh* mosque had no side walls, merely a single huge *mihrab* wall to orientate the congregation and a *minbar* from which an *imam* addressed the crowd. The original Karakhanid *mihrab* wall with its finely carved terracotta plates still stands as a rare pre-Mongol survivor, but the colonnaded gallery and glazed polychrome tiles of the portal were only added in the 16th century.

Further west at the next road junction stands the **Dzhubari Madrassah**, a functioning female madrassah where some 70 young Uzbek and Tajik girls learn embroidery, etiquette and the Koran, and the **Volidoi Abdul Aziz Khudaydad Mosque**, a recently re-opened 17th-century district mosque. From here follow Jeibor (ex-Oktyabryskaya) Street southwest for a few hundred metres to ponder the site where the Soviet Army first entered the holy city of Bukhara, the old Sheikh Jalal gates. Alternatively head north up Khabzinab (ex-Ordzhani) Street into the old Iranian section of the town and then turn two blocks west to the crumbling **Kaliph Khudaydad Ensemble**. This crumbling 18th-century collection of a mosque, *khanagha* and submerged *sardoba* (covered pool) is in a sorry state but the beautifully-carved wood panels are undergoing loving restoration by a renegade band of old men who, impatient with the pace of Islamic reconstruction, have taken the initiative. *Sardobas* were once a matter of life and death to this desert oasis and were scattered throughout the town and its caravan routes. A second example, the Sardoba Ishan-i-Imla, lies a few hundred metres away in a schoolyard.

A five-minute walk north of the Ark leads to the **Khazreti Imam Cemetery**, where engraved reflections of the deceased lead the way to the high dome of the central mosque and associated *hauz*, *tacharatkhana*, and six *hujra* cells. The open-air tomb of Khazreti Imam lies on a northern bank, next to an underground chamber heavy with the scent of Zoroastrian beliefs and adorned with the symbols of sainthood.

Suburban Excursions

SITORAI MAKHI KHOSA

Popularly known as the Emir's Summer Palace, this charming and nauseating collection of dwellings and state rooms was built by the Russians in 1911 for the last Emir Alim Khan, as an inducement to get him out of the Ark fortress and safely ensconced in a strategic and cultural no-man's-land on the edge of town.

By the end of the 19th century, the emirs of Bukhara actually spent little time in their official residence, the Ark, but rather flitted between winter layover in Shakhrisabsz, summer suburban residence in the now destroyed Shirgaron Palace and the safe haven of Karmana. It was a physical dislocation that merely reflected a wider cultural confusion as the modern sparked with the medieval. By now the ruler of Central Asia's most fanatical bastion of Islam paid annual visits in his private train to the banquets and balls of St Petersburg's Winter Palace or to his fashionable dacha on the Crimean coast, as his son read Dostoevsky and tried to reconcile a four-year military education in St Petersburg with the medieval theology taught in Bukharan madrassah. With its uneasy mix of Russian and Central Asian architecture and traditions, Alim's summer palace offers an intriguing symbol of, and insight into, the lifestyle of an emir trying to bridge two worlds and of an emirate caught between two ages.

■ SIGHTS

From the discordant designs and alien red majolica of the front gate, go swiftly past the emir's wine cellar (now a book shop) and servants' quarters of the *hauli birun,* or outer courtyard, and into the main reception halls of the inner *darun* courtyard, site of the First Congress of the Bukharan Soviet on 6 October 1920 and present-day **Museum of Applied Arts**. The bed chambers of the emir lie in the northwest corner of the courtyard, next to the lime-green ganch *iwan,* and still contain the emir's bed, while the wedding-cake-white ganch and mirrored glass of the next door reception room give it the name White Hall. From here a small corridor decked with Persian and Turkoman prayer carpets leads to the emir's games room, banquet hall, secretary's office and tea room. Quirky cross-cultural items to look out for include a mechanical calendar, statue of Peter the Great, early Russian fridge, a mirror that multiplies forty times, a 16th-century Chinese sugar bowl and photographs of the last two emirs. Nearby is a recent statue of local craftsman Shirin Muradov, who decorated much of the palace.

Further into the complex, to the left, stands the Octagonal Palace and **Museum of National Costume**. Starting from the southern entrance and walking clockwise, room one has a display of thin *yaktab* summer robes with Russian influenced collars, a horsehair *paranja* and a 1928 photograph of the emir's unveiled concubines, room three holds examples of *gulduzi* gold embroidery, including one robe entirely covered in two years' worth of work, and the central octagonal dining room contains the robes of the emir and his wives. Other rooms hold skullcaps that were traditionally worn underneath one's turban, *munisak* wedding robes and Aladdin-style slippers with curled toes. Robes in Central Asian society were a major indicator of wealth, a signal of a woman's marital status (married women had their sleeves sewn together), a traditional gift given to foreign visitors and even a form of tax payment.

Further south lie the harem quarters, pool and viewing platform, from where it is

Emir's Summer Palace, Bukhara

said Alim would savour the view of his naked concubines frolicking in the waters below and toss a ripe apple to the beauty who had most captivated his heart. Once chosen, the fortunate girl would be washed in donkey's milk (the emir found the odour strangely arousing) and delivered to his bed chambers. The liberation of the harem was one of the Soviets' more pleasing duties:

> *The storming of the harem took place under strict vigilance and nothing unpleasant happened. The begums, of course, behaved like scared rabbits, but the sight of the husky young men scrambling for them must have made some impression on them. Able-bodied young men seeking their favour was a new experience to women whose erotic life naturally could not be satisfied by a senile old man. At the end it was a pleasing sight—the secluded females allowing themselves to be carried away by proud men.*

> M N Roy (quoted by Peter Hopkirk)

Today the building houses a **Museum of Needlework**, with examples of contrasting *suzaine* needlework from Urgut and Shakhrisabsz and a mock-up of a traditional house with a *beshik* cradle and *sunduk* chests. South of the pool is the site of the emir's zoo, famous for its peacocks and elephant, later transferred to Moscow.

After the fall of Bukhara, Alim Khan fled his palace for Afghanistan. His wife and children were taken to Moscow by the Soviets, where his second son became a major-general in the Soviet army, until the League of Nations ruled that the emir's family should be allowed to join him in Afghanistan. The emir harboured brief hope of regaining power through logistical support of the *basmachi* movement, but finally died in Kabul in 1952.

The palace is situated in the northern suburbs of the city and is serviced by bus numbers 9 or 17. Closed Wednesdays.

BAKHAUDDIN NAKHSHBANDI ENSEMBLE

> *If you sow the seed of good it will grow into seven ears and then yield seven hundred good deeds.*

> Nakhshbandi

Bukhara's holiest ensemble is a place of shrines, stories and superstitions, of burgeoning faith and parallel Islam. It is also the burial place of one of Sufic Islam's founders and holiest saints, Khazreti Mohammed Bakhauddin (Baha-al-din) Nakhshbandi (1318–1389).

Bakhauddin (The Decoration of Religion) was born a few kilometres from the present complex in the town of Kasri Orifon into a family of metalworkers, from where he took the name Nakhshbandi (Engraver of Metals). He came under the early influence of Abdul Khaliq Gijduvani (see page 222) and as a married man spent 12 years in the employ of Tamerlane's nephew Khalil Sultan after which, according to the Encyclopedia of Islam, he devoted himself to "the care of animals for seven years and road-mending for another seven". This last vocation is not quite as bizarre as it may sound, for Nakhshbandi espoused a life of hard work, self-reliance and modesty, encouraging all his pupils to learn a trade as he himself had done. His 11 principles of conduct were based on a retreat from authority, spiritual purity and a rejection of ostentation or ceremony, principles that were stretched to their limit by the Nakhshbandi brotherhood's early rejection of communism in the 1920s and subsequent tacit support for the *basmachi* revolt.

The shrine itself is steeped in superstition. Pilgrims circle and kiss Nakhshbandi's tombstone, tie rags, money and wishes around the tree said to have sprouted from his staff and cook offerings and sacrifices in the specially-built mass kitchens after these wishes have been granted. The site is also permeated with the holy Sufic number seven; in the seventh month the saint came into the world, in his seventh year he knew the Koran by heart and at the age of 70 he breathed his last. In the nearby museum a display of seven lambskins refers to the traditional seven tenge fee to the site and in Central Asian funerals male friends of the deceased jostle to carry the coffin for the expected seven steps.

The spiritual focus of any visit is the large *mazaar* encasing the black tombstone of the saint, traditionally known as the Stone of Desire, and the 20 graves of past pilgrims that include the Khans Abdul Aziz and Abdullah II. The holy courtyard is enclosed by the Abu'l Faiz Khan Mosque (1720), now used as a women's mosque, and the Muzaffar Khan Mosque, built 150 years later. The architectural centre of the complex is the huge *khanagha* built in the same year as the tomb (1544) by the Uzbek chief Abdul Aziz Khan; a cool, cubed building equipped with 48 hujra cells and crowned by a huge 30-metre (98-foot) high dome.

In 1993, on the 675th anniversary of Nakhshbandi's birth, the complex was restored and revamped with Turkish and Pakistani money (including a personal donation of $45,000 from ex-President Özal of Turkey) and unveiled in a great show of international Muslim brotherhood. The event marked not only the reconnection of Uzbekistan with the international Muslim community, but also formalized the rebirth of official religion, a process that had started under *perestroika* and will continue to underscore the new Islamic orientation of an independent Central Asia.

The complex lies a ten-minute drive (bus number 60 from the Ark) northeast of Bukhara.

CHOR BAKR NECROPOLIS

In 970 Imam Sayid Abu Bakr and his three brothers Fazl, Ahmed and Hamed, all direct descendents of the Prophet, were laid to rest in the village of Sumitan, seven kilometres west of Bukhara. They instilled the site with an immediate sanctity that soon attracted legions of the rich and famous clamouring to claim holiness by association.

The initial harbingers of the four (Chor) Bakr's holy entourage were the Khojorum sect of Sufic dervishes who based their brotherhood around the holy graves. From 1559–1563 Abdullah Khan commissioned the *khanagha,* mosque and madrassah that still make up the hearts and bones of the complex, as well as a series of outlying parks and pavilions that have since been lost. The complex was catapulted through the ranks of Bukhara's holiest sites and during the course of the following few centuries hundreds of family members of both the khan and the local dynasty of Juybar sheikhs were buried in a street of tombs reminiscent in layout, if not decoration, of the Shah-i-Zindah in Samarkand.

The complex is approached from a gatehouse and walkway that leads to the central square, dominated by the twin façade of the mosque (left), dervish *khanagha* (right) and connecting *hujra* cells of a madrassah and summer mosque. Decoration is sparse, concentrated mainly in the mosque tympanum and dome and *khanagha* dome, but the symmetry of the ensemble, linked by a belt of twin level loggias, lends it an imposing air. Buildings to the left of the mosque include defunct *korikhana*s and *chillakhana*s (places of retreat, especially for the sick) and also a functioning *takharatkhana,* or wash house, where pilgrims still perform their ablutions in individual cubicles. Two main streets of crumbling mausoleums lead off to the north and northwest and scattered tombs cover the surrounding area like fallen leaves. The tomb of Abu Bakr is said to be the one to the right of the walled passage leading to the west. The site crumbles in a shroud of silence that befits its role as the domain of the dead, but it is still infused with an air of unrestored grandeur that makes it well worth the visit.

Buses to Sumitan leave from the main bazaar. Those taking taxis should bargain for a return trip and ensure that the driver waits, as transport back to Bukhara can be elusive.

KAGAN

When the representatives of the Devil's Wagon arrived at Bukhara to obtain the khan's permission to build the next leg of the Transcaspian Railway, the emir demanded just recompense paid in German silver shipped all the way from Hamburg and an assurance that the railway would not pass within ten miles of the holy city. Within a few years, local Bukharans could be found squatting in railway carriages for hours waiting for the remarkable sensation of locomotion, the emir could be found riding in a mock carriage in his summer palace as servants fluttered bits of coloured paper outside the window to give the impression of speed and the rival Russian cantonment of Kagan was in full swing.

Today the primary reason to visit Kagan, apart from catching a train, is to see the spectacular turn-of-the-century **Tsarist Palace** rise from the railway city like a creamy white wedding cake. In 1895 Emir Abdul Ahad, enthused with the architectural glories of St Petersburg after attending the coronations of Alexander III and Nicholai II, and informed of the tsar's impending Central Asian grand tour, decided to commission a 300,000-rouble replica of a tsarist palace. Eight years later the gem was complete but Nicholai failed to arrive, overtaken by wider political events. The palace was adopted by the tsarist Russian Political Commissar until the Soviets handed it over to the railway proletariat as a social club in 1920. Today it houses a fledgling Museum of the Railway, but the palace is more remarkable for the rich luxury of its exterior and banqueting hall and as a flash of decadence in a working-man's town.

Kagan also has a busy market and a small **Russian Orthodox Church**, whose allegedly beautiful interior lies locked away, even on Sunday, as Russians leave town in an ethnic exodus. *Marshrutnoe* minibuses leave for Kagan from the Lyab-i-Hauz.

Bukhara Practical Information

TRANSPORT
Four flights a day leave for Tashkent for US$60–70 one-way. Tickets can be reserved at the Hotel Bukhara (see Tatyana, front desk) but must be paid for at the airport (bus number 10), renovated in late 1997. The **bus station** three kilometres to the north of the city centre serves all major towns except those to the east (Karshi, Shakhrisabsz etc) which depart from the Shark (East) station. There are four buses a day to Tashkent (11–12 hours), five to Samarkand (5–6 hours) and one to Urgench (7–8 hours). All **trains** depart and arrive at Kagan, ten kilometres (six miles) east of Bukhara, for Tashkent, Urgench and Moscow. By far the easiest way to get around outside the old town is by taxi. Almost any car can be flagged down, but arrange the price first.

ACCOMMODATION
The Bukharan B&B revolution is spreading countrywide. In the city itself, a growing number of reasonably priced, well serviced and charming private homes show up the over-priced, dysfunctional state hotels.

Sacha's B&B, 13 Molodyozhnaya Street (tel. 36522, 33890, fax 235593, e-mail: sashlen@bukhara.silk.org)
The earliest and most comfortable homestay, Sacha's is the darling of Tashkent's expat scene. Ex-Intourist guide Sacha speaks excellent English and offers facilities from modern bathrooms and sauna to vegetarian meals and city tours. Located ten minutes' walk east of the Lyab-i-Hauz, in a backstreet running parallel to Nyzami

Street, behind the Navoi school. Prices at present float between US$15–20 for a single and $25–30 for a double.

Mubinjon's Bukhara House, 4 Ishoni Pir (tel. 42005)
An earthier, more traditional and cheaper alternative is this beautifully decorated Tajik house, perfectly located 300 metres (330 yards) south from Lyab-i-Hauz and much enlivened by young daughter Bibi Khanum. Four rooms are arranged around a courtyard equipped with tea *kan* and beds come in the traditional shape of a mattress on the floor. Basic washing facilities, but Mubinjon can point you towards excellent *hammam* (baths). Rooms can be hot in summer, cold in winter. Price is negotiable at around $12–15. Contact Raisa Achmedovna on 23398/37277 or direct (no English).

Sasha & Son B&B, 3 Ishoni Pir, (tel. 244966)
Sasha's second venture (a third will be open when you read this) occupies the restored residence of a Jewish merchant; beds or mats available, 5 rooms, 9 people, US$25 each, dinner US$6

Other traditional style Bukharan houses include: Lyab-I-Hauz B&B, 7 Husainova, tel. 242484, US$25; Nootfillo's B&B, 15 Vavilova St, tel. 45151, US$15; Mosque Balyand B&B, 18 Uritskiy, tel. 236434, US$15; Bafo B&B, 103 Deputatskaya, tel. 31556, US$8-10; e-mail: bafo@bukhara.silk.org

Hotel Bukhara (new), 8 Prospect Navoi, (tel. 30024, fax 31033)
The city's premier tourist hotel is Indian-built and soon to be managed by the German team running Tashkent's Shodlik Palace. Two restaurants, four bars, shops, pool, and other facilities. Singles/doubles US$70/90.

Hotel Bukhara (old), 8 Muminov Kuchasi, (tel. 30124, fax 31359)
Next door is a familiar Intourist behemoth, recently renovated to three stars and home to most group tours. Offers 183 rooms, bar, café, restaurant, tours and shop. Singles/doubles US$35–50/40–60.

Hotel Varakhsha, 5 Prospect Navoi, (tel. 34582, fax 36396)
Renovated to two stars, the Varakhsha has rooms from US$20–30 and a decent restaurant.

Hotel Gulistan, 19 M. Ikbola St, (tel. 38311)
Standard ex-Soviet rooms and service for US$10–30.

Hotel Zerafshan, 7 M. Ikbola St, (tel. 34173)
Cheapest of the official hotels (c.US$5 in sum); spartan rooms, temperamental water and staff.

Kukeldash Madrassah Lyab-i-Hauz, Anbar (ex-Pushkin) Street
Basic accommodation (no toilets) with obvious but limited charm, reluctant to accept foreigners. A better bet for that madrassah experience is the Amin Khan Madrassah in Khiva.

FOOD

Eating out is a classless struggle in Bukhara; it matters little how much you are prepared to spend—it is still hard to find anything open or edible, let alone both. Lunch is rarely a problem as Uzbek staples can be found in the bazaars, Lyab-i-Hauz, Registan *chaikhana* etc. An evening meal, however, can be a problem. The best bet is to arrange a home meal through your B&B. An inoffensive and dependable mainstay is the Hotel Bukhara restaurant, whose top-floor juice bar is a fine place to see the sun set over a round of kebabs. Fried chicken is good in both the Zerafshan and Varakhsha Hotels and the latter has good beer in the annex bar and regular open-air shashlik. The *chaikhana* on Hamza St, a block east of the Hotel Bukhara, offers a good selection when open. Stock up on food at the old bazaar near the Chashma Ayub and modern bazaar two

Bolo Hauz mosque, Bukhara

blocks east of the Hotel Bukhara. Remember Babur's warning that Bukharan dried fruits form a powerful laxative.

SHOPPING

Most tourist sites sell souvenirs on the side; the Divanbegi Khanagha sells Uzbek clothes and paintings, the Divanbegi Madrassah sells good quality jewellery and engraved plates, the Art Gallery sells paintings and pottery, the Ark sells books, postcards and knives, the Ulug Beg Madrassah sells everything, the Tok-i-Furushon sells clothes, hats and gold embroidery, the Gold Embroidery Factory sells what you think it sells, plus waistcoats and other clothes, the Tok-i-Zargaron sells metalware as does the Gaukushan Madrassah and the Sitorai Makhi Khosa also stocks a good range of quality souvenirs. For Uzbek champagne and Rasputin Vodka head for the new bazaar and for skullcaps check out the bazaar by the Chashma Ayub. Mubinjon has some old antiques of varying quality in his homestay. The Bukhara Artisans' Development Centre, located across from the Lyab-i-Hauz pool inside the Saifuddin Caravanserai, is intended as a living museum in which artisans demonstrate both their skills and their products, and a number of handicrafts are for sale. There is a similar setup in Samarkand [see page 180].

Travel Agencies

Salom Travel, Apt 61, Bldg 11, Prospect Navoi, tel./fax 37277, e-mail: raisa@salom. bukhara.silk.org. Salom's Raisa Gareyeva is one of the pioneers of post-Intourist travel in Uzbekistan; her agency offers a very comprehensive range of services, from visa invites to complete Central Asia packages and extensive B&B network.

Bukhara Information & Culture Centre, beside Lyab-i-Hauz, tel. 42246, e-mail: bicc@bukhara.silk.org. A wide range of tourist & business information; ask about 'Humo' puppet theatre in Nadir Divanbegi Madrassah.

Bukhara-Tourist (formerly Uzbektourism/Intourist), old Hotel Bukhara, tel. 30124, fax 31359. Can organize transport and a stable of generally good guides for standard and offbeat sites from archaeological digs to cheetah/gazelle reserves, folk dance displays and a collective farm.

Bukhara-Visit, 7/73 Djami St, Microrayon 5, tel./fax 64600; e-mail: visit@b1.silk. glas.apc.org. Young, enthusiastic agency offering tours, transport and accommodation.

Farkhad & Maya, farkhad@bukhara.silk.org. Traditional B&B, plus tourist services
Bafo, 103 Deputatskaya, tel.31556; e-mail: bafo@bukhara.silk.org

Telephone

International and local calls can be made from the Hotel Bukhara or nearby at the cheaper telecommunications office, 200 metres east of the hotel.

Banks

The Hotel Bukhara will take money from you in a wide variety of shapes and sizes, but for cash advances on a Visa card try the National Bank at 10, Muminov Kuchasi.

Around Bukhara

Hakkim Mullo Mir Khanagha

Hidden deep in the village of Chilangu, about 20 kilometres (12 miles) from the nearest tourist, lies the unassuming grave of Sheikh al-Islam Emir Hussein Mullo Mir (died 1587) and the enormous *khanagha* built a century later in the shadow of his name. The dervish house has a complicated layout and its imposing four storey portal makes it seem larger than it actually is. Five staircases lead to a series of *hujra* cells arranged around the central mosque and a further two staircases lead up corner pylons to access the third-storey roof and chimneys of the cells below. The whole building is as solid as a rock and is set afloat on a sea of grasses and graves.

An excellent time for individuals to visit is Friday lunchtime, when local *aksakals* emerge from the surrounding fields like iron filings to a magnet to celebrate Friday *namaz* with feasting and communal prayer. A trainee *imam* usually sounds the call to prayer with hands cupped around his ears to catch the words of Allah. After individual prayer the *imam* ascends the *minbar* pulpit and addresses the congregation, after which he leads them in communal prayer. Then a donations book is read out and the tightfisted are grilled in silent shame. A small foreign donation will normally be rewarded with an entry into the book. Chilangu is best reached by taxi from Bukhara or Romitan. Follow the P-68 turnoff at Galasiya from the main M-37.

VARAKHSHA

Bunyat Bukhar was drinking wine in his palace at Varakhsha, secure in the knowledge that he was the ruler of the richest city in Mavarranawahr, when two horsemen bearing the Caliph's standard appeared as two clouds of dust on the horizon. They rode up into the fortress, dismounted and, without saying a word, drew their swords and cut off his head. They accused him of aiding and abetting the heretic Mokanna, proclaimed the end of the Bukhar Khudat line and departed.

With the death of Bunyat in 782 came the slow decline of the city of Varakhsha, a city older and bigger than Bukhara, home to Hephalite kings and Sogdian princes and staging post on the eight-day caravan trail to Khorezm. Today Uzbektourism and Sacha offer tours into the Kyzyl Kum to see its southern citadel, but its most famous find, a series of pre-Islamic wall paintings depicting hunters on elephants fighting off leopards and griffins and a state reception scene complete with crouching, winged camels supporting a royal throne, are held in Tashkent museums.

AFSHONA

The languid *kishlak* of Afshona slumbers in a bed of white-dusted cotton fields and gurgling irrigation canals and were it not for its one world-famous son would enjoy its torpor like any other neglected Uzbek hamlet. But in 980 Ali ibn-Sina, or Avicenna (980–1037), was born here and the city was thrust into the limelight of international attention. The **Avicenna Museum** was unveiled on the 1,000th anniversary of his birth and contains some interesting items, such as fearsome-looking turn of the century Uzbek surgical hooks and pliers, but with few captions in English it is perhaps best appreciated by those with a focused interest.

PAIKEND

The Copper City of Paikend was once the greatest trading city in Transoxiana, equipped with the 1,000 fortified, representative *rabads* set up by every self-respecting city in the region and the finest mosque this side of the Oxus. The Arabs destroyed the city after pilfering a pearl 'the size of a pigeon's egg' during 50 days of plunder and it never truly recovered, even after repeated resuscitation by the Karakhanid Arslan Khan. Today Uzbektourism can take specialists to its faint remains, 60 kilometres (40 miles) southwest of Bukhara.

Khorezm

The distant lands of Khorezm are formed and fed by the Amu Darya delta and its history is inextricably linked to the river, like Egypt's to the Nile. Its turbid waters prise apart the red and black deserts on either side to colour the desert island oasis with a fragile smear of green. It divided Turkic from Persian and provided a cradle for Central Asia's earliest civilization, only to shift course like a restless nomad, turning marsh into baked desert, killing cities at a whim. Today it is dammed, channelled and bled dry to quench thirsty cotton quotas and only then allowed to limp, exhausted and spent, into the dying arms of the Aral Sea.

Today this land of shifting rivers, trade routes, capitals and nomads is divided into the Khorezm oblast and Karakalpak Autonomous Republic and still maintains its distinct character. It echoes little of Ferghana's religious revival, but enjoys the best of Central Asia's incorrigible hospitality. Winter snows that froze the Oxus and the summer furnace that forced European visitors "like the Mussulmans, to remain immovable on the same spot without doing anything at all, not even thinking" still sandwich the tourist season and the region is generally unaccustomed to tourism, but hardy souls will be attracted to its desert citadels, ancient capitals and the Aral Sea.

Khiva

Khiva is the most intact and most remote of Central Asia's Silk Road cities, the final destination of a trip back through the centuries from socialist Tashkent to medieval slave town. Where Samarkand leaves the imagination exhausted, Khiva's khanate romance is plain to see and where Urgench lies restricted to two dimensions, Khiva revels in all four, as visions of the past float through its narrow streets like superimposed film.

HISTORY
Khiva has existed for as long as trade caravans have pulled up alongside the sweet waters of its Khievak Well, on a transcontinental pit-stop from Gurganj to Merv. Shem, the biblical son of Noah, is said to have marked out the city walls during a fiery desert mirage and as early as the tenth century the town entered Arab chronicles. But regional dominance only arrived in the 16th century, as nomadic Uzbek tribes swept through the oasis to found the khanate of Khorezm in 1511. By the end of the century Khiva had replaced the dying Kunya Urgench and assumed the mantle of capital.

Harem, Tash Hauli Palace, Khiva

The early years of the khanate were racked by instability, infighting and invasion by the rival Shaybanid clan of Bukhara and the region was unable to develop into anything more than a loose confederation of semi-independent clans whose unity depended largely upon the strength and charisma of its khan. The accession of Abul Gazi Khan in 1642 and his son Anusha Khan in 1663 finally ushered in the formative age of Khivan consolidation. The entire population of Gurganj was repatriated to Khiva and military expansion took war to the gates of Bukhara and Meshed. The khan even found time to write a history of Khiva and his Mongol ancestors; forced to, he claimed, for none of his subjects were sufficiently educated to do it for him.

The 18th century saw a return to tribal anarchy and accelerated political disintegration. Kungrad Uzbeks fought Mangit Uzbeks, northern Aral tribes seceded, Yomut Turkomans revolted and the Persian Nadir Shah conquered and held the town from 1740–47. In 1770 the Kungrad Inaks finally wrested power. Succeeding khans such as Mohammed Amin (1792–1800), Mohammed Rakhim (1806–1825) and Alla Kuli (1826–1842) again managed to control the cycle of tribal massacre and revenge, to centralize the state, improve irrigation and restore and expand traditional borders. Trade with Russia and the Volga boomed at Bukhara's expense, fuelling rapid urbanization and reconstruction. The khanate spread from the Aral to Merv and the scholars of Khiva became the leading exponents of Chagatai Turkic literature.

Yet Khiva still remained little more than a desert hideout for slave-traders, brigands, thieves and even pirates. Treachery and murder suffused daily life and trade always took second place to theft.

By the mid-19th century, Russian and Khivan spheres of influence began to clash on the threshold of Central Asia as Khiva found itself drifting towards fatal confrontation with a rising power. Russia was growing increasingly impatient with the abduction of its subjects into slavery and the plundering of its caravans by Khivan Turkomans. The Tsarists were also keen to restore lost pride after two disastrous expeditions to Khiva.

In 1717 Prince Bekovich had been sent by Tsar Peter to investigate the twin rumours of Khorezmian gold and a water route to India along the former bed of the Oxus. At the city gates his 4,000 troops had been warmly welcomed, congenially divided up to find accommodation and then viciously slaughtered. Bekovich himself was flayed alive and his skin stretched over a drum. The murders went unforgotten but unpunished and the khan drew conceit from his desert fastness. A century later, another Russian officer, Nikolai Muraviev, was detained for two months in Khiva while the court debated how to kill him, only to return to St Petersburg six months later, haunted by a message secreted in the barrel of his gun pleading for the release of the city's 3,000 Russian slaves and burning with plans for a swift and painless invasion. Thus in the winter of 1839–40 one General Perovsky led 5,000 troops and 10,000 camels into the snowy wastes of the Kyzyl Kum to teach the barbarian khan a lesson. Within one month his snow-blind troops were wading through a metre of snow, his camels were dying at a rate of 200 a day and packs of wolves shadowed the growing trail of frozen, starving bodies. The Russians admitted a second defeat and had still not managed to fire a shot.

As the Great Game heated up, Khiva grew in importance as a strategic stepping stone to Merv, Herat and British India beyond. Russian spies like Count Nicolai Ignatiev reconnoitred the region, armed with little more than pretexts (in his case the gift of an organ for the khan, which could only be ferried down the strategic water links of the Amu Darya), while British officers like Abbott and Shakespeare hurried to diffuse Russia's *causus belli*: the slave trade.

On 29 May 1873 Russian troops simultaneously arrived at Khiva's gates from Orenburg, Krasnovodsk, Tashkent and Kazalinsk and even the last-ditch release of 26 Russian prisoners by the panic-stricken khan failed to prevent them entering the city:

> *We began to see small groups of men in the lateral streets, in dirty ragged tunics and long beards, with hats off, bowing timidly to us as we passed. These were the inhabitants, and they were not yet sure whether they would all be massacred or not. With what strange awe and dread they must have gazed upon us as we passed, dust-covered and grimy after our march of 600 miles over the desert, which they had considered impassable. Grim, stern, silent and invincible, we must have appeared to them like some strange, powerful beings of an unknown world.*

MacGahan, Campaigning on the Oxus and the fall of Khiva, 1874

During the tsarist period, a motley crew of eccentric foreigners somehow made it to the town. In 1875 Fred Burnaby, six foot four in his socks, strong enough to carry a small pony under his arm and hold a billiard cue outstretched at the tip, fluent in seven languages but still described by Henry James as "opaque in intellect, indomitable in muscle", finally shook off his Russian minders in the desert and persuaded his guide to detour to Khiva by suggesting that he buy his brother-in-law's horse. In 1898 Robert Jefferson rode his bicycle, in a conscious echo of Burnaby's trip, from Catford in South London to Khiva in south Khorezm, surviving Kazakh witches, churches hovering upside down in the middle of the desert (a mirage) and a rousing sendoff from the cycling club of Orenburg. Both it seems suffered cultural confusions; Burnaby shocked a local barber by ordering his face shaved instead of his head and misunderstood local admiration over the toughness of his horse (he regaled its remarkable stamina, whilst the Turkoman complained that it would be difficult to eat), while Jefferson encountered either blind terror or uncontrollable laughter whenever he rode his magic bicycle, "an instrument which no true Mohammedhan ought to have anything to do with".

However, the khanate was fast approaching the end of its life. A series of nomad

Khiva
Хива

1 Telephone, Post Office
2 Museum
3 War Memorial
4 Hospital
5 Hotel Khorezm
6 Kosh Darvaza
7 Al Khorezmi Museum
8 Nurullah Bai Palace
9 Isfandiyar Khan Palace
10 Mohammed Rakhim Khan Madrassah
11 Restaurant
12 Cinema
13 Sayid Mohammed Khan Madrassah
14 Sheikh Kalander Bobo Mausoleum
15 Bika Jun Bika Ensemble
16 Magamed Magrum Madrassah
17 Gulsava Minaret
18 Sayid Magrumjan Complex

19 Tort Shalbaz
20 Museum
21 Cotton Mill
22 Koi Darvaza
23 Naspurush Mad.
24 Bazaar
25 Sayid Niaz Sheliker Mosque
26 Carpet Market
27 Palvan Kari Complex
28 Abdal Bobo Complex
29 Minaret

NOTE
* an asterisk next to the name of a street indicates that the old (Soviet) name is still in use at the time of going to press

C = chaikana

rebellions led by the Yomut Turkoman Junaid Khan rocked the town, culminating in the assassination in 1918 of Isfandiyar Khan. On 27 April 1920 the Khorezm People's Republic was proclaimed and Khan Abdullah abdicated, later to die in a Soviet prison hospital. Restless local *basmachi* continued to hound the region and in February 1924 15,000 Turkoman besieged the town for three and a half weeks until Soviet reinforcements eventually pacified all revolt. In 1922 the region gained promotion to a Soviet Republic and in 1924 joined the republic of Uzbekistan.

SIGHTS: ICHAN KALA

Since 1967 Khiva's status as a museum city has ensured it remains the most homogenous collection of architecture in the Islamic world, deep-frozen, immune to time and lost in romantic imagination. The renegade city of thieves and slave-traders, this "den of iniquity lost in the desert sands", has been tamed by Soviet "spite, contempt or fear" (Philip Glazebrook, 1991) into a showcase city without a soul. Today, however, Khivans are returning cautiously to the Ichan Kala, as if awakening from a bad dream, and traditional building work continues apace. Tourists and wedded couples still outnumber local families, but in the soft light of dawn and dusk the quiet riot of Central Asian life again murmurs behind baked-mud walls.

Khiva's kernel *shakhristan* is wrapped in a 2.2-kilometre (1.4-mile) belt of

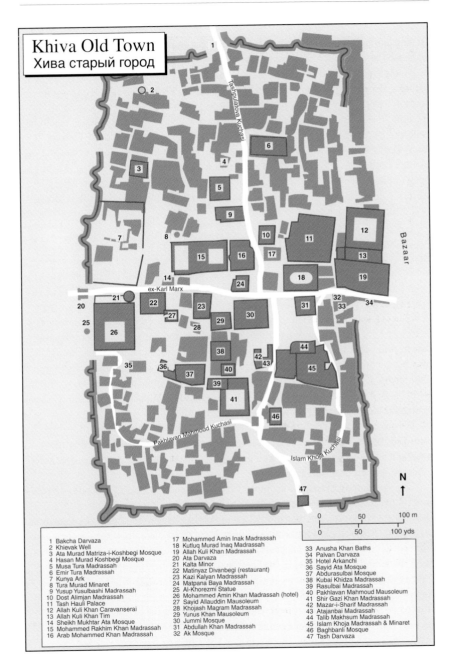

Khiva Old Town
Хива старый город

N ↑

0	50	100 m
0	50	100 yds

1 Bakcha Darvaza
2 Khievak Well
3 Ata Murad Matriza-i-Koshbegi Mosque
4 Hasan Murad Koshbegi Mosque
5 Musa Tura Madrassah
6 Emir Tura Madrassah
7 Kunya Ark
8 Tura Murad Minaret
9 Yusup Yusulbashi Madrassah
10 Dost Alimjan Madrassah
11 Tash Hauli Palace
12 Allah Kuli Khan Caravanserai
13 Allah Kuli Khan Tim
14 Sheikh Mukhtar Ata Mosque
15 Mohammed Rakhim Khan Madrassah
16 Arab Mohammed Khan Madrassah
17 Mohammed Amin Inak Madrassah
18 Kutluq Murad Inaq Madrassah
19 Allah Kuli Khan Madrassah
20 Ata Darvaza
21 Kalta Minor
22 Matinyaz Divanbegi (restaurant)
23 Kazi Kalyan Madrassah
24 Matpana Baya Madrassah
25 Al-Khorezmi Statue
26 Mohammed Amin Khan Madrassah (hotel)
27 Sayid Allauddin Mausoleum
28 Khojash Magram Madrassah
29 Yunus Khan Mausoleum
30 Jummi Mosque
31 Abdullah Khan Madrassah
32 Ak Mosque
33 Anusha Khan Baths
34 Palvan Darvaza
35 Hotel Arkanchi
36 Sayid Ata Mosque
37 Abdurasulbai Mosque
38 Kubai Khidza Madrassah
39 Rasulbai Madrassah
40 Pakhlavan Mahmoud Mausoleum
41 Shir Gazi Khan Madrassah
42 Mazar-i-Sharif Madrassah
43 Atajanbai Madrassah
44 Talib Makhsum Madrassah
45 Islam Khoja Madrassah & Minaret
46 Baghbanli Mosque
47 Tash Darvaza

crenellated, bastioned **city walls** that stands as old as the city it protects. Parts of the walls are thought to date from the fifth century, but the strongest sections were added by Arang Khan, son of Anusha Khan, in 1686–1688. Most visitors today enter the city within a city through its western Ata Darvaza (gate), rebuilt 40 years ago after the original was pulled down to open the medieval city to motor traffic. To the north lie the double-sided guardrooms of the Bakcha Darvaza, where customs duties would be collected from the caravans arriving from Urgench. To the south are the Tash or Stone Darvaza (1830–40), whose twin stairwells lead up to a first-floor viewing platform and to the east lie the Palvan Darvaza. These gates would seal the town from dusk to dawn and offer protection to a city plagued by nomadic raids and desert storms. It is still possible to walk along the city walls from the northern Bakcha Gate to the edge of the Ark.

■ MOHAMMED AMIN KHAN MADRASSAH

Pass through the Ata Darvaza and back in time. The double façade of celled shops to the right belong to the Mohammed Amin Khan Madrassah (1852–1855), the largest of its kind in the city with a capacity of 250 Islamic students, or rather 137 romantic tourists, as the madrassah today houses the Hotel Khiva. The seminary was so large that parts of the city wall had to be demolished to make way for it. The impressive, restored portal leads to a left hand mosque/hotel bar and a classic courtyard layout that in times past held sessions of the city's supreme Muslim court. Access to the twisting corridors is largely unfettered, to reveal unique double roomed cells that look uncharacteristically outwards and also a series of rooms in the northeast corner of the madrassah that allow reluctant access to the Kalta Minaret. To the side of the madrassah sits a brooding statue of al-Khorezmi.

Debate rages over the future of the madrassah. UNESCO would like to see the cannibalized seminary restored to an original purity, but local chiefs say that the hotel echoes its original purpose well enough and that it may well set a precedent for other similar cultural transformations.

The madrassah's patron, Mohammed Amin Khan (r.1843–1855), was one of Khiva's most illustrious khans. He restored the khanate's former territories, captured Merv, pacified the Saryk clan and then shifted his murderous gaze to the Tekke Turkoman in several epic battles fought in the wastes of the Kara Kum. Then, in a curious show of trust, he left the subjugated Tekke in the bloody hands of the Yomut and Uzbek tribes. Soon the Yomut were fighting the Tekke, the Tekke were fighting the Uzbeks and the Uzbeks were fighting the Yomut, until the exasperated Medamin finally hurled the Yomut leader off a Khivan Minaret. He succeeded briefly in uniting the squabbling tribes, but only against himself and, shortly afterwards, on the eve of an attack on Serakhs (on the current Iranian border), he was decapitated by a rogue Tekke horseman and Khiva was left vulnerable to regular Turkoman ravage for the next 70 years.

The death of Medamin overshadows the nearby **Kalta Minor** or Short Minaret, commissioned by the khan in 1852 to stand (at over 70 metres/230 feet) as the biggest in the Islamic world, but abandoned in the wake of his death at a frustrated 26 metres (85 feet). Others say that the architect had secretly agreed to build an even larger minaret for the emir of Bukhara and that he was thrown off the minaret for his treachery. The Kalta Minor is girdled in a typically Khivan shade of jade green so rich that it seems to have sucked all the decoration out of the exhausted city into one glorious reservoir of colour. Sixty four corkscrew steps lead up the truncated tower to reveal the structure in cross section and a fine view of the city.

■ THE KUNYA ARK

The khans of Khiva had several residences during the century before Soviet rule, including the Tash Hauli of Allakuli Khan and Nurullabai Palace of Isfandiar, but the Kunya Ark, or Old Fortress, remains the original and has for centuries provided fortified refuge during times of uncertainty. The foundations of the Ark date from the fifth century, but most of the complex was added to piecemeal in the 19th century by successive khans.

Pass through the main entrance gate and turn right for the gorgeous tilework of the **summer mosque** (1838), where cool blues and whites flash in a concentrated burst of colour and floral arabesques spiral up side walls like creeping ivy. The tiles were made by local masters Ibadullah and Abdullah Jin, who also decorated large parts of the Tash Hauli and Pakhlavan Mahmoud Mausoleum. In the corner of this small courtyard lies the old mint which funded the expansionary exploits of Rakhim Khan I from 1806–1825. Today the mint holds a collection of coins, medals and silk banknotes, dense with dawning socialist suns, from the early Khorezm Republic and a mock-up of a blacksmith's workshop where Khivan coins were minted.

Return from the mint to the main courtyard, original home to the offices of court advisers, and head west for the **Kurinish Khana or Throne Room** (1804–06), where the khan would grant public audience, either in the open summer *iwan* or in a warm winter yurt set upon its circular brick platform. It was here that the Russian Captain Muraviev was finally granted a royal audience after seven weeks of deliberation when his fate hung in the balance. The small court has beautiful ceiling decoration and geometric tilework, with fine ganch and a decorated *mihrab* in the room behind. It was here that the wooden throne of the khan, built in 1816 and gilded in silver, traditionally stood until it was carted off to the Armour Chamber of St Petersburg's Hermitage Museum by the victorious Russians. The Uzbeks are now in negotiations to retrieve their stolen heritage and figures of up to two million dollars are bandied about as rumoured Russian reimbursement.

From the throne room head north into the derelict former stables and armoury and thence either straight on to the finely decorated *iwan* of the khan's harem chambers (1806), or west into the fortified heart of the Ark, the **Ak Sheikh Bobo Bastion**. This core citadel, set against the city walls, is the oldest building in Khiva and foundations from the site are contemporary with the ancient Khorezmian fortresses, such as Toprak Kala, scattered in the surrounding deserts. While those citadels died of thirst, the Khivan heart grew into the Khanate, to be used as a hermitage by Mukhtar Vali, the White Sheikh, and then as a watchtower and gunpowder arsenal. The top platform provides a classic Khivan profile, but dim lower halls require torchlight.

Just outside the main gates lies the most recent **Zindan** city jail (1910) equipped with manacles, flails and a series of pictures recreating fiendish tortures and executions. A telling insight into the Khivan judicial system was provided by an unflinching vizier in response to Burnaby's concerns over potential culprits who denied guilt: 'We beat him with rods, put salt in his mouth, and expose him to the burning rays of the sun, until at last he confesses.'

View from Jummi Minaret, Khiva

Walk across the main square, past Khiva's deepest well, to the shimmering blue *pishtak* of the **Mohammed Rakhim Khan Madrassah** (1871), noted for its unusual front courtyard and heavy corner towers. The façade tilework was restored in September 1994 on the 150th birthday of Rakhim Khan (also known by the pen name of Feruz) and more cosmetic touches were added by the crew of Sally Potter's film *Orlando*. The Khivan Craft Centre opened here in 1998.

The madrassah currently houses a confused museum, tenuously organized around the life of Feruz. Exhibits begin in the left-hand chamber with an old flag of the Khanate of Khiva (whose five stars represent the five pillars of Islam) and an exhibition of local clothes and armour. The central rooms continue with a nervous mix of poetry and axes, an ornately inscribed robe belonging to the city head judge, or Kazi Kalyon, and a collection of flag poles inscribed with the Arabic word Allah, used by different regiments of the khan's army to distinguish them in battle. The right-hand mosque holds some fascinating turn of the century photographs of Feruz and Isfandiyar Khan, decorated in Russian military awards and flanked by turbaned viziers and smooth-looking Russian generals.

Feruz is an intriguing Central Asian character; the khan who, not unlike Bukhara's Abdul Ahad, straddled two ages and had the unenviable task of reconciling Russian domination with the fierce, nomadic independence of his subjects. On his three trips to St Petersburg he picked up a private printing press which produced nothing but his own poetry, he learned how to smoke and proudly bought a telephone, even though there was no connecting line for hundreds of kilometres. Back in Khiva he forced his harem into the most fashionable corsetry of the day and pressured his finance minister into learning how to play his grand piano. In 1873 he finally signed away his independence to become the tsar's 'obedient servant' and entered the Cossack Army as major-general. He died of a heart attack on 16 August 1910, aged 65, and was buried in the Magrumjan Complex outside the Ichan Kala.

South of the madrassah, past the rebuilt Sheikh Mukhtar Ata Mosque and Matinyaz Divanbegi Madrassah (now the Restaurant Khiva), lies in rest the **Tomb of Sayid Allauddin**. This Mongol-era 14th-century tomb is known as the earliest standing building in Khiva and was built by Kulyal Emir around the beautiful *sagana* tombstone of the Nakhshbandi Sufic master Sayid Allah ad-Din (died 1303). Its stunning ceramics probably came from Gurganj (Kunya Urgench).

Join the main east-west street that strings the old town monuments together and turn right, past the long-suffering tourist camel that moved Phillip Glaze-

Kalta Minaret and Ark, Khiva

Khivan Rough Justice

They looked like lambs in the hands of their executioners. Whilst several were led to the gallows or the block, I saw how, at a sign from the executioner, eight aged men placed themselves down on their backs upon the earth. They were then bound hand and foot, and the executioner gouged out their eyes in turn, kneeling to do so on the breast of each poor wretch; and after every operation he wiped his knife, dripping with blood, upon the white beard of the hoary unfortunate.

Ah ! cruel spectacle ! As each fearful act was completed, the victim liberated from his bonds, groping around with his hands, sought to gain his feet! Some fell against each other, head against head; others sank powerless to the earth again, uttering low groans, the memory of which will make me shudder as long as I live.

A treatment of prisoners such as I have described is indeed horrible; but it is not to be regarded as an exceptional case. In Khiva, as well as in the whole of Central Asia, wanton cruelty is unknown; the whole proceeding is regarded as perfectly natural, and usage, law and religion all accord in sanctioning it. The present khan of Khiva wanted to signalise himself as a protector of religion, and believed he should succeed by punishing with the greatest severity all offences against it. To have cast a look upon a thickly-veiled lady, sufficed for the offender to be executed by the Redjm according as religion directs. The man is hung, and the woman is buried up to the breast in the earth near the gallows, and there stoned to death. As in Khiva there are no stones, they use kesek (hard balls of earth). At the third discharge, the poor victim is completely covered with dust, and the body, dripping with blood, is horribly disfigured, and the death which ensues alone puts an end to her torture.

The Khan has affixed the punishment of death, not only for adultery, but to other offences against religion, so that in the first years of his reign, the Ulemas were even obliged to cool his religious zeal; still no day passes, but some one is led away from an audience with the Khan, hearing first the fatal words pronounced, which are his doom, 'Alib barin' (away with him).

I had almost forgotten to mention that the Yasaul led me to the treasurer to receive the sum for my daily board. My claim was soon settled; but this personage was engaged in so singular an occupation that I must not omit to particularise it. He was assorting the khilat *(robes of honour) which were to be sent to the camp, to reward those who had distinguished themselves. They consisted of about four kinds of silken coats with staring colours, and large flowers worked in them in gold. I heard them styled four-headed, twelve-headed, twenty-headed, and forty-headed coats. As I could see upon them no heads at all in painting or embroidery, I demanded the reason of the appellation, and I was told that the most simple coats were the reward for having cut off four heads of enemies, and the most beautiful a recompense for forty heads, and that they were now being forwarded to the camp. Some one proceeded to tell me 'that if this was not an usage in Roum, I ought to go next morning to the principal square, where I should be a witness of this distribution.'*

Accordingly, the next morning I did really see about a hundred horsemen arrive from the camp covered with dust. Each of them brought at least one prisoner with him, and amongst the number, women and children, also bound either to the tail of the horse or to the pommel of the saddle; besides all of which, he had buckled behind him a large sack containing the heads of his enemies, the evidence of his heroic exploits. On coming up he handed over the prisoners to the Khan, or some other great personage, then loosened his sack, seized it by the two lower corners, as if he were about to empty potatoes, and there rolled the bearded or beardless heads before the accountant, who kicked them together with his feet until a large heap was composed, consisting of several hundreds. Each hero had a receipt given to him for the number of heads delivered, and a few days later came the day of payment.

Arminius Vambery, Travels in Central Asia (1864)

brook to say: "I saw the suffering in the camel's eye and knew what I hated about Khiva in Soviet hands". Turn right again at the Kazi Kalyan Madrassah, built by the chief judge Salim Akhun (whose robe stands displayed in the Feruz Museum) and now an uninspiring Museum of Music, and continue down a closeted, mud-walled street (paved for President Mitterand's visit in 1994) of madrassah workshops, miscellaneous mausoleums and *kori khana* hostels to the holiest necropolis in Khiva.

■ PAKHLAVAN MAHMOUD MAUSOLEUM

> *To crush one hundred Caucasian mountains with a pestle,*
> *To languish one hundred years in prison,*
> *To dye the sky red with the blood of one's heart,*
> *Is easier than to pass one moment with a fool.*

Pirar Vali (1247–1325), four-lined stanza carved above his tomb.

Pakhlavan Mahmoud the Hercules of the East, Palvan Pir the *kurash* wrestler-saint, Pirar Vali the antireligious Persian poet, Mahmoud the district furrier, all died here, one and the same, in 1325 to enter local folklore as a hero of both brain and brawn and to become the adopted patron saint of Khiva. Over the years a small mausoleum grew up over the site of Mahmoud's original furrier shop, but it was not until 1810-1835 that the tomb was given its present glory by the Kungrad khans of Khiva, as they transformed the shrine into the last great family mausoleum erected in Central Asia and the most renowned building in the city.

The complex is entered through the early southern portal, dated to 1701 by an inscription on the carved gate, and leads to a pretty courtyard with *hujra* cells to the left, the main *khanagha* and mausoleums straight ahead and an open summer mosque and well to the right. The introspective and dizzying decoration saturates everything in multiple shades of blue from the piercing to the languid, while above floats the turquoise ball of the high dome, restored after heavy snow dragged off its tiles in winter 1993. The main hall covers the sarcophagi of Abdul Gazi Khan (left, r.1643-1663), Anusha Khan (right, r.1663-1674/81) and Mohammed Rakhim Khan I (centre, r.1806-1825), but the true focus of adoration lies adorned with local folk motifs in a left-hand chamber, behind an ornate screen inlaid with ivory. A further mausoleum dating from 1913 was originally designed to commemorate Isfandiyar Khan, but he was assassinated outside the city walls and could not be buried here and so today it contains only the tomb of Isfandiyar's mother and son, Timur. A man was traditionally buried with his mother rather than his wife, because of the large number of wives and concubines a khan could amass in one lifetime. The tomb of Alla Kuli Khan also lies to the right of the main hall but is occasionally locked away.

The Soviet era saw the popular tomb close in 1959 when pilgrims were 'invited' to attend antireligious lectures here and transformed in 1979 into The Khorezm Museum of Revolutionary History. Today awkward newlyweds and childless hopefuls throng Khiva's holiest spot. All visitors to the tomb should leave their shoes by the entrance.

A labyrinth of layered tombs surrounds the holy magnet, bricked up when full, and even the remains of a Zoroastrian ossuary can be seen sunk into the earth outside the right-hand wall of the complex.

Opposite the mausoleum is the **Shir Gazi Khan Madrassah** (1718-1720), built by 5,000 Persian slaves abducted from Meshed. The slaves were promised their freedom in return for their labour, but as the construction neared completion Shir Gazi began to murmur discontent over its construction and the slaves, sensing perfidy in the air, lynched their master inside his own madrassah. An inscription above the entrance stoically reads: "I accept death at the hands of slaves." The khan is also famed as one of the greatest historians to write in Chagatai Turkic. His tomb is said to stand in the western chamber, next to the adjoining Rasulbai Madrassah.

Today, the madrassah holds a Museum of Medicine whose two main halls contain little of authenticity to detract from the local personality cults of ibn-Sina and al-Khorezmi. There are also displays dedicated to the Turkoman Poet Makhtum Kuli who studied here for several years until, it seems, he had studied everything his teachers had to teach.

■ ISLAM KHODJA MADRASSAH AND MINARET (1908-10)
As Khiva slowly emerged blinking into the 20th century, the pressing need for reform became apparent to certain members of the court of Isfandiyar Khan. At the cutting edge of these reforms was the Grand Vizier, Islam Khodja, who rapidly earned the love of the people by commissioning a public school and hospital, and the wrath of the clergy by initiating a series of educational reforms. In 1913 he was assassinated on the orders of his arch enemy Nazar Beg, with the tacit permission of the khan, but not before he had time to commission this madrassah (1908) and minaret (1910). The project was destined to be the last monumental architectural achievement of the Central Asian khanates, not least because its architect was buried alive by Isfandiyar in the wake of the assassination cover-up.

At a height of 44.8 metres (146 feet) the minaret stands only two metres shorter than the Kalon in Bukhara, but is almost 800 years younger. Its tapering bands of green glazed tiles lead up to the tallest watchtower in Khiva, essential for spotting roving bands of man-stealing Turkomans, even in 1910. Wooden steps lead up to the height of the original madrassah entrance and another 98 continue up to the clerestory.

The 42 rooms of the madrassah now hold Khiva's finest museum, displaying local applied arts ranging from women's embroidered *chetvan* robes to the original carved wooden plaque of the Ata Darvaza and from plates emblazoned with the insignia of the Uzbek SSR to Turkoman tiaras. The mosque is crowned with a characteristically Persian-shaped dome.

Opposite the madrassah is the first Russian school built in Khiva (1912), now a Museum of Education where skullcaps and soviet medals, portraits of al-Khorezmi and Yuri Gagarin and black-and-white photographs of idealistic Uzbeks congregating under Lenin's stern gaze provide some fine cultural collisions, as clips from the Soviet dream fade from propaganda into history, from menace into disbelief.

One hundred metres south of the Islam Khodja Minaret lies the Baghbanli District Mosque (1809), whose Corinthian carved columns rank as some of the most beautiful in the city.

■ JUMMI MOSQUE (1788)

A deep, monastic calm pervades Khiva's centrally placed Friday Mosque, providing a cool, dim, almost subterranean retreat from the bright desert heat. Two puddles of light echo around a petrified forest of pillars in deepening shades of gloom and provide life for two outstretched trees, which have long since outgrown their static home.

Around the trees a vertical formation of 213 pillars, each 3.15 metres (10 feet) apart, exhibits a millenium long spread of Khivan history. The four oldest pillars were rescued from the dying Khorezmian capital of Kath in the tenth century and were joined 100 years later by a further 17 pillars that still stand. The most recent mosque was completed at the end of the 18th century. For once, the focus of a mosque, the mihrab, seems strangely incidental.

An exhibition of carved wood complements the working examples of karagatcha pillars and the tsarist carriage in the corner was a gift from Alexander II. The odorous minaret climbs 81 steps and 33 metres (100 feet) to provide an unfettered panorama of deeply-etched streets.

Opposite the Friday Mosque lies the small **Matpana Baya Madrassah** (1905), today an anachronistic ex-Soviet Museum of Atheism that recruits some strange thinkers to the cause, including Darwin and al-Beruni. Recent vandalism, such as the destruction of Lenin's face, does not bode well for the future of the museum. The northern side of the chaikhana square is faced by the **Mohammed Amin Inak Madrassah** (1785) which, in its modern role as the local marriage registration office, provides the source for many a marzipan tour of the old town. Inak is best known as the first of the Kungrad dynasty of khans which came to dominate centuries of Khivan history.

■ EASTERN ENSEMBLE

Continue east to the bustling heart of the mid-19th century Khivan revival, an intense section of town where arches, domes, *iwans*, tilework and terracotta all mix into the religious and the secular, the royal and the public.

The small **Abdullah Khan Madrassah** (1855), built by the Khan's mother when he was just 17, now houses a patchy Natural History Museum which reminisces over a lost heritage. Next to the madrassah is the tiny **Ak** or **White Mosque** (1838-42), whose beautiful carved doors offered the district sheltered winter prayer. Its small-scale congregation was roused by its small-scale minaret. The 340-year-old public **Anusha Khan Baths** (1657), behind, were built for the Khan Abul Gazi's son Anusha as part of a reward for saving his father's life against the Bukharan forces at Karmana. Anusha also received several hundred servants and the city of Khazarasp. The pools and heating ducts of the baths are sunk deep into the ground to prevent heat loss and cubicle domes rise from the roof like a spine of soap bubbles.

The Eastern city gate, the **Palvan Darvaza** (1804), was the main artery connecting the inner city with the bustling markets outside. Its 60-metre (195-foot) long, domed tunnel, large enough for a truck, is lined by deeply recessed cells which evolved over time from slave pens into shops, as the 19th century yielded to the 20th. The outer gates were also a place of announcements, decrees, executions and punishment, where runaway slaves were nailed to the gates by their ears in public humiliation.

The imposing raised platform of the **Kutluq Murad Inaq Madrassah** (1804-1812) was once home to a thriving local market, but today it gives hushed access to a tantalizing exhibition of the early black-and-white photographs of Khudai Bergan Divanov, one of the only Khivans to document the city's meteoric transition from medieval citadel to Soviet Republic. Divanov was later executed in Stalin's purges, accused of advocating Khorezmian independence.

The madrassah is noted for the traditional but rare terracotta plaques decorating its corner towers and the covered, subterranean *sardoba* accessed by damp steps from the internal courtyard. Kutluq himself, the uncle of Allah Kuli Khan, is said to be buried under the floor of the main porch, at present under the watchful eye of a cartoon cutout of

Khivan wedding,
Pakhlavan Mahmoud mausoleum

strongman Pakhlavan Mahmoud. He was stabbed in the back while in a conciliatory embrace with a rival Turkoman leader, and it is said that, after the subsequent massacre of the Yomut forces by the incensed Khivan population, six days hard labour were needed to dispose of all the dead bodies.

Directly opposite, the second-largest college in Khiva, the **Allah Kuli Khan Madrassah** (1834), introduces a series of buildings that all bear the royal stamp of one of Khiva's greatest khans. The building is locked, but its artistic energy is publicly aired in the piercing blue tilework of the city's highest portal. At the time of construction, space was limited in this busy part of town but the city walls, it seems, were more flexible than the plans of the Khan. Not only were parts of the walls demolished to accommodate the 99 cells of the royal madrassah, but the existing 17th century Khojamberdiby Madrassah (1688) was coldly sliced in two to provide student access, thereby endowing it with the popular nickname of the Saddlebag or **Khurjum Madrassah**. The madrassah now holds a tourist coffee bar.

The cool, bubbled cupolas of the **Allah Kuli Khan Tim** (1835-38), also known as the Serai Bazaar or Palace Market, link the inner town to the main bazaar and also to the huge **Allah Kuli Khan Caravanserai** (1832), now the wonderfully exotic location of the distinctly proletarian Univermag department store. In the 1830s huge trade caravans carrying Karakul pelts, Turkestan melons frozen in lead cases of ice, fine silks and cotton would regularly set off across the deserts to Orenburg and Astrakhan and return with samovars, furs, sugar and guns as Khivan-Russian trade reached fever pitch. One hundred and sixty years later, Russian goods have dried up and the state shop lies as bare as the surrounding Kara Kum. Just outside, the free-market bazaar booms and prices rocket, leaving many Uzbeks and Turkomans angry, bewildered and longing for the golden days of Brezhnev's Union.

■ TASH HAULI PALACE

> *Luxury to the nomad Mongol meant the embroideries and textiles with which he lined his tent. When he settled in the towns, all he asked was that his palaces and mosques should create a similar effect with the facings of ceramics.*
>
> Rene Grousset, *Empire of the Steppes*, 1939

The introspective and labyrinthine corridors of the Stone Palace comprised the stylized world of Allah Kuli Khan (1826–42) and his extravagant entourage. The palace was first commissioned by the impatient khan in 1830 in a move that reflected a shift in emphasis from the west to the east of the city. When royal architect Usto Nur Mohammed Tajikhan timidly suggested that the 163 rooms and three courtyards could never be completed in the stipulated three years he was promptly impaled and replaced by Kalender Khivaki and famous tile decorator Abdullah Jin. The palace was finally completed some eight years later, but only with the help of over 1,000 slaves.

Museum staff now hide in the gatehouse where, in 1876, Frederick Burnaby met a "guard of thirty or forty men armed with scimitars all attired in long flowing silk robes of various patterns, bright coloured sashes being girt around their waists, and tall fur hats surmounting their bronzed countenances" and also a band of effeminate *bacha*, or dancing boys, ready to entertain.

The first section of the palace to be built was the **Harem** (1830-32), home to the Khan (first room on left) and his four legal wives in the five comfortable southern *iwans* and to female relatives and Persian serving girls in more austere quarters to the north. The royal rectangle is decorated with a sober riot of the finest china blue tilework and is complemented by beautifully carved, slim, wooden pillars on carved marble bases. Fine painted ceilings, whose details were painted before assembly and then suspended upon hooks from the ceiling, provide a festive tone but the ice-blue right-angles of the courtyard still hint at the oppressive boredom of harem life, residents being forbidden to leave the high palace walls and with only an elderly, decrepit despot as company. Note the holy swastika-like emblem carved into the columns of the far *iwan*, next to the entrance of the Museum of Khivan Crafts.

A secret corridor, or *dolom*, to which only the khan was permitted access, joins the private world of the harem to the public offices of the court. The eastern court-yard, the **Ishrat Hauli** (1832-34), served as a reception court where, in winter, visiting Turkoman, Uzbek or Kazakh clan leaders or even the khan himself would pitch a yurt on the raised circular platform in preparation for a welcome feast or royal audience. It was here that Abbott met Alla Kuli Khan and suffered the unenviable task of explaining to a sniggering court why England was ruled by a young woman (Victoria) and why her future husband would not later assume control of the crown. It was also where Mohammed Rakhim Khan II ("a cheery sort of fellow") entertained Burnaby and where Vambery blessed the effeminate Khan Sayyid Mohammed. The courtyard is covered in glistening wall to wall tilework with second-floor calligraphy courtesy of the Chagatai poet Ogahi. The khan's throne room occupied the second floor and summer guest rooms surrounded it.

The third courtyard is the similarly laid out **Arz Hauli** or Court of Law (1837–38), where the khan would dispense justice for an expected four hours a day. All three courtyards were built at separate times and so all have individual gatehouses, but the Arz Hauli has two heavily guarded and complicated exits: one for acquittal, the other for execution. Again, tile decoration is at its most opulent with cucumber and medallion motifs crowding the walls, in a formal synthesis of local designs. The view from the roof of the Stone Palace is timeless:

> *It was now near midnight and the silent, sleeping city lay bathed in a flood of glorious moonlight. The palace was transformed. The flat mud roofs had turned to*

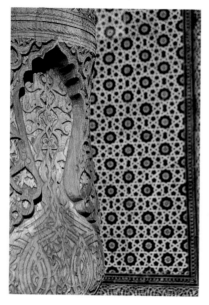

Harem detail, Khiva

marble; the tall slender minarets rose dim and indistinct, like sceptre sentinels watching over the city...Far away the exterior walls of the city, with battlements and towers, which in the misty moonlight looked as high as the sky and as distant as the horizon. It was no longer a real city, but a leaf torn from the enchanted pages of the Arabian Nights.

J Macgahan, Campaigning on the Oxus and the Fall of Khiva, (1874)

■ OFF THE BEATEN TRACK
Just west of the Tash Hauli lies the renovated **Uch Avlioli or Three Saints Mazar**, first built in 1549 and renovated in 1821. One dry summer in the 16th century three brothers faced agricultural ruin along with the rest of the poor farmers when a rich beg refused to open the canal sluices of his fields to irrigate the surrounding farmland. The brothers prayed for rain and when it came their crops were saved, the wicked beg's were flooded and the brothers graduated into bigger business: religious sainthood. The building opposite the tomb is a summer mosque.

During the 19th century madrassah would open and close according to the level of royal support and, as now, not all were open at any one time. Today's misused madrassahs include the Emir Tura Madrassah (1870), built for the brother of Mohammed Rakhim II, the Arab Mohammed Khan Madrassah (1616 rebuilt 1838), now the museum archives, the Musa Tura (Prince Moses) Madrassah (1841), named after the grandson of Alla Kuli Khan and the Dost Alimjan Madrassah (1882), now a wood-carving workshop.

The most enigmatic surviving evidence of a pre-khanate Khiva, the **Khievak Well**, lies sunk in a private courtyard in the northwest corner of the inner town. The well was the original desert source that attracted camel caravans and early settlers to the area and which gave its name, Khievak, to the early city.

Piled up against the inside of the southern city wall lies a confused tumble of graves and holy tombs attended by chanting pilgrims and prayer rags.

SIGHTS: DISHAN KALA

For all its monumental splendour, the Ichan Kala can leave one strangely cold. To see mosques function, deals struck, Turkoman *tilpaks* made and donkeys and *arbas* rather than camels ridden, the visitor must take the rare step out of the Ichan Kala into the Dishan Kala, from the royal city to the merchant suburbs. Here, amongst the cobweb of *aryks,* is where the medieval meets the Soviet and where the medieval stands in better shape. Although it rarely figures in tourist itineraries, its neglected sights still have much to offer.

■ THE BAZAAR

The bazaar spills out from the Palvan Gates and Allah Kuli Khan Tim into the surrounding square, as it has done for centuries.

Next to the Palvan Gate and modern carpet market, the nine-domed **Sayid Niaz Sheliker Bai Mosque** (1842) today acts as a surrogate Friday Mosque and its regular call to prayer performs mouth-to-mouth resuscitation on the old town, providing a lone cry in a skyline of silent minarets.

The next door **Palvan Kari Minaret** stands unique like a cylindrical, Central Asian Rapunzel's tower, while further on the **Abd al Bobo Mausoleum** holds the grave of the 12th-century Khorezmshah Atsiza of Gurganj and marks the site of Khiva's old slave market, where seminomadic slave raiders would turn over their half-starved merchandise and briefly atone for their sins in the nearby mosque. The Naspurush madrassah next to the melon bazaar now holds the bazaar committee.

North of the bazaar on Budennaga St lies the exhausted Tort Shalbaz Ensemble (1885) with mosque, minaret, *khanagha* and *sardoba.*

■ AL-KHOREZMI MUSEUM

This new and deceptively named museum traces the birth of the Khorezm People's Republic as the Khanate hurdled the 18th and 19th centuries to come crashing into the 20th. A series of remarkable photographs show sternfaced, idealistic, young, revolutionary Turkoman crowding the Kunya Ark for the 1920 proclamation of the Republic and the Amin Khan Madrassah for the first Communist Party Conference and also women burning the veil in a mass meeting in the Nurabullai Palace in

Harem detail, Khiva

1925. It also exhibits a painting of Lenin wearing a striped *khalat* presented to him in 1920 by the fledgling republic, as well as a model of the 1924 four-day assault on the city waged by the *basmachi* leader Junaid Khan when, according to the tinted glass of Soviet myth, the Islam Khodja Minaret was used as a radio tower to summon from distant Ferghana the first plane ever to be seen in Khiva, which subsequently strafed and bombed the terrified brigand forces.

North of the museum lies the Kosh Darvaza Gate, one of ten gates in the ten-kilometre (six-mile) outer wall and so-called because its confident design allowed traffic to enter the city in two directions simultaneously. There are also monuments to those who fell in the 1920 revolution and 1941–45 Great Patriotic War and the first hospital built in Khiva in 1912.

■ SAYID MAGRUMJAN (1884)

This monumental ensemble of mausoleums, known locally as the Chadruli Ishan, gets its name from the dead khan (*marhum khan*) Sayyid Mohammed, who is buried here with his son Mohammed Rakhim Khan II, grandsons Isfandiyar Khan and Timur Gazi and father-in-law of Isfandiyar and vizier, Islam Khodja. Local custom forbade anyone who died outside the city walls to be brought back into the inner town for burial and so Mohammed (who lived outside the city) was buried in the main hall next to the larger tomb of Feruz. Isfandiyar and Islam Khodja (who were both murdered outside the city) were buried together, assassin and victim, in a separate side building. The adjoining madrassah is now used as a piano school.

■ NURULLAH BAI PALACE (1906–1912)

The fortified courtyards of Isfandiyar Khan's residence today languish in a largely sorry state of disrepair, but the modern-style reception hall is still in good condition, enshrined as a holy Soviet site to commemorate the first people's government set up here on 26 April 1920 as well as the revolutionary writer Niyazi Hamza who lived and worked here during 1922 and 1923. It is here that Isfandiyar Khan is said to have been murdered in 1918 by Turkoman assassins. The palace is worth a visit for its mind-spinning decoration. The courtyard square was home to the first Lenin in Central Asia until he was replaced by the popular khan Mohammed Rakhim II.

■ WESTERN GATES

Close to the Ata Darvaza lies the **Bika Jun Bika Ensemble** (1894), a mosque, madrassah, minaret and video bar complex built by a rich local merchant to honour the sister of Mohammed Rakhim II. Next door lies the tomb of Sheikh Kalander Bobo, a 16th-century dervish and holy man.

Further to the southwest lies the Magamed Magrum Madrassah and local *mahallya* centre, here called *elat* in local dialect, and on the southwest fringe of the outer city the Gulsava minaret of the former Ashir Magrum Mosque still stands, disconnected from history, in the garden of a local family.

Further west lies the site of the 19th-century Rafanek Summer Palace, now a school for the blind, and the **Shakhimardan Cemetery**, one of seven cemeteries claiming to be the resting place of Caliph Ali, brother-in-law of the Prophet Mohammed.

AROUND KHIVA

Khorezm is studded with obscure mausoleums and holy sites, many of which predate the khanate by several hundred years and any of which provide ample excuse for an exploratory foray into the *kishlaks* and cotton fields of the Khorezmian countryside, where, after all, some 80 per cent of the local population live. They are most conveniently seen in a half-day hired taxi, but all are served by public bus.

Head east through the Koi Darvaza Gates of the outer city wall towards the town of Gandymian, where in 1873 Mohammed Rakhim signed away the independence of his khanate and all lands north of the Oxus. Two kilometres past the huge cotton-ginning factory lies the **Atajan Tura Ensemble**, named after the Khivan prince royal who received the Russian forces while his brother, the khan, hid in the surrounding desert. The mosque, baths and well stand in excellent condition and provide a creative home for yet more woodcarvers. Next door is a functioning *hammam* where one can buy a wash, massage, shave and haircut for the princely sum of 20 cents.

■ CHADRA HAULI

This unusual, four-storeyed, stepped tower looks as if should be squeezed into a gap between high-rise buildings. It is actually the 19th century out-of-town summer residence of a local nobleman or rich merchant, desperate to escape the baking streets of the Ichan Kala. Above a ground floor stables and storehouse rise two diminishing living quarters which form a *bala khana* (from where we get the English balcony), whose high and easily defended *iwans* point north to catch the cool prevailing breezes. The tower echoes the *kushka* form of the much older Ak Sheikh Bobo Bastion in the Ark in a remarkable continuity of style and, as the only one of its kind to survive, it gives a rare peek into non-nomadic country life. The Chadra Hauli lies in a collective farm (Rosmat Madaminov, ex-Frunze) two kilometres past the hamlet of Sayat, some 11 kilometres (7 miles) east of Khiva. A local caretaker can unlock the tower.

In the town of Sayat lies the renovated Bibi Hadj Bibi Mazaar and Mosque, focus of female prayers and Friday communal plov.

■ SHEIKH MUKHTAR VALI MAUSOLEUM

This extraordinarily complex building lies near the village of Ostana, 20 kilometres east of Khiva in Chapaev Kholkhoz and can be easily combined with a low-key visit to the Chadra Hauli. Mukhtar Vali was a holy man from Khorasan and rival of Pachlavan Mahmoud, who lived as a hermit in Khiva and was buried here with his brother-in-law, the equally holy Sayid Ata, a deputy of the Sufic master Yasawi. In 1287 a tomb was built in the wake of the Mongol storm and the final touches were added in 1807 by Mohammed Rakhim Khan I. The 22-metre (71 feet) high drum spills down into a profusion of sub domes and side rooms on two storeys which over the years have provided regular pilgrim refuge from Turkoman raids. The 16-sided drum diffuses soft light through ganch grills and a heavy still saturates every nook and cranny. If locked, local imam Ismael Ibraghim will provide the key and doubtless invite everyone present for tea.

■ KUBLA TOZA BEG SUMMER PALACE (1893-1913)

The summer residence of Mohammed Rakhim Khan II stands halfway between the European and Central Asian worlds, two kilometres southwest of Khiva. Craftsmen from St Petersburg brought square windows and large doorways to the traditional pillared *iwans* of the servants' courtyard and girikh designs of the green ganch reception rooms. The palace was restored for Mohammed Rakhim Khan's 150th birthday in 1992, but today its three courtyards languish in peaceful neglect. Kubla Toza means New Orchard.

KHIVA PRACTICAL INFORMATION

■ TRANSPORT

Marshrutnoe minibuses provide a regular shuttle between Urgench and Khiva (35 kilometres/22 miles), stopping at the Western Gates of Khiva's old town and a minibus rank 100 metres (110 yards) from the Urgench bus station, on Al-Khorezmi St. Minibuses depart when full but stop running after about 6 pm. Buses are cheaper but inconvenient, as the bus station is merely an informal gathering of routes in the north end of town. Taxis will make the trip for a few dollars. Buses, trains and planes to other destinations leave from Urgench.

■ ACCOMMODATION

Staying the night in Khiva is recommended to anyone more interested in a moonlit stroll around the silent shadows of an Islamic citadel than a hot shower and good food. It helps to have Khiva written on your visa, not just Urgench.

Hotel Khiva (Amin Khan Madrassah) (tel. (36237) 54945/54942)
The only option for romantic amateurs chasing a Silk Road dream. Student cells come equipped with private bathroom and bath, wardrobe and desk and a view of the city walls from your balcony. Water can be temperamental and a mosquito repellent is

advisable. A sunken *chaikhana* in the courtyard provides tea and soft drinks. Known officially as the Hotel Khiva. Singles/doubles US$30/40 a night.

Hotel Arkanchi, 10 Pakhlavan Mahmoud Street, (tel. 52230)
Bossman Hussein Sabur and his family provide impressive homestay hospitality in more modern and comfortable surroundings than the neighbouring madrassah. Beds consist of the traditional mattress on the floor and the food is the best in Khiva ($3 for non-guests). Price $25 a night with all meals included, plus free entry to all Khivan sites.

Hotel Khorezm 5, 50 Let Oktyabr Street, (tel. 53566)
An out of town alternative to the Hotel Khiva with less charm but better facilities.

■ FOOD
The plush surroundings of the Restaurant Khiva in the Matinya Madrassah comprise a reliable option if you can gain entry. The bazaar provides bread, honey, fruit, salad, melons, shashlik and fried fish, but rarely after lunch. Other options for the desperate include fried chicken and soup at the Restaurant Grill Bar opposite the Nurullah Bai Palace and cheap basics at state *chaikhanas* opposite the north and west gates. The *chaikhana* next to the Abdal Bobo has the best atmosphere and fried reservoir fish.

(left) *Film extras, Khiva* (right) *Jummi minaret, Khiva*

■ SHOPPING

Karakul *tilpak* hats are sold in the bazaar and wild Turkoman *chorma* hats are irregularly sold with books and postcards near the Sayyid Allauddin Mausoleum in the Ichan Kala. Striped robes, or *don* in local dialect, also pop up occasionally.

Urgench

Urgench is a flat, grey Soviet city with all of Tashkent's faults and few of its saving graces. It is however the gateway to Khorezm and the home of most group travel. For those with time to kill the city offers a bustling modern market and a plethora of Soviet monuments, including those to the Martyrs of the Revolution and the 20 Komsomol members murdered by Tekke *basmachi* on the banks of the Syr Darya in 1922. Lenin quite literally disappeared overnight in 1992, but al-Khorezmi still stands tall outside the Hotel Urgench. Cotton motifs dominate the city, adorning everything from apartment blocks to street lights and in the autumn months the city empties into the surrounding cotton fields and cotton harvests monopolize local news.

PRACTICAL INFORMATION

■ TRANSPORT

Getting to Khiva has never been easy and although Urgench is the transport hub of the region problems persist. Those coming by train from Russia can merely step off the train at Urgench, but from Tashkent distances are large and it pays ($80) to mix in a flight one-way to or from Tashkent. Up to four flights a day connect Tashkent to Urgench's newly renovated airport, with bi-weekly connections to Bukhara, Fergana, Namangan and Moscow. Trains go north to Nukus and Moscow and south to Bukhara and Tashkent, but can be booked up for days. Local trains are packed. Buses serve most destinations but distances can be great (Bukhara takes seven hours). Taxis can be persuaded to take the desert run to Bukhara for cash dollars. Those arriving by plane will probably have their visas checked by OVIR.

■ ACCOMMODATION

Hotel Khorezm, 2, Al Beruni Street, Urgench 740008 (tel. (36222) 65408, 65666, fax. 66108). Singles/doubles $22–42/44/70 depending on season; treble for 'liux' rooms. This carbon copy of the Hotel Shakhrisabsz is the best place to stay in Urgench and the tourist base for the region, providing clean rooms with reliable water and air conditioning. Uzbektourism also works out of the hotel offering guides ($3 per hour) and cars ($12 per hour, seats four). Visa cards accepted. Guides include the excellent Svetlana and helpful Saida and good German-and French-speaking guides are also available.

Hotel Jeihun, 28 Al Khorezmi Street, Urgench 740000 (tel. 66249, 60809)
A cavernous new hotel with spacious rooms with bath, fridge and TV. Singles/doubles $35–50, plus $4 breakfast. Jeihun means 'muddy' and is the Arabic name for the Oxus.
Hotel Urgench, 27 Pachlavan Mahmoud (ex Kommunistichskaya) Street, Urgench 740001 (tel. 62022)
Catering largely to locals with small, grimy rooms but cheap at under $10 in sum.
Olympic Hotel, Sportivnaya Street, near Olympic Stadium (tel. 69325, 64514)
Another budget option, but with an inconvenient location. Price $5.
Train Station
Travellers have stayed in a converted railway sleeper carriage in this basic hotel (no water), $2.

■ TRAVEL AGENCIES
Uzbektourism, 26 Al Khorezmi St (tel. 66455, 63405, 63171, fax 67630)
Most tourists arrange excursions through the Hotel Khorezm, but staff can arrange trips to Kunya Urgench, Toprak Kala etc for the same prices. English speakers should talk to Sophia.

The Desert Sites

It is hard to believe that the arid and baked plains of Khorezm were once a densely populated marshland stalked by tigers, traversed by boats and inhabited by Messagetae Scythians. As the Amu Darya forced its way into the Aral Sea around 2000 BC, the region slowly drained and dried. The Messagetae, Great Scythian nomads, held sway by the sixth century BC. These horseback archers practised a form of group marriage and killed off elders to de-burden the tribe. Their finest victory came in 529 BC with the death of Persian emperor Cyrus the Great. As rivers changed course, irrigation canals became fragile desert lifelines controlled by feudal lords, vulnerable to nomadic incursions and tribal war. Whenever irrigation canals were destroyed, stranded cities withered and died, leaving skeletons of past glory strewn in the desert like the water marks of a high tide.

TOPRAK KALA
This 2,000-year-old ruined city fortress, 350 by 500 metres (1,150 by 1,640 feet) and framed by the brooding Sultan Vais Mountains, is the most dramatic and best explored in the region. The settlement grew up around the first century BC to peak around the third century under Kushan patronage as the capital of the region, until

THE DEATH OF TAMERLANE

After spending the autumn of 1404 feasting outside Samarkand and enriching the glory of the city, Tamerlane advanced an army of 200,000 men against China. He had chosen the hardest winter in memory. As his Arab biographer recorded, "scorched by the cold, their noses and ears fell off . . if a man spat, his spittle, warm though it might be, froze to a ball before it reached the ground". By late January the 69-year-old warrior lay stricken by fever in Otrar. Hot drugs and ice-packs made him "foam like a camel dragged backwards with the rein", until his doctors conceded defeat and to the sound of crashing thunder the "Hand of Death gave him the cup to drink" on February 18, 1405.

Embalmed with musk and rose-water, his body returned in an ebony coffin for burial in the Gur Emir. According to Johann Schiltberger, a Bavarian captive in Samarkand, Tamerlane suffered posthumous regret—"the priests that belong to the temple heard him howl every night during a whole year . . . His friends went to his son and begged that he would set free . . . the craftsmen his father had brought to his capital, where they had to work. He let them go, and as soon as they were free, Tamerlane did not howl anymore."

Although an inscription on his grave threatened "Were I alive, the world would tremble", and locals warned of disaster surpassing Tamerlane's atrocities if his body were disturbed, Soviet scientist Gerasimov won permission to exhume. He began in the dead of night on June 22, 1941. Within hours came the news of Hitler's invasion of Russia. The investigation revealed a man tall

superseded by Kath in 305 AD. The later collapse of Kushan and White Hephalite rule left the region open to devastating Turkic raids which destroyed irrigation canals and lead to the depopulation of the town in the sixth century.

The huge royal citadel dominates the rectangular city and, together with the still-strong city walls, provides an eloquent testament to the fragility of medieval life. Although the three-acre citadel is clearly etched by a series of internal courtyards, rooms and decorative niches and is surrounded by three, three-storeyed, 25-metre (81-foot) high towers, the strength of the site lies in its general impact rather than fine details. Three main halls have, however, been identified by archaeologists: the

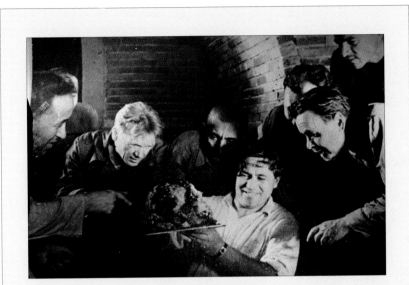

Gerasimov admires Tamerlane's skull

for his race, a tuberculosis sufferer and lame from wounds to both right limbs. Red hair still clung to the skull from which Gerasimov reconstructed a bronze bust. When Ulug Beg was exhumed, his severed head was found beside his body, proof of his son's treachery. The findings were written in Chinese waterproof ink on fine 19th-century Kokandi paper, and sealed in glass and marble, as the skeletons were reinterred with Muslim burial rites at the end of 1942. Five weeks later came news of the German surrender at Stalingrad, the turning point of the Great Patriotic War.

state Hall of Kings, decorated with royal portraits; the Hall of Victories, whose seated pantheon included the Hellenistic god Nike; and the Hall of Black Guards, named after the portraits of Indian guardsmen recruited into the Khorezmian army. Southern rooms formed the inner quarters of the royal family. An armoury stood to the southeast. Leather parchments carrying Khorezmian script, wall paintings depicting river reeds, tigers, stylized red hearts, fantastic griffins and dancing couples were all recovered by Professor Tolstov's 1938 desert excavations and have since been sent to St Petersburg's Hermitage Museum.

The area to the south of the citadel provided an elite home to twelve large extended clan houses, each holding hundreds of people and linked by a narrow grid of streets. Today only the central mound of a dynastic fire-worshipping temple can be made out. Five minutes' drive to the west lies **Kyzyl Kala**, a small fortified dwelling on two floors, accessed by a blind-side gatehouse. Also visible from the fortress is the reportedly impressive **Ayaz Kala**, a further 60 kilometres (40 miles) into the Kyzyl Kum.

The desert sites are best visited combined as a half- or full-day taxi trip from Urgench, crossing the Oxus either near Beruni or Turt Kul (Petro Alexandrovsk). Karakalpak buses go from Beruni as far as Bustan, a few kilometres from the site, but few cross the river from Urgench.

KOI KRYLGAN KALA

Another fascinating skeleton of antique sophistication, the Fort of the Dead Rams, lies approximately 30 kilometres southeast of Toprak Kala, best approached from the city of Turt Kul.

The fort forms two astonishing and perfectly concentric circles of 42 metres (135 feet) and 87 metres (285 feet) in diameter. The inner citadel, originally used as a burial ground for Khorezmian rulers, for cult rites and even astronomical observations, forms a ten-metre high drum covering a central courtyard and six side rooms. Between the inner and outer walls servants' and artisan rooms spread out radially towards the nine towers of the city defences. The site is best appreciated from the air.

Excavations from the site have revealed ossuaries, drinking horns, Scythian headdresses and Khorezmian inscriptions in an Aramaic script and indicate that the site was inhabited from the fourth century BC to the fourth century AD as a dynastic centre.

Other sites in the area include the huge city walls of **Guldursan** (between Turtkul and Toprak Kala), destroyed by Mongol retribution in 1221, the imposing raised Zoroastrian altar of **Chilpak Kala** (close to the Amu Darya road between Mangit and Nukus) and the remote desert forts of Dzhanbas Kala, Yakke Parsan and Dzhampik Kala.

Excursion to Turkmenistan: Kunya Urgench

An intriguing excursion can be made from either Urgench or Nukus into the neighbouring republic of Turkmenistan, to the sudden, silent remains of the ancient capital of Khorezm.

HISTORY

Gurganj has oscillated through history between sophisticated, cultural metropolis and distant, desert backwater; three times sacked by invading nomad empires, three times to rise from the ashes in an intense burst of cultural energy. The city flowered, fell and bloomed again.

Gurganj's early history is documented only in the distant annals of Chinese ambassadors, but we know that by the time Arab forces were invited into Khorezm to help solve its civil war, the city was one of the three largest towns in Khorezm, subject to the ruling Afraghid Khorezmshah at Kath (or Al-Fir). As Kath declined in the wake of the Arab destruction and was gradually washed away by the Amu Darya, rival Gurganj flourished as steppe trade links with the Khazar and Bulghar in southern Russia grew. A Khorezmian delegation even visited the royal court of Kiev in a futile attempt to persuade its prince of the obvious advantages of Islam as a state religion. The prince declined the offer, after hearing that conversion entailed not only circumcision but moreover a life devoid of alcohol, and accepted the Orthodox faith instead. In 995 Emir Mamun of Gurganj overthrew the Afraghids, murdered the Khorezmshah and united the oasis under its new capital.

Mongol victim,
Kunya Urgench

Under the 23-year rule of Mamun and his son Mamum II (999-1017), Gurganj fostered the state-sponsored Academy of Learning that sparkled with the individual brilliance of al-Beruni and ibn-Sina, as commercial power made the tricky transition into political strength and cultural excellence. The city grew into a cosmopolitan mix of transcontinental traders, dervish missionaries and even Melkite and Nestorian Christians, whose frozen Turkestan melons were famed throughout the Islamic world and shipped in leaded boxes of chipped snow to the courts of Baghdad.

In 1017 Mamun II was killed by patriots who objected to the submissive moves made to the expanding Ghaznavid empire, but it was a move which only opened the door for Ghaznivid and Seljuk annexation into the rising tide of Turkic domination. But under the new dynasty of Khorezmshah in the mid-12th century the nominal Seljuk yoke was shrugged off and history's spotlight again fell upon the city. Under Tekkesh (1172-1200) and his son Mohammed II (1200-1220), the Gurganj revival conquered territory from Afghanistan to Iraq and Azerbaijan. The Mongol historian Juvaini described the pre-Mongol town: "Khorezm was the dwelling place of the celebrities of mankind, its environs were receptacles for the rarities of the time, its mansions were resplendent with every kind of lofty idea".

In 1219 the Khorezmshah committed a grave mistake. His conceit inflamed by Genghis Khan's acceptance of him as one of his best 'sons', he ordered a 500-camel Mongol caravan murdered in the Khorezmian border town of Otrar and a gold bar "the size of a camel's hump" confiscated. In a rare piece of Mongol diplomacy, three envoys were sent across the steppes to demand the head of the Otrar governor, Inalchiq, but Gurganj's unambiguous reply was to kill one and burn the others' beards. This dishonour deflected Genghis' rage from India to Central Asia and within two years Otrar, Bukhara and Samarkand had all fallen and a dark cloud had descended outside the gates of Gurganj. Mohammed somehow managed to escape but was pursued relentlessly to the ends of the earth, eventually to die of exhaustion on a remote island in the Caspian Sea. The governor of Otrar had molten silver poured into his eyes. The population of Gurganj was counted, every Mongol soldier was ordered to slay 24 inhabitants, the Gurganj dam was destroyed and the town was washed away by the Oxus. "Khorezm became the abode of the jackal and the haunt of the owl and the kite." (Juvaini).

The city was miraculously revived by trade that had been united into the lands of the Golden Horde and by 1366 had become "the largest, greatest, most beautiful and most important city of the Turks", a city that "shakes under the weight of its population". ibn-Battuta continues to describe a city so busy that a man could not move in the throng, where Friday absentees from the mosque were publicly beaten and fined five dinars and from where boats sailed the Oxus to Termez. The local Sufi dynasty filled a power vacuum left by the weakening Hordes but soon trod on the toes of Tamerlane's rapidly expanding empire. In 1379 Tamerlane attacked Gurganj, but found the chivalry to offer its besieged and hungry ruler a selection of the first melons of the season, just arrived from Termez. The khan angrily threw the melons into the moat, giving the golden dish to the gatekeeper, and battle began. In 1388 Tamerlane ordered the rebellious city destroyed once and for all, barley sown upon its charred remains and its artisans abducted to Samarkand. The city never really recovered and its handful of inhabitants were finally relocated by Abul Gazi Khan of Khiva in the 17th century.

SIGHTS

The majority of sights lie scattered in a baked and levelled plain like charred tree trunks after a forest fire, giving the eerie impression that Timur's troops left the still smoking wreckage just a few hours ago.

The first monument reached from the north is the unique **Turabeg Khanum Mausoleum**, built in 1370 in honour of the Princess Turabeg, daughter of the Golden Horde's Uzbek Khan and wife of Kutluk Timur. The central six-sided chamber merges to a 12-sided transition zone and a 24-windowed drum of twelve metres diameter. The inner dome is inlaid with a starry swirl of unrestored tilework, while the exterior rosettes in blues, yellows and browns point to a cosmopolitan past. The northern room is the burial vault of the Gurganj Sufi dynasty.

Over the road and past the restored 19th century Sayid Akhmed Mazar, towers the tallest minaret in Central Asia, the 62-metre (200-foot) high **Kutlug Timur Minaret** (1320–30). The chimney-stack tower contains 143 steps and would have been built by workmen standing on the inside. At the top an exterior wooden platform would have supported a faint call to prayer. Around the minaret lie the remains of a kiln and *sardoba*; fire and water for the production of local ceramics.

The blue-tiled tent design of the **Sultan Tekkesh Mausoleum** (1200) rises on 16 sides to commemorate one of the greatest rulers of Gurganj's golden age. The building, known locally as the Sharif Sheikh, used to hold a state library and college.

The holy **Forty Mullah's Hill** is said to contain the original Mamun Academy of Science, home to ibn-Sina and al-Beruni and the centre of the fiercest resistance to the Mongol invasion, and thus its bloodiest retribution. Tortured skulls protrude from the excavations and add a human dimension to the historical sackings repeatedly endured by the city.

The 12-sided **Fakhr-ad-din Razi** or **Il Arslan Tomb** is either named after the father of Sultan Tekesh who ruled Gurganj from 1156–1172 or the local scientist Razi, depending upon your sources. The bricks of its rich eastern terracotta facing were laid on the ground, covered in clay, carved, baked individually and then reassembled to make up the remarkably intense trim.

The base of the **Mamun II Minaret** lies anchored in the ground to the south like a tree stump that the Mongols failed to uproot. Shards of tilework and an inscription examined in 1952 date the pre-Mongol minaret and Friday mosque to the year 1011. The minaret was paid for by Khorezmshah Mamun himself "in humility toward religion, and to approach God, may his mention be great, and with the desire for recompense in this world and the hereafter." (as inscribed on the minaret). It is even conjectured that al-Beruni, court vizier at the time, may have influenced the construction with the idea of using it as an astronomical observation tower.

Further south lies the gate portal of the **Tash Kala Caravanserai**, site of the reluctantly resettled 16th-century town, and to the southeast lies the 13th century **Ak Kala** fortress, a prime example of what happened to fortresses that stood against the Mongol fighting machine. To the east lies the popular holy tomb of Divan-i-Burkh.

Back in the modern Turkoman town, the twin **Najmaddin Kubra** (1321–33) **and Sultan Ali** (1580) **Mausoleums** lie separated by the holy shade of a *karaman* tree. The intense floral and *girikh* tilework and inscriptions of ultramarine rank alongside the most beautiful in Central Asia. Kubra (1145–1221), an important figure in the intellectual development of Sufism and founder of the Kubrawiya sect of dervishes, was born in Khievak in 1145, travelled widely in Egypt, studied in Tabriz and settled in Gurganj. The Islamic martyr was killed waging a jihad against the Mongol forces after he had decided not to make the city invisible to the enemy. He is famous for his saying that the 'ah' in 'Allah' forms the very sound we make with every breath. Khorezmshah Sultan Ali was the ruler of Gurganj when Jenkinson visited the town in the mid-16th century.

The unassuming tomb of Piryar Vali is said to hold the father of Pakhlavan Mahmoud and the nearby Tash Mosque and Madrassah (1903–08) house a local museum.

■ **FURTHER AFIELD**

Some 50 kilometres (30 miles) west, along the legendary former route of the Oxus, lies the ruined city of **Dev Kesken**, visited by Anthony Jenkinson in 1558, when it was one of a ring of rich cities skirting the southern fringe of the Ust'urt plateau and its trade routes to Russia.

PRACTICAL INFORMATION

■ **VISAS**

At present there is some confusion over the status of day-trips into Turkmenistan. Routes from Urgench theoretically involve an international border-crossing, and travellers are advised to try to obtain a Turkoman visa at the embassy in Tashkent. However, if an excursion is arranged with Uzbektourism, they will normally arrange a one-day visa with their Turkoman Intourist contacts. Travellers in a taxi or public bus may find themselves open to a small on-the-spot 'fine', but should remind the authorities that there is little choice. Low-key border crossings from Nukus/Khojeli or Mangit are unlikely to cause any problem. Problems will normally arise if you are planning to spend the night in Kunya Urgench, making a day trip doubly attractive.

■ **TRANSPORT**

Uzbektourism can provide a car and driver for $80 a day, but a cheaper bet is to arrange a price with a local taxi driver, agreeing costs for petrol, fines and detours before you set out. Several people in Khiva can arrange this. Public buses run from Urgench to Dashkovuz and then on to Kunya

New Uzbek emblem

Urgench and also from Khojeli, near Nukus, direct to Kunya Urgench. An early start is essential.

Turkoman currency is the *manat*, currently trading at about five manat to one Uzbek sum, but Uzbek sum is widely accepted. There are hotels in Kunya Urgench, Dashkovuz and Khojeli, in extreme cases of emergency.

Nukus

Nukus is a grim, spiritless city of bitter pleasures whose gridded avenues of socialism support a centreless town, only to peter out around fading fringes into an endless wasteland of cotton fields punctuated by the random, surreal exotica of wild camels loitering in neglected apartment blocks. It is the capital of Karakalpakstan, an ill-defined autonomous republic inside Uzbekistan and thus the regional centre and transport hub of the republic.

The **Karakalpak** (Black Hat), whose ethnic umbrella gives the republic its *raison d'etre*, are a Turkic people whose language, traditions and clan structure have closer links to the Kazakh than the Uzbek and whose physiognomy owes more to the nomadic Mongol than to the settled Persian. Their ancestral heartland was tradition-ally centred upon the lower Volga and Syr Darya rivers and northern Aral, but to-wards the end of the 18th century the clans were gradually driven southwest into the Amu Darya delta by relentless Kazakh aggression. Their signed treaty of friendship with the ambassador of Peter the Great in 1722 meant little in these new lands and they were made reluctant and unruly subjects of the Khans of Kungrad and later Khiva. In 1827 a Karakalpak rebellion held the town of Kungrad for a time but it was bloodily suppressed by Khivan forces. In 1873 Karakalpak lands were ceded to Russia and rose restlessly under Soviet rule through the ranks of nationality from an autonomous oblast in the Kazakh republic (1925), to autonomy in the Russian Federation (1930), to an autonomous republic in its own right (1932), to an autonomous republic inside the Uzbek republic (1936). In these dizzy days of ethnic assertiveness the republic's status is somewhat ambiguous, but practical autonomy stretches little further than a national flag, em-blem and TV station. Approximately 30 per cent of the population are ethnic Karakalpak, 30 per

Al-Khorezmi

cent Uzbek and 30 per cent Turkoman. Only 2 per cent are Russians, descended mainly from Cossack fishermen, and most of these are leaving.

Today the land is characterized by impending ecological disaster and entrenched popular Islam, a heady mix of environmentalists and pilgrims and a tiny trickle of tourists.

SIGHTS

The city itself is of limited interest to either tourists or inhabitants and is best used as a base for visits to the Aral Sea and Kunya Urgench. Once you are here, however, its three affiliated museums are a must.

The **Karakalpak State Museum**, on the corner of Karakalpakstan and Mustakillik Streets, offers many wide-ranging insights into the region. The first hall concentrates on the region's dying or dead natural history, with satellite maps of the Aral Sea taken from 1957–1988 and stuffed examples of extinct species that once inhabited the reedy marshes of the Oxus delta and the stony desert of the Ust'urt plateau. The very last Turan Tiger, caught and stuffed in 1972, stands glassy-eyed in a corner, its final moment of extinction frozen for all to mourn. Models of Toprak and Koi Krylgan Kala line the next hall, beside photographs of Tolstov's intrepid looking camel expeditions into the surrounding deserts. Karakalpak armour leads to a fine historic spread of Turkestan roubles, Bukharan Republic notes and Soviet currency emblazoned with 'Workers of the World Unite' in seven languages. There are also excellent examples of Karakalpak and Turkoman clothes and jewellery; the medium through which local nomadic creativity traditionally found its greatest artistic outlet.

Above the museum is the **Igor Savitsky Art Gallery**, home to one of the finest collections of Soviet avant-garde art from the 1920s and 30s; an age of relative artistic freedom before the demands from the 'centre' changed in the mid 1930s and Stalinist socialist realism became the only acceptable form of Soviet art. Nukus's backwater obscurity enabled Savitsky to collect a wide spread of artistic life, from local folk art to Russian icons, at a time when the more celebrated museums in Moscow and St Petersburg had their wrists ideologically tied. Today the museum holds some 80,000 exhibits ranging from the Khorezmian art of Toprak Kala to Karakalpak cubism, which the very knowledgeable and English-speaking director, Marinika Babnazarova, can place into sharper context. Now that funding from Moscow has dried up, the sale of local paintings and visiting donations provide the only source of meagre revenue.

A few hundred metres left, out of the museum, hides the affiliated **Museum of Applied Arts**, where further fine examples of local fabrics, traditional dress and silver jewellery point to a distinct cultural tradition that is still hinted at today in local faces, although not local dress.

The **Centre Progress English School** (31 Utepova Street, a ten-minute walk southeast of the Hotel Tashkent) is an oasis of enthusiastic and excellent English and

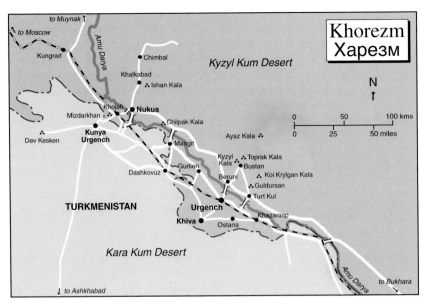

is recommended to anyone in search of conversation with bright young Karakalpaks, in need of translators or guides, or even just a cup of tea. (Tel. (36122) 72459.)
The statue opposite the Nukus Theatre pays tribute to Berdachi (1827–1900), Karakalpak's greatest poet and statesman.

PRACTICAL INFORMATION

■ TRANSPORT
There are a theoretical five flights a day to Tashkent and one weekly to Moscow. Long-distance trains depart from nearby Khojeli. Local buses to and from Khojeli, Muynak and Beruni leave from the southern bus station (bus numbers 1 or 6), next to the train station, as does the 3 pm bus to Urgench, Bukhara and Samarkand. Buses to Khalkabad and Chimbai depart from the northeast station.

■ ACCOMMODATION
Tashkent Hotel, Berdachi (ex Turtkulsky Street)
The best option in town with rooms on ten floors with television, fridge, heating, air-con and hot water. The adjoining restaurant is also the best place to eat. Single $20.
Nukus Hotel, Karakalpakstan (ex-Karl Max Street),
An outrageous $20 is demanded for cockroach-ridden rooms with disgusting bathrooms. A potential local sum price of about $2 makes it more attractive for budget travellers. An underground orgy of taped MTV, vodka and mutton takes place nightly in the basement video bar.

THE SEA THAT IS FLEEING ITS SHORES

The Aral Sea no longer exists. The two rivers that replenish the 60km³ of water lost every year by evaporation no longer reach the sea, bled dry by the unyielding quotas of a cotton monoculture and a command economy. Sea level is dropping by one metre every year and the chemical cocktail of pesticides and defoliants let into the sea from the leaching of cotton fields is being concentrated and deposited as a crust, as thousands of kilometres of sea bed turn to salty dust. The area of the sea has halved in 30 years, and its volume has quartered. The island in the middle of the sea has linked emerging arms to either shore to create a land bridge that separates the southern sea from the northern. In 1840, English captain James Abbott heard of an enchanted castle on the island "from which there is no return", where dragons guarded treasure vaults girdled by flaming quicksands. In Soviet times the island was equally dangerous as the secret home of a biological weapons testing ground.

The Aral Sea is not a local problem. The Aral straddles Kazakhstan and Uzbekistan, waters are diverted from it to feed Turkmenistan, and its water source lies locked in the glaciers of Kyrgyzstan and Tajikistan. Sandstorms carry chemical salts, the dry tears of the Aral, into the atmosphere to deposit them as far away as Ferghana, Georgia and the Arctic coast. The shrinking sea no longer moderates the extreme continental climate of the closed environment. Summers are getting hotter, winters colder and cotton yields are plummeting. Russia, as the 'centre', is also intricately linked to both the problem and its solution, especially now that the crisis has taken a wider ethnic dimension as a symbol of Russian exploitation and Soviet obsession with the domination of nature.

The Aral Sea has no solution. In 1987 the Politburo finally shelved its plan to divert water from two Siberian rivers to stabilize the sea. In February 1994 and 1995 the leaders of the five Central Asian states met in a now annual conference to formulate a cohesive rescue plan, but none can afford to cut back on cotton production and none have the necessary funds to combat the problem. Theoretical hopes hang on a pipeline artery from the Caspian Sea, the planting of vegetation on the shores of the Aral to slow erosion and even a scheme to artificially stimulate rain clouds in the Aral basin. The shrinking of the Aral was noticed in 1868 by Eugene Schuyler. Perhaps now, well over a century later, the best hope for the Aral Sea lies concealed in this very fact—hidden in the wider sweep of nature. What man has created, only nature can now redress.

ARAL STATISTICS

<u>1960–1992</u>
Level of sea: 53.4m (175.2ft) to 36.9m (121.1ft)
Area of sea: 67,388 km^2 (26,012 miles^2) to 33,300km^2 (12,852 miles^2)
Volume: 1092.4 km^3 to 290km^3
33,000 km^2 of sea floor has so far been exposed.
In Muynak cancer of the gullet is 18 times the national average.
Species of mammals recorded in the Aral region have dropped from 70 to 30.
Species of birds have dropped from 319 to 168.
All 24 species of fish have disappeared.
Salt content (1960): 10g/litre (1987): 27g/litre.
Average daily temperature extremes in the region have gone up by 3.3^{0}C (7^{0}F).
The Aral Sea is dropping by one metre every year.

Aral victim; beached trawler, Muynak

■ **FOOD**

The bazaar is located 400 metres (440 yards) north of the Hotel Tashkent and has several basic eateries. The café of the Tashkent Hotel serves coffee and sausage if its restaurant is closed.

■ **HEALTH**

If you plan to work or stay in Karakalpakstan for any length of time you should invest in a water filter and procure medical advice from the UN clinic in Tashkent.

AROUND NUKUS

All around Nukus the Amu Darya is bullied, cajoled, channelled, funnelled and squeezed into a maze of canals, lakes and hydroelectric dams, of which the most impressive to visit is at **Takiatash**, 12 kilometres (7.5 miles) southwest of Nukus. Its Soviet power, originally earmarked for Turkmenistan, now lies on Uzbek soil and is only one of many subjects presently under discussion as the two republics attempt to disentangle their countless connecting threads.

Some 15 kilometres (9 miles) west of Nukus and 4 from Khojeli, on the road to Kunya Urgench, lie the holy sites of **Mizdarkhan** and **Yusup Ishan**, two enormous cemeteries of several thousand graves which spill over the only two hills on the horizon, each like a mini Jerusalem on the steppe. The larger of the two, Mizdarkhan, was once an important centre of handicrafts set on the trade crossroads to Gurganj, until it was destroyed by Tamerlane en route to larger things in Gurganj.

The cemetery gets its popular name, Mazlum Khan Slu, from the restored mausoleum and ablutions hall of the same name, skilfully constructed underground at the beginning of the 14th century. The beautiful (*slu*) Mazlum Khan was the Juliet-like daughter of the city *hakkim* who died for her love of the Romeoesque *hakkim* of the rival town of Yusup Ishan. Other tombs include the seven-cupolaed, 25-metre- (80-foot-) long sarcophagus of the giant Shamun Nabi, said to have grown an inch every year for several centuries, the crumbling 11th-century tomb of Caliph Yejereb and the holy hill of Jumurat Khasap, where Khorezmian majolica and Mongol coins have been discovered. Close to the cemetery lies the ancient walled city of Gaur Kala and the sister cemetery of Yusup Ishan.

On the eastern fringes of Khalkabad, 40 minutes' drive from Nukus, lie the 150-year-old remains of the frozen feudal village of **Ishan Kala** (Fortress of the Elders). Individual buildings are clearly defined and include the ten-metre- (33-foot-) high walls of the citadel, a central Friday mosque and the holy tomb of local Sufic elder Ata Ula Ishan. On Fridays, the nearby mosque is a boundless source of colourful Turkoman clothes, hospitality and *plov*.

Some 90 kilometres (55 miles) southeast of Nukus lies the **Badai Tugai Nature Reserve** for endangered species.

Muynak and the Aral Sea

The water that serveth all that country is drawn by ditches out of the River Oxus, unto the great destruction of the said river, for which it cause it falleth not unto the Caspian Sea as it hath done in times past, and in short time all that land is like to be destroyed, and to become a wilderness for want of water, when the river of Oxus shall fail.

Anthony Jenkinson, 1558

Hidden in one of the most obscure corners of the former Soviet Union lies one of its darkest secrets; the disappearance, in a single lifetime, of the Aral, once the fourth largest inland sea in the world. The landlocked port of Muynak stands as a silent witness to its death throes and, like Chernobyl and Semipalatinsk, points to what were, until *glasnost*, the unmentioned costs of the Soviet experiment.

Muynak was once the largest port on the Aral, a finger of coast where a significant part of the Aral catch was processed and canned. In 1921 as the Volga region suffered a terrible famine, Lenin appealed to the Aral fleet for help and within days 21,000 tonnes of fish had been dispatched, saving thousands of Russian lives. Today it is a nightmarish town of stagnant, corrosive pools and deserted factories, the victim of a Soviet crusade to overcome nature. Not a single fish can survive in the sea, 10,000 fishermen have lost their jobs and Muynak has lost its *raîson d'être*. The only reason to visit it is a macabre one; to witness the death throes of the sea and the dramatic sight of dozens of deserted fishing boats rusted at their moorings, submerged in sand, riding the crest of a sand dune, 100 kilometres (60 miles) from the shoreline.

To visit the **ship's graveyard** continue north through the town from the bus station for two kilometres and head northeast, over the crunchy, white top soil of salt and sea shells, towards the large canning factory. A solitary taster of the debacle ahead lies on display at the bus station and a wider view of the area can be gained from the northern promontory

Muynak used to be a closed, forbidden town, but today little fuss is made if your papers are in order. Uzbektourism will even provide transport if needed and aerial tours of the sea itself can be arranged either at Nukus airport or in Tashkent (tel. 320626). Public buses depart twice a day from Nukus and take three to four hours. The town can be comfortably visited as a day trip from Nukus with your own transport otherwise the basic Hotel Muynak, four kilometres north of the town, can supply accommodation at approx $3. Staying overnight greatly increases potential problems with OVIR.

The Stream of Ages

Travelling thus Eastwards, and arrested at each forward step by some relic of a dead civilisation, or of a glorious but forgotten past, the imagination of the European cannot but be impressed with the thought that he is mounting the stream of the ages, and tracing towards its remote source the ancestry from which his race has sprung. His feet are treading in an inverse direction the long route of humanity. The train that hurries him onward into new scenes seems at the same time to carry him backward into antiquity, and with every league that he advances the mise en scene recedes into a dimmer distance. History lies outspread before him like the page of a Chinese manuscript, to decipher which he must begin at the bottom and work his way up to the top...

In these solitudes, moreover, the traveller may realise in all its sweep the mingled gloom and grandeur of Central Asian scenery. Throughout the still night the fire horse, as the natives have sometimes christened it, races onwards, panting audibly, gutturally, and shaking a mane of sparks and smoke. Itself and its riders are alone. No token or sound of life greets eye or ear; no outline redeems the level sameness of the dim horizon; no shadows fall upon the staring plain. The moon shines with dreary coldness from the hollow dome, and a profound and tearful solitude seems to brood over the desert. The returning sunlight scarcely dissipates the impression of sadness, of desolate and hopeless decay, of a continent and life sunk in a mortal swoon. The traveller feels like a wanderer at night in some deserted graveyard, amid crumbling tombstones and and half-obliterated mounds. A cemetery, not of hundreds of years but of thousands, not of families or tribes but of nations and empires, lies outspread before him; and ever and anon, in falling tower or shattered arch, he stumbles upon some poor unearthed skeleton of the past.

George Curzon, Russia In Central Asia, *1889*

Language Guide to Uzbek and Russian

While Russian remains the most useful language for the traveller, Uzbek is now the state language and, more importantly, will break the ice on any occasion, opening up the bounteous world of Uzbek hospitality. Part of the Eastern Turkic group of languages, Uzbek diverged from other Central Asian tongues in the early 14th century. Known as Chagatai, or old Uzbek, it was enriched by poet Alisher Navoi (1441–1501) to rival the literary pretensions of Arabic and Persian, source of numerous loanwords. By the time of the Bolshevik Revolution, Chagatai was quite divorced from the colloquial language. In 1923, a new Uzbek language was adopted, using a modified Arabic alphabet. To speed literacy campaigns and isolate the Uzbeks' Islamic past, Arabic was replaced by Latin in 1927. In 1940, Cyrillic superseded Latin as Sovietization was stepped up.

The process is now in reverse. In 1989, Uzbek was reinstated as the official language of the republic. In 1993, parliament agreed to a transition to a Latin script, similar to Turkey's, while madrassah nationwide reintroduce Arabic through the Koran. Although Uzbeks remained among the least linguistically Russified peoples of the former Soviet Union—bazaars were Uzbek-only zones—further education and a place in the hierarchy demanded Russian language ability. The current changes, common to all Central Asia, are forcing many intellectuals and politicians to rediscover their roots.

A smattering of Uzbek will benefit the traveller when among the Kazakhs, Kyrgyz and Turkoman, and also among the Uighur in northwest China's Xinjiang Autonomous Region, for all these people speak mutually intelligible Turkic languages, at least to some degree. Only Tajikistan stands out, for its Persian-based population use a language more akin to Farsi. Since independence, a number of local English-Uzbek phrasebooks have become intermittently available, though the best choice is Lonely Planet's *Central Asia Phrasebook*. While Latin alphabet street signs *are* appearing, there is confusion over the exact script to be used and a lengthy transition from Cyrillic may ensue. An approximation of likely reforms is given below.

Many people in the travel industry are Russian and while English speakers are on the increase, elementary Russian is still essential for a successful trip. Budget travellers should make an effort to master survival phrases, a number of which are listed on pages 319 and 320. It is most advised that you take a comprehensive Russian phrasebook and dictionary on your trip. The table on page 318 lists new Latin Uzbek next to Uzbek Cyrillic while the right-hand column gives an approximation of the English pronunciation. Please note that Uzbek Cyrillic has three additional letters that correspond to the new Latin Uzbek letters.

Uzbek Latin	Uzbek Cyrillic	Equivalent Sound in English
Aa	Аа	*ah*
Bb	Бб	*b* (pronounced *p* when ending word)
Cc	Цц	*ts*
Dd	Дд	*d* (pronounced *t* when ending word)
Ee	Ее	*yeh* or *eh*
Ff	Фф	*f*
Gg	Гг	*g* as in *gull* (pronounced *k* when ending word)
Hh	Хҳ	aspirated *h*
I i	Ии	*ee*
J j	Йй	*y* as in *you*
Kk	Кк	*k*
Ll	Лл	*l*
Mm	Мм	*m*
Nn	Нн	*n*
Oo	Оо	*o* as in *lone* or *ah* when its syllable is *unstressed*
Pp	Пп	*p*
Qq	Ққ	hard *k*
Rr	Рр	*r*
Ss	Сс	*s*
Tt	Тт	*t*
Uu	Уу	*u* as in *loot*
Vv	Вв	*v* pronounced *f* when ending word
Xx	Хх	*kh* as in Scottish *loch*
Yy	Яя	*ya* as in *yard*
Zz	Зз	*z*
CHch	Чч	*ch* as in *chop*
Ḡḡ	* Ғғ	*ga*, gutteral sound
J̵j̵	Жж	*zh* like *s* sound in *measure*
Ññ	* Нг нг	*ng* as in *sing*
Ōō	* Ўў	*oh*
SHsh	Шш	*sha*
there are no Latin equivalents for these five sounds {	Щщ	*sh'ch* as in fresh cheese
	Ъъ	hard sign, silent, divides syllables of words
	Ьь	soft sign, silent, softens preceding consonant
	* Ээ	*eh*
	Юю	*yoo*
	Ыы	open *I* as in *pin*
Ëё	Ёё	*yo* as in *yacht*

© 1998 Odyssey Publications Ltd

*Cyrillic characters marked thus: * are particular to Uzbek Cyrillic.*

ENGLISH	RUSSIAN	UZBEK
Hello	*zdravstvuityeh*	*assalom alaykum* (may peace be unto you) (and upon you-*alaykum assalom*)
Goodbye	*da svidaniya*	*khair*
Thank you	*spaseeba*	*rakhmat*
Please	*pazhalusta*	*markhamat / iltimos*
Yes	*da*	*kha*
No	*nyet*	*yoq*
How are you?	*kahk deelah?*	*yakshimisiz?*
(very) well / good	*(ocheen) kharasho*	*(juda) yakhshi*
bad	*plokha*	*yomon*
How much?	*skolka stoet?*	*nyech pul/kancha pul?*
expensive	*daragoi*	*qimmat*
cheap	*deeshoviy*	*arzon*
I want...	*ya hachoo...*	*menga...kerak*
Do you have...?	*...yest?*	*sizda...bormi?*
Where is..?	*gdyeh...?*	*...kayerda?*
I want a ticket to...	*adin bilyet dah..., pazhalusta*	*mengga...gacha bilet kerak*
I don't speak Russian	*ya nye gavaryu pa Russki*	
I don't speak Uzbek		*men Uzbekcha bilmayman*
Do you speak English?	*Vi gavaritye pa Angliski?*	*siz Ingliz tilida gapirasizmi?*
I don't understand...	*Ya nye panemaiyoo...*	*men...bilmayman*
What is your name?	*kahk vas zavut?*	*isminggiz nima?*
my name is...	*meenya zavut...*	*mening ismim...*
Where are you from?	*vi ahtkoodah?*	*siz qaerdan kildingiz?*
I am from...	*ya eez...*	*men...kelaman*
England	*Anglia*	
America	*Amerika*	
Canada	*Kanada*	**[Use Russian names]**
France	*Frantsia*	
Germany	*Germania*	
Are you married?	(women) *vi zhamuzim?*	*turmushga chikkanmisiz?*
	(men) *vi zhinati?*	*uylanganmisiz?*
I am married	(women) *ya zamuzhim*	*turmushga chikkanman*

ENGLISH	RUSSIAN	UZBEK
I am married	(men) *ya zhinat*	*uylanganman*
Any children?	*dyety yest?*	*bolalaringiz bormi?*
What is your job?	*kto vi pa prafessiy?*	*kasbingiz nima?*
Old Town	*starriy gorad*	*eski shakhar*
Restaurant	*restoran*	*ashkhana*
Hot	*zharka*	*issiq*
Cold	*khalodniy*	*sovuq*
Big	*balshoya*	*katta*
Small	*mahlinki*	*kichik*
Beautiful	*kraseevah*	*chiroilee*
Hotel	*gostinitsah*	*mekhmonkhona*
Room	*nomeer*	*khona*
I am hungry	*ya goladin*	*mening qornim och*
I have diarrhoea	*oo meenya panoss*	*mening ichim ketayapti*
One	*adin*	*bir*
Two	*dva*	*ikki*
Three	*tree*	*uch*
Four	*chyetyri*	*turt*
Five	*pyat*	*besh*
Six	*shest*	*olti*
Seven	*syem*	*yetti*
Eight	*vosym*	*sakkiz*
Nine	*dyeveet*	*toqqiz*
Ten	*dyeseet*	*on*
Eleven	*adinatsat*	*on bir*
Twelve	*dvenatsat*	*on ikki...*
Twenty	*dvatsat*	*yigirma*
Thirty	*tritsat*	*ottiz*
Forty	*sorak*	*qirq*
Fifty	*peedyesyat*	*ellik*
Sixty	*shestdyesyat*	*oltmish*
Seventy	*syemdyesyat*	*yetmish*
Eighty	*vosymdyesyat*	*sakson*
Ninety	*dyevinosta*	*toqson*
Hundred	*sto*	*yuz*
Thousand	*tisicha*	*bir ming*
Two thousand	*dveye tisicha*	*ikki ming*

Glossary

Ak/Kara/ Kyzl/Kok	white/black/ red/blue
Aksakal	lit. white beard, elders
Arba	two-wheeled traditional cart
Aryk	irrigation channel
Baiga	Kyrgyz game of polo using a goat corpse
Basmachi	lit. bandits, 1920s resistance movement
Beg/Bai	rich man, district governor
Chapan	long striped Uzbek cloak
Darya	river
Dastarkhan	lit. table cloth, food offered to guests
ibn	(Arabic) son of
Ishan	Leader of Sufi brotherhood, elder
Jaddid	Islamic reform movement as opposed to qadim
Kalym	bride price, paid by bride groom
Khalat	(Rus.) see chapan
Khodja	gentleman, person of distinction
Kishlak	rural Uzbek settlement (Kyrgyz = aul)
Kolkhoz	(Rus.) collective farm
Kosh Begi	Prime Minister
Kuchasi	street
Kum	desert (sands)
Malhallya	lit. neighbourhood, committees / social conventions
Maktab	traditional Islamic school

Mavarannahr	(Arabic) lit. the land beyond the river Oxus/Transoxiana
Namazgokh	summer, festival
Navruz	New Year festival, beginning of spring
Noz	green snuff, placed under the tongue
Oblast/Raion	Soviet administrative region
Paranja	traditional women's dress (Iranian Chador)
Piala	tea bowl
Qadim	classical movement as opposed to Jadid
remont (Rus.)	under repair
Sayyid	claimed descendant of the prophet
Suzaine	needlework
Tandyr	brick oven used to cook non bread, samosas etc.
Tariqat	path of Sufi Islam
Ulitsa (Rus.)	street

ARCHITECTURAL GLOSSARY

Ark	Inner citadel, forming the medieval town with a shakhristan
Balakhana	balcony, upper room
Birun/Darun	external/internal
Chorsu	lit four ways, crossroads
Chortak	lit four arches, domed structure on squinch
Cupola	dome
Dalon	passage, walkway

Darskhana	madrassah lecture room
Darvaza	gate
Ganch	alabaster carving
Girikh	lit knot, branching floral motif within star-shaped pentograms
Guldasta	corner tower
Gumbaz	dome
Gurkhana	tomb chamber
Hammam	Turkish baths
Harem	lit. forbidden, women's living quarters
Hauz	pool
Hauli	palace
Hujra	student's cell in madrassah
Iroki	star-shaped stalactite ornament
Iwan	covered pillared portico or vaulted portal
Jummi	Friday, thus a mosque which should house the city congregation on Friday
Khana	house, dwelling
Khanagha	dervish hostel
Kitabkhana	library
Korikhanah	where the blind recite from the Koran and receive alms
Kosh	double, pair
Kufic	Arabic calligraphic script
Kundal	gilded, polychromatic paintwork using glue paints
Kurgan/Kushk	fortress (Sogdian)
Mazar	grave/cemetery/place of visit
Madrassah	Islamic seminary college
Mianserai	entrance hall
Mihrab	niche that orientates a mosque to Mecca
Minbar	mosque pulpit
Minor	minaret
Muqarna	alabaster stalactite corner squinches
Pishtak	adorned portal
Quiblah	wall orientated to Mecca
Rabat	caravanserai, fortress of Islam, town suburb
Registan	lit. sandy place, square
Sardoba	lit. cool water (Tajik), covered water reservoir
Serai	palace
Shakhristan	inner town around an ark
Squinch	corner arch forming the transition from square to dome
Takharatkhana	hall for ablutions
Tash	stone (as in Tashkent and Tashkurgan)
Tepe	fort (also *tyube*)
Tim/Tok	bazaar with one entrance/crossroads/bazaar
Tympanum	space over portal between lintel and arch
Ziaratkhana	prayer room, place of pilgrimage
Zindan	Prison

Recommended Reading

In London, try amongst others the Traveller's Bookshop, 25 Cecil Court, near Leicester Square, (tel. 0171 836–9132) or Edward Stanford's, 12 Long Acre, Covent Garden, (tel. 0171 836–1321). For maps in the USA try Russia/Central Asia Travel Resources, 117 N 40th St, Seattle, WA 98103.

TRAVEL LITERATURE

Akchurin, Murat. *Red Odyssey*. (Secker & Warburg, 1992.) An underground soviet 'On the Road', tracing a Moscovite Tartar's tour of Central Asia, haunted by the ethnic violence of a crumbling union.

Bailey, F M. *Mission To Tashkent*. 1946 (Oxford University Press, 1992.) A dry but remarkable behind-the-scenes revelation of a British spy's fun and games with the Bolsheviks, only cleared by the British government in 1946.

Burnes, Alexander. *Travels in Bokhara* (vol 2). 1834 (Oxford University Press, 1973.) Classic Great Game tale and portrait of the Bukharan Emirate.

Curzon, George. *Russia in Central Asia*. 1889 (Frank Coss & Co, 1967.) Wonderfully politically incorrect view of native life, told with great wit and bravado by the 25-year-old future Viceroy of India.

Graham, Stephen. *Through Russian Central Asia*. (Cassell & Co, 1916.) Lyrical odyssey.

Hopkirk, Kathleen. *Central Asia—a Travellers Companion*. (John Murray, 1993.) Absorbing compendium of traveller's tales that spills over into Chinese Turkestan.

Krist, Gustav. *Alone Through the Forbidden Land*. 1937 (Ian Faulkner, 1992.) Tall stories from a disguised Austrian ex-prisoner of war/carpet-seller.

Maclean, Fitzroy. *Eastern Approaches*. 1949 (Penguin 1991.) Riotously funny romp through Uzbekistan dodging secret police. Only one third of the book covers Central Asia. Maclean's *To the Back of Beyond* is a large format complement written 25 years later.

Maillart, Ella. *Turkestan Solo*. 1934 (Century Travellers, 1985.) Indomitable voyage around Kyrgyzstan and Uzbekistan by Peter Fleming's erstwhile travel companion.

Moorhouse, Geoffrey, *Apples in the Snow*. (Hodder & Stoughton, 1990.)

Schuyler, Eugene. *Turkistan*. 1876 (Routledge & Keegan Paul, 1966.) Another classic full of valuable insight and charm but hard to find.

Terzani, Tiziano. *Goodnight Mr. Lenin*. (Picador, 1992.)

Thubron, Colin. *The Lost Heart of Central Asia*. (Heinneman, 1994.) Fascinating account of post-Soviet Central Asia.

HISTORY

Hambly, Gavin. *Central Asia*. 1969. An excellent historical overview

Hookham, Hilda. *Tamburlaine the Conqueror.*

Hopkirk, Peter. *The Great Game.* (Oxford University Press, 1991.) Gripping portrayal of heroes and lunatics during Turkestan's most stylish modern era.

Hopkirk, Peter. *Setting the East Ablaze.* (Oxford University Press, 1986.) A slightly more prosaic account of the Bolshevik's early 20th-century tussles with British spies and *basmachi*.

Nicolle, David. *The Age of Tamerlane.* Sharq/UNESCO. *Amir Timur in World History*, Tashkent, 1996. Tamerlane's birthday inspired this comprehensive, well-illustrated work.

MODERN UZBEKISTAN

Critchlow, James. *Nationalism in Uzbekistan.* (Westview Press, 1991.) Thorough and lucid portrayal of modern Uzbekistan.

Banuazizi, Ali. *The New Geopolitics of Central Asia* (I.B. Taurus, 1995.) Traces the modern history of Central Asia and assesses the impact of independence within a regional context.

Gleason, Gregory. *The Central Asian States: Discovering Independence* (Westview, Boulder, Colorado/Oxford, England, 1997)

Hiro, Dilip. *Between Marx and Mohammed.* (Harper Collins, 1994.) Detailed review of Central Asia's 20th century. Now in paperback.

Rashid, Ahmed. *The Resurgence of Central Asia* (Zed Books, 1994). Excellent introduction to the region.

Taheri, Amir. *Crescent in a Red Sky* (Hutchinson, 1989.) Very readable study of Russia's turbulent relationship with Islam.

ART AND ARCHITECTURE

Knobloch, Edgar. *Beyond the Oxus.* (Ernest Benn, 1972.) Illustrated meander through the history, art and architecture of Transoxiana.

SOUVENIR PHOTO BOOKS

Naumkin, V. *Samarkand; Caught in Time*, (Garnet Publ., Reading 1992) Collection of turn of the century photographs. Other volumes cover Khiva and Bukhara.

Bukhara; A Museum in the Open. (Tashkent, 1991.) Excellent souvenir regularly for sale in Bukhara. Other volumes cover Khiva and Samarkand.

GUIDEBOOKS AND MAPS

Maier, Frith. *Trekking in Russia and Central Asia* (The Mountaineers, 1994)

Whittell, Giles. *Central Asia* (Cadogan, 1996)

Central Asia: A Travel Survival Kit (Lonely Planet, 1996)

WEBSITES

Cyber Uzbekistan (http://www.cu-online.com/~k_a/uzbekistan/) - your best port of call, with links to all worthwhile Uzbek-related sites.

Index